The SQL Server 7.0 Handbook:

A Guide to Microsoft Database Computing

Ken England and Nigel Stanley

Digital Press

Boston ● Oxford ● Auckland ● Johannesburg ● Melbourne ● New Delhi

Butterworth-Heinemann suports the efforts of American Forests and the
Global ReLeaf program in its campaign for the betterment of trees, forests,
and our environment.

Library of Congress Cataloging-in-Publication Data

England, Ken, 1955–
    The SQL Server handbook : a guide to Microsoft database computing
/ by Ken England and Nigel Stanley.
      p. cm.
    ISBN 1-55558-201-X (pbk. : alk. paper)
    1. Database management.   2. SQL server.   I. Stanley, Nigel.
    II. Title.
    QA76.9.D3E64 1999
    005.75'85—dc21   99-30942
                    CIP

British Library Cataloguing-in-Publication Data

A catalogue record for this book is available from the British Library

The publisher offers discounts on bulk orders of this book.
For information, please contact:

Manager of Special Sales
Butterworth–Heinemann
225 Wildwood Avenue
Woburn, MA 01801–2041
Tel: 781-904-2500
Fax: 781-904-2620

For information on all Digital Press publications available, contact our World Wide Web
home pages at: http://www.bh.com/digitalpress

10 9 8 7 6 5 4 3 2 1

Composition: P.K.McBride, Southampton
Printed in the United States of America

The SQL Server 7.0 Handbook

2

Contents

Preface

This book is based on Version 7.0 of Microsoft SQL Server, which was released toward the end of 1998. This version provides a technically sophisticated and fully-functional database management system for the Microsoft Windows NT operating system, which can be run on Intel Pentium-based platforms or the Compaq 64-bit AXP processor commonly known as Alpha.

Building on the success of previous versions, version 7.0 is a major rewrite of Microsoft's popular database management system. The database engine has been reengineered to provide a database architecture that will be able to support the demands for database technology over the next 10 to 12 years. Version 7.0 is designed to scale from small Windows 95/98 computers to large symmetric multiprocessing servers, to be easy to administer, and to support large data warehouses.

The growing popularity of Windows NT and SQL Server among customers, software development companies, and consulting firms has prompted us to write this book. It is intended to be a comprehensive introduction to the extensive capabilities offered by SQL Server and a text in which we can impart some of our experience.

This book is definitely not intended to be a rehash of the documentation set. It is intended to be a text where readers, whether they are developers, database administrators, people performing a technical database evaluation, or computer professionals looking to broaden their horizons, can gain a good overview of the product in one book.

This book is also not intended to focus on SQL Server alone, but to position SQL Server within the rest of the Microsoft database family and to look at SQL Server application development.

SQL Server 7.0 provides a powerful and easy-to-use graphical management tool known as the SQL Server Enterprise Manager. It is now possible to almost completely forget about the system-stored procedures that can be found in earlier versions of SQL Server. In this book, however, we have chosen to provide numerous examples of the use of system-stored procedures as well as the SQL Server Enterprise Manager. We have done this because we believe that this will be useful for readers who have worked with earlier versions of SQL Server and also readers who are familiar with Sybase SQL Server.

The chapters are written to follow one another in a logical fashion, building on some of the topics introduced in previous chapters. The structure of the chapters is as follows:

- Chapter 1 introduces the components of Microsoft SQL Server and the Microsoft SQL Server 7.0 architecture.

- Chapter 2 describes the SQL Server installation process and upgrading from previous versions of SQL Server.

- Chapter 3 introduces the creation and management of SQL Server 7.0 databases and their files.

- Chapter 4 presents the data definition features in SQL Server 7.0, such as the creation of tables and views.

- Chapter 5 introduces the data manipulation features in SQL Server 7.0, including how to retrieve and store data.

- Chapter 6 introduces advanced data manipulation features, such as flow control, stored procedures, and extended stored procedures.

- Chapter 7 presents the data integrity features in SQL Server, including referential integrity constraints and triggers.

- Chapter 8 describes database administration activities including backup, restore, the SQL Server Profiler, and automating administration.

- Chapter 9 introduces the SQL Server security architecture including roles and permissions.

- Chapter 10 describes indexed access and the function of the optimizer, as well as techniques to observe and influence its strategy and locking.

- Chapter 11 introduces the distributed capabilities in SQL Server 7.0 such as heterogeneous distributed joins and replication.

- Chapter 12 explores Microsoft Transaction Server and COM, and their role in developing SQL Server applications.

- Chapter 13 introduces data warehousing and the new OLAP cube technology.

- Chapter 14 introduces visual tools and SQL Server development.

To relate a little background about the authors—Ken tends to focus on the server, especially in the performance and tuning space. Nigel deals more with the development side and new technologies.

To this end, Ken has written Chapters 3, 4, 5, and 6, which focus on creating databases, creating objects in databases, and manipulating data through Transact-SQL. He has also written Chapter 7 about SQL Server 7.0 data integrity, Chapter 9 about security, Chapter 10 on indexing and locking, and Chapter 11 on distributing data. He has also written about the SQL Server Profiler and database backup/restore in Chapter 8.

Nigel has written Chapters 1 and 2 concerning the SQL Server 7.0 architecture and installation/upgrade process. He has written development oriented chapters—Chapter 12 on Transaction Server, Chapter 13 on data warehousing, and Chapter 14 on developing applications with SQL Server 7.0. He has also written about alerts, jobs, operators, and the web assistant in Chapter 8.

Acknowledgments

Most of all, we would like to thank Margaret England and Rue Stanley for their long suffering while we were writing this text.

Thanks also to Michael and Katy England for their long suffering while I was locked in my study writing this text. Writing about databases is, unfortunately, not an activity in which most of the family can join. Because of this, writing and being sociable are usually mutually exclusive!

As well as the friends and colleagues who encouraged us with this book, we would like to give an extra special thanks to the following people:

A very special thank you to Keith Burns who always has a bubbling enthusiasm for SQL Server; our colleagues at ICS Solutions for helping to put SQL Server on the map; and Dr. Jeff Middleton for debating many SQL Server and related topics while on 20 mile hikes!

Another special thanks goes to Phil Sutherland and Pam Chester at Butterworth-Heinemann. Many thanks to our other friends in Microsoft, without whose skill and hard work SQL Server 7.0 would not be the excellent product it is today.

Ken England

Nigel Stanley

February 1999

1

SQL Server Architecture

1.1 Introduction

This chapter will give the reader a good understanding of the general *make up* of Microsoft SQL Server version 7.0, including the architectural changes between version 6.x and 7.

By the end of this chapter a reader should have a good grasp of the SQL Server architecture and feel happy about starting the steps of installing and building a server. It is not the intention of this chapter to give a blow by blow account of product installation, more an expansion of areas that may be of interest to the database administrator.

1.2 Major Changes to SQL Server Version 7.0

Without a doubt SQL Server version 7.0 (code named SPHINX in beta) is a massive change to the SQL Server product line. It is really Microsoft's first opportunity to rewrite the product and finally move away from the Sybase legacy, and to incorporate new Microsoft-centric features such as integrated management tools, reduced cost-of-ownership features, and improved concurrency with row-level locking. Here is an overview of the new features that will be covered later on in the book.

New Graphical Tools:

- ◆ Microsoft Management Console (MMC) that hosts a new Enterprise Manager administration tool.

- ◆ SQL Executive replaced with new SQL Server Agent for job (new name for tasks) management.

- ◆ SQL Server Query Analyzer with new features to recommend best use of indexes.

- SQL Server Profiler to monitor SQL Server activity and assist in optimizing queries, log changes, and administration tasks.

Improved Features to Minimize Administration:

- No more disk devices or segments, instead SQL Server now has files that can grow and shrink in line with database size.

- Memory manager now works intelligently with the operating system to make best use of available memory.

- System statistics automatically updated.

- New security model that is better integrated with Windows NT.

- Better data import/export management with Data Transformation Services enabling complex data scrubbing and manipulation via OLEDB.

- Improved replication, including multi-site updates, improved third party interfaces, and improved tools for monitoring.

- New English Query tool to improve database reporting and reduce end user requirement to learn complex SQL.

Improved Locking and Querying:

- Full, dynamic locking model that determines the most effective locking mechanism based on system cost.

- Row-level locking now fully implemented.

- Query optimizer rewritten to allow parallel queries with new merge join and hash algorithms.

- Distributed queries between SQL Server databases and SQL Server and another OLEDB data source.

- Local cursors.

- Index tuning wizard.

New Architecture

- Pages are now 8K, with associated 64K extents.

- Extents can now contain data from multiple tables to save space.

- Better support for very large databases with improved online backups and restores that are now fully incremental and easier to manage within file groups.

- DBCC now has improved performance.

- Limits improved on table numbers in queries and columns per table.

- SQL Server now available for Windows 9.x.

- Support for Windows 2000 64-bit memory.

- Support for UNICODE.

- Support for recursive triggers.

- New Transact-SQL statements including ALTER PROCEDURE, ALTER TABLE, ALTER TRIGGER, and ALTER VIEW.

1.3   Overview of Windows NT

Although this is a book about Microsoft SQL Server and related technologies, Windows NT technology is a crucial foundation stone. All examples and experiences related in this book refer to the Windows NT SQL Server product.

Windows NT shipped to the market place on August 31st, 1993 to mixed reviews. The release of the product followed nearly seven years of tough development, lead by operating system guru Dave Cutler, formerly of Digital Equipment Corporation, where he lead the development team for the OpenVMS operating system.

Windows NT is the most powerful member of the Microsoft Windows family designed for high-end workstation or multiprocessor servers. The key features of Windows NT are:

- Manageability—The use of the Windows 9.x graphical user interface gives users a familiar environment. For the database user this is useful, as graphical tools have been built to manage SQL Server and remove a lot of the tedium of writing SQL scripts.

- Security—Windows NT is designed to be certified to U.S. Department of Defense C2 level security. SQL Server 6.x could integrate into the Windows NT security model, but version 7 has taken that integration a step further with a complete rewrite of the SQL Server security model.

- Multithreading—Any application can be written to take advantage of multithreading, so that an application's processes can be multitasked, for example executing one query while building another and printing a third. Windows NT also supports preemptive multitasking, so that applications are forced to yield processor time as opposed to cooperative multiprocessing in 16-bit versions of Windows that rely on the application yielding processor time to other applications. For example, in the past, a poorly written Windows 3.1 application could consume all the system resources and prevent other applications from operating.

- Symmetric Multiprocessing—With microcomputers that support multiple processors, Windows NT can "load balance" work across multiple processors to give improved performance. A query's performance can be improved by threading it across processors balanced with other work. Version 7 of SQL Server is now better positioned to use the multiple processor architecture of Windows NT.

1.3.1   Windows NT 4.0 Enterprise Edition

Microsoft has been aggressively positioning itself as a scalable platform vendor with Windows NT, and Windows NT 4.0 has been repositioned with the introduction of NT 4.0 Enterprise Edition. The Enterprise Edition is seen as a stepping stone to Windows 2000 and has a number of key features:

- Enhanced support for applications. Three GB application support for applications compiled to take advantage of the additional address space (4 Gigabyte Memory Tuning [4GT]). SQL Server 6.5 has a special version compiled to use the 3GB address space as opposed to today's limit of 2GB.

- Support for 8-way SMP servers.

- System clustering based upon "Wolfpack" cluster technology, providing 2-node high-availability clusters on standard PC server hardware.

- Option Pack containing Microsoft Transaction Server and Message Queue.

1.3.2   Windows 2000 (Windows NT 5.0)

At the time of writing, Microsoft has made further public announcements regarding Windows NT 5.0. Seen as a major upgrade to version 4.0, version 5.0 will finally deliver upon the much promised "Cairo" technology set. NT 5.0 is critical to Microsoft, in fact senior executives have made it public that they are "betting the business" on the success of the product. Some may see that as the reason for product delay, others that Microsoft is focused on an excellent version 1.0 product. To put Windows NT 5.0 in perspective, NT 3.51 contained 4 million lines of code and NT 5 contains over 26 million. NT 5 will deliver some key technology the SQL Server user and developer could utilize, and listed below are some of the key highlights:

- Active Directory technology that will expose a set of object-oriented interfaces into the Active Directory Service Interface (ADSI). It will also have support for the Lightweight Directory Access Protocol API (LDAP) and Microsoft Mail API (MAPI) support.

- Intellimirror, part of the Microsoft attempt to repel the attack of the NC/thin client by reducing the administrative overhead of an NT server. This is designed to mirror a user's data onto a server in an "intelligent" manner, meaning that a user's data and desktop appearance can be restored to any client automatically. Those readers with experience managing a network will immediately see some benefits here.

- Application installer that should remove the time consuming DLL management required to update and reconfigure a client PC. The application using the app installer will work with Windows NT to determine the DLLs required on installation and then hand over to the operating system for completion.

- Microsoft Management Console will become the central window for application administration snap-in tools. Readers will see more on the use that SQL Server makes of this later.

1.4 | SQL Server Architecture

SQL Server can be thought of as a family of products, tightly integrated to offer a good suite of complimentary services. Version 6.x introduced this concept with the use of SQL Distributed Management Objects that have now been built upon and expanded.

SQL Server RDBMS

The *SQL Server RDBMS* component is the database engine responsible for data storage, security, and integrity.

SQL Server Enterprise Manager/MMC

The SQL Enterprise Manager tool was used for day-to-day administration duties, including setting up and configuring stored procedures, triggers, tables, and other SQL objects in SQL Server 6.x. The Microsoft Management Console (MMC) is the new user interface for SQL Server and other BackOffice server product management. This shared console concept provides a consistent environment for SQL Server and other "snap-in" administration tools. The SQL Server MMC snap-in console is still called SQL Server Enterprise Manager.

SQL Server Web Assistant

Web enablement of Microsoft applications followed the redirection of the company toward the Internet in 1994/95. SQL Server 6.5 had a Web Assistant that enabled the publishing of SQL Server data into HTML format on a once only or scheduled basis. This has been extended in version 7.0 to include the import of data from an HTML page.

SQL Server Query Analyzer

The query management engine on SQL Server 7.0 has been changed considerably from 6.x. The query analyzer tool has also received a facelift. SQL Server Query Analyzer provides the SHOWPLAN option that is used to report the methods chosen by the SQL Server optimizer to retrieve data.

SQL Server Profiler

SQL Trace is now called SQL Server Profiler. SQL Server Profiler captures a continuous picture of server activity in real-time. By picking the items and events that need monitoring, including Transact-SQL statements and batches, object usage, locking, security events, and errors, SQL Server Profiler can filter these events, showing only the significant events that a DBA may have chosen. A recorded trace against the same or another server can be replayed to assist in the administration of a server.

SQL Server Agent

The *SQL Executive* in SQL Server 6.x was responsible for the management of administrative tasks such as the alerting of operators. SQL Executive is now called *SQL Server Agent*, but is still responsible for managing jobs, alerts, operators, and notifications, as well as replication.

SQL Distributed Management Objects (DMO)

On top of the RDBMS engine we have the *SQL Distributed Management Objects (DMO)* component that is an *Object Linking and Embedding (OLE) 2.0* layer of objects used for the distributed management of servers. These objects interfaced to the graphical management tools in SQL Server 6.x.

Other Services

Replication is the component that is responsible for sending data to remote servers that have requested it. *Host gateways* are used to access remote data in non-SQL Server format. *DB-Library* is the client/server interface to SQL Server usually used by developers using the C programming language. *Embedded SQL* is used with the COBOL interface to SQL Server. *Open Data Services (ODS)* is another application programming interface (API) which enables gateways to be constructed to operate across the data enterprise. The API consists of C functions and macros used for creating two types of server applications—applications that are initialized as Open Data Services servers and that support user connections and user queries, and applications called *extended stored procedures* that are added directly to SQL Server and accessed by making procedure calls to SQL Server.

There are more than 200 client applications that can combine with Microsoft SQL Server to create client server based solutions. These include the popular *Office* type applications from Microsoft including Access, Excel, and Word and from other vendors, products such as Business Objects, Paradox, and dBASE.

1.5 SQL Server System Databases

Once SQL Server has been installed, one of the things it does is create a number of system databases and files.

1.5.1 The Master Database

The *master* database is the *controller* of the databases and operations within an SQL Server. It contains, among other things, the system stored procedures and system tables that contain server configuration information. The default database for users following logon is "master," and so this should be changed to another database the user is likely to need on a regular basis. There is no need for most users to access the master database—indeed this must be avoided to prevent problems that may affect the entire SQL Server installation. The system administrator (SA) account will still require the master database as its default. The master database is located on Master.mdf, with the log (4MB) on Mastlog.ldf.

NOTE: Due to its critical nature, the master database should be backed up each time a database object in it is changed or created.

1.5.2 The Model Database

The *model* database is effectively a template used for each new database that is created on a SQL Server system. Contained within the model database are all of the system tables that are required for each database, and if changes are made to the model database then they will be reflected in every database created after that change. Typical changes to the model database include the addition of user-defined datatypes. Again care must be taken as to who actually accesses the model database as the changes he or she makes will be perpetuated throughout the system. The model database is located in the Model.mdf file. The transaction log file is located on the Modellog.ldf file.

1.5.3   The Tempdb Database

The *tempdb* database is a shared work area that is used by all databases in an SQL Server system. This temporary area is cleared each time the system is closed down and, when users log out, temporary tables will automatically be removed from *tempdb*. Subqueries frequently use the GROUP BY function or users undertake a lot of activity directly on the temporary tables. The database is located on the Tempdb.mdf file. The associated transaction log is located in the Templog.ldf file.

1.5.4   The Pubs Database

The *pubs* database is used for demonstration and example work. You should install this database to follow the examples that are found throughout this book. It is located on the Pubs.mdf file. The database's transaction log is located on the Pubs_log.ldf file.

However, for those of you who are familiar with the pubs database provided with SQL Server 4.21, the pubs database has been updated to reflect the new product enhancements in SQL Server 6.0 and beyond:

- Addition of international data to test sorts and character sets.
- Three new tables *employees*, *jobs*, and *pub_info*.
- The *publishers* table has a new country column.
- Referential integrity is now enforced with primary and foreign key constraints.
- More complex triggers have been provided.
- The *pub_info* table contains text and graphics data.
- All defaults and rules have been changed to use the DEFAULT and CHECK constraints respectively.

1.5.5   Northwind Database

For those readers that are familiar with Microsoft Access, the workgroup database product Northwind will need no introduction. It is a demonstration database from a fictitious company called Northwind Traders. Northwind is installed automatically by running the instnwnd.sql file with the osql utility.

1.5.6 The Msdb Database

SQL Server 7.0 uses a database called *msdb* to provide support for the *SQL Agent*. It is located on the Msdbdata.mdf file. The database's transaction log is located on the Msdblog.ldf file.

Table 1.1 *Summary of System Databases and Files Created*

Database	Data File	Log Files
Master	Master.mdf	Mastlog.ldf
Model	Model.mdf	Modellog.ldf
MSDB	Msdbdata.mdf	Msdblog.ldf
Northwind	northwnd.ldf	northwnd.mdf
Pubs	Pubs.mdf	Pubs_log.ldf
Temp	Tempdb.mdf	Templog.ldf

1.6 SQL Server Files

SQL Server databases and files are discussed in detail in Chapter 3. For now it is worth mentioning that SQL Server version 7.0 introduces a major change to the internal structure of the database. Devices no longer exist; instead SQL Server uses a file analogy that contains various database objects. There are three file types:

♦ Primary—Every database has one primary file that references other files that may be used. This has the default file extension of .mdf.

♦ Secondary—Data that is not contained in the primary file is held in one or more secondary files that have the extension .ndf.

♦ Log—Logged information used in the database recovery process. A database has at least one log file that has the extension .ldf.

The file extensions are not enforced by SQL Server and the developer or administrator is able to create their own extensions. This is not advisable, and the authors recommend that the defaults be always employed. The files are referred to by two names, the internal logical name used by SQL Server and the external operating system name, both of which must adhere to their respective naming conventions.

1.7   Pages and Extents

SQL Server 7.0 still uses pages and extents. A page is the most granular storage unit used by SQL Server and is 8KB in size, giving 128 pages per megabyte. Each page has a header that contains system type information such as object owner, free space on the page, and the nature of the page. The header amounts to 96 bytes, and is then followed by the data rows that are placed sequentially. A row cannot span multiple pages, but has now increased in size to 8060 bytes excluding attached text and image data that is now stored in separate pages. At the end of the table there is a row offset table containing the offset of the rows within the page.

There are seven page types now used in SQL Server:

Table 1.2 *Page Types in SQL Server*

Page	Contains
Data	Data rows
Index	Index entries
Log	Log records
Page Free Space	Maps free space available on pages
Index Allocation Map	Maps extents used by a table or index
Text/Image	Text and image data
Global Allocation Map	Maps allocated extents

An extent is a set of 8 contiguous pages (64K and 16 extents per MB) and is the basic unit used by SQL Server to allocate space for tables and indexes. Extents can either be uniform or mixed. A uniform extent only allows ownership and use by a single object. A mixed extent can contain shared data from 8 separate objects. Any new table or index created is allocated space in a mixed extent. As soon as it has increased in size to cover eight pages it will be allocated space from uniform extents.

1.8   Space Management

Internally, SQL Server needs to work hard to ensure disk space is allocated and used efficiently. This can have a direct impact on the performance of a server installation.

Allocation information is held in a set of tightly packed pages that reduce disk activity needed to retrieve allocation data. Due to the contiguous nature of these pages they are often found in memory, further improving retrieval time. Minimizing the chaining together of these allocation pages further reduces contention.

SQL Server uses a Global Allocation Map (GAM) page type to record extent allocation. Covering up to 4GB of data containing 64,000 extents, the page contains 1s or 0s to indicate allocation usage. Another type of GAM called a Secondary Allocation Map (SGAM) covers the use of mixed extents that have a minimum of one unused page. SQL Server applies an algorithm to the GAM and SGAM data to establish where to place a mixed or uniform extent within the database.

The amount of free page space is held (surprisingly!) on a Page Free Space page that covers 8000 pages and contains a bitmap to indicate the percentage of the page that is full with data.

1.9 Text and Image Data

As mentioned before, text and image data values are not stored as an integral part of the data row, rather in a separate data collection of their own. The data page that contains a text or image value actually has a 16-byte pointer to the physical storage location of the text or image data, which is a collection of 8K pages organized in a b-tree structure. This gives significant performance improvements in retrieving the data over the previous versions of SQL Server that used page chaining.

2

Installing and Upgrading to SQL Server 7.0

Microsoft put a lot of effort into easing the installation process. Windows NT was known for some time internally at Microsoft as the "Half Hour OS" because it was straightforward to install and configure. SQL Server 7.0 has received some improved installation routines, and work has been put into the various wizards to assist the administrator with most of the basic setup routines. Nevertheless, there are some key preparations that need to be taken to ensure the installation runs as smooth as possible, which we have covered below. This chapter will also explore the upgrade process for those who have an existing SQL Server database they wish to move to version 7.

The first, and probably most paramount, recommendation the authors will make is that you should always back up any sensitive data that exists on the installation server—especially if you are upgrading from a previous version of SQL Server.

The other steps are as follows:

- If you are installing SQL Server onto an existing server always shut down any SQL Server-dependent services.

- Close down the Windows NT Event Viewer and Regedt.exe programs to provide a clean system.

- Check for sufficient disk space and processor type. SQL Server will need an Intel Pentium 166 MHz or higher, Pentium PRO, or Pentium II. A typical install will take up to 170MB for the product alone, excluding user databases, which should be sized 1.5 times larger than a SQL Server 6.x database. Appropriate service packs will need to be added to the underlying operating systems. Suitable network adapters will, naturally, be required for network connectivity.

- Disable the write caching on the system disk controller if you have it activated. Write caching can cause problems with SQL Server data integrity, as the log mechanism may believe that data has been committed to disk where in fact it has been placed into cache by the cache controller. This has become more of an issue recently with the general acceptance of disk-based caching on NT-based servers. There are some instances where disk caching may have been placed on a system for the purpose of using it as a data server, but the authors recommend a serious review of this in light of possible data integrity problems.

♦ Create a Windows NT user account that will be used by the SQL Server Agent service and another for the SQL Server service. The account may be shared but it must be a member of the Windows NT Administrators group and have the "login as a service" option enabled, as well as a number of other attributes that may be found in the online documentation.

♦ Ensure that any domain, server, or user names contain legal SQL Server characters. SQL Server will take its name from the server.

♦ Select a character set and sort order.

The choice of character set determines which types of characters SQL Server will recognize in the stored data. If the incorrect character set is chosen on installation, then databases will need to be rebuilt and the data reloaded. A character set contains 256 characters, of which the first 128 are identical for each character set but the remaining 128, called the *extended character set*, are different. The extended characters contain the language-specific characters such as diacritical marks and specialized accents. If databases are to use these extended characters, the same character set must be chosen on the client and the server.

SQL Server has the choice of a number of character sets. The default is 1252 (ISO Character Set [Latin 1 or ANSI]).

The installation process will need to know which sort order is required. The sort order governs the collation and presentation of data produced by a query. If the incorrect sort order is selected on installation and a change is needed then the databases will need to be rebuilt and the data reloaded. A choice of sort orders is provided by SQL Server. The *Binary* sort order is the simplest and fastest sort order to use as the collating sequence is based on the numeric value of the characters in the installed character set. A *dictionary* sort order will not perform as quickly as one based on binary character sorting.

The default sort order for SQL Server is *dictionary order case insensitive*. The authors recommend that this sort order is chosen.

- Decide on your security model. SQL Server allows for NT Authentication or SQL Server Authentication. See Chapter 9, "Security."

- Log onto the Windows NT system with administrative privileges.

The installation process itself, once you have a suitably configured server, is straightforward and is a question of following the installation program and wizards. New users should go with the default options offered until they have gained some more experience in customizing an SQL Server.

2.1   Unattended Installation

If unattended installation is required, then SQL Server 7.0 makes this as easy as possible. Unattended installation prevents you from having to respond to prompts from the setup program so that it just runs through preconfigured scripts. Obviously this is most useful for those wanting to create a set of identically configured servers. The one thing that you can't do from here is remote server installation. The file used to contain the options is called the setup initialization file, and exists as SQL setup.iss in the \mssql7\install directory.

2.2   Pre-Upgrade Considerations

Upgrading databases is a horrible job at the best of times. Data needs to be backed up, server time needs to be scheduled, bosses need to be reassured. And once the server has been upgraded, you need to make sure it will work again.

Microsoft recognized this problem a while ago, and SQL Server 7.0 has received major attention in this area. There are two routes that the DBA can take to upgrade—"side by side" or "computer to computer." This chapter will take you through the upgrade process, and smooth the way for you.

The first thing that you need to do is a comprehensive backup of your system. If the latest service packs have not been installed, then load them now so that your 6.x system is as up to date as possible. If you are a proud holder of a version 4.21 installation you need to upgrade to at least version 6.0, as version 4.21 direct to version 7.0 upgrade is not supported. If space is an issue then you can get a better estimate of the required disk storage by running the Database Estimation Utility.

2.3   How to Run the Database Estimation Utility

*   Start the upgrade wizard.

*   Logon to your existing system as SA.

*   Click through the wizard until you reach the "use the default configuration" or "edit the default" screen.

*   You now get to the upgrade layout utility. Click "advanced" and then click onto an object in the proposed 7.0 database layout. "Drive summary" gives the estimated size of the version 7.0 files and the free disk space left on the local drives.

The upgrade process will use memory and tempdb space—so increase your memory to the most you can afford, and increase tempdb to at least 25MB. You also need at least 200MB of disk capacity free for the upgrade files—the more the merrier, as SQL Server needs room to maneuver when playing with the SQL files.

If you are running with SQL Server replication, then you must ensure that the distribution database is upgraded to version 7.0 before the subscribing servers. Once the distributor is upgraded then you can roll out the subscriber upgrades at a more leisurely pace, as version 7.0 will support replication out to 6.x subscribers.

2.4   Summary of Pre-Upgrade Actions

*   Back up the SQL Server 6.x database installation.

*   Install the latest SQL Server service pack.

*   Install SQL Server 7.0.

*   Set **tempdb** to at least 25 MB in the SQL Server 6.x installation.

*   Set the **memory** option to as high a value as appropriate in the SQL Server 6.x installation.

*   Check that all database users have logins in the **master** database.

*   Ensure that you upgrade all databases that are dependent on other databases.

*   Give a username and password to the MSSQLServer service in the SQL Server 6.x and SQL Server 7.0 installations, instead of using the local system account.

*   Stop replication services and empty the transaction log.

*   Shut down all applications and services that use SQL Server.

2.5   Hardware and Software Needed for the Upgrade

- ◆   Hard disk space

    In addition to the hard disk space used by SQL Server version 7.0, you need approximately 1.5 times the size of the existing 6.x databases.

- ◆   Operating system

    Microsoft Windows NT Server version 4.0 with SP4 or later.

    Windows NT Workstation 4.0 with SP4 or later.

- ◆   SQL Server 6.0 with SP4.

    SQL Server 6.5 with SP4 or later.

- ◆   Network Protocols and Named Pipes

    SQL Server 6.x and 7.0 must be set to listen to the default pipe,

    ```
    \\.\pipe\sql\query
    ```

    Named Pipes is required even for a tape backup upgrade.

2.6   Upgrade Choices

The SQL Server upgrade is fairly straightforward, and gives you a choice to upgrade in the most convenient way for your installation. The upgrade process refers to the existing SQL Server 6.0 installation as the export server and the 7.0 installation as the import server.

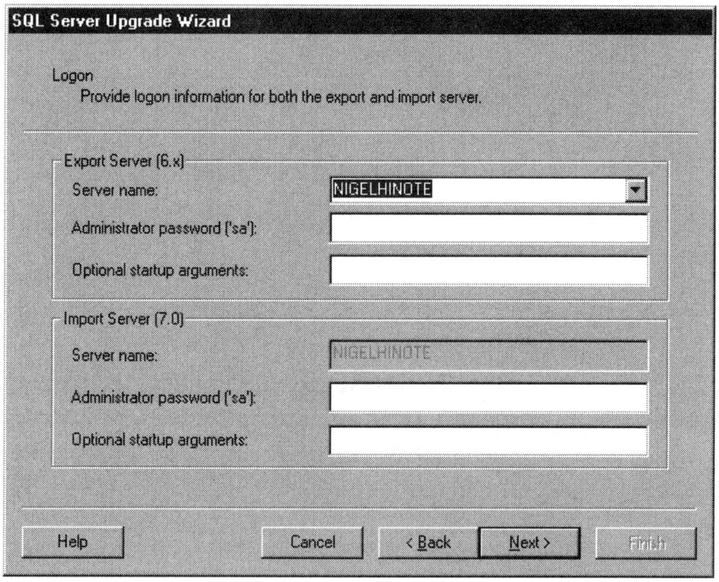

Figure 2.1

Upgrade Wizard — Identifying the Import and Export Servers

2.6.1   Named Pipe Upgrade

This is designed for users with plenty of disk space, as the pipeline enables the Wizard to transfer data from the memory of the version 6.0 server direct to the version 7.0 server. This method is also the fastest and most reliable, and has the added advantage of leaving the 6.0 server intact if you wish to go back to it. The downside to this is that you cannot reclaim any 6.0 diskspace until you delete it from the server.

Figure 2.2

Upgrade Wizard —
Choosing the Data Transfer
Method

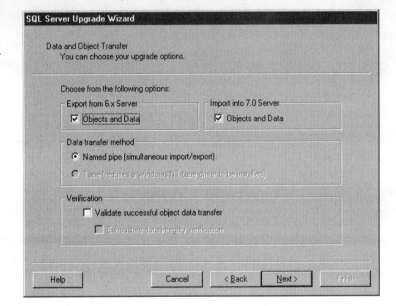

2.6.2   Tape Backup

This is designed for users with low disk space, as the 6.0 databases are backed up to tape device. The original installation is deleted and the 7.0 server installed into its place. You must remember that the backup of a 6.x database to tape is different to the transfer to tape option used by the upgrade wizard. The former will create a backup or dump device and the latter will produce a tape of objects ready for the upgrade process.

Hint: If you have opted to allow the Wizard to backup your installation to tape, then you must remember to remove the tape from the drive, as the wizard will preformat the tape before transferring the 6.x objects for upgrade.

2.7   Upgrade Verification

SQL Server upgrade is pretty robust, but if you are a bit nervous then you can switch on a couple of verification options.

◆   Object and data transfer verification

The upgrade wizard makes a list of all the objects, data rows, and configuration settings on the 6.0 server, upgrades to version 7.0, and then compares the 6.0 list with the actual objects and data on the 7.0 server. If there is a discrepancy, then the upgrade wizard will report it.

◆   Exhaustive data integrity check

A check sum is applied by the wizard to ensure that all objects and rows are transferred.

Figure 2.3

Upgrade Wizard—During the Upgrade Process SQL Server Dynamically Switches between SQL Server Versions Installed on the Server

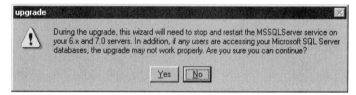

2.8   SQL Server 7.0 Database Configuration

The upgrade wizard gives a choice about the configuration of the version 7.0 databases

◆   Use the default database configuration

The size of the database files is estimated as if they were to contain all of the objects and data from the 6.x server. No allowance is made for any free space in the files and they are physically placed in the same location as the 6.x devices.

◆   Use databases and logs that you have already created in SQL Server 7.0

No user databases are created by the wizard, instead these must be manually created before the upgrade wizard is started.

◆   Use an SQL script file that you provide

As it says, the wizard will use a script that has been previously created.

When upgrading the master database there are three configuration options. With the server configuration option all options relevant to a 7.0 installation are transferred, such as logins and server configurations that are applicable to version 7.0. The replication settings option will upgrade all of the articles, subscriptions, and publications of the selected database as well as the distribution database. Finally, the SQL Executive settings can be transferred and run as SQL Server Agent tasks.

ANSI NULLS

This option controls how SQL Server compares null values in queries and other SQL operations, and can have an impact on the values returned to the end user. For example, with ANSI_NULLS set to ON, the Transact-SQL operators EQUAL (=) and NOT EQUAL (<>) will return false when one of the values is NULL. With ANSI_NULLS set OFF, you will find a true or false returned dependent upon one or both arguments being NULL.

When upgrading from version 6.x, the ANSI_NULLS option must be set to either ON or OFF. For database tables the ANSI_NULLS setting is not important, as the columns will retain their version 6.x NULL or NOT NULL settings, but for database objects it can be very important. SQL Server 6.x resolves the ANSI_NULLS option for stored procedures and triggers at query execution time, but SQL Server 7.0 will resolve the setting at creation time.

QUOTED_IDENTIFIER

Double quote marks (") can have ambiguous meaning in SQL Server. With the QUOTED_IDENTIFIER set OFF, the double quote mark will delimit a character string. With the option set ON, the double quote will delimit an identifier such as a column name. Double quotes need to be used if a name contains illegal characters such as spaces or punctuation marks.

For example, consider the following T-SQL statement:

```
SELECT "Nigel"
FROM Authors
```

With QUOTED_IDENTFIER set to ON, "Nigel" would be interpreted as the column named Nigel. If it is set OFF, "Nigel" would be a constant string equivalent to Nigel. This interpretation depends on the value of the QUOTED_IDENTIFIER when the object containing the double quote, such as a stored procedure, is created. During upgrade the setting of the QUOTED_IDENTIFIER determines how all objects behave when they have been recreated. To avoid confusion and if you are unsure of the correct setting, you can use the MIXED option, which will convert all objects containing double quotes as if the QUOTED_IDENTIFIER was ON, and if any object fails that process, then it receives a QUOTED_IDENTIFIER setting of OFF.

Figure 2.4
Upgrade Wizard — Choosing the ANSI Nulls and Quoted Identifier Settings

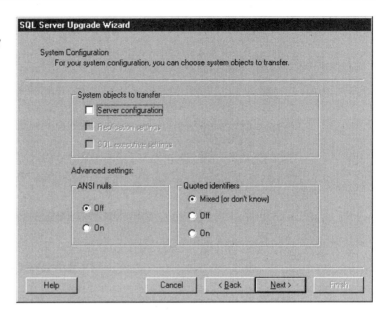

2.9 Side-by-Side Upgrades

This is the method of installing SQL Server 7.0 onto the same server that is running your 6.x installation. If you have plenty of disk space free then this is the preferred method, as you can directly "pipeline" the data from one SQL Server to another, keeping your source SQL Server intact during the transfer process. If it all goes horribly wrong at least you can go back to the operational SQL Server and pretend to your boss that you were only practicing. To put some context around pipeline upgrades, a 1GB 6.x database has been upgraded in under 1 hour, with an 80GB 6.x ERP installation being upgraded in 14.5 hours. Obviously this upgrade time is a function of the number of objects, volume of data, indexes used, and so on, but it gives some idea of the likely time scale.

2.10 Computer-to-Computer Upgrades

The first thing to note is that this upgrade method is not available to servers that use replication, as replication uses a lot of server-to-server communication based on computer names. Computer-to-computer upgrades connect a server running a 6.x installation on a network to a computer running SQL Server 7.0 elsewhere on a network. You can connect via a direct pipeline to the source server, or connect to a tape drive on the network.

2.11   SQL Server Compatibility

The SQL Server compatibility level defines the way in which a database will operate once upgraded from version 6.x. By default, the compatibility level will be set to that of the source database, and the general advice is not to adjust this level for upgraded databases immediately. Even though the compatibility level is set to 6.x, the upgraded database will still be able to access SQL Server features such as row level locking. Any new databases created will have their compatibility level set by the MODEL database, and by default will be set for the SQL Server 7.0 level.

Figure 2.5

Upgrade Wizard — Choosing the System Code Page. Leave the Default Setting for Most Applications.

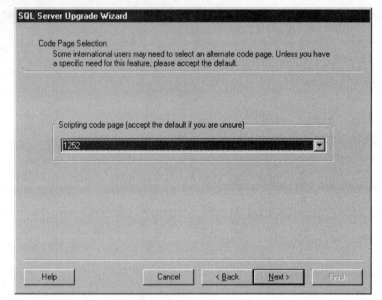

2.12   Log Files Created during Upgrade

Every time the Upgrade Wizard is run, a folder will be created under the SQL Server \UPGRADE folder which will be named after the server name, plus the date and time when the folder was created, giving a unique folder containing upgrade information.

Each step of the upgrade process will write information into this folder, giving a catalogue of actions that can be reviewed after the upgrade. The file extension .OK indicates a successful transfer, and a file extension .ERR indicates an error, and will list the objects that were not upgraded and the reason why.

In addition the directory \WinNT contains two files:

Table 2.1 *\WinNT Directory Files*

File	Description
Sqlupgrade.ini	List of .err files that are displayed by the Script Interpreter
Upgrade.ini	Used to set defaults and run pre- and post-task applications, if required

Files in the \Mssql7\Upgrade directory:

Table 2.2 *\MSSQL7\Upgrade Directory Files*

File	Description
Status.log	Used for remote checking of upgrade status to see the current task being executed
Check65.ini	A command prompt argument sent to Check65.exe
Upgrade.ini	Scripted file for the upgrade
<6.x server>_<date>_<time> directories	Directory containing objects for each run of the SQL Server Upgrade Wizard

Files in the object directories are named with either a .out or a .err extension, depending on the success of the task.

Figure 2.6

Upgrade Wizard — Selecting Which Databases Need to be Upgraded. Upgtest is a User Database.

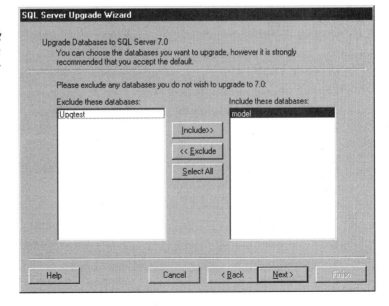

Table 2.3 *Files in the Object Directories*

File	Description
Layout.ini	A component of the wizard used for communication between the Upgrade Wizard and the layout utility.
~backup.ini	Used to backup, delete, and manually restore SQL Server 6.*x* data files during taped upgrades.
<dbid><db>.ini	Files used by layout.exe to cache the user settings for the current upgrade.
Changedbo.sql.out / .err	List of each statement that passed after the change DBO task has been run.
Check65 - <dbid><db>.out / .err	Output from check65.exe created while checking the SQL Server 6.*x* databases for inconsistencies.
Check65 - <dbid><db>_err.out / .err	Errors from check65.exe created while checking the SQL Server 6.*x* databases for inconsistencies.
Cleantempdb.bat	Used to delete the SQL Server 7.0 **tempdb** files after a successful upgrade.
Cleantempdb.sql.out / .err	Output from deleting the SQL Server 7.0 **tempdb** files after a successful upgrade.
Convload1.sql.out / .err	Sets configuration options.
Convload2.sql.out / .err	Adds logins, local groups, and other objects.
Createdb.sql.out / .err	Creates user databases and the SQL Server 7.0 **tempdb**.
Creating Databases.out / .err	Output from creating the SQL Server 7.0 **tempdb** and user databases.
Dboptions.sql.out / .err	Status of database options that were set and passed.
Dropping temporary tempdb files.out / .err	Success of dropping **tempdb** files.
Export and Import via Named Pipe - <dbid><db>.out / .err	Success of exporting data from SQL Server 6.*x* and importing into SQL Server 7.0 during a named pipe backup.
Export Data - <dbid><db>.out / .err	Success of exporting data from SQL Server 6.*x* in a tape backup.
Import Data - <dbid><db>.out / .err	Success of importing data into SQL Server 7.0 from a tape backup.
Export Database Objects - <dbid><db>.out / .err	Success of exporting objects from SQL Server 6.*x*.
Export Database Owners.out / .err	Success of exporting database owners from SQL Server 6.*x*.

File	Description
Export Logins - <#>.out / .err	Success of exporting logins from SQL Server 6.*x*.
Export Server Settings from Master.out /.err	Success of exporting server settings from SQL Server 6.*x*.
Export SQL Executive Settings.out / .err	Success of exporting SQL Executive settings.
Import Database Objects - <dbid> <db>.out / .err	Success of importing objects into SQL Server 7.0.
Import Logins - <#>.out / .err	Success of importing logins into SQL Server 7.0.
Import Server Settings from Master.out /.err	Success of importing server settings into SQL Server 7.0.
Import SQL Executive Settings - <#> .out / .err	Success of importing SQL Executive settings into SQL Server Agent in SQL Server 7.0.
Logininfo.sid	Integrated login mapping.
Loginmap.txt	Integrated login mapping.
Marking database upgrade status - <dbid><db>.out / .err	Success of marking which databases have been upgraded.
Marking database upgrade status - <dbid><db>.sql.out / .err	Marks database upgrade status.
Modifying scripts.out / .err	Success of removing stored procedures that are not to be created in SQL Server 7.0.
Msdb6in.sql	**msdb** integrated logins run against SQL Server 7.0.
Pre60to7.sql	Upgrades **msdb** from SQL Server 6.0 to SQL Server 7.0.
Pre65to7.sql	Upgrades **msdb** from SQL Server 6.5 to SQL Server 7.0.
Preparing MSDB for upgrade - <#>.out /.err	Success of preparing **msdb** for upgrade.
Preparing SQL-DMO for upgrade.out / .err	Success of preparing SQL-DMO for upgrade.
Replupd.out / .errreplupd_erro.out / .err	Success of updating replication settings.
Setting Database Options.out / .err	Success of setting database options in SQL Server 7.0.
Upgrade Complete.ini	Lists upgrade options and success codes for each upgrade task and object type.
Upgrade.log	Lists success code, start time, and stop time for each task in the Script Interpreter, created when the Script Interpreter exits or restarts after a failed task.
Upgrade.reg	Registry entries for the upgrade Data Source Name used by many of the ODBC applications in the upgrade process.
<dbid><db> directories	Database-specific directories for each upgraded database, including master.

Specific directories for each of the databases contain these files:

Table 2.4 *Files in Database Specific Directories*

File	Description
<6.x server>.master.bak (only in the master database directory)	Backup of stored procedure script before the Modify Scripts task is run
<6.x server>.<db>.bnd.out / .err	Table column bindings
<6.x server>.<db>.def.out / .err	Defaults
<6.x server>.<db>.dr1.out / .err	DRI to be created before data transfer (clustered keys)
<6.x server>.<db>.dr2.out / .err	DRI to be created after data transfer (nonclustered keys)
<6.x server>.<db>.fky.out / .err	Foreign key constraints
<6.x server>.<db>.gr1.out / .err	Groups
<6.x server>.<db>.id1.out / .err	Indexes to be created before data transfer (clustered indexes)
<6.x server>.<db>.id2.out / .err	Indexes to be created after data transfer (nonclustered indexes)
<6.x server>.<db>.LGN	Creates logins
<6.x server>.<db>.prc.out / .err	Stored procedures
<6.x server>.<db>.prv.out / .err	Permissions
<6.x server>.<db>.rul.out / .err	Rules
<6.x server>.<db>.tab.out / .err	Tables
<6.x server>.<db>.trg.out / .err	Triggers
<6.x server>.<db>.udt.out / .err	User-defined data types
<6.x server>.<db>.usr.out / .err	Users
<6.x server>.<db>.viw.out / .err	Views

2.13 Switching between SQL Server Versions

The general recommendation is to install version 7.0 and 6.x side by side, and remove the older version when you are happy that version 7.0 is up and running as it should be. Although both versions can be installed together on a machine, only one may be run at any one time. To make this switching between versions as easy as possible, Microsoft has created an SQL Server Switch Utility that can be run from the START menu. This resets the registry keys and the program group to the alternative version. It takes a minute or so to run, and will prompt you to turn off any running SQL Server service prior to switching over. It's a useful utility, and is also available from the command line as **Vswitch.exe**

Figure 2.7

The SQL Server Version Switch

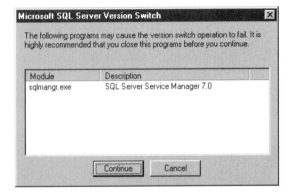

Figure 2.8

*Upgrade Wizard—
Choosing the Database
Configuration for the
Version 7.0 Installation*

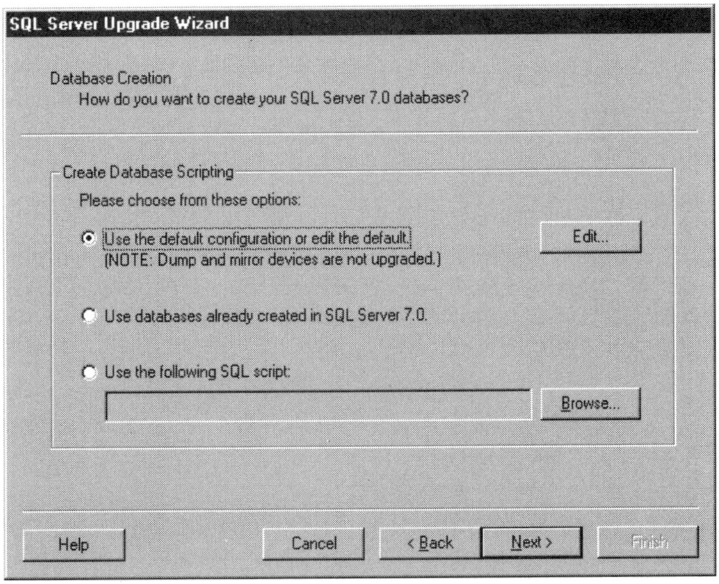

Figure 2.9
Upgrade Wizard—Once
Complete Confirms the
Upgrade Choices

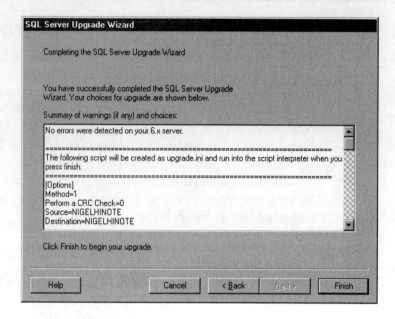

2.14   Deinstalling Version 6.x

Once you are happy that version 7 is working well, remove the old installation by using the Remove SQL Server 6.x application on the Start menu. That will ensure that the directories are cleaned up and recover the space for future use.

3

Creating and Managing Databases

3.1 Introduction

A database contains all the tables, views, indexes, triggers, stored procedures, and user data that, together, help to make up an application. An SQL Server will typically host many databases. Usually individual databases are backed up, restored, and integrity-checked and so a database can also be thought of as a unit of administration.

Databases can be created using the SQL Enterprise Manager, Transact-SQL, or the Database Creation Wizard and this chapter will describe how databases are created and managed.

Depending on the requirements of the system, a database may consist of two files—a data file and a transaction log file. However, Microsoft SQL Server 7.0 is capable of supporting large and complex database topologies. In fact, a database can be as large as 1,048,516 TB and can consist of 32,767 files. A data file size can be as large as 32 TB and a log file size can be as large as 4 TB. This is large enough for most organizations!

By default only members of the fixed server roles *sysadmin* or *dbcreator* have sufficient permission to create databases unless CREATE DATABASE permission has been granted to other users. Note, *sa* is a member of the *sysadmin* role.

3.2 The Structure of a Database

An SQL Server 7.0 database consists of at least two operating system files—one for data and one for the transaction log.

Unlike databases and database devices in previous versions of SQL Server, a database cannot share its files with any other database and the database data and transaction log cannot reside in the same file.

There are three file types that may be found associated with a SQL Server 7.0 database.

The *primary data file* is the starting point of the database and contains the pointers to the other files in the database. All databases have a single primary data file. The recommended file extension for primary data files is .mdf.

Databases may also have *secondary data files* to hold data that does not fit on the primary data file. Some databases may not have any secondary data files, while others have multiple secondary data files. The recommended file extension for secondary data files is .ndf.

Log files hold all of the log information used to recover the database. There is at least one log file for each database. The recommended file extension for log files is .ldf.

The primary data file will hold the system tables and, typically, user tables. For most users, placing all their database tables in this file and placing the file on a suitable RAID configuration will be sufficient. For some users, their user tables may be too large to place in a single file as this would mean that the file would be too large to place on one of their storage devices. In this case, multiple data files—a primary and multiple secondary files—may be used. User tables would then be created and populated. SQL Server would allocate space from each file to each table so that the tables were effectively spread across the files and, consequently, the physical storage devices.

Figure 3.1 shows a simple database topology using a single file to hold the system tables and user tables and a single file for the transaction log. The files reside on separate physical storage devices that may be single disks or RAID configurations.

Figure 3.1
A Simple Database Topology

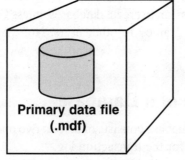 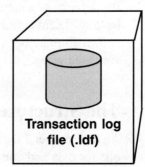

**Primary data file
(.mdf)**

**Transaction log
file (.ldf)**

Physical storage device D: **Physical storage device E:**

Figure 3.2 shows a more complex database topology using multiple files to hold the system tables and user tables and multiple files for the transaction log. The files reside on separate physical storage devices that may be single disks or RAID configurations.

Figure 3.2

A More Complex Database Topology

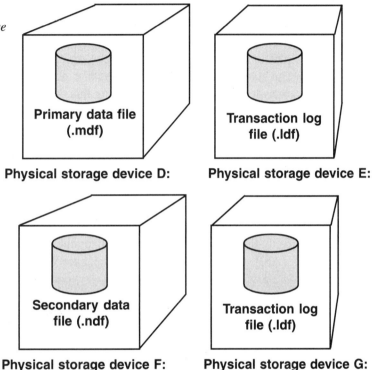

Primary data file (.mdf)

Physical storage device D:

Transaction log file (.ldf)

Physical storage device E:

Secondary data file (.ndf)

Physical storage device F:

Transaction log file (.ldf)

Physical storage device G:

For those users with even greater database performance and size requirements, *filegroups* may be used. The role of a filegroup is to gather data files together into collections of files into which database tables, indexes, and text/image data can be explicitly placed. This gives the database administrator great control over the placement of these database objects. Perhaps two database tables that are very heavily accessed can be separated into two filegroups that consist of two sets of data files residing on two sets of physical storage devices. The tables could also be separated from their nonclustered indexes in a similar fashion. Nonclustered indexes are described in Chapter 10. From an administration perspective, individual filegroups can be backed up, allowing a large database to be backed up in parts.

Some rules govern the use of filegroups. Transaction logs are never members of filegroups—only data files are. Also data files can only be a member of one filegroup.

For most users, though, the use of filegroups and multiple data and transaction log files will not be necessary to support their performance and administration requirements. They will use one data file and one transaction log file. Though they will not use user-defined filegroups, even in this simple case the database will contain a filegroup known as the *primary* filegroup. This will contain the system tables and user tables. It will also be the *default* filegroup. The default filegroup is the filegroup into which tables, indexes, and text/image data are placed when no filegroup is specified as part of their definition. Any filegroup can be made the default filegroup, and there is a school of thought that advocates always creating a single user-defined filegroup and making this the default filegroup when the database is first created. This ensures that the system tables alone reside in the primary filegroup and all user data resides in the user-defined filegroup separate from them.

3.3   Creating Databases

Databases can be created by means of the Create Database Wizard, the SQL Server Enterprise Manager, or the Transact-SQL CREATE DATABASE statement. As the Create Database Wizard is merely a wrapper around the SQL Server Enterprise Manager, database creation dialog boxes will not be discussed further here. Creating a database with the SQL Server Enterprise Manager is accomplished as follows:

⇨   Expand the server group and expand the server

⇨   Right-click *Databases*, then click *New Database*

⇨   Enter the name, file, size, and attribute information for each data file

⇨   Enter the name, file, size, and attribute information for each transaction log file

⇨   Click *OK*

Depending on how large the database will be, this may take a considerable length of time. In this case using a Transact-SQL script may be a better bet if you don't want to wait a while before you can use the SQL Server Enterprise Manager again.

The SQL Server Enterprise Manager *Database Properties* dialog box is shown in Figure 3.3.

As can be seen in Figure 3.3, various properties can be set for each data and transaction log file. The *Filename* of the file is the name by which it is referred within SQL Server, for example, by various system-stored proce-

Figure 3.3

The Database Properties Dialog Box

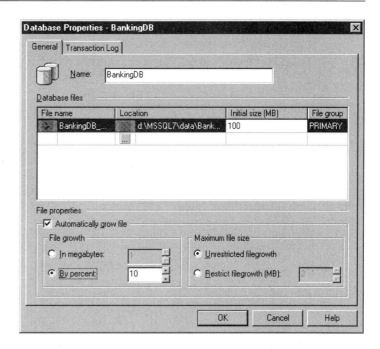

dures such as *sp_helpfile*. The location is the physical storage location where the file will reside. A filegroup may also be entered for data files other than the primary at this point, in which case the secondary data file will be placed in that filegroup. Other attributes of the file relate to size and growth, which will be discussed shortly.

An example of creating a database using the Transact-SQL CREATE DATABASE statement follows:

```
CREATE DATABASE BankingDB
ON PRIMARY
(   NAME = BankingData,
    FILENAME = 'd:\data\BankingData.mdf',
    SIZE = 200MB,
    MAXSIZE = 800MB,
    FILEGROWTH = 40MB )
LOG ON
(   NAME = 'BankingLog',
    FILENAME = 'e:\data\BankingLog.ldf',
    SIZE = 100MB,
    MAXSIZE = 500MB,
    FILEGROWTH = 50MB )
```

Like the SQL Server Enterprise Manager, a name is specified for the file, this time with the *NAME* option, and a physical location with the *FILENAME* option. The *ON* keyword introduces a list containing one or more data file definitions and the *LOG ON* keyword introduces a list containing one or more transaction log file definitions.

The *PRIMARY* keyword identifies the list of files following it as files that belong to the primary filegroup. The first file definition in the primary filegroup becomes the primary file, which is the file containing the database system tables. The *PRIMARY* keyword can be omitted, in which case the first file specified in the CREATE DATABASE statement is the primary file.

Regardless of the mechanism by which a database is created, size and growth information may be specified. The *Initial size (MB)* in the SQL Server Enterprise Manager and the *SIZE* keyword in the CREATE DATABASE statement specify the initial size of the file. In Transact-SQL, the units are, by default, megabytes, although this can be specified explicitly as in the example by using the suffix *MB*. If desired, the file size can be specified in kilobytes using the *KB* suffix in Transact-SQL.

In SQL Server 7.0, when a data file or transaction log file fills it can automatically grow. In previous versions of SQL Server, if a data file or transaction log file filled, applications received error messages and the database administrator had to then intervene. In the SQL Server Enterprise Manager, a file is allowed to automatically grow by checking the *Automatically grow file* check box. This is, in fact, checked by default. In Transact-SQL, the file, by default, will be allowed to grow unless the *FILEGROWTH* keyword is set to 0. When a file grows, the size of the growth increment is controlled by the *File growth* property in the SQL Server Enterprise Manager and the *FILEGROWTH* keyword in Transact-SQL. The growth increment can be specified as a fixed value, such as 10 megabytes, or as a percentage. This is the percentage of the size of the file at the time the increment takes place. Therefore, the size increment will increase over time. In Transact-SQL, the *FILEGROWTH* value can be specified using the suffix MB, KB, or %.

The file may be allowed to grow until it takes up all the available space in the physical storage device on which it resides, at which point an error will be returned when it tries to grow again. Alternatively, a limit can be set using the *Restrict filegrowth (MB)* text box in the SQL Server Enterprise Manager or the *MAXSIZE* keyword in Transact-SQL. The *MAXSIZE* value can be specified using the suffix MB or KB.

Note: Every time a file extends the applications using the database during the file extension operation may experience a performance degradation. Also, extending a file multiple times may result in fragmented disk space. It is advisable, therefore, to try and create the file with an initial size that is estimated to be close to the size that will ultimately be required by the file.

The following example shows a CREATE DATABASE statement that will create a database consisting of multiple data and transaction log files:

```
CREATE DATABASE BankingDB
ON PRIMARY
( NAME = BankingData1,
  FILENAME = 'd:\data\BankingData1.mdf',
  SIZE = 50MB,
  MAXSIZE = 200MB,
  FILEGROWTH = 25MB),
( NAME = BankingData2,
  FILENAME = 'e:\data\BankingData2.ndf',
  SIZE = 50MB,
  MAXSIZE = 200MB,
  FILEGROWTH = 25MB)
LOG ON
( NAME = BankingLog1,
  FILENAME = 'f:\data\BankingLog1.ldf',
  SIZE = 50MB,
  MAXSIZE = 200MB,
  FILEGROWTH = 25MB),
( NAME = BankingLog2,
  FILENAME = 'g:\data\BankingLog2.ldf',
  SIZE = 50MB,
  MAXSIZE = 200MB,
  FILEGROWTH = 25MB)
```

The following example recreates the multiple file BankingDB database created in the previous example, but this time a user-defined filegroup *Filegroup1* is created. As the file named *BankingData2* follows the filegroup definition, it is placed in this filegroup. This means that tables, indexes and text/image data can be explicitly placed in this filegroup if required. If no filegroup is specified on the object definition, the object will be created in the DEFAULT filegroup, which, unless it is changed, is the primary filegroup.

```
CREATE DATABASE BankingDB
ON PRIMARY
( NAME = BankingData1,
  FILENAME = 'd:\data\BankingData1.mdf',
  SIZE = 50MB,
  MAXSIZE = 200MB,
  FILEGROWTH = 25MB),
FILEGROUP Filegroup1
( NAME = BankingData2,
  FILENAME = 'e:\data\BankingData2.ndf',
  SIZE = 50MB,
  MAXSIZE = 200MB,
  FILEGROWTH = 25MB)
LOG ON
( NAME = BankingLog1,
  FILENAME = 'f:\data\BankingLog1.ldf',
  SIZE = 50MB,
  MAXSIZE = 200MB,
  FILEGROWTH = 25MB),
( NAME = BankingLog2,
  FILENAME = 'g:\data\BankingLog2.ldf',
  SIZE = 50MB,
  MAXSIZE = 200MB,
  FILEGROWTH = 25MB)
```

Various attributes of a database can be modified after it has been created. These include increasing and reducing the size of data and transaction log files, adding and removing database and transaction log files, creating filegroups, changing the DEFAULT filegroup, changing database options, changing the name of the database, and changing its ownership.

These operations are achieved by using the ALTER DATABASE statement, DBCC SHRINKFILE and DBCC SHRINKDATABASE and the system stored procedures *sp_dboption, sp_renamedb,* and *sp_changedbowner*. Most of these operations can also be changed through the SQL Server Enterprise Manager. Let us first look at increasing the size of a database.

3.4   Increasing the Size of a Database

To increase the size of a database, data and transaction log files may be expanded by using the SQL Server Enterprise Manager or the Transact-SQL ALTER DATABASE statement. Increasing the size of a file in the SQL Server Enterprise Manager is merely a case of entering a new value in the *Space allocated (MB)* text box, as shown in Figure 3.4.

Figure 3.4

Increasing the Size of a Database File

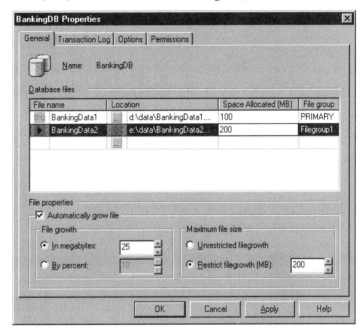

In Transact-SQL, the ALTER DATABASE statement is used:

```
ALTER DATABASE BankingDB
   MODIFY FILE
   (NAME = BankingData2,
    SIZE = 100MB)
```

Note that file attributes such as MAXSIZE and FILEGROWTH may also be modified with an ALTER DATABASE statement, but only one attribute may be specified at any one time.

Note: Only members of the *db_owner* and *db_ddladmin* fixed database roles and members of the *sysadmin* and *dbcreator* fixed server roles may alter a database. Fixed database and server roles are discussed in Chapter 10.

To increase the size of a database, data and transaction log files may be added:

```
ALTER DATABASE BankingDB
  ADD FILE
  (NAME = BankingData3,
  FILENAME = 'h:\data\BankingData3.ndf',
  SIZE = 50MB,
  MAXSIZE = 200MB,
  FILEGROWTH = 25MB)
```

Note that to add a transaction log file the ADD LOG clause is used.

To add a file to an existing user-defined filegroup, the ADD FILE .. TO FILEGROUP syntax is used.

```
ALTER DATABASE BankingDB
  ADD FILE
  (NAME = BankingData3,
  FILENAME = 'd:\data\BankingData3.ndf',
  SIZE = 50MB,
  MAXSIZE = 200MB,
  FILEGROWTH = 25MB)
  TO FILEGROUP FileGroup1
```

Figure 3.5

Adding a New File to an Existing Filegroup

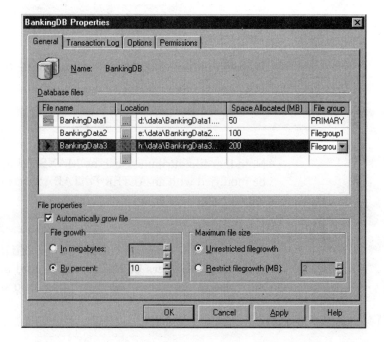

In the SQL Server Enterprise Manager, adding a new file to an existing filegroup is achieved by selecting the appropriate filegroup from the drop-down *File group* list as shown in Figure 3.5.

Note: A file that already exists in the database cannot be subsequently added to another filegroup.

3.5   Decreasing the Size of a Database

There are a number of mechanisms that can be used to decrease the size of a database. On one hand a database can be simply flagged to allow automatic database shrinkage to occur at periodic intervals, needing no effort on the part of the database administrator, but also allowing no control. On the other hand, DBCC statements can be used to manually shrink a database or individual database files; these DBCC statements provide the database administrator the greatest control over how the shrinkage takes place. In between, the SQL Server Enterprise Manager provides a means to shrink a database that can be scheduled under the control of the database administrator.

Before we look at shrinking a database it is worth considering why we might want to do it. Obviously, shrinking a database in a way that physically releases space back to the operating system is an attractive proposition if space is limited on the server and disk space must be shared amongst applications. However, if space is taken away from a database and is used by another application, it is no longer available for use by that database again. If the database is likely to grow and need the space in the short term, it is pointless to release the space. Also, the process of expanding the database files in increments, as just discussed, is not necessarily efficient as the act of extending the file may impact the performance of applications and the file extents may end up being fragmented around the disk drive.

However, if a database has grown in an uncharacteristic fashion because a large amount of data has been added and then removed, it makes sense to release the space that is not likely to be needed again. With these thoughts in mind, let us look at how a database and its files may be shrunk.

3.5.1   The Autoshrink Database Option

A database option can be set that makes a database a candidate for automatically being shrunk. Database options and how to set them are discussed shortly. At periodic intervals a database with this option set may be shrunk if there is sufficient free space in the database to warrant it. Note that the database administrator has no control over exactly what happens and when.

3.5.2   Shrinking a Database in the SQL Server Enterprise Manager

A database may be shrunk using the SQL Server Enterprise Manager. To do so:

⇨   Expand the server group and expand the server.

⇨   Expand *Databases*, then right click the database to be shrunk.

⇨   Select *All Tasks* and *Shrink Database*.

⇨   Select the desired options.

⇨   Click *OK*.

The SQL Server Enterprise Manager *Shrink Database* dialog box is shown in Figure 3.6.

Figure 3.6

Shrinking a Database Using the SQL Server Enterprise Manager

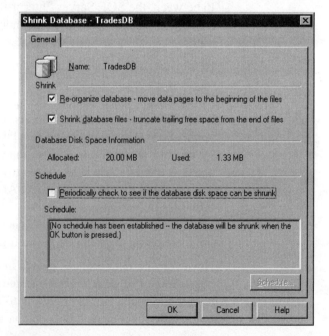

The dialog box offers two options concerning database shrinkage. These are to reorganize the data in the database files by relocating pages at the end of the file to the beginning of the file and to truncate the files, releasing the free space at the end of the file back to the operating system. At least one of these options must be set. These options map to the DBCC statement options described next. Note that the SQL Server Enterprise Manager allows a schedule to be set so that the database can be checked periodically to see if it can be shrunk, however, it does not let the database administrator specify by how much the database is shrunk.

3.5.3 Shrinking a Database Using DBCC Statements

The greatest control over database file shrinkage is provided by two DBCC statements—DBCC SHRINKDATABASE and DBCC SHRINKFILE. The first statement considers all the files in the database when attempting to shrink it. The second statement only considers the named file.

The SQL Server Enterprise Manager actually executes a DBCC SHRINKDATABASE when it is used to shrink a database.

Let us first consider DBCC SHRINKDATABASE. The syntax diagram for this statement is as follows:

```
DBCC SHRINKDATABASE
( database_name [, target_percent]
[, {NOTRUNCATE | TRUNCATEONLY}]
)
```

The target percent parameter is the desired percentage of free space left in the database file after the database has been shrunk. If this parameter is omitted, SQL Server will attempt to shrink the database as much as possible.

The NOTRUNCATE and TRUNCATEONLY options map onto the options available in the SQL Server Enterprise Manager *Shrink Database* dialog box. The NOTRUNCATE option ensures that any free file space produced by relocating data is kept within the database files and not given back to the operating system. If the database files were examined with Windows Explorer before and after the shrink operation, no change in file size would be observed.

The TRUNCATEONLY option ensures that any free space at the end of the data files is returned to the operating system but no data is relocated within the files. If the database files were examined with Windows Explorer before and after the shrink operation, a change in file size may be observed. The *target_percent* parameter is disregarded when the TRUNCATEONLY option is used.

If neither of these is specified, data is relocated in the files and the free space at the end of the files is released to the operating system.

The operation of shrinking a database is not quite so straightforward as it first appears. Various restrictions come into play and you may not always see shrinkage as large as you may expect. For example, a database file cannot be shrunk using DBCC SHRINKDATABASE to smaller than the size at which it was first created. Also a database cannot be shrunk smaller than the model database (a DBCC SHRINKFILE can shrink a file smaller than its initial size). Data files and transaction log files are also treated differently. In the case of data files, each file is considered individually. In the case of transaction log files, all the files are treated as if they were one contiguous lump of transaction log.

Do not expect a transaction log to shrink immediately. It is marked for shrinking and will physically shrink when it is truncated after a transaction log backup. Of course, a database can never be shrunk smaller than the amount of data it currently holds.

Let us now consider DBCC SHRINKFILE. The syntax diagram for this statement is as follows:

```
DBCC SHRINKFILE
( {file_name | file_id }
{ [, target_size]
| [, {EMPTYFILE | NOTRUNCATE | TRUNCATEONLY}]
}
)
```

The target size parameter is the desired size to which the database file should be shrunk. If this parameter is omitted, SQL Server will attempt to shrink the file as much as possible.

The NOTRUNCATE and TRUNCATEONLY options have the same meaning as for DBCC SHRINKDATABASE. The EMPTYFILE option moves the data contained in the file to other files that reside in the same filegroup and stops the file being used to hold new data. This option is most often used to prepare a file for removal from the database. It could not otherwise be removed if it contained data.

3.5.4   Removing Database Files

Files may be removed from the database by using the ALTER DATBASE statement. Neither data files nor transaction log files can be removed from a database if they contain data or transaction log records. In the case of data files, the DBCC SHRINKFILE statement with the EMPTYFILE option can be used to move data out of the file that is to be removed to other files in the same filegroup. This is not possible in the case of transaction log files. The transaction log will have to be truncated to remove transaction log records before the removal of a transaction log file is possible.

The following example removes a file from the BankingDB database created earlier:

```
ALTER DATABASE BankingDB
    REMOVE FILE BankingData2
```

Removing a file using the SQL Server Enterprise Manager is merely a case of selecting the file to remove and pressing the *Delete* key, as shown in Figure 3.7.

Figure 3.7

Removing a File with the SQL Server Enterprise Manager

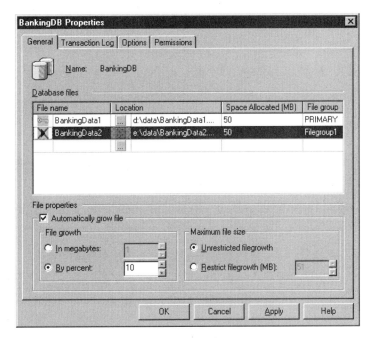

A filegroup may also be removed:

```
ALTER DATABASE BankingDB
    REMOVE FILEGROUP FileGroup1
```

However, a filegroup cannot be removed if it contains files.

3.6   Modifying Filegroup Properties

The properties of a filegroup may be changed. Filegroup properties can be READWRITE, READONLY, and DEFAULT. The READWRITE property is typically the property that most filegroups have. This means that objects such as tables and indexes in the filegroup can be both retrieved and changed. The READONLY property is the opposite of the READWRITE property in that those objects in a filegroup with the READONLY property set cannot be changed; they can only be retrieved. The primary filegroup cannot have this property set.

The DEFAULT property is typically set on the primary filegroup. A filegroup with this property set is used to store objects whose definition does not include a target filegroup specification. The DEFAULT property can be set on a filegroup other than the primary filegroup but only one filegroup in a database can have this property set. The following example sets the READONLY attribute on the filegroup FileGroup1:

```
ALTER DATABASE BankingDB
    MODIFY FILEGROUP FileGroup1 READONLY
```

Note: Setting the properties READONLY or READWRITE requires exclusive use of the database.

3.7   Setting Database Options

Database options are the *attributes* of a database and control the way it behaves and its capabilities. The database options are listed in Table 3.1 below.

Table 3.1 *Database Options*

Settable options	Meaning
ANSI null default	This option controls the database default nullability. If a table column is created without specifying NULL or NOT NULL the default behavior is to create the column with NOT NULL. However, the ANSI standard specifies that the column should be created with NULL. Set this option to follow the ANSI standard. It is recommended that NULL or NOT NULL is always explicitly specified to avoid confusion.

ANSI nulls	This option controls the result of comparing NULL values. If it is set, comparisons to a null value evaluate to NULL, not TRUE or FALSE. When not set, comparisons of non-Unicode values to a NULL value evaluate to TRUE if both values are NULL.
ANSI warnings	This option controls whether warnings are issued if, for example, NULL values appear in aggregate functions.
auto create statistics	This option controls whether statistics are automatically created on columns used in the search conditions in WHERE clauses.
auto update statistics	This option controls whether existing statistics are automatically updated when the statistics become inaccurate because the data in the tables has changed.
autoclose	This option controls whether a database is shutdown and its resources released when the last user finishes using it.
autoshrink	This option controls whether a database is a candidate for automatic shrinking.
concat null yields null	This option controls whether NULL is the result of a concatenation if either operand is NULL.
cursor close on commit	This option controls whether cursors are closed when a transaction commits.
dbo use only	This option controls whether access to a database is limited to members of the db_owner fixed database role only.
default to local cursor	This option controls whether cursors are created locally or globally when this is not explicitly specified.
merge publish	This option controls whether the database can be used for merge replication publications.
offline	This option ensures that the database is closed and shutdown cleanly and marked offline.
published	This option allows the database to be published for replication.
quoted identifier	This option controls whether identifiers can be delimited by double quotation marks.
read only	This option controls whether a database can be modified.
recursive triggers	This option controls whether triggers can fire recursively.
select into/bulkcopy	This option allows non-logged operations to be performed against a database.
single user	This option limits database access to a single user connection.
subscribed	This option allows the database to be subscribed for publication.
torn page detection	This option allows incomplete I/O operations to be detected.
trunc. log on chkpt.	This option allows the inactive portion of the transaction log to be truncated every time the CHECKPOINT process activates.

To set a database option the SQL Server Enterprise Manager or the system stored procedure *sp_dboption* can be used.

To use the SQL Server Enterprise Manager:

⇨   Expand the server group and expand the server.

⇨   Expand *Databases*, then right click the database whose options are to be set.

⇨   Select *Properties*.

⇨   Select the *Options* tab and the required options.

⇨   Click *OK*.

The SQL Server Enterprise Manager *Options* tab is shown in Figure 3.8.

Figure 3.8
Setting Database Options

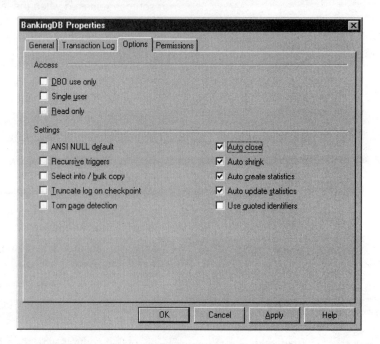

Because some options, for example replication options, are set by other parts of the SQL Server Enterprise Manager, the options displayed in the *Options* tab are a subset of the available database options.

To set a database option using Transact-SQL:

```
EXEC sp_dboption BankingDB, 'READ ONLY', TRUE
```

3.8 Displaying Information about Databases

Information about databases can be obtained through the SQL Server Enterprise Manager or various Transact-SQL statements. We have already seen the properties page that is displayed when a database is right clicked and *Properties* selected. This shows us quite a lot of information, such as the files that comprise the database. An example of this is shown in Figure 3.7. If a database is mouse clicked, a *taskpad* is displayed in the SQL Server Enterprise Manager as shown in Figure 3.9.

Figure 3.9

Viewing the Details of a Database

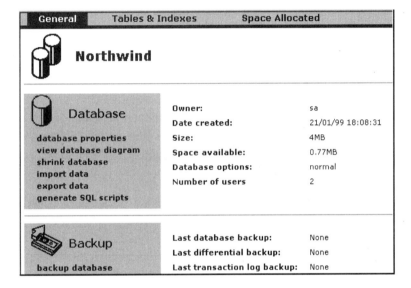

A database administrator can "drill down" by clicking on, for example, *Space Allocated*. The resultant output is shown in Figure 3.10.

Figure 3.10

Displaying Space Allocation Information

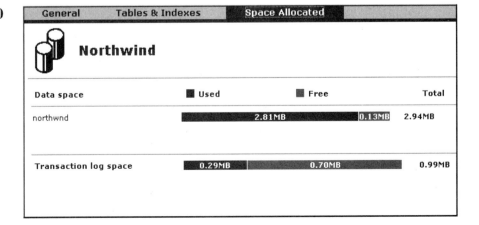

In Transact-SQL, the *sp_helpdb* system stored procedure is very useful:

```
EXEC sp_helpdb
```

name	db_size	owner	dbid	created	status
Banking	1500.00 MB	sa	6	Jul 23 1998	no options set
Derivatives	25.00 MB	sa	8	Jul 18 1998	no options set
master	17.00 MB	sa	1	Jul 12 1998	trunc.log on chkpt.
model	1.00 MB	sa	3	Jul 12 1998	no options set
msdb	8.00 MB	sa	5	Jul 23 1998	trunc.log on chkpt.
pubs	3.00 MB	sa	4	Jul 30 1998	trunc.log on chkpt.
tempdb	2.00 MB	sa	2	Jul 19 1998	select into/bulkcopy

This outputs one row for each database on the server. The *db_size* column is the total size of all the files in the database.

A database name can be specified as a parameter:

```
EXEC sp_helpdb banking
```

name	db_size	owner	dbid	created	status
Banking	1500.00 MB	sa	6	Jul 23 1998	no options set

Name	fileid	filename	filegroup	size	maxsize	growth	usage
bankingdata	1	d:\mssql7\data\bankingdata.mdf	PRIMARY	1024000 KB	Unlimited	1024 KB	data only
bankinglog	2	d:\mssql7\data\bankinglog.ldf	NULL	512000 KB	Unlimited	1024 KB	log only

This displays information about the files in the database. Other useful system stored procedures that can be used to obtain information about files and filegroups are *sp_helpfile* and *sp_helpfilegroup*. Another useful system stored procedure is *sp_spaceused,* which returns space usage information.

3.9   Renaming and Dropping a Database

Occasionally, it may become necessary to rename a database. This can be done with the system stored procedure *sp_renamedb* (or *sp_rename* with an object type of database). This is an operation that cannot be done through the SQL Server Enterprise Manager.

```
EXEC sp_renamedb Northwind, Westwind
```

To rename a database it must be put into single user mode.

To drop a database use the DROP DATABASE statement:

```
DROP DATABASE Westwind
```

The database must not be in use and the connection that is executing the DROP DATABASE statement must do it in the context of the master database.

Note: Once a database has been dropped it is permanently deleted. Only a restore from a backup can get it back.

The owner of a database, usually but not necessarily the person who created it, can be changed with the *sp_changedbowner* system stored procedure:

```
EXEC sp_changedbowner 'Mary'
```

4

Defining Database Objects

4.1   Introduction

In this chapter we will look at the *Data Definition Language* (DDL) capabilities in SQL Server 7.0. The DDL is used to define various objects that are typically found in an SQL Server database and include:

* Tables
* User-defined data types
* Views
* Indexes
* Stored Procedures
* Triggers

In this chapter we will discuss tables, user-defined data types, and views in detail. Indexes, constraints, stored procedures, and triggers will be explored in later chapters.

In the next chapter we will look at the *Data Manipulation Language* (DML) capabilities in SQL Server. DML is used to manipulate the data that can be found in the tables in an SQL Server database.

4.2   Methods for Creating SQL Server Objects

Historically, database management systems used proprietary languages to create their data structures, such as tables and views. The disadvantage of this approach was that every database management system had its own unique way of describing its metadata (data that describes data such as a column definition) and querying its user data. Knowledge gained using one product was not easily transportable to another product. In an effort to solve this problem, the standards bodies defined a standard language for relational database management systems known as *Structured Query Language* (SQL). This is defined by the American National Standards Institute (ANSI), the International Standards Organization (ISO), and standards bodies from around the world. It is adopted by most vendors of relational database management systems.

SQL Server is no exception and provides its version of SQL known as *Transact-SQL*. It should be noted that the SQL Standard is a *living* document and the standard is continually evolving. At any given point in time the database management system vendors will support a subset of the standard to greater or lesser extents. So beware, the SQL provided by vendors is likely to be very similar but not completely so.

Creating objects and manipulating them in SQL Server can be achieved with Transact-SQL. It is not the only method, however, as SQL Server provides graphical tools that can also be used. Which method is used is a matter of preference and we will introduce both approaches. Database administrators who are already familiar with earlier versions of SQL Server will be used to typing Transact-SQL. New users will probably find that it is easier to use the SQL Server Enterprise Manager. It should be noted that the Transact-SQL definitions of objects can be reverse-engineered from the objects themselves irrespective of the method used to create them.

Note: It is worth keeping a textual Transact-SQL definition of the objects present in SQL Server. This provides a means of recreating lost definitions and can also form part of the database documentation as well as be a tool for recreating definitions on other database management systems.

The tools used to create and manage objects include:

♦   OSQL—a command line utility that accepts individual Transact-SQL statements or groups of them known as *batches*. This utility accesses SQL Server using the ODBC Application Programming Interface (API).

♦   ISQL—a legacy command line utility that accepts individual Transact-SQL statements or batches. This utility accesses SQL Server using the older DB-Library API.

♦   The Query Analyzer—a graphical tool that executes individual Transact-SQL statements or batches and also provides a graphical representation of the way SQL Server executes queries (a query plan). The

Query Analyzer can be thought of as a graphical superset of OSQL and ISQL and so these command line utilities will not be described separately.

♦ The SQL Server Enterprise Manager—a graphical tool that can be used for creating and managing SQL Server objects instead of using textual Transact-SQL statements. It is also used to administer local and remote servers.

There are other graphical tools such as the SQL Performance Monitor and the SQL Server Profiler that are used for monitoring the performance of a database.

4.2.1 The Query Analyzer

The Query Analyzer can be invoked from the SQL Server menu: *Start → Programs → SQL Server 7.0 → Query Analyzer*. It can also be started from the *Tools* menu in the SQL Server Enterprise Manager. When it is selected the user is presented with a window as shown in Figure 4.1.

Figure 4.1
The Query Analyzer Window

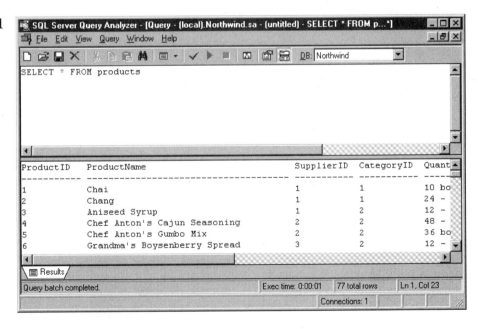

In Figure 4.1, the user has typed a query into the *Query Pane* and has executed the query by hitting the CTRL+E or ALT+X keys or mouse-clicking the *Execute* button (the green arrow). The result of the query has been displayed in the *Results Pane*.

The Query Analyzer has many capabilities but we will save the description of these to Chapter 6 where we will be typing in a multitude of DML statements!

4.2.2 SQL Server Enterprise Manager

The SQL Server Enterprise Manager can be invoked from the SQL Server menu: *Start → Programs → SQL Server 7.0 → Enterprise Manager*. When it is selected the user is presented with a window as seen in Figure 4.2.

Figure 4.2
The SQL Server Enterprise Manager.

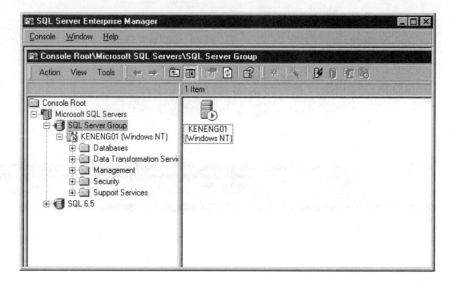

The SQL Server Enterprise Manager is a "snap-in" to the Microsoft Management Console (MMC). The MMC provides a consistent user interface for Microsoft's BackOffice® server management environment.

As can be seen from Figure 4.2, the server KENENG01 is visible in the *console tree*. This is because KENENG01 is the local server and this is detected automatically. Other servers must be registered. This is performed with the *Register Server* wizard. The database administrator can manage many SQL Servers on the network and there are many features of the SQL Server Enterprise Manager that facilitate this. In this chapter, however, we will focus on those features used to manage objects such as tables.

If the *Databases* folder is expanded and the chosen database is expanded, a list of folders becomes visible in the console tree, as shown in Figure 4.3. In the *details pane*, on the right of the console tree, information about the selected database is displayed.

Figure 4.3

Expanding the Database Folder

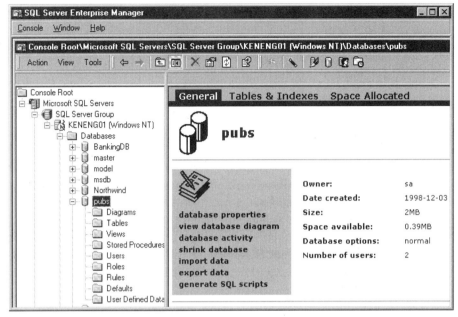

There are various routes into the SQL Server Enterprise Manager to arrive at a properties page that will allow the database administrator to perform a particular task and we shall explore some of these. Of course, in many instances a wizard is at hand to help. As a general rule of thumb, if a folder is right-clicked the option to create a new object in it is displayed. If an object is right-clicked and the *Properties* option selected, various attributes of the object can be set.

In Figure 4.3 the system databases appear in the list of databases. Specifying that this should happen also causes the system tables to be displayed along with user tables. This tends to clutter the display and so we will turn this attribute off. However, the place to do this is not intuitive. Here is what we must do:

⇨ Expand the server group and expand the server.

⇨ Right-click the server and click *Edit SQL Server Registration properties.*

⇨ Click *Show system databases and system objects.*

⇨ Click *OK.*

When first using the SQL Server Enterprise Manager, database administrators typically expect this attribute to be set as part of the server properties. It is not, however, a server property. It is a property of the individual server registration in the SQL Server Enterprise Manager.

As can be seen from Figure 4.3, there are a number of menu options labelled *Action*, *View*, and *Tools* on the *command bar*. The *Action* menu is equivalent to right-clicking an object. The options presented are the same and these depend on what object is selected in the console tree or details pane. Also, depending on which object is selected, various *command buttons* are displayed. For example, if a specific object such as the database *pubs* or the table *authors* is displayed, the *Delete* option in the *Action* menu is displayed and the *Delete* button is highlighted.

Note: Usually a *Refresh* button is present on the command bar. This forces the metadata cache on the SQL Server Enterprise Manager client to be refreshed. It will reread the system tables on the server. If this is not done a change made by another connection may not be displayed by the current SQL Server Enterprise Manager session.

The *Tools* menu presents a list of tools such as the Query Analyzer, SQL Server Profiler, and Database Maintenance Planner.

4.3   Creating Tables, User-Defined Data Types and Views

In relational databases, such as SQL Server, data is stored in tables. Examples of tables are those in the *pubs* database including the *titles* and *authors* tables. Usually, a table represents some real-world object that is relevant to a company's business, sometimes referred to as an entity. A table may contain a number of rows that are instances of an entity. For example, the *authors* table contains a number of rows, one for each author. The rows consist of columns, which represent attributes of the entity. For example, the *authors* table consists of a number of columns that are attributes of the entity author, such as the author's name and address. Figure 4.4 shows the *Authors* table in the pubs database and five rows from it.

Figure 4.4
The Authors Table

au_id	au_lname	au_fname	phone	address	city	state	zip	contract
172-32-1176	White	Johnson	408 496-7223	10932 Bigge Rd.	Menlo Park	CA	94025	1
213-46-8915	Green	Marjorie	415 986-7020	309 63rd St. #411	Oakland	CA	94618	1
238-95-7766	Carson	Cheryl	415 548-7723	589 Darwin Ln.	Berkeley	CA	94705	1
267-41-2394	O'Leary	Michael	408 286-2428	22 Cleveland Av. #14	San Jose	CA	95128	1
274-80-9391	Straight	Dean	415 834-2919	5420 College Av.	Oakland	CA	94609	1

At a point in the database design cycle it becomes necessary to physically create the tables that until now merely existed as part of a logical design.

By now a number of decisions should have been made, such as:

- The tables that are to be created in the database.

- The columns that comprise the tables.

- The data types, size, and precision of those columns.

- Default values for columns.

- Legal values for columns.

- Nullability for columns.

- The columns in a table that constitute the primary keys.

- The columns in a table that constitute the foreign keys.

- The views that are to be created in the database.

- The indexes that are to be created on a table.

Assuming this is so, let us now look at how tables, user-defined data types, and views are created. We will look at how to create these objects in Transact-SQL and the SQL Server Enterprise Manager.

4.3.1 Creating Tables

Tables are created with the CREATE TABLE Transact-SQL statement or with the SQL Server Enterprise Manager. The attributes of a table will be described using the CREATE TABLE statement and then we will look at creating a table with the SQL Server Enterprise Manager.

Basically, creating a table is simply a case of naming the table and listing the columns that it will be comprised of:

```
CREATE TABLE titleauthor
    (
    au_id      ID,
    title_id   TID,
    au_ord     TINYINT    NULL,
    royaltyper INT        NULL
    )
```

The only items that need to be considered initially are the names of the columns and the table itself, the data types of the columns and whether the columns allow *null* values. There are a number of other attributes concerning, for example, database integrity and we shall cover these in later chapters.

In the above example the data types are *TINYINT, INT, ID,* and *TID*. TINYINT and INT are known as *system data types,* whereas ID and TID are known as *user-defined data types*. These will be described on the following pages.

If a column is flagged as NOT NULL this means that a value for the column must be supplied when a row is inserted into the table. A value can either be supplied explicitly by the application issuing the INSERT statement or by means of a DEFAULT definition. DEFAULT definitions will be described in Chapter 8. If the attribute NULL is specified, the row can be inserted without a value being supplied for the column or a DEFAULT definition being defined on it. NULL represents the fact that a value is missing, that is, undefined. What happens if you do not specify NULL or NOT NULL in the column definition? The answer is somewhat complicated. The behavior depends on the setting of database options and session options. It is always best to explicitly state whether a column allows null values or not as part of its definition.

Note: A table may contain a maximum of 1024 columns.

If a table is created, in what database does it reside? Prior to creating a table, a database context must be created, that is, the database environment must be declared. In the Query Analyzer, a database can be selected from the list box. In Transact-SQL this is achieved with the USE statement:

```
USE pubs
```

Tables may now be created in the pubs database. To create a table in another database another USE statement can be issued:

```
USE oldpubs
```

The two classes of data types used for table columns are system and user-defined data types. As their names suggest, system data types are those data types that SQL Server provides, whereas user-defined data types are defined by the database designer using the system data types as building blocks. User-defined data types can be specific to a database or, if they are created in the model database, to all the databases in a SQL Server created after the user-defined data types were placed in the model.

How to create user-defined data types will be discussed shortly. First it is worth looking at the types of system data types available. It is useful to group these into categories, as listed below:

◆   Character

◆   Unicode

- ❖ Numeric
- ❖ Monetary
- ❖ Date and Time
- ❖ Binary
- ❖ Text and Image
- ❖ Special

Character

The character data types typically hold alphanumeric characters but can also hold symbols, depending on the character set chosen at SQL Server installation time. Character data types can be specified as CHAR(n) and VARCHAR(n). However, to maintain compatibility with the SQL-92 standard, the synonyms CHARACTER and CHARACTER VARYING can be used instead of CHAR and VARCHAR respectively.

A CHAR(n) column can be considered to be a fixed length of "n" characters up to a maximum of 8000. If a CHAR(100) column is created it will take up 100 bytes whether 1 or 100 characters are stored in it.

In contrast, a VARCHAR(n) column can be considered to be a variable length of "n" characters up to a maximum of 8000. If a VARCHAR(100) column is created it will take up only the space it actually needs. If 10 characters are stored in it, considerably less space will be used than if 100 characters are stored in it. Hence, use of a VARCHAR data type could save disk space if a column contained character data that varied in length throughout the table, such as a person's last name. However, a VARCHAR(n) data type may require more processing than its CHAR(n) equivalent when it is updated.

Note: An UPDATE statement may cause a column defined with a VARCHAR data type to increase in size such that there is no longer sufficient space on the database page to accommodate the row. In this situation, the row will migrate to a new page, leaving a forwarding pointer at its old position. This is similar to a forwarding address you may leave if you move.

If the amount of character data to be stored in a CHAR or VARCHAR column exceeds 8000 characters, the TEXT data type can be used. This is described later in the chapter.

Unicode

The Unicode standard uses 2 bytes to represent a character instead of the single byte used in traditional character sets. Traditional character sets could only represent 256 characters due to the 1 byte (256 bit combinations) limitation. This meant that characters from different foreign languages could not all be held in one character set—there were just too many of them. As the Unicode standard uses 2 bytes there are 65,536 possible bit combinations. This means that there are enough combinations to hold all the characters typically found in business use around the world. It does, of course, mean that twice the storage space is used to hold a string than using a traditional character set.

The Unicode data types are NCHAR, NVARCHAR, and NTEXT. As you may suspect, NCHAR and NVARCHAR are the Unicode equivalent of CHAR and VARCHAR. The NTEXT data type is the Unicode equivalent of the TEXT data type that we shall discuss shortly.

Because of the 2 byte storage requirement, the NCHAR and NVARCHAR data types can hold a maximum of 4000 characters, that is, you may specify a maximum string length of NCHAR(4000) and NVARCHAR(4000).

The NTEXT data type can hold a maximum of 1,073,741,823 characters.

Numeric

There are a number of ways of representing numbers in SQL Server. Numbers can be whole numbers (integers) and decimal and fractional numbers.

Note: To achieve the maximum precision of 38, SQL Server must be started with the "p" startup parameter, otherwise the maximum precision is 28.

Integer

The integer data types are very common. They hold whole numbers with no fractional or decimal part, the range being determined by the actual integer data type in use. The integer data types available are TINYINT, SMALLINT, and INT. The TINYINT data type uses 1 byte to hold integers that fall in the range 0 to 255. The SMALLINT data type uses 2 bytes to hold integers that fall in the range -32,768 to 32,767. The INT data type uses 4 bytes to hold integers that fall in the range -2,147,483,648 through 2,147,483,647.

Mathematical expressions can use the integer data types but if you use integers when dividing be careful—the result is truncated not rounded. For example, if you divide 5 by 3 you will get the result 1. You may expect the result of 1.666666 to be rounded up to 2, but it is truncated instead.

Note: To maintain compatibility with the SQL-92 standard, the synonym INTEGER can be used instead of INT.

Decimal

The DECIMAL data type can store up to 38 digits and these can all be to the right of the decimal point. When defining a DECIMAL data type the *precision* and *scale* may be specified. A precision and scale can be specified in the form DECIMAL[(p[,s])] where p is the precision, that is the maximum number of digits stored on both sides of the decimal point, and s is the *scale,* which is the maximum number of digits stored right of the decimal point. For example, DECIMAL (7,4) could represent 345.6687.

The storage requirements of the DECIMAL data type depend on the precision. For example, a precision of 8 would need 5 bytes of storage whereas a precision of 15 would need 9 bytes of storage.

Note: The synonym NUMERIC can be used instead of DECIMAL and, to maintain compatibility with the SQL-92 standard, the synonym DEC can be used instead of DECIMAL.

Approximate Numeric

Approximate numeric data is also known as floating point data. The FLOAT and REAL data types are used to hold floating point data. The real data type uses four bytes of storage to hold floating-point numbers in the range -3.40E+38 to 3.40E+38 with seven-digit precision. The float data type uses eight bytes of storage and can hold floating point numbers in the range -1.79E+308 to 1.79E+308 with fifteen-digit precision.

The FLOAT data type is specified as FLOAT(n) where n is the number of bits used to hold the mantissa using scientific notation. For example, if n is between 1 and 24 inclusive, the precision is 7 and the storage used is 4 bytes. If n is between 25 and 53 inclusive, the precision is 15 and the storage used is 8 bytes.

Note: To maintain compatibility with the SQL-92 standard, the synonym DOUBLE PRECISION can be used instead of FLOAT(53). Note that REAL is equivalent to FLOAT(24).

Money

This data type holds money amounts. Money data types can be specified as SMALLMONEY or MONEY. The SMALLMONEY data type uses four bytes of storage to hold money amounts in the range -214,748.3648 to +214,748.3647 with ten-thousandth of a monetary unit accuracy. The MONEY data type uses eight bytes of storage to hold money amounts with ten-thousandth of a monetary unit precision in the range -922,337,203,685,477.5808 to +922,337,203,685,477.5807. The DECIMAL data type can be used if four decimal places are not enough accuracy. The currency sign can prefix the value when it is inserted, for example, £45.88.

Date and Time

This data type holds date and time values. The DATETIME data type uses 8 bytes of storage. The base date is defined as January 1st, 1753 and the maximum date that can be held is December 31, 9999. The date is held to an accuracy of one three-hundredth of a second. There is also a SMALLDATETIME data type that uses four bytes of storage to hold date and time values with an accuracy of one minute. The base date for the SMALLDATETIME data type is defined as January 1st, 1900 and the maximum date that can be held is June 6, 2079.

Binary

This data type holds binary data in the form of hexadecimal numbers. In a similar way to the character data types described above, there are BINARY(n) and VARBINARY(n) data types. The BINARY(n) and VARBINARY(n) data types can hold a maximum of 8000 bytes. Examples of binary data would be a Microsoft Excel spreadsheet or a bitmap picture.

If the amount of character data to be stored in a BINARY or VARBINARY column exceeds 8000 bytes, the IMAGE data type can be used.

Text and Image

The TEXT data type and IMAGE data type are used to hold character data and binary data that exceeds 8000 bytes. The NTEXT data type is used to hold Unicode data greater than 8000 bytes. TEXT and NTEXT data is interpreted as a stream of characters, whereas IMAGE data is interpreted as a stream of bits.

A column defined with the TEXT or IMAGE data types can hold 2,147,483,647 characters or bytes respectively. As mentioned previously, a column defined with the NTEXT data type can hold a maximum of 1,073,741,823 characters, as each character uses two bytes of storage.

Special

There are a number of data types that cannot be conveniently grouped with the others.

Bit

The BIT data type can hold the values 0 or 1 (or null). A single bit within a byte is used, so eight columns of a BIT data type can be held in one byte.

Timestamp

The TIMESTAMP data type holds a value that is updated every time a row containing it is updated or when the row is initially inserted. It holds a value that is unique in the database. Its main use is as a check to see if a row has been changed since a user last read it.

Uniqueidentifier

The UNIQUEIDENTIFIER data type holds a 16-byte hexadecimal value used to specify a globally unique identifier value. This will be described shortly.

4.3.2   User-Defined Data Types

User-defined data types may be created based on the system data types just described. This is useful when a number of tables must contain the same column definition. This is a common situation. For example, the pubs database uses the *title_id* column in the *titles*, *titleauthor*, *sales,* and *roysched* tables. Creating and using user-defined data types ensures that the data type, length, and nullability of the columns is the same.

Creating and managing user-defined data types is described later in this chapter.

4.3.3   Identity Columns

In a table, one column may be designated as being an identity column. This means that SQL Server automatically generates the column's data whenever a new row is added to the table. Typically, user applications do not explicitly supply a value for an identity column.

To be eligible, a column must not allow null values and must be either an integer data type, that is, TINYINT, SMALLINT, or INT, or be a DECIMAL or NUMERIC data type with zero scale.

When defining the identity property for a column, a *seed* and *increment* value are specified. The seed value is the value used for the first row inserted into a table. The increment is the value added to the last value used to obtain the new value for the next row. The following example specifies that the *CustID* column has the identity property with a seed value of ten and an increment of two.

```
CREATE TABLE customer
  (
  CustID    INT       NOT NULL IDENTITY (10,2),
  CustName  CHAR(20)  NOT NULL
  )
```

Various functions can be used to display information about a column with the identity property. For example, the functions IDENT_INCR(), IDENT_SEED() and @@IDENTITY can be used to find the increment, seed value, and last inserted identity value respectively. Functions are described in Chapter 6.

4.3.4   Computed Columns

A column in a table may be defined as a *computed column*. A computed column does not take up any space in the table, as it does not actually hold data. Rather, it is materialized when rows from the table are selected. The definition of a computed column is an expression involving columns from the same table. The example below defines a computed column, *Area*, as the product of two other columns:

```
CREATE TABLE PropertyLand
  (
  PlotNo INT,
  Length INT,
  Width INT,
  Area AS Length * Width
  )

SELECT * FROM PropertyLand
```

```
PlotNo      Length     Width      Area
_____      _____     _____     _____

1           23         23         529
2           786        6554       5151444
3           3          5          15
```

Because computed columns do not hold data, values cannot be specified for them when a row is inserted into a table or when a row is updated. Also, they cannot be used as a column in an index.

4.3.5   The UNIQUEIDENTIFIER Data Type

As mentioned previously, the UNIQUEIDENTIFIER data type holds a 16-byte hexadecimal number. A column defined with the UNIQUE-IDENTIFIER data type is used to hold a globally unique identification number (GUID). A GUID is a number that is unique across the servers in a network and is typically used by SQL Server to support merge replication. However, it can be used by any application.

The UNIQUEIDENTIFIER data type is used in conjunction with the NEWID() function to assign a globally unique value. The example below creates a table with a UNIQUEIDENTIFIER data type used for the *OrdID* column. It has a DEFAULT definition specifying the NEWID() function. When a row is inserted into the table, the NEWID() function generates a globally unique value for the column. This value is then displayed in the SELECT statement. The SELECT and INSERT statements are described in Chapter 5 and DEFAULT definitions are described in Chapter 7.

```
CREATE TABLE Orders
    (
    OrdID    UNIQUEIDENTIFIER    NOT NULL DEFAULT NEWID(),
    PartID   CHAR(10)            NOT NULL,
    Qty      INT
    )


INSERT INTO Orders (PartID,Qty) VALUES ('VH776JK987',23)


SELECT * FROM Orders
```

```
OrdID                                        PartID      Qty
_____        _____  ___

FBA9A4D4-ADC5-11D1-8573-0060088ECA3B         VH776JK987  23
```

As a table may have a number of columns using the UNIQUEIDENTIFIER data type, it is useful to designate one of these columns to uniquely identify the rows in the table. This is achieved by the use of the ROWGUIDCOL property. For example:

```
CREATE TABLE Orders
    (
    OrdID   UNIQUEIDENTIFIER   NOT NULL
            DEFAULT NEWID()    ROWGUIDCOL,
        :

        :
```

Note: Only the operators =, <>, IS NULL, and IS NOT NULL can be used with a UNIQUEIDENTIFIER data type column.

4.3.6   Creating Tables using the SQL Server Enterprise Manager

As mentioned previously, tables can be created using the SQL Server Enterprise Manager. To do so:

⇨ Expand the server group and expand the server.

⇨ Expand *Databases* and expand the database in which the table is to be created.

⇨ Right-click the *Tables* folder and click *New Table.*

⇨ Enter a name for the table.

⇨ Enter a definition for each column including a name and data type and where appropriate a length, precision, and scale

⇨ Enter other column attributes such as *Allow Nulls, Default Value, Identity,* and *RowGuid.*

⇨ Close the window, saving the definition.

An example of the *New Table* dialog box is shown in Figure 4.5 below.

Another way to create tables is to use a database diagram. A database diagram can be created through the SQL Server Enterprise Manager. To do so:

⇨ Expand the server group and expand the server.

⇨ Expand *Databases* and expand the database in which the table is to be created.

⇨ Right-click the *Diagrams* folder and click *New Database Diagram.*

Figure 4.5

*The New Table
Dialog Box*

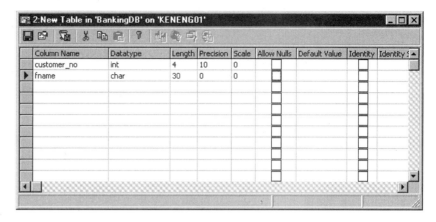

⇨ Click *Next* on the *Welcome* page of the wizard.

⇨ On the *Select Tables to be Added* page, choose the tables to add to the diagram.

⇨ Click *Next* and *Finish*.

This will create a database diagram, an example of which is shown in Figure 4.6.

Figure 4.6

*The Database
Diagram of the
BankingDB
Database*

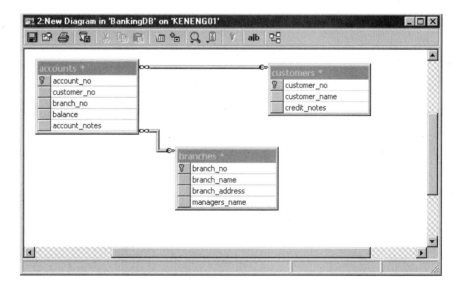

To create a new table click the *New Table* button and enter a name for the new table when prompted. In the grid, enter a definition for each column including a name and data type and where appropriate a length, precision, and scale, as described earlier.

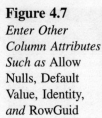

Figure 4.7

Enter Other Column Attributes Such as Allow Nulls, Default Value, Identity, *and* RowGuid

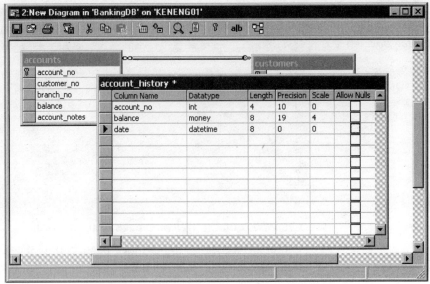

A table may be created through a GUI tool such as the SQL Server Enterprise Manager or database diagram as we have just seen. However, there may still be a requirement to hold the definition of the table in the form of a CREATE TABLE script. Some reasons for this may be for mass deployment, security, or to e-mail the table definition to a colleague. Whatever the reason, generating a CREATE TABLE script from an existing table is easily accomplished. To do so:

⇨   Expand the server group and expand the server.

⇨   Expand *Databases* and expand the database holding the table to be scripted.

⇨   Expand the *Tables* folder and right-click the table to be scripted.

⇨   Click *All Tasks* and *Generate SQL Scripts*.

⇨   In the *Generate SQL Scripts* dialog box, select the object to be scripted and formatting attributes as well as scripting options.

⇨   Click *OK*.

⇨   Specify the name of the file to hold the script and click *Save*.

An example of the *Generate SQL Scripts* dialog box is shown in Figure 4.8.

We have just seen how to create tables through Transact-SQL using the CREATE TABLE statement, the SQL Server Enterprise Manager, and a database diagram. We have also seen a number of properties that relate to columns in tables such as data types and nullability. Once a table is created,

Figure 4.8

The Generate SQL Scripts Dialog Box

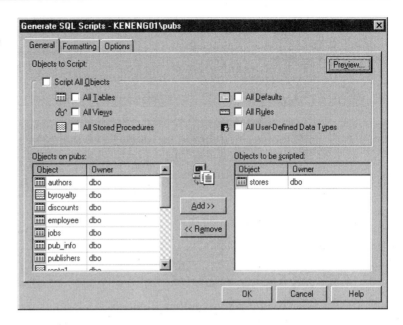

however, it will become necessary eventually to change it. The next section discusses how existing tables containing data can be modified.

4.3.7 Altering Tables

Once a table is created it may be subsequently altered with the ALTER TABLE Transact-SQL statement or the GUI tools such as the SQL Server Enterprise Manager and database diagram. Unlike previous versions of SQL Server, SQL Server 7.0 is very flexible when it comes to changing tables. A table or column name can also be changed using the *sp_rename* system-stored procedure or the GUI tools. The following lists some of the changes that may be performed:

- Changing a table name.

- Adding a column that allows NULL values.

- Adding a column that does not allow NULL values but has a DE-FAULT definition.

- Removing a column.

- Changing a column data type, length, scale, and precision.

- Changing a column nullability.

- Changing a column name.

4.3.8   Changing a Table Name

Occasionally it may become necessary to change the name of a table. This is accomplished with the system-stored procedure *sp_rename*:

```
EXEC sp_rename authors, writers
```

Note: Care should be taken when using this stored procedure as other objects that are based on the table and refer to it by name, such as a view, will be affected.

To rename a table using the SQL Server Enterprise Manager, right-click the table and choose *Rename*.

4.3.9   Adding a Column that Allows NULL Values

To add a column that allows NULL values use the ALTER TABLE statement:

```
ALTER TABLE branches
    ADD branch_area   CHAR(4)   NULL
```

To use the SQL Server Enterprise Manager:

⇨   Expand the server group and expand the server.

⇨   Expand *Databases* and expand the database holding the table to be changed.

⇨   Expand the *Tables* folder and right-click the table to be changed.

⇨   Click *Design Table*.

⇨   Enter the name of the new column, select a data type, and check *Allow Nulls*.

⇨   Close the *Design Table* dialog box, saving the changes.

An example of the *Design Table* dialog box is shown in Figure 4.9.

Adding a new column that allows NULL values through a database diagram is similar to using the *Design Table* dialog box. Right-click the table in the database diagram and click *Column Properties*. Either select the next blank row after the existing columns and add the new column as described above, or right-click an existing column and click *Insert Column* to insert the new column before the existing one, then save the database diagram. Note that this technique to insert the column in any position in the table also applies to the *Design Table* dialog box.

Figure 4.9

Adding a New Column in the Design Table *Dialog Box that Allows NULLs*

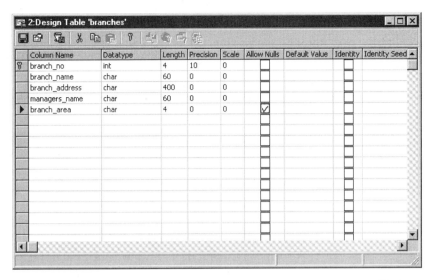

4.3.10 Adding a Column that Does Not Allow NULL Values but Has a Default Definition

To add a column that does not allow NULL values but has a default definition, use the ALTER TABLE statement:

```
ALTER TABLE branches
    ADD branch_area CHAR(4) NOT NULL DEFAULT 'DP77'
```

This statement will affect every row in the table as it will add the column to the table and then update the column with the DEFAULT definition value for every row. If a new row is added to the table and a value is not supplied for the new column, the default value will be placed in the column.

Figure 4.10

Adding a New Column in the Design Table *Dialog Box that Does Not Allow NULLs*

To use the SQL Server Enterprise Manager, the *Design Table* dialog box is used to add the new column as described previously. However, *Allow Nulls* is not checked but a value is entered into the *Default Value* column as shown in Figure 4.10.

Adding a new column that disallows NULL values but specifies a default value through a database diagram is similar to using the *Design Table* dialog box. Right-click the table in the database diagram and click *Column Properties*. Enter the column details as described previously.

Note: Unlike using the ALTER TABLE statement, adding a column that disallows NULL values through the SQL Server Enterprise Manager or a database diagram is accomplished by generating a script. This script creates a new table with a new name and the new properties, copying the data from the table being changed to the new table, removing the old table, and renaming the new table. Constraints and indexes will also be created on the new table. On a large table, these actions could take a while and use a lot of disk space, so be aware of the difference in using the GUI tools that create new tables and the ALTER TABLE statement that does not.

4.3.11   Removing a Column

To remove a column use the ALTER TABLE statement:

```
ALTER TABLE branches
    DROP COLUMN branch_area
```

There are a number of restrictions that govern whether a column can be removed or not. Some of the restrictions that will stop you from removing a column from a table are that the column must not be:

 •   Used in a DEFAULT definition.

 •   Used in a PRIMARY KEY, FOREIGN KEY, UNIQUE, or CHECK constraint.

 •   Used in an index.

 •   Used in a computed column.

 •   Used in replication.

There are other restrictions but these are the ones that you are most likely to trip over.

To use the SQL Server Enterprise Manager to remove a column the *Design Table* dialog box is used. Right-click the column to be removed and click *Delete Column.*

Removing a column through a database diagram is similar to using the *Design Table* dialog box. Right-click the column in the database diagram and click *Delete Column.*

Note: Unlike using the ALTER TABLE statement, removing a column through the SQL Server Enterprise Manager or a database diagram will generate a script that creates a new table as previously described.

4.3.12   Changing a Column Data Type, Length, Scale, and Precision

The data type of a column in the table can be modified as long as the existing data in the column can be implicitly converted to the new data type. To change the data type of a column use the ALTER TABLE statement:

```
ALTER TABLE authors
   ALTER COLUMN city VARCHAR(30)
```

In the above example the *city* column in the *authors* table is a VARCHAR(20), which has been increased to a VARCHAR(30). This operation succeeds as would be expected. However, in the example below, an attempt is made to change the *city* column to a VARCHAR(10). This fails because some of the city names are longer than 10 characters, for example, "Salt Lake City."

```
ALTER TABLE authors
   ALTER COLUMN city VARCHAR(10)

Server: Msg 8152, Level 16, State 9
String or binary data would be truncated.
The statement has been aborted.
```

Suppose we insert a new row into the *Sales* table:

```
INSERT sales VALUES ('8042', 'P724','1994-09-14', 300,
'Net 60', 'MC2222')
```

The *qty* column is a SMALLINT data type. What happens if we try and change this to a TINYINT?

```
ALTER TABLE sales
ALTER COLUMN qty TINYINT
```

```
Server: Msg 220, Level 16, State 2
Arithmetic overflow error for data type tinyint, value
= 300.
The statement has been aborted.
```

Again, the data type SMALLINT cannot be converted to a TINYINT as this data type is not large enough to hold the data.

Can we change the *qty* column SMALLINT to a CHAR(6)?

```
ALTER TABLE sales
ALTER COLUMN qty CHAR(6)
```

This works fine, the CHAR(6) data type can hold the data in the column. Suppose we insert a new row:

```
INSERT sales VALUES ('8042', 'P729','1994-09-14',
'400', 'Net 60', 'PS2091')
```

Can we change the column back to a SMALLINT?

```
ALTER TABLE sales
ALTER COLUMN qty SMALLINT
```

There is no problem. The character strings now held in the *qty* column are all numbers. But suppose before we change the *qty* column back to a SMALLINT we insert this row:

```
INSERT sales VALUES ('8042', 'P769','1994-09-14',
'40Q', 'Net 60', 'BU1032')
```

Could we now change the column back to a SMALLINT?

```
ALTER TABLE sales
ALTER COLUMN qty SMALLINT

Server: Msg 245, Level 16, State 1
Syntax error converting the varchar value '40Q   ' to a
column of data type smallint.
The statement has been aborted.
```

Of course, it is not possible. A value of "40Q" cannot be converted to a SMALLINT.

A number of other restrictions apply when considering changing column attributes. The column cannot be of data type TEXT, IMAGE, NTEXT, or TIMESTAMP and it cannot be a computed column or be used in a computed column. Also it cannot be a column that is being replicated and it cannot be used in an index (with some exceptions). These are just a few of the restrictions—there are others.

In the case of PRECISION and SCALE, these can be changed for the DECI-MAL data type:

```
ALTER TABLE discounts
ALTER COLUMN discount DECIMAL (5,3)
```

To use the SQL Server Enterprise Manager to change a column, the *Design Table* dialog box is used. Edit the properties of the column to be changed. Close the *Design Table* dialog box, saving the changes.

Changing a column through a database diagram is similar to using the *Design Table* dialog box.

Note: Unlike using the ALTER TABLE statement, changing a column through the SQL Server Enterprise Manager or a database diagram will generate a script that creates a new table as previously described.

4.3.13 Changing a Column Nullability

The nullability of a column can be modified. A column that does not allow NULL values can be changed to a column that does, as long as it is not a column participating in a PRIMARY KEY constraint. PRIMARY KEY constraints will be described in Chapter 7. A column that allows NULL values can be changed to a column that does not, as long as it does not contain any NULL values. To change the nullability of a column use the ALTER TABLE statement:

```
ALTER TABLE stores
ALTER COLUMN stor_name VARCHAR(40) NOT NULL
```

To use the SQL Server Enterprise Manager to change the nullability of a column, the *Design Table* dialog box is used. Check or uncheck *Allow Nulls* for the column. Close the *Design Table* dialog box, saving the changes.

Changing the nullability of a column through a database diagram is similar to using the *Design Table* dialog box.

Note: Unlike using the ALTER TABLE statement, changing the nullability of a column through the SQL Server Enterprise Manager or a database diagram will generate a script that creates a new table as previously described.

4.3.14   Changing a Column Name

Occasionally it may become necessary to change the name of a column. This is accomplished with the system-stored procedure *sp_rename*:

```
EXEC sp_rename 'dbo.authors.au_lname', 'lastname', 'COLUMN'
```

Note: Care should be taken when using this stored procedure as other objects that are based on the column and refer to it by name such as a view will be affected.

To use the SQL Server Enterprise Manager to rename a column, the *Design Table* dialog box is used. Change the name for the column. Close the *Design Table* dialog box, saving the changes.

Changing the name of a column through a database diagram is similar to using the *Design Table* dialog box.

4.3.15   Dropping Tables

To drop a table the DROP TABLE statement is used. This removes the table from the database and also any indexes or triggers created on the table, as well as any permissions. No user can be accessing the table while it is being dropped. Disk space used by the table and its indexes will be released to be used by other database objects as required:

```
DROP TABLE authors
```

The SQL Server Enterprise Manager can be used to drop a table. To do so right-click the table name and then select *Delete, Drop All,* and *OK.*

Note: Care should be taken when dropping tables as other objects that are based on the table and refer to the table by name, such as a view, will be affected.

4.3.16   Showing Table Details

A common requirement is to display details about a table, perhaps its columns or its indexes or maybe the space that it uses. There are a number of system-stored procedures that are useful in this respect and the main ones are described below.

The *sp_help* system-stored procedure with no parameters displays a list of objects in the database. Because a database object name in SQL Server 7.0 is an NVARCHAR(128), it is a lot easier to read the output if the results are displayed in a grid as shown in Figure 4.11.

Figure 4.11
The Results of sp_help *in a Grid*

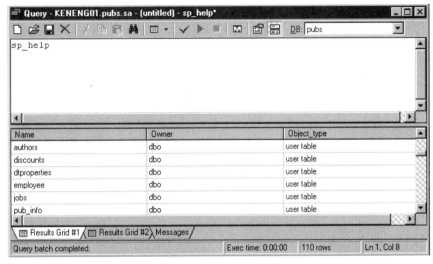

An object name, such as a table name, can also be entered as a parameter, as shown in Figure 4.12.

Figure 4.12
The Results of sp_help objectname *in a Grid*

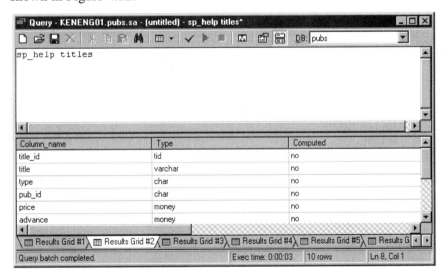

Note: There are a number of *Results Grids* returned by this system-stored procedure when used with an object name.

In the SQL Server Enterprise Manager, various displays return information about a table. We have already seen the *Design Table* dialog box. The table name can also be right-clicked and *Properties* chosen. The display is shown in Figure 4.13.

Figure 4.13
Table Properties

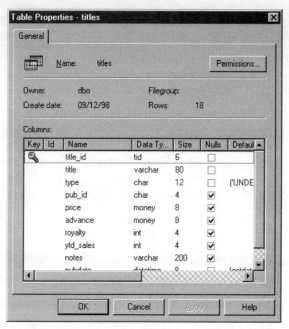

The *sp_spaceused* system-stored procedure can be used to display details about the space usage associated with a table:

```
EXEC sp_spaceused accounts
```

name	rows	reserved	data	index_size	unused
accounts	10000	27616 KB	26672 KB	880 KB	64 KB

In the SQL Server Enterprise Manager, space usage by tables can be displayed by clicking the database name in the console tree and then *Tables and Indexes* in the Details Pane as shown in Figure 4.14.

4.3.17   Information Schema Views

As well as using system-stored procedures to find out information about tables, there are also other mechanisms that can be used. Functions are one mechanism and these will be described in Chapter 6. In previous versions of SQL Server, developers and database administrators could also interrogate the SQL Server system tables to find out information.

Figure 4.14
Checking Table Space Usage through the SQL Server Enterprise Manager

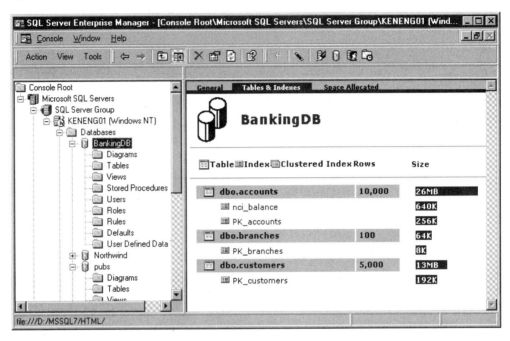

Microsoft recommends that system tables not be queried directly to obtain information about the structure of tables and other system objects. SQL Server 7.0 introduces a new mechanism to obtain catalog (system table) information that is portable between different SQL-92 database management systems. This new mechanism uses views of the catalog known as *information schema* views.

SQL Server supports a three-part naming convention as does SQL-92, however, the names are not the same. The following list shows the relationship between the different names as these names are used in the information schema views:

Server	SQL-92
database	catalog
owner	schema
object	object
user-defined data type	domain

There are 17 information schema views. On the whole, their names are self-explanatory. For example, the *TABLES* information schema displays information about tables and views in the current database, as shown in Figure 4.15.

Figure 4.15
*Using
Information
Schema Views*

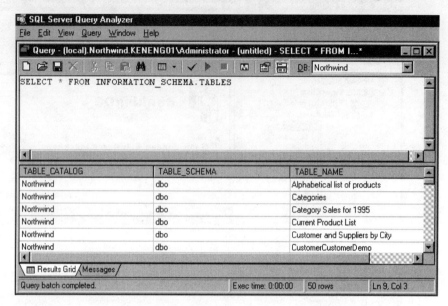

The information schema views are:

INFORMATION_SCHEMA.CHECK_CONSTRAINTS

INFORMATION_SCHEMA.COLUMN_DOMAIN_USAGE

INFORMATION_SCHEMA.COLUMN_PRIVILEGES

INFORMATION_SCHEMA.COLUMNS

INFORMATION_SCHEMA.CONSTRAINT_COLUMN_USAGE

INFORMATION_SCHEMA.CONSTRAINT_TABLE_USAGE

INFORMATION_SCHEMA.DOMAIN_CONSTRAINTS

INFORMATION_SCHEMA.DOMAINS

INFORMATION_SCHEMA.KEY_COLUMN_USAGE

INFORMATION_SCHEMA.REFERENTIAL_CONSTRAINTS

INFORMATION_SCHEMA.SCHEMATA

INFORMATION_SCHEMA.TABLE_CONSTRAINTS

INFORMATION_SCHEMA.TABLE_PRIVILEGES

INFORMATION_SCHEMA.TABLES

INFORMATION_SCHEMA.VIEW_COLUMN_USAGE

INFORMATION_SCHEMA.VIEW_TABLE_USAGE

INFORMATION_SCHEMA.VIEWS

4.3.18   Temporary Tables

The tables that have been described so far in this chapter are permanent tables in the sense that, once they are created, they will exist until they are explicitly dropped. SQL Server also provides the capability of creating temporary tables. They can be used to hold data that do not need to exist after the connection in which they were created finishes.

Two types of temporary tables can be created: *local* and *global*. Local temporary tables have a table name prefixed with a # character, as shown below:

```
CREATE TABLE #Temp1
   (EmpID    CHAR (6),
    Code     TINYINT)
```

A local temporary table is only visible to the connection that created it and it will disappear when the connection terminates.

Global temporary tables have a table name prefixed with two # characters, as shown below:

```
CREATE TABLE ##Temp2
   (EmpID    CHAR (6),
    Code     TINYINT)
```

A global temporary table is visible to all the connections on the server. It will disappear when no connection uses it. In fact, when the connection that created it terminates, no new connection can use the global temporary table. When all the current connections using it terminate, it will disappear.

Temporary tables are created in the system database known as *tempdb*, not the current user database.

4.3.19   Creating Views

Views are virtual tables that do not physically hold data, but rather act like a window into the physical tables that were defined with the CREATE TABLE statement. They can be considered to be a stored query. Views can be created in a database with the CREATE VIEW Transact-SQL statement, SQL Server Enterprise Manager, or the Create View Wizard. To the end-user, a view looks like a table and generally can be treated as if it were a table, however, there are some restrictions concerning the updating of views.

The physical tables on which views are based are called *base* tables. Views can contain subsets of the rows or columns found in a base table or a combination of base tables and can be used to replace often used selection and join operations. Views may also be used to enforce security. A user may be allowed to retrieve data through a view, but not from the underlying base table. Views also provide another level of abstraction in a database as a view can hide from the user the fact that it is comprised of a number of base tables. Because of this, a database administrator can often change the definition and number of base tables in a view without the user being aware that the change has occurred. Views can also provide a different representation of the data in a base table, perhaps by converting underlying data types or by substituting more meaningful representations of the underlying data. For example, in the underlying data the BIT data type may be changed into a meaningful phrase by using a CASE.

Suppose we wish to create a view that limits the number of columns that are displayed from the *authors* table. Perhaps we only want to provide a view that displays the author ID, last name, and first name. This is shown pictorially in Figure 4.16.

Figure 4.16

The AuthorsNamesVW View

au_id	au_lname	au_fname	phone	address	city	state	zip	contract
172-32-1176	White	Johnson	408 496-7223	10932 Bigge Rd.	Menlo Park	CA	94025	1
213-46-8915	Green	Marjorie	415 986-7020	309 63rd St. #411	Oakland	CA	94618	1
238-95-7766	Carson	Cheryl	415 548-7723	589 Darwin Ln.	Berkeley	CA	94705	1
267-41-2394	O'Leary	Michael	408 286-2428	22 Cleveland Av. #14	San Jose	CA	95128	1
274-80-9391	Straight	Dean	415 834-2919	5420 College Av.	Oakland	CA	94609	1

Authors Table

au_id	au_lname	au_fname
172-32-1176	White	Johnson
213-46-8915	Green	Marjorie
238-95-7766	Carson	Cheryl
267-41-2394	O'Leary	Michael
274-80-9391	Straight	Dean

AuthorsNamesVW View

To see how such a view is created in Transact-SQL we need to look at the (simplified) definition of the table first:

```
CREATE TABLE authors
    (
    au_id       ID,
    au_lname    VARCHAR(40)    NOT NULL,
    au_fname    VARCHAR(20)    NOT NULL,
    phone       CHAR(12)       NOT NULL,
    address     VARCHAR(40)    NULL,
    city        VARCHAR(20)    NULL,
```

```
state     CHAR(2)        NULL,
zip       CHAR(5)        NULL,
contract  BIT            NOT NULL
)
```

Creating this view is simple; we merely have to list the columns we require:

```
CREATE VIEW AuthorsNamesVW
        AS SELECT au_id, au_lname, au_fname
        FROM authors
```

Note: The definition of a view can be encrypted using the WITH ENCRYPTION clause.

If we used a Transact-SQL SELECT statement to query this view we would see the following data returned:

au_id	au_lname	au_fname
172-32-1176	White	Johnson
213-46-8915	Green	Marjorie
238-95-7766	Carson	Cheryl
648-92-1872	Blotchet-Halls	Reginald
672-71-3249	Yokomoto	Akiko
:		
:		
998-72-3567	Ringer	Albert

In fact, we can change the names of the columns if we wish. This can be useful if we are creating views for different groups of users who might use different names to refer to the same piece of data:

```
CREATE VIEW AuthorsNamesVW
  (
  Badge_Number,
  Last_Name,
  First_Name
  )
  AS SELECT au_id, au_lname, au_fname
  FROM authors
```

We would now see more meaningful column headings:

Badge_Number	Last_Name	First_Name
172-32-1176	White	Johnson
213-46-8915	Green	Marjorie
⋮		
⋮		

Note: A view can refer to a maximum of 1024 columns.

The above views have limited the number of columns from the *authors* table that can be seen. Suppose that we often wanted to see details for authors who lived in the state of Utah. We would use a WHERE clause in the view to filter the rows returned.

```
CREATE VIEW UTAuthorsNamesVW
   (
   Badge_Number,
   Last_Name,
   First_Name
   )
   AS SELECT au_id, au_lname, au_fname
   FROM authors
   WHERE state = 'UT'
```

A Transact-SQL SELECT statement using this view would in fact now only return two rows:

Badge_Number	Last_Name	First_Name
899-46-2035	Ringer	Anne
998-72-3567	Ringer	Albert

Views can contain mathematical expressions, such as the following view that displays the difference between the high royalty range and low royalty range from the *roysched* table:

```
CREATE VIEW RoyaltyRangeSizeVW
   (
   ID,
   RangeSize
   )
```

```
AS
SELECT title_id, (hirange - lorange) FROM roysched
```

Views can contain functions. A very useful function that can be used in views is the Transact-SQL CONVERT function that converts datatypes. Functions are described in Chapter 6:

```
CREATE VIEW WhenPublishedVW
    (
    titleid,
    published
    )
    AS
    SELECT title_id,CONVERT(CHAR(10),pubdate,106) FROM titles
```

This view formats the *pubdate* column into a style preferable to the user.

Often views are defined as the combination of more than one base table. If we look at the *sales* table we find a column *stor_id* which identifies a bookstore. However, it is merely a four-character identifier. If we look at the *stores* table we also find the *stor_id* column together with the name and address of the store. We can create a view that combines these two tables using the *stor_id* column. The definitions of the base tables are as follows:

```
CREATE TABLE sales
    (
    stor_id          CHAR(4)         NOT NULL,
    ord_num          VARCHAR(20)     NOT NULL,
    ord_date         DATETIME        NOT NULL,
    qty              SMALLINT        NOT NULL,
    payterms         VARCHAR(12)     NOT NULL,
    title_id         TID
    )

CREATE TABLE stores
    (
    stor_id          CHAR(4)         NOT NULL,
    stor_name        VARCHAR(40)     NULL,
    stor_address     VARCHAR(40)     NULL,
    city             VARCHAR(20)     NULL,
    state            CHAR(2)         NULL,
    zip              CHAR(5)         NULL
    )
```

Suppose we wish to create a view that lists the quantity of books sold to each store displaying the store name, the quantity sold, the sale date, and the title id of the book. We could use the following Transact-SQL statement to create the view that performed a join of the two base tables *sales* and *stores*:

```
CREATE VIEW SalesByStoreVW
    (
    store_name,
    quantity_sold,
    date_of_sale,
    book_ID
    )
    AS SELECT stor_name, qty, ord_date, title_id
    FROM stores LEFT OUTER JOIN sales
    ON stores.stor_id = sales.stor_id
```

This view will return the following data:

store_name	quantity_sold	date_of_sale	book_ID
Barnum's	75	13 Sep 1985 0:00	PS2091
Barnum's	50	24 May 1987 0:00	PC8888
News & Brews	10	14 Sep 1985 0:00	PS2091
News & Brews	40	15 Jun 1987 0:00	TC3218
News & Brews	20	15 Jun 1987 0:00	TC4203
News & Brews	20	15 Jun 1987 0:00	TC7777
:			
:			
Fricative Bookshop	35	21 Feb 1988 0:00	BU2075

The SQL Server Enterprise Manager can be used to create views. To do so:

⇨   Expand the server group and then the server.

⇨   Expand *Databases* and expand the database in which the view is to be created.

⇨   Right-click *Views*.

⇨   Select *New View*.

⇨   Add the tables, columns, and criteria as required.

Designing a view in the SQL Server Enterprise Manager is shown in Figure 4.17.

Figure 4.17

Designing a View in the SQL Server Enterprise Manager

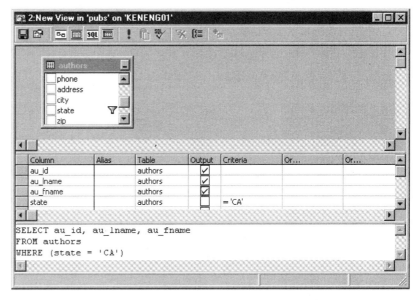

The Create View Wizard can also be used to create views.

4.3.20 Renaming Views

Like a table, it may become necessary to change the name of a view. This is accomplished with the system-stored procedure *sp_rename*:

```
EXEC sp_rename SalesByStoreVW, SalesByShopVW
```

Care should be taken when using this stored procedure as other objects that are based on the view and refer to the view by name, such as another view, will be affected.

To rename a view using the SQL Server Enterprise Manager, right-click the view name and then select *Rename* and type in a new name for the view.

To find which objects are dependent on the view use the SQL Server Enterprise Manager.

⇨ Expand the server group and expand the server.

⇨ Expand *Databases* and expand the database holding the view.

⇨ Click *Views*.

⇨ Right-click the view.

⇨ Select *All Tasks* and *Display Dependencies*.

An example dependency output is shown in Figure 4.18.

Figure 4.18
View Dependencies

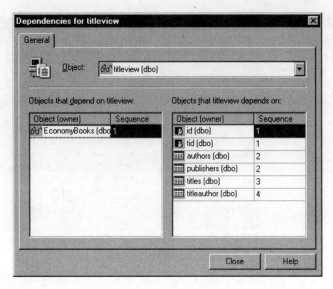

4.3.21 Altering Views

A view can be altered using the ALTER VIEW statement:

```
ALTER VIEW SalesByStoreVW
    (
    store_name,
    quantity_sold,
    date_of_sale,
    book_title
    )
AS SELECT stor_name, qty, ord_date, title_id
FROM stores INNER JOIN sales
ON sales.stor_id = stores.stor_id
```

The SQL Server Enterprise Manager can also be used to edit existing views. To do so right-click the name of the view and choose *Design View*. The dialog box shown in Figure 4.17 is displayed.

4.3.22 Dropping Views

To drop a view the DROP VIEW statement is used. This removes the view from the database:

```
DROP VIEW SalesByStoreVW
```

The SQL Server Enterprise Manager can be used to drop a view. To do so right-click the view and then select *Delete* and *Drop All*.

4.3.23   Showing View Details

A common requirement is to display details about a view. There are a number of system-stored procedures that are useful in this respect, the main ones being *sp_help* and *sp_helptext*. We have discussed the system-stored procedure *sp_help* before but we have not yet covered *sp_helptext*.

The system-stored procedure *sp_helptext* can be used to display the definition of the CREATE VIEW Transact-SQL statement:

```
EXEC sp_helptext AuthorsNamesVW
```

```
text
```

```
CREATE VIEW AuthorsNamesVW AS SELECT au_id, au_lname, au_fname
FROM authors
```

Apart from the dialog boxes we have already seen, a view definition can be displayed by right-clicking the view and selecting properties. This is shown in Figure 4.19.

Figure 4.19
View Properties

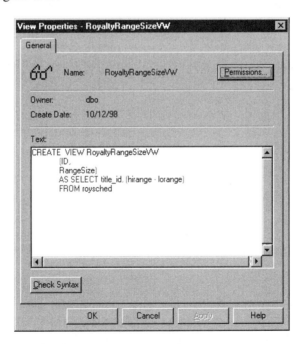

4.3.24   Extra Considerations when Dealing with Views

When creating a view, there are some restrictions that must be observed. View definitions can include other views but view nesting is limited to 32 levels. A view cannot contain the clauses ORDER BY, COMPUTE, or

COMPUTE BY and neither can it contain the INTO keyword. These will be discussed in subsequent Data Manipulation Language (DML) chapters. Indexes and triggers cannot be created on a view and views cannot be created on temporary tables.

There are also restrictions concerning the modification of data through a view. An UPDATE or INSERT statement must only specify columns from one base table in the view. For example, suppose view V1 is defined as a join of tables T1 and T2. Table T1 contains columns C1 and C2 and table T2 contains columns C1 and C3. An UPDATE statement could update column C2 or column C3 but not both.

If a view only contains a subset of the columns in a table, then the columns not contained in the view must have a DEFAULT definition or allow NULL values if an INSERT statement is to be allowed against the view. For example, suppose a table T1 contained columns C1, C2, and C3, and a view V1 was defined on table T1 but only contained columns C1 and C2. To insert a row through V1, C3 would have to have a DEFAULT definition or allow NULL values, otherwise there would be no way a value could be supplied for it and the INSERT statement would fail.

A view definition may also contain the WITH CHECK OPTION clause. Consider the following view definition:

```
CREATE VIEW EconomyBooksVW
  (
  ID,
  Price
  )
  AS
  SELECT title_id, price FROM titles WHERE price < 10
  WITH CHECK OPTION
```

Selecting rows from the view produces the following output:

```
SELECT * FROM EconomyBooksVW

ID        Price
_____    _____

BU2075    2.9900
MC3021    2.9900
PS2106    7.0000
PS7777    7.9900
```

Suppose an attempt is made to update the book with ID "PS2106" so that its price is increased to $12:

```
UPDATE EconomyBooksVW
  SET price = $12.00
  WHERE ID = 'PS2106'
```

```
Server: Msg 550, Level 16, State 1
```
The attempted insert or update failed because the target view either specifies WITH CHECK OPTION or spans a view that specifies WITH CHECK OPTION and one or more rows resulting from the operation did not qualify under the CHECK OPTION constraint.
The statement has been aborted.

Without the CHECK OPTION clause, this column update would have been allowed. However, this clause ensures all data modification statements executed against the view obey the criteria set within SELECT statement in the view definition. Hence, if a row is updated through a view, the clause ensures that the row remains present in the view after the update has completed.

If a SELECT statement contains items in the SELECT list that are derived from mathematical expressions or functions, a row cannot be inserted into the view and the derived column cannot be updated. If the SELECT statement contains an aggregate function such as AVG, COUNT, SUM, MIN, MAX, GROUPING, STDEV, STDEVP, VAR, or VARP or a clause such as GROUP BY, UNION, DISTINCT, or TOP, the view data cannot be changed. These functions and clauses are covered in Chapter 6.

4.4   User-Defined Data Types

As discussed earlier in this chapter, SQL Server provides a number of system data types. In addition, SQL Server enables a database designer to define his or her own data types, known as *user-defined data types*. This capability is useful when a number of tables must share the same definition for a column and it is therefore important to make sure that the columns have the same data type, length, and nullability. An example of this would be a human resources database where the column representing the employee ID number appears in many tables.

To create a user-defined data type in the SQL Server Enterprise Manager:

⇨   Expand the server group and expand the server.

⇨   Expand *Databases* and expand the database in which the user-defined data type is to be created.

⇨   Right-click the *User-Defined Data Types* folder and click *New User-Defined Data Type.*

⇨   Enter a name for the user-defined data type.

⇨   Enter the attributes of the user-defined data type such as the system
     data type on which it is based, its length, and nullability.

⇨   Click *OK*.

⇨   An example of the *New User-Defined Data Type* dialog box is shown
     in Figure 4.20.

Figure 4.20

Creating a User-Defined
Data Type

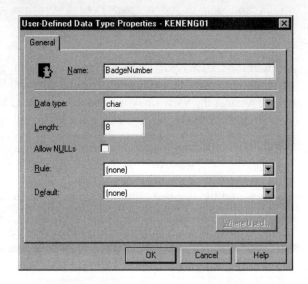

To create a user-defined data type with Transact-SQL, use the *sp_addtype*
system-stored procedure.

```
EXEC sp_addtype BadgeNumber, 'CHAR(8)', 'NOT NULL'
```

Note that the parentheses in the CHAR(8) in the example generate a requirement to use single quotation marks. This can be irritating trying to
remember to use single quotation marks for different data types. It may be
easier to use single quotation marks all the time for consistency. Always
use single quotation marks around NOT NULL and NULL.

Once a user-defined data type has been defined it can be used in a table
definition:

```
CREATE TABLE employee
    (
    Badge        BadgeNumber,
    LastName     CHAR(20)        NOT NULL,
    FirstName    CHAR(20)        NOT NULL
    )
```

If required, the NULL and NOT NULL option of the user-defined data type can be overridden in the table definition:

```
CREATE TABLE employee
    (
    Badge       BadgeNumber    NULL,
    LastName    CHAR(20)       NOT NULL,
    FirstName   CHAR(20)       NOT NULL
    )
```

Hint: Suppose a user-defined data type is going to be used in many databases. It can be defined in the model database. As the model database is effectively a template from which user databases are created, the user-defined data type will automatically be created in future user databases on the server. This can help to enforce a company's internal database standards.

To remove a user-defined data type from a database using the SQL Server Enterprise Manager, right-click the user-defined data type and choose *Delete*. Alternatively, use the *sp_droptype* system-stored procedure:

```
EXEC sp_droptype height
```

If the user-defined data type is being used in a table definition it cannot be dropped:

```
EXEC sp_droptype BadgeNumber

Server: Msg 15180, Level 16, State 1
Cannot drop. The data type is being used.
```

object	type	owner	column	data type
employee	U	dbo	badge	badge_number

To rename a user-defined data type using the SQL Server Enterprise Manager, right-click the user-defined data type and choose *Rename*. Alternatively, use the *sp_rename* system-stored procedure.

To display information about a user-defined data type, right-click the user-defined data type in the SQL Server Enterprise Manager and select *Properties*. The *Where Used* button may be selected to display a list of tables where the user-defined data type is used. Alternatively, use the *sp_help* system-stored procedure.

4.5   The *Pubs* Example Database

Now that we have discussed tables, views, and user-defined data types we can introduce the *Pubs* database. This is an example database that Microsoft uses in their SQL Server documentation and is an ideal database with which to demonstrate SQL Server concepts.

There are 11 tables in the pubs database:

- Authors
- Discounts
- Employee
- Jobs
- Pub_info
- Publishers
- Roysched
- Sales
- Stores
- Titles
- Titleauthor

Figure 4.21
The Pubs Database

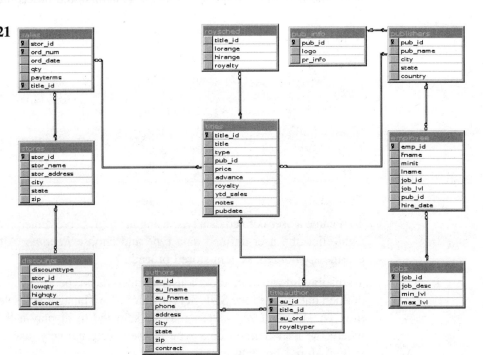

These tables are described in detail in the *Microsoft SQL Server for Windows NT* documentation, however, Figure 4-21 shows the relationships between the tables. Note that we have occasionally added rows to the pubs database and so the results displayed in some of our examples might differ slightly from the results you might obtain.

The *authors* table contains details about the authors held in the database and the *titles* table contains details about the books held in the database. An author can write many books and a book can be written by a number of authors. Hence, there is a many-to-many relationship between authors and titles. This is resolved by using the *titleauthor* table, which participates in a one-to-many relationship with the authors and titles tables. The *titleauthor* table also holds extra information such as the order in which the authors are named and their royalty split.

The *stores* table contains details about the bookstores that stock books. A store can purchase many books and a book can be purchased by a number of stores. Hence, there is a many-to-many relationship between *stores* and *titles*. This is resolved by using the *sales* table, which participates in a one-to-many relationship with the *stores* and *titles* tables. The *sales* table represents the purchases by bookstores of a given book at a given time. Participating in a one-to-many relationship with *stores* is the *discounts* table, which represents discount levels awarded to individual stores.

Participating in a one-to-many relationship with *titles* is the *publishers* table, as a publisher publishes many books, and participating in a one-to-many relationship with *titles* is the *roysched* table, which holds royalty details. Each publisher has an entry in the *pub_info* table that holds details about the publisher as well as their logo in text and image data types. There is a maximum of one *pub_info* row for a publisher.

Participating in a one-to-many relationship with *publishers* is the *employees* table, which represents people employed by the publisher. Each employee has a *job_id* column that relates the *jobs* table to the employee. The jobs table contains job information such as the job description.

Note: SQL Server 7.0 also installs the Northwind database. This is the same learning database that is present in Microsoft Access.

5

Manipulating Database Data

5.1   Introduction

The previous chapter discussed elements of the *Data Definition Language* (DDL) capabilities found in SQL Server. As we saw, DDL is used to define various objects that are typically found in a SQL Server database including tables and views.

In this chapter we will discuss the *Data Manipulation Language* (DML) capabilities in SQL Server. DML is used to manipulate the user data in the database, typically inserting it into tables, updating it, querying it, and deleting it. Note that although we usually think of DML as manipulating user data, it can also be used to manipulate system data that is stored in SQL Server system tables, although doing this is not generally encouraged.

In this chapter we will cover the following DML topics:

- ◆   Querying and sorting data.
- ◆   Joining tables.
- ◆   Aggregates.
- ◆   Built-in functions.
- ◆   Inserting data into tables.
- ◆   Updating data in tables.
- ◆   Removing data from tables.

The intention of this chapter is not to be a definitive reference book on using Transact-SQL statements, rather it is to give the reader a taste of some of the possibilities. For a definitive text, the *Building SQL Server Applications: Transact-SQL Reference* book should be consulted. Advanced topics such as flow control and stored procedures will be covered in the next chapter.

It was seen in Chapter 4 that the SQL Server Enterprise Manager is used to manipulate database objects. It can also be used to manipulate user data and we will look at this capability later in the chapter. First of all, we will look at how data can be managed using Transact-SQL through the Query Analyzer tool.

5.2   Basic Relational Terms

This chapter will not attempt to describe relational concepts as it is assumed that the reader will be familiar with these. However, it is worth revisiting a few points.

As discussed in the previous chapter, in relational databases such as SQL Server, data is stored in tables and a table is comprised of rows and columns.

In the relational model, a column or number of columns is designated as a *primary key*. A row must be uniquely identified by its primary key, therefore, a primary key value cannot occur more than once in a table. This also means that a primary key cannot contain NULL values, that is, a column that constitutes a primary key must contain a value. In the *titles* table, the primary key is the unique identifier of a book represented by the column *title_id*. Each book's *title_id* value is unique throughout the database. No two books may have the same value for *title_id*.

Columns in one table may appear in other tables to establish a relationship between the tables. These columns are called *foreign keys*. In the *pubs* database, the *sales* table contains a column *title_id*. This is a foreign key and establishes a relationship between the *titles* table and the *sales* table.

Other common terms that are often found in the relational world are *selection*, *projection*, and *join*. A selection operation forms a subset of the rows in a table usually by applying some condition, such as the authors who live in Utah. A projection operation removes columns from the rows being retrieved by forming a stream of rows with only specified columns present.

A *join*, probably one of the most powerful relational operations, allows data from more than one table to be combined. Typically, data from more than one table is joined by relating certain meaningful columns from the tables. In the *pubs* database a common operation would be the joining of the *title* and *sales* tables over the *title_id* column to produce a report concerning book sales.

5.3   The Query Analyzer

Before we start to investigate the Transact-SQL statements themselves it is worth taking a tour of the Query Analyzer. The Query Analyzer can be launched from the SQL Server 7.0 start menu or from the *Tools* button in the SQL Server Enterprise Manager. A typical Query Analyzer session is shown in Figure 5.1.

Figure 5.1
*Executing a
Query to
Display
Results as Text*

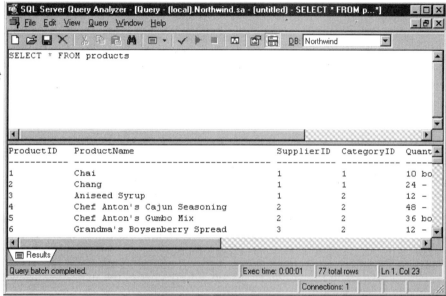

The user has typed a query into the *Query Pane* and has executed the query. The result of the query has been displayed in the *Results Pane*. The *Results Pane* can be hidden or displayed by selecting *Window → Hide Results Pane* or *Window → Show Results Pane* or by mouse-clicking the *Show/Hide Results Pane* button.

Note the Query Analyzer color codes the query to assist the developer in writing correct Transact-SQL syntax.

Execution of the query has been performed by mouse-clicking the *Execute* button. In fact, a number of buttons, *Current Mode, Parse Query, Execute Query, Cancel Executing Query,* and *Display Estimated Execution Plan* control how the query is processed. The *Execute* button displays the query result in the *Text* form shown in Figure 5.1 or *Grid* form shown in Figure 5.2. The choice of display, *Text* or *Grid,* is controlled by the *Current Mode* button.

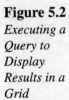

Figure 5.2
Executing a
Query to
Display
Results in a
Grid

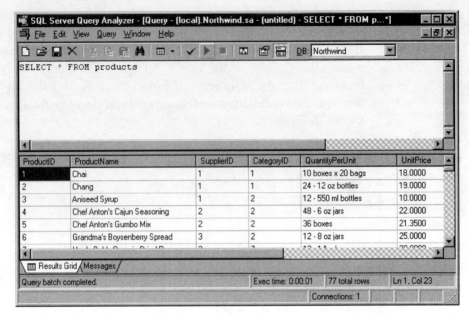

The text form is similar to previous versions of SQL Server. Sometimes this display is not easy to read as long character columns mean that excessive horizontal scrolling needs to be performed (execute *sp_help* to see what we mean). In this case executing the query into a grid is often a better choice, as shown in Figure 5.2.

The *Parse Query* button simply checks the query syntax without actually executing the query. If you execute a long-running query you will notice that the *Cancel Executing Query* button is highlighted. This might stop that query. The function of the *Display Estimated Execution Plan* button will be described in Chapter 10. It shows the query plan that the query optimizer has chosen to execute the query in the most efficient fashion.

You may have typed many queries in the query pane but you do not have to execute them all—you can select just the ones you want to execute and you can even select just parts of queries. All you need to do is highlight one or more queries or parts of queries before you execute the query. Query execution can also be achieved by keystrokes. CTRL+E or ALT+X produce the same result as mouse-clicking the *Execute* button. CTRL+T sets the execute mode to *Results in Text*. CTRL+D sets the execute mode to *Results in Grid*.

Other useful keystrokes are F1 to invoke help, SHIFT+F1 while selecting a Transact-SQL statement to get help on that statement, and ALT+F1 while selecting an object such as a table to get information about that object.

There are others, but now that you know about help, what better way to seek out new keystrokes yourself! (OK, we're not that mean—CTRL+Z will undo your mistakes.)

Before you execute queries you will want to establish a database context to execute those queries in. This can be done by selecting your database from the list box [Northwind ▼].

You can save your hard work by mouse-clicking the *Save Query/Result* button 🗁🖫 or retrieve previously saved Transact-SQL statements by mouse-clicking the *Load SQL Script* button.

The new query button 🗋 creates a new, blank query pane for you to work in. But take note that each new query pane creates a new connection to the server as can be seen from the *Connections*: information at the bottom of the Query Analyzer window. These connections will consume memory and can interact with one another in terms of locking.

If you do create a new query how do you remove it? There are two possibilities. You can mouse-click the cross ✖ at the upper right hand corner of the query pane which will remove the query and the connection or you can mouse-click the *Clear Query Window* button that will empty the pane but not remove the query pane or connection.

Various query options can be set using the *Query Options* button 🖻. This displays the window as shown in Figure 5.3.

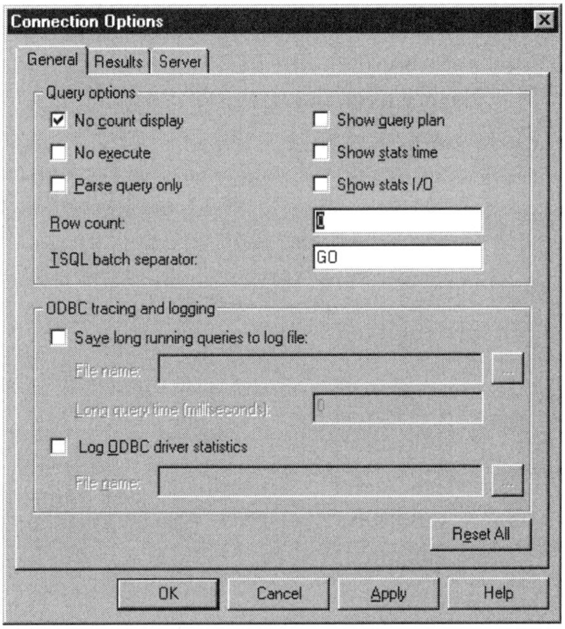

Figure 5.3

The Query Options Dialog Box

There are a number of query options that can be set. For example, the option *No Count Display* specifies that the number of rows affected by the query is not displayed after the result set. We will have this option specified for many of our examples. The option *Row Count* specifies a limit on the number of rows a query will return; the default value of 0 ensures that all rows are returned.

The other connection option tabs allow for the customization of the results display and various server options such as the query timeout.

Right-clicking the query pane also displays many of the menu items just described.

So, with the Query Analyzer tool at our disposal, let us quickly start to execute some Transact-SQL statements.

5.4   Querying and Sorting Data

The most frequently used Transact-SQL keyword is almost certainly SE-LECT. It is used to query the data in the database tables and to return subsets of the rows and columns based on specified criteria. In this chapter we will explore the many SELECT options. First, though, we must choose the database that holds the data we need to query. To do this we simply issue the Transact-SQL USE statement:

```
USE pubs
```

Once we have selected our database we can begin to query data. The simplest form of the SELECT statement is that used to query all the rows and all the columns in a table:

```
SELECT * FROM discounts
```

discounttype	stor_id	lowqty	highqty	discount
InitialCustomer	NULL	NULL	NULL	10.50
VolumeDiscount	NULL	100	1000	6.70
CustomerDiscount	8042	NULL	NULL	5.00

```
(3 row(s) affected)
```

The * character is a shorthand way of saying that all the columns in the table should be displayed. All the columns could be listed but for a large table this might be tedious.

Note: When writing production applications it is good practice to list all the columns. This assists in documentation and makes the SELECT statement independent of any future addition of columns to the table.

In the above example the rowcount is displayed. For many of the queries executed in this chapter, rowcount will be turned off using the Query Options Dialog box, as shown in Figure 5.3, to aid clarity.

5.4.1   Working with Columns

To limit the number of columns returned we can list them instead of using the * character:

```
SELECT discounttype, stor_id, discount FROM discounts

discounttype        stor_id     discount
----------------    --------    --------

Initial Customer    NULL        10.50
Volume Discount     NULL        6.70
Customer Discount   8042        5.00
```

Note that the full name of a database object such as a table is more complex than that implied above. It is in fact:

```
[[[server.][database].][owner].]object
```

The fuller version is used to resolve ambiguity and, if there is none, a shorter version can be used. For example, if we are working in the context of a specific database residing on the local server, the database name and server name can be omitted.

The default column header for an item in the select list, if it is a column, is the name of that column. A column name like *stor_id* might not be meaningful to some users so a SELECT statement has syntax to allow the columns to be given different names. If the item in the select list is not a column, and we will meet examples of this shortly, then it will not have a column header by default. Here is an example of giving a column a non-default column header:

```
SELECT discounttype, stor_id AS bookstore, discount FROM discounts

discounttype        bookstore   discount
----------------    --------    --------

Initial Customer    NULL        10.50
```

```
Volume Discount        NULL          6.70
Customer Discount      8042          5.00
```

Note that this is the ANSI SQL-92 method, which is the preferred approach. There are other traditional methods that are worth seeing as they are fairly common:

```
SELECT discounttype, stor_id bookstore, discount FROM discounts

SELECT discounttype, bookstore = stor_id, discount FROM discounts
```

Text can be added to the item list in the SELECT statement:

```
SELECT 'The Answer is: ', discounttype, stor_id AS bookstore,
discount FROM discounts
```

	discounttype	bookstore	discount
The Answer is:	Initial Customer	NULL	10.50
The Answer is:	Volume Discount	NULL	6.70
The Answer is:	Customer Discount	8042	5.00

Even mathematical expressions can be placed in the list of columns:

```
SELECT discounttype, stor_id AS bookstore, discount, discount *
1.175 FROM discounts
```

discounttype	bookstore	discount	
Initial Customer	(null)	10.5	18.3750
Volume Discount	(null)	6.7	11.7250
Customer Discount	8042	5.0	8.7500

As before, we can name the column but this time we have more than one word in the column name so we must enclose it in single quotation marks:

```
SELECT discounttype, stor_id AS bookstore, discount, discount *
1.175 AS 'Inc UK VAT'
FROM discounts
```

discounttype	bookstore	discount	Inc UK VAT
Initial Customer	(null)	10.5	18.3750
Volume Discount	(null)	6.7	11.7250
Customer Discount	8042	5.0	8.7500

To readers from the United Kingdom this column will be familiar, although perhaps not popular!

So far we have always returned every row from the table. We might wish to remove rows from the result set with duplicate values in a column. We can do this with the DISTINCT keyword. Suppose we wish to list the *state* column from the *stores* table to display the states where there are stores:

```
SELECT state FROM stores
```

```
state
--

WA
CA
CA
WA
CA
OR
```

SQL Server displays 6 rows but some of them, for example CA, appear more than once. We can use the DISTINCT keyword to remove multiple occurrences of a value from the *state* column:

```
SELECT DISTINCT state FROM stores
```

```
state
--

CA
OR
WA
```

Now only 3 rows have been returned and they are all distinct values—the duplicates have been eliminated.

5.4.2   Working with Rows

To return a subset of the rows in a table based on some criteria the WHERE clause is used. This is a very common form of the SELECT statement and there are many operators that can be used in the WHERE clause.

Simple WHERE Conditions

By using the operators supplied with SQL Server various conditions may be specified on a SELECT statement. Simple comparisons may be performed as in the following examples:

```
SELECT title FROM titles WHERE title_id = 'MC2222'

title
_____

Silicon Valley Gastronomic Treats

SELECT title_id FROM sales WHERE qty > 30

title_id
_____

PS2091
BU2075
PC8888
TC3218
```

Specification of a range of values may be made with the BETWEEN operator:

```
SELECT title_id, qty FROM sales WHERE qty BETWEEN 10 AND 15

title_id     qty
_____     ___

PS2091       10
MC3021       15
BU1032       10
BU7832       15
MC2222       10
PS3333       15
```

The BETWEEN operator is inclusive so BETWEEN 10 AND 15 includes the values 10 and 15. To specify an exclusive range use > and <. The following example would, in fact, return zero rows.

```
SELECT title_id, qty FROM sales WHERE qty > 10 AND qty < 15
```

Note: If you put the range in the wrong way, don't expect SQL Server to guess what you really meant—it will not and you will get zero rows returned.

We can easily find rows outside a specified range:

```
SELECT title_id, qty FROM sales WHERE qty NOT BETWEEN 10 and 50
```

```
title_id     qty
_____     ___

PS2091       75
PS2091       3
BU1032       5
```

A check can be made to see if a value is in a list. A common example is U.S. states:

```
SELECT pub_name FROM publishers WHERE state IN ('NH', 'MA')
```

```
pub_name
_____

New Moon Books
```

We can easily find rows where a column value is not in a list:

```
SELECT pub_name FROM publishers WHERE state NOT IN ('CA', 'DC')
```

```
pub_name
_____

New Moon Books
Five Lakes Publishing
Ramona Publishers
GGG&G
Scootney Books
Lucerne Publishing
```

Simple text matching is provided:

```
SELECT title_id, title FROM titles WHERE title LIKE '%oo%'
```

```
title_id title
_____ _____

BU1111   Cooking with Computers: Surreptitious Balance Sheets
MC3026   The Psychology of Computer Cooking
TC3218   Onions, Leeks, and Garlic: Cooking Secrets of the Mediterranean
```

In this example the % wildcard is used that represents any string of zero or more characters. Here is an example of using the _ wildcard character that is used to represent exactly one character:

```
SELECT title_id, title FROM titles WHERE title LIKE '_oo%'
```

```
title_id  title
_____  _____

BU1111    Cooking with Computers: Surreptitious Balance Sheets
```

Here are some other useful wildcards that can be used:

The [ ] wildcard represents any single character within the specified range, for example, [a-g] or set, for example, [bcpt]. Using the ^ character allows us to search outside the range or set, for example, any single character not within the specified range [^a - g]) or set [^bcpt).

To list all books whose titles begin with "I", "s" or "t:"

```
SELECT title_id, title FROM titles WHERE title LIKE '[ist]%'
```

```
title_id  title
_____  _____

PS2091    Is Anger the Enemy?
PC8888    Secrets of Silicon Valley
MC2222    Silicon Valley Gastronomic Treats
BU7832    Straight Talk About Computers
TC7777    Sushi, Anyone?
BU1032    The Busy Executive's Database Guide
MC3021    The Gourmet Microwave
MC3026    The Psychology of Computer Cooking
```

To list all books whose titles begin with any character in the range "a" to "e" inclusive:

```
SELECT title_id, title FROM titles WHERE title LIKE '[a-e]%'
```

```
title_id  title
_____  _____

PC1035    But Is It User Friendly?
PS1372    Computer Phobic AND Non-Phobic Individuals: Behavior
          Variations
BU1111    Cooking with Computers: Surreptitious Balance Sheets
PS7777    Emotional Security: A New Algorithm
```

The case sensitivity of these comparisons depends on whether a case-sensitive sort order was chosen when SQL Server 7.0 was installed.

Note: To search for the wildcard values themselves, for example to search for "%,"use the ESCAPE clause. To perform more sophisticated searches use the Full-Text search capability.

A column that allows NULL values can be tested to see if a NULL value is present:

```
SELECT title FROM titles WHERE price IS NULL

title
```

```
The Psychology of Computer Cooking
Net Etiquette
```

NULL values were introduced in Chapter 4. They usually make life more complicated because they are not values as such. If a column contains a NULL value, it is perhaps because the application did not supply a value for the column when the row was inserted. NULL values are not equivalent to zero, a zero-length string, or blank.

If NULL values are to be compared the result depends on whether ANSI standard behavior is turned on with the SET ANSI_NULLS option. If this option is turned on then this is the result of a query that compares NULL values:

```
SELECT title FROM titles WHERE price = NULL

title
```

Note that zero rows are returned. This is because the ANSI behavior is such that comparing two values where one is set to NULL results in UNKNOWN, not TRUE or FALSE. However, if the SET ANSI_NULLS option is turned off:

```
SELECT title FROM titles WHERE price = NULL

title
```

```
The Psychology of Computer Cooking
Net Etiquette
```

This results because turning the SET ANSI_NULLS option off enables a Transact-SQL (non-ANSI) extension, which allows TRUE or FALSE to be returned when comparing NULL values.

Note: This is dangerous and confusing. The same query appears to behave in two ways and return different result sets depending on the setting of an option. Running the same query under ISQL and OSQL will give these two different results, as the setting is on for OSQL and off for ISQL. We suggest that you ensure the setting is kept on to adhere to the ANSI behavior and use IS NULL and IS NOT NULL for NULL.

To summarize, these are the most *common* operators used to compare values:

Table 5.1 *The Most Common Operators Used to Compare Values*

Operator	Action
=	Checks equality between two expressions
<>	Checks if two expressions are not equal
!=	Checks if two expressions are not equal
>	Checks if one expression is greater than the other
>=	Checks if one expression is greater than or equal to the other
!>	Checks if one expression is not greater than the other
<	Checks if one expression is less than the other
<=	Checks if one expression is less than or equal to the other
!<	Checks if one expression is not less than the other
LIKE	Checks if the character string matches a pattern
BETWEEN	Defines an inclusive range of values
IS [NOT] NULL	Checks for NULL values or for values that are not NULL
[NOT] IN	Checks if the value of an expression is in or not in a list of values

More Complex WHERE Conditions

Simple WHERE clauses can be combined with the logical operators AND, OR, and NOT to enable more complex SELECT statements to be written. For example, it might not be sufficient that we specify the name of a city in a WHERE clause as there may be more than one city with the same name in different states. Instead we might choose to specify the state as well as the city:

```
SELECT pub_name FROM publishers WHERE city = 'Boston' AND state = 'MA'
```

```
pub_name
_____

New Moon Books
```

Note that both these conditions must be true so only publishers who are based in Boston and Massachusetts are displayed. The OR logical operator can be used to display rows when any of the conditions are true as opposed to all of them being true using the AND operator. If we wished to display the publishers that were based in the state of California or the city of Washington we could use the OR operator:

```
SELECT pub_name FROM publishers WHERE city = 'Washington' OR
state = 'CA'
```

```
pub_name
_____

Binnet & Hardley
Algodata Infosystems
```

Suppose we wished to display all the publishers except those based in New Hampshire. In this case we could use the NOT operator that effectively reverses the condition following it:

```
SELECT pub_name FROM publishers WHERE NOT state = 'CA'
```

```
pub_name
_____

New Moon Books
Binnet & Hardley
Five Lakes Publishing
Ramona Publishers
Scootney Books
```

The logical operators AND, OR, and NOT can be combined in a WHERE clause. Knowing which logical operator is executed first can be confusing and so the authors strongly recommend that parentheses be used to clarify the order in which the operators are evaluated.

Displaying Data in Order

The relational model does not stipulate in what order data is returned from a query unless a specific order is requested. If a specific order is not requested, the order in which the table rows are returned is undefined. The order is often governed by the order in which data was inserted into a table, the access method chosen by the query optimizer to retrieve it, and whether the query was executed in parallel. In other words, you cannot assume in what order data will be returned and it is dangerous to do so.

If the data must be returned in a particular order, it is important to ask SQL Server to ensure that the data is sorted before returning it by the use of the ORDER BY clause:

```
SELECT au_lname, au_fname FROM authors ORDER BY au_lname
```

```
au_lname            au_fname
-----------------   -----------

Bennet              Abraham
Blotchet-Halls      Reginald
Carson              Cheryl
DeFrance            Michel
  :
  :
```

In the above example, the table rows from the *authors* table are displayed in ascending order of their last name. Ascending order is the default but we could have explicitly specified that we wanted ascending order:

```
SELECT au_lname, au_fname FROM authors ORDER BY au_lname ASC
```

We could have asked for the results in descending order:

```
SELECT au_lname, au_fname FROM authors ORDER BY au_lname DESC
```

More than one column can be used in the ORDER BY clause:

```
SELECT au_lname, au_fname FROM authors ORDER BY au_lname ASC,
au_fname DESC
```

In the above example the results will be sorted by ascending last name and, within the same last name, descending first name.

5.4.3   Combining Data from Multiple Tables

We have concentrated so far on SELECT statements operating on a single table. As was mentioned in Chapter 4, often two or more tables must be operated on simultaneously. The idea is that the tables are combined to form a result that looks like a set of rows from one table. The operations that are often used to combine the rows from more than one table are the *join* and the *union* and these operations are now described. Another way of combining the results of more than one table is to use a *subquery* as described later in this chapter.

Combining Data by Joining Tables

Suppose we wished to display a list of books that each publisher publishes, containing the name of the publisher and the title of the book. These two pieces of information are not held in any one table. The publishers name is held in the *publishers* table and the title of the book is held in the *titles* table as shown from their (simplified) definitions below:

```
create table publishers
    (pub_id      CHAR(4)        NOT NULL,
     pub_name    VARCHAR(40)    NULL,
     city        VARCHAR(20)    NULL,
     state       CHAR(2)        NULL,
     country     VARCHAR(30)    NULL)


create table titles
    (title_id    tid,
     title       VARCHAR(80)    NOT NULL,
     type        CHAR(12)       NOT NULL,
     pub_id      CHAR(4)        NULL,
     price       MONEY          NULL,
     advance     MONEY          NULL,
     royalty     INT            NULL,
     ytd_sales   INT            NULL,
     notes       VARCHAR(200)   NULL,
     pubdate     DATETIME       NOT NULL)
```

We must combine the information in these two tables and we do this by using a join operation to bring the two tables together. How do we know which book relates to which publisher? There must be some way of relating the rows in the two tables, otherwise joining them will not produce a sensible result. There is, in each of the tables, a column named *pub_id* that is the identifier that uniquely identifies each publisher and specifies the publisher of each book. It is this column that we will use to relate the rows from each table. Rows from each table with the same *pub_id* will be matched together:

```
SELECT publishers.pub_id, pub_name, title
   FROM publishers INNER JOIN titles
   ON
   publishers.pub_id = titles.pub_id
   WHERE type = 'business'
```

pub_id	pub_name	title
1389	Algodata Infosystems	The Busy Executive's Database Guide
0735	New Moon Books	You Can Combat Computer Stress!
1389	Algodata Infosystems	Straight Talk About Computers
:		
:		

Note that the ON clause contains the statement that is used to relate the rows in the two tables, namely that a *pub_id* column from the row in one table must equal the *pub_id* from the row in the other table. Note that there is no need to display the *pub_id* column if that is not desired.

In this example, the columns that are used in the ON clause to relate the rows have the same name in both tables—*pub_id*. This may or may not always be the case. However, because they have the same name, mentioning just *pub_id* to name a column in the list of columns to be displayed would be ambiguous, therefore, the column name must be qualified with the table name.

Another way to do this is by using a *table alias*. This is usually a convenience but is sometimes necessary, for example when a table is joined with itself. The above example can be written using table aliases as:

```
SELECT p.pub_id, pub_name, title
FROM publishers AS p INNER JOIN titles AS t
ON
p.pub_id = t.pub_id
WHERE type = 'business'
```

Note: You cannot mix both methods, that is, using full table names and table aliases to qualify columns in the same query. The AS is optional.

The join operation can be thought of as a concatenation of rows from the *publishers* table with the appropriate matching rows from the *titles* table. It is therefore important to specify the correct relationship between the tables in the ON clause, otherwise the wrong rows will be concatenated.

The FROM clause specifies the type of join, in this example an INNER JOIN is to be performed. There are other types of joins as we shall see shortly.

In many cases the operator that joins the table will be the equals sign (=), however, the greater than (>), greater than or equal to (>=), less than (<), less than or equal to (<=), not equal to (<> or !=), not greater than (!>), and not less than (!<) operators are also valid.

Note: The join syntax we will describe in this chapter is the ANSI standard syntax. This syntax, we feel, is clearer and more concise than the old syntax as the join type is explicitly stated. The join condition is specified in its own ON clause and it is not possible using this syntax to forget to relate tables with a join condition.

The above example is known as a two-way join because two tables are joined together. More than two tables can be joined together and doing this is merely a case of adding extra tables and the relevant conditions in the ON clause of the SELECT statement. For example, to find out information concerning the quantity of computer books sold to particular bookstores, the *titles*, *sales*, and *stores* tables must be joined:

```
SELECT stor_name, title, ord_date, qty
    FROM stores
    INNER JOIN sales ON stores.stor_id=sales.stor_id
    INNER JOIN titles ON sales.title_id = titles.title_id
    WHERE type = 'popular_comp'
```

stor_name	title	ord_date	qty
Bookbeat	But Is It User Friendly?	22 May 1993 0:00	30
Barnum's	Secrets of Silicon Valley	24 May 1993 0:00	50

It is possible, in theory, to join many tables together. However, in practice doing this can adversely affect performance. Many tables must be accessed and the query optimizer must also work hard to look at the many options now available to it for efficient processing of the join. Small inefficiencies in the inner tables can become large if they are iterated through many times. Alternative ways of formulating the query, perhaps in stages, may sometimes be preferable.

Note: If you do write complex joins involving many tables don't leave performance to chance. Check to see what query plan the query optimizer has produced and test the query on realistic data—not 10 rows! We will see how to look at what the query optimizer has decided is a good plan in Chapter 10.

Outer Joins

Suppose we now look at a join of the *titles* and *sales* tables:

```
SELECT titles.title_id, title, ord_date, qty
 FROM titles INNER JOIN sales
 ON titles.title_id = sales.title_id
```

title_id	title	ord_date	qty
BU1032	The Busy Executive's	1994-09-14 00:00:00.000	5
PS2091	Is Anger the Enemy?	1994-09-13 00:00:00.000	3
PC8888	Secrets of Silicon V	1993-05-24 00:00:00.000	50
:			
:			
PC1035	But Is It User Frien	1993-05-22 00:00:00.000	30

```
(21 row(s) affected)
```

We've chopped the title to fit the result set across the page. There are 21 rows returned by this inner join.

It is possible that a book does not have any sales associated with it. In this case no information would be returned about the book. Only *titles* with matching rows in the *sales* table would be displayed. This is a characteristic of an inner join—to produce a row in the result set, rows must be present in each table that match on the join condition.

Perhaps this is not what we want as we may wish to also see the books that have not sold. To ensure that books that have no matching sales appear in the result set produced by the query alongside books that have matching sales, we can use an *outer join*. There are three types of outer join—left, right, and full.

To specify an outer join we can use *outer join* in the from clause. A left outer join ensures that rows from the left table are returned even if there are no matching rows in the right table. A right outer join ensures that rows from the right table are returned even if there are no matching rows in the left table. A full outer join is equivalent to performing a left outer join and a right outer join. In other words, rows from the left table are returned even if there are no matching rows in the right table and rows from the right table are returned even if there are no matching rows in the left table.

A left outer join of the titles and sales table would return rows for books that had no sales:

```
SELECT titles.title_id, title, ord_date, qty
 FROM titles LEFT OUTER JOIN sales
 ON titles.title_id = sales.title_id
```

title_id	title	ord_date	qty
BU1032	The Busy Executive's	1994-09-14 00:00:00.000	5
PS2091	Is Anger the Enemy?	1994-09-13 00:00:00.000	3
PC8888	Secrets of Silicon V	1993-05-24 00:00:00.000	50
:			
:			
PC9999	Net Etiquette	NULL	NULL
:			
MC3026	The Psychology of Co	NULL	NULL
:			
PC1035	But Is It User Frien	1993-05-22 00:00:00.000	30

```
(23 row(s) affected)
```

The result set is now 23 rows as it contains two additional rows for books with no sales. Note how these rows have NULL displayed in the columns from the right table.

Cross Joins

A join that does not have a join condition produces the *cartesian product* of the tables involved in the join. The number of rows in the result set is the number of rows in the first table multiplied by the number of rows in the second table:

```
select * FROM titles CROSS JOIN sales
```

The above example returns a result set consisting of 378 rows! This type of join has limited use.

Unions

Another way of combining data from multiple tables is to use the *union* operator. A union operation is similar to the operation of appending a file to another one, only with the union operation we are dealing with relational tables. Suppose that instead of one *sales* table there is a sales table for American sales and one for European sales. Their definitions might be identical except for their names:

```
CREATE TABLE sales_america
  (
  stor_id    CHAR(4),
  ord_num    VARCHAR(20),
  ord_date   DATETIME,
  qty        SMALLINT,
  payterms   VARCHAR(12),
  title_id   TID
  )

CREATE TABLE sales_europe
  (
  stor_id    CHAR(4),
  ord_num    VARCHAR(20),
  ord_date   DATETIME,
  qty        SMALLINT,
  payterms   VARCHAR(12),
  title_id   TID
  )
```

To combine data from the two tables in a query we could use the *union* operator:

```
SELECT stor_id, title_id, qty FROM sales_america
UNION
SELECT stor_id, title_id, qty FROM sales_europe
```

stor_id	title_id	qty
6380	PS209	13
6380	BU103	25
7066	PC8888	50
7067	TC4203	20
7067	TC7777	20

7067	TC3218	40
7131	PS3333	15
:		
:		
9055	PS2091	15
9055	MC3021	18
9055	PS2106	18
9055	PS7777	18
9820	MC222	27
9820	BU7832	11
9820	BU2075	26
9966	BU103	27
9966	MC3021	11
9966	BU1111	18
9966	PC1035	22

There are a number of restrictions that apply to the use of the union operator. The SELECT statements should contain the same number columns in the select and these should be in the same order for each SELECT statement to be unioned. These restrictions are not unreasonable. Also we would expect that the columns in the select list of the SELECT statements should have the same datatypes.

Transact-SQL is not, in fact, as restrictive as this. Columns that contain data to be unioned may have different datatypes as long as SQL Server can make an implicit datatype conversion.

Any number of SELECT statements can be unioned so long as these rules are obeyed. The individual SELECT statements in a union cannot have their own ORDER BY clause. A single ORDER BY clause may be placed after the last SELECT statement in the union and this will then govern the order of the result set from the union operation. Note that the UNION operator automatically eliminates duplicate rows from the result set. If this is not the desired behavior use UNION ALL.

5.4.4   Performing Calculations on Data

Transact-SQL has a number of useful functions that can be used to perform operations such as adding up the data in a column and finding the number of rows in a table. These are often known as *aggregate* functions. The use of aggregate functions is very common and SQL Server 7.0 supplies the following:

SUM   adds up the values in a column or expression.

AVG   averages the values in a column or expression.

COUNT   counts the number of values in a column or expression.

COUNT (*)   counts the number of rows returned from a query.

MIN   finds the smallest value in a column or expression.

MAX   finds the largest value in a column or expression.

VAR   finds the statistical variance of all values in the given expression.

VARP   finds the statistical variance for the population for all values in the given expression.

STDEV   finds the statistical standard deviation of all values in the given expression.

STDEVP   finds the statistical standard deviation for the population for all values in the given expression.

Examples

Find the total number of sales:

```
SELECT SUM(qty) FROM sales
```

```
_____

493
```

It is probably more readable to give a decent column heading:

```
SELECT SUM(qty) AS Total FROM sales
```

```
Total
_____

493
```

Find the average number of sales:

```
SELECT AVG(qty) AS Average FROM sales
```

```
Average
_____

23
```

Find the total number of rows in the authors table with a non null value in the state column:

```
SELECT COUNT(state) AS 'Total Count' FROM authors

Total Count
_____

23
```

Find the total number of rows in the authors table with a distinct non null value in the state column:

```
SELECT COUNT(DISTINCT state) AS 'Distinct Count' FROM authors

Distinct Count
_____

8
```

Find the total number of rows in the authors table:

```
SELECT COUNT(*) AS 'Number of Authors' FROM authors

Number of Authors
_____

24
```

Find the lowest value in the price column in the titles table:

```
SELECT MIN(price) AS 'Least Expensive Book' FROM titles

Least Expensive Book
_____

2.9900
```

Find the highest value in the price column in the titles table:

```
SELECT MAX(price) AS 'Most Expensive Book' FROM titles

Most Expensive Book
_____

22.9500
```

Find the lowest value in the last name column in the authors table:

```
SELECT MIN(au_lname) AS 'Name' FROM authors

Name
_____

Bennet
```

Find the statistical variance of all price values in the titles table:

```
SELECT VAR(price) AS 'Variance' FROM titles

Variance
_____

46.82581166666666
```

Find the statistical standard deviation of all price values in the titles table:

```
SELECT STDEV(price) AS 'Standard Deviation' FROM titles

Standard Deviation
_____

6.8429388179835904
```

The GROUP BY Clause

It is often useful to use the above aggregate functions in conjunction with the *GROUP BY* clause. As its name suggests, this clauses groups data together when returning results.

Instead of returning the total number of authors we could return the number of authors in each state:

```
SELECT state, COUNT(*) FROM authors GROUP BY state

state
____        _____

CA        15
IN        1
KS        1
MD        1
MI        1
OR        1
TN        1
UT        2
```

Again, we could provide a more meaningful heading:

```
SELECT state, COUNT(*) AS 'Total' FROM authors GROUP BY state

state   Total
____    _____

CA        15
IN        1
```

:

:

The other aggregate functions can be used with GROUP BY:

```
SELECT stor_id, SUM(qty) AS 'Total Quantity' FROM sales
GROUP BY stor_id
```

stor_id	Total Quantity
6380	8
7066	125
7067	90
7131	130
7896	60
8042	80

Earlier we saw how to filter the rows returned from a SELECT statement with a WHERE clause. The WHERE clause may be used with a SELECT statement involving the GROUP BY clause, however, to place conditions on the groups themselves, the HAVING clause is used:

```
SELECT state, COUNT(*) AS 'Total' FROM authors GROUP BY
state HAVING COUNT(*) > 1
```

state	Total
CA	15
UT	2

In the above example, the earlier SELECT statement is modified to limit the results to states where the number of bookstores is greater than one.

The COMPUTE and COMPUTE BY Clause

Other clauses that may be used with the aggregate functions are *COMPUTE* and *COMPUTE BY*:

```
SELECT stor_id, qty FROM sales
ORDER BY stor_id
COMPUTE SUM(qty) BY stor_id
```

stor_id	title_id	qty
6380	BU1032	5
6380	PS2091	3

```
sum
_____

8

stor_id       title_id    qty
____          _____    ___

7066          PC8888      50
7066          PS2091      75

sum
_____

125               :

                  :

                  :

stor_id       title_id    qty
____          _____    ___

8042          MC3021      5
8042          BU1032      10
8042          BU1111      25
8042          PC1035      30

sum
___-

80
```

Unlike the previous examples we have seen using aggregate functions, the use of the COMPUTE clause causes the summary values to be displayed as extra rows. Also, we can see the detail lines, which means that the display is more like a report. Multiple aggregations can be performed:

```
SELECT stor_id, qty FROM sales
  ORDER BY stor_id
  COMPUTE SUM(qty), AVG(qty) BY stor_id

stor_id       title_id    qty
____          _____    ___

6380          BU1032      5
6380          PS2091      3
```

```
sum          avg
_____ _       _____
8            4
  :
  :
```

A grand total can also be displayed:

```
SELECT stor_id, qty FROM sales
   ORDER BY stor_id
   COMPUTE SUM(qty)

stor_id       title_id   qty
_____         _____   ___
6380          BU1032     5
6380          PS2091     3
  :
  :
8042          BU1111     25
8042          PC1035     30


sum
_____
493
```

The ORDER BY clause must be used if COMPUTE or COMPUTE BY is used in a SELECT statement in order to group the relevant rows together.

The COMPUTE and COMPUTE BY clauses are, however, Transact-SQL enhancements that are not found in the ANSI SQL-92 standard.

Note: It is generally recommended that COMPUTE and COMPUTE BY not be used but, rather, the ROLLUP clause is used (see later) if aggregation is to be performed using Transact-SQL.

The CUBE Operator

The CUBE operator is used in conjunction with the GROUP BY clause to aggregate values into a multidimensional cube. Every possible combination of the columns specified in the GROUP BY clause is output. Suppose we have a table that represents the wine sales of a small specialist wine shipper. Here is a table containing sales information:

```
SELECT * FROM wines
```

Name	Country	Region	Style	Vintage	Qty_sold
Cotes du Souris	France	Rhone Valley	Red	1994	156
Ch. Montagne	France	Rhone Valley	Red	1997	196
Ch. des Loup	France	Pauillac	Red	1996	111
Ch. Marble	France	Pauillac	Red	1995	223
Ch. Marble	France	Pauillac	Red	1992	105
Pouilly les Chaux	France	Graves	White	1998	111
Domaine de Brouette	France	Graves	White	1997	88
Ch. Beret	France	Pessac-Leog	White	1997	45
LA Blush	France	California	Rose	1997	97
Bel Air	USA	California	Rose	1996	123
Pierre Brut 678	France	Loire Valley	Sparkling	1997	145
Napa Brut	USA	California	Sparkling	1996	201
Blue Line Brut	Australia	Victoria	Sparkling	1997	209
Tarr Caylor	England	East Sussex	Sparkling	1996	167
Barbarello	Spain	Andalusia	Fortified	1997	55
Madeira d'Olusia	Portugal	Madeira	Fortified	1998	77

```
(16 row(s) affected)
```

Suppose we wish to examine the number of wine cases we have sold by country and style. We can use the GROUP BY clause we have just met to achieve this:

```
SELECT country, style, SUM(qty_sold) AS 'Cases Sold' FROM wines
GROUP BY country, style
ORDER BY country, style
```

Country	Style	Cases Sold
Australia	Sparkling	209
England	Sparkling	167
France	Red	791
France	Rose	97
France	Sparkling	145
France	White	244
Portugal	Fortified	77

```
Spain          Fortified      55
USA            Rose           123
USA            Sparkling      201
```

```
(10 row(s) affected)
```

We can immediately see the number of wine cases sold of each category in each country. The result set has reduced in size from the 16 rows from the non-aggregated table to the 10 rows of the aggregated table. The ORDER BY clause was added just to make the result easier to read—it is not mandatory. What this result set does not easily tell us is the total number of wine cases sold across all categories and all countries, or the total number of French wines sold, or the total number of sparkling wines sold. Sure, we could reach for the calculator but this gets tedious when the result set contains tens of thousands of rows!

This is where the CUBE operator comes to the rescue. Let us execute the Transact-SQL statement again but this time we will add a CUBE:

```
SELECT country, style, SUM(qty_sold) AS 'Cases Sold' FROM wines
GROUP BY country, style
WITH CUBE
ORDER BY country, style
```

```
Country        Style          Cases Sold
_____         _____          _____

NULL           NULL           2109
NULL           Fortified      132
NULL           Red            791
NULL           Rose           220
NULL           Sparkling      722
NULL           White          244
Australia      NULL           209
Australia      Sparkling      209
England        NULL           167
England        Sparkling      167
France         NULL           1277
France         Red            791
France         Rose           97
France         Sparkling      145
```

```
France              White           244
Portugal            NULL            77
Portugal            Fortified       77
Spain               NULL            55
Spain               Fortified       55
USA                 NULL            324
USA                 Rose            123
USA                 Sparkling       201


(22 row(s) affected)
```

Notice that there are now 22 rows in the result set. The CUBE operator has added rows. Upon investigation, it can be seen that the addition of the CUBE operator has inserted new rows containing NULL values in various columns. For example, one row has a NULL value in the *Country* and *Style* columns and the *Cases Sold* column contains the total of all the cases sold. Another row contains "France" in the *Country* column and NULL in the *Style* column. Here, the *Cases Sold* column contains the total of all the cases sold for France, irrespective of the style. Other rows contain NULL in the *Country* column and a value in the *Style* column. Here, the *Cases Sold* column contains the total of all the cases sold for a style, irrespective of the country.

In fact, all the possible combinations are displayed. If we were to GROUP BY the *Name, Country, Region, Style,* and *Vintage* columns, many rows would be returned with all possible combinations.

However, suppose that the underlying data contains NULL values. It then becomes difficult to decide whether the NULL values in the result set are generated by the CUBE operator or were there in the table already. This is where the *GROUPING* function comes in handy. This function returns a 0 if the NULL comes from the data or 1 if it is generated by the CUBE operator. It is useful to use the GROUPING function with the CASE function to substitute a string for the NULL returned by the CUBE operator. The CASE function is described later in this chapter.

Note: Microsoft SQL Server OLAP Services, as discussed in Chapter 13, is the recommended way of creating multidimensional cubes.

The ROLLUP Operator

The ROLLUP operator is similar to the CUBE operator in that it is used in conjunction with the GROUP BY clause to aggregate values. However, the ROLLUP generates a result set showing aggregates for a hierarchy of values in the selected columns rather than every possible combination. For this reason, the ROLLUP operator is sensitive to the order of the columns in the GROUP BY clause. Using our wine table as before:

```
SELECT country, style, SUM(qty_sold) AS 'Cases Sold' FROM wines
GROUP BY country,  style
WITH ROLLUP
ORDER BY country, style
```

Country	Style	Cases Sold
NULL	NULL	2109
Australia	NULL	209
Australia	Sparkling	209
England	NULL	167
England	Sparkling	167
France	NULL	1277
France	Red	791
France	Rose	97
France	Sparkling	145
France	White	244
Portugal	NULL	77
Portugal	Fortified	77
Spain	NULL	55
Spain	Fortified	55
USA	NULL	324
USA	Rose	123
USA	Sparkling	201

(17 row(s) affected)

It can be seen that a sum of wine cases is displayed for a given style within a country, a given country, and all countries. The GROUPING function can also be used with the ROLLUP operator. The use of the ROLLUP operator is recommended over the use of the COMPUTE BY clause.

The TOP Clause

The TOP clause limits the number of rows returned in the result set of a query. Consider the following query:

```
SELECT title_id, qty FROM sales ORDER BY qty DESC
```

title_id	qty
PS2091	75
PC8888	50
TC3218	40
BU2075	35
PC1035	30
MC3021	25
PS2106	25
PS7777	25
BU1111	25
TC4203	20
TC7777	20
:	
:	
PS209	13

```
(21 row(s) affected)
```

There are 21 rows returned that we have ordered by descending *qty* column values. Note that for these examples we will display the number of rows returned to aid clarity. Let us limit the result set to 6 rows using the TOP clause:

```
SELECT TOP 6 title_id, qty FROM sales ORDER BY qty DESC
```

title_id	qty
PS2091	75
PC8888	50
TC3218	40
BU2075	35
PC1035	30
MC3021	25

```
(6 row(s) affected)
```

Using the TOP clause has enabled us to limit the number of rows returned. Comparing this result set to the complete result set of 21 rows shows us that there are in fact four rows with a *qty* column value of 25. This is not obvious from the result set of six rows. To ensure that all rows with a *qty* column value of 25 are returned and not "chopped off" in the middle we can use the WITH TIES clause:

```
SELECT TOP 6 WITH TIES title_id, qty FROM sales ORDER BY qty DESC
```

title_id	qty
PS2091	75
PC8888	50
TC3218	40
BU2075	35
PC1035	30
MC3021	25
PS2106	25
PS7777	25
BU1111	25

```
(9 row(s) affected)
```

This obviously returns more rows that the six we asked for but it does enable us to see if there are any ties. We can also find the top N% of the rows in the table:

```
SELECT TOP 10 PERCENT title_id, qty FROM sales ORDER BY qty DESC
```

title_id	qty
PS2091	75
PC8888	50
TC3218	40

```
(3 row(s) affected)
```

There are 21 rows in the table so 10% would return 2.1 rows. We cannot, of course, return part of a row so this is rounded up and 3 rows are returned. If required, the WITH TIES clause can also be used with TOP PERCENT.

5.4.5   Using Subqueries

So far we have looked at SELECT statements that manipulate data from one or more tables. It is permissible to nest a SELECT statement inside another SELECT statement and this is called a subquery. By using subqueries, more than one table can be manipulated in a similar way to using joins. In many instances the use of subqueries and joins is interchangeable.

```
SELECT stor_name FROM stores WHERE stor_id IN (SELECT stor_id FROM sales)
```

```
stor_name
_____

Eric the Read Books
Barnum's
News & Brews
Doc-U-Mat: Quality Laundry and Books
Fricative Bookshop
Bookbeat
```

In the above example we are asking for the name of every store that has sold a book, in other words, that appears in the *sales* table.

We could, of course, have written this using a join:

```
SELECT stor_name FROM stores
INNER JOIN SALES
ON stores.stor_id = sales.stor_id
```

```
stor_name
_____

Eric the Read Books
Eric the Read Books
Barnum's
Barnum's
:

:

Bookbeat
Bookbeat
Bookbeat
Bookbeat
```

However, this would have resulted in 21 rows being returned as each row from the *stores* table would be matched with each row from the *sales* table matching that store. In this case a DISTINCT keyword would be useful to display the same output. However, note one point about the above join. We can display values from columns in the *sales* table. It is not possible to display columns from the inner SELECT statement in a subquery.

We can use a WHERE clause in the inner query:

```
SELECT stor_name FROM stores WHERE stor_id IN
  (SELECT stor_id FROM sales WHERE qty > 10)
```

```
stor_name
_____

Barnum's
News & Brews
Doc-U-Mat: Quality Laundry and Books
Bookbeat
Fricative Bookshop
```

In the above example we are asking for name of every store that has purchased more than 10 copies of any book (at a given date).

There are, however, restrictions on a SELECT statement that appears in a subquery. For example, the text and image data types are not allowed in the select list of subqueries and a subquery cannot include ORDER BY, COMPUTE, or INTO. It can, however, use TOP in conjunction with an ORDER BY clause.

A common use of a subquery is in conjunction with the EXISTS clause. Suppose we want to list the authors who live in the same state as a publisher:

```
SELECT au_lname, state FROM authors WHERE EXISTS
  (SELECT * FROM publishers WHERE publishers.state = authors.state)
```

```
au_lname        state
_____     ___

White           CA
Green           CA
Carson          CA
O'Leary         CA
Straight        CA
Bennet          CA
Dull            CA
```

```
Gringlesby      CA
Locksley        CA
Yokomoto        CA
Stringer        CA
MacFeather      CA
Karsen          CA
Hunter          CA
McBadden        CA
```

We can see that the only state where there are both authors and publishers is California. This is known as the *intersection* of the *authors* and *publishers* table over the *state* column and is, in fact, a set-theory operation. Another set-theory operation is *difference*. The difference operation applied to the *authors* and *publishers* table over the *state* column is the set of authors who do not live in the same state as a publisher. We can use NOT EXISTS to produce this difference operation:

```
SELECT au_lname, state FROM authors WHERE NOT EXISTS
  (SELECT * FROM publishers WHERE publishers.state = authors.state)
```

```
au_lname          state
_____       ___

Smith             KS
Greene            TN
Blotchet-Halls    OR
DelCastillo       MI
DeFrance          IN
Panteley          MD
Ringer            UT
Ringer            UT
```

5.4.6   Functions

In SQL Server there are a number of functions that are available for use in Transact-SQL. Because they are *built into* the product they are known as *built-in* functions. These built-in functions are useful in many different areas and can be grouped into three categories:

+ Rowset functions that can be used like table references in an SQL statement.

+ Aggregate functions that work on a list of values but return a single summary value.

♦   Scalar functions that operate on a single value and then return a single value.

Rowset functions consist of the following

OPENQUERY	OPENROWSET
CONTAINSTABLE	FREETEXTTABLE

The *OPENQUERY* and the *OPENROWSET* functions are typically used with heterogeneous queries, that is, queries that access data from remote non-SQL Server data sources.

An OPENQUERY function allows a pass-through query to be executed on a linked server that is an OLEDB data source. The OPENQUERY function can be referenced in the FROM clause of a query as if it were a table name, hence its rowset function classification.

The OPENROWSET function can also be referenced in the FROM clause of a query as if it were a table name. The difference is that, unlike the OPENQUERY function, the OPENROWSET function does not execute on a linked server, instead it includes all the connection information necessary to access remote data from an OLEDB data source.

These functions will be discussed further in Chapter 11.

The CONTAINSTABLE and FREETEXTTABLE are used with the Full Text search capability.

Aggregate functions consist of the following:

AVERAGE	COUNT	SUM	MIN	MAX
VAR	VARP	STDEV	STDEVP	

These functions were discussed earlier in this chapter and will not be discussed again.

The largest group of functions is the scalar functions. The categories of these functions are shown in Table 5.2.

Some examples of these scalar functions follow:

Configuration:

1. Find the current version and service pack level of SQL Server:

```
SELECT @@VERSION

Microsoft SQL Server  7.00 - 7.00.517 (Intel X86)
    Jun 19 1998 17:06:54
    Copyright (c) 1988-1998 Microsoft Corporation
    Standard version on Windows NT
```

Table 5.2 *Categories of Functions*

Category	Explanation
Configuration	Provides information about the current configuration
Cursor	Provides information about cursors
Date and Time	Provides date and time operations
Mathematical	Provides mathematical operations
Metadata objects	Provides information about the database and database
Security	Provides information about users and roles
String	Provides string operations
System	Provides information about values, objects, and settings
System Statistical	Provides statistical information about the system
Text and Image	Provides text and image operations

2. Find the server process ID of the current connection:
```
SELECT @@SPID
```

```
___
15
```

Cursor:

1. Find the status of cursor AuthCurs:
```
DECLARE AuthCurs CURSOR FOR SELECT * FROM authors

OPEN AuthCurs

SELECT CURSOR_STATUS('global',' AuthCurs')
```

```
___
1
```

This status means that the result set of the cursor has at least one row.

Date and Time:

1. Find the current date and time:
```
SELECT GETDATE()
```

```
_____
1998-09-30 17:37:15.723
```

2. Extract the name of the month from the current date and time:

```
SELECT DATENAME(month, GETDATE())
```

```
September
```

3. Add four days to the current date and time:

```
SELECT DATEADD(day, 4, GETDATE())
```

```
1998-10-04 17:43:22.533
```

4. Finds the number of days that have elapsed between a date and the current date and time:

```
SELECT DATEDIFF(day, 'Oct 26 1955',GETDATE())
```

```
15680
```

5. Find the day number of the year:

```
SELECT DATEPART(dy, GETDATE())
```

```
273
```

Note: The functions DAY(), MONTH(), YEAR() are special cases of the DATEPART() function.

Mathematical:

1. Find the cosine of an angle in radians:

```
SELECT COS(1.0)
```

```
0.54030230586813977
```

2. Find the smallest integer greater than or equal to the given numeric expression:

```
SELECT CEILING(23.23)
```

```
24
```

3. Find the largest integer less than or equal to the given numeric expression:

```
SELECT FLOOR(23.23)
```

```
___
23
```

4. Find the value of the given expression raised to the specified power:

```
SELECT POWER(2,10)
```

```
_____
1024
```

5. Find the natural logarithm and base-10 logarithm of the given expression:

```
SELECT LOG(2.0), LOG10(2.0)
```

```
_____    _____
0.69314718055994529        0.3010299956639812
```

Metadata:

1. Find the object identification number:

```
SELECT OBJECT_ID ('authors')
```

```
_____-
117575457
```

2. Find whether the object has the specified property:

```
SELECT OBJECTPROPERTY (OBJECT_ID('authors'),'ISTABLE')
```

```
--
1
```

Note: Check the SQL Server 7.0 documentation for the list of properties, as it is rather comprehensive.

3. Find whether the database has the specified property:

```
SELECT DATABASEPROPERTY ( 'pubs','ISREADONLY')
```

```
--
0
```

Security:

1. Find if the current user is a member of the specified fixed server role:

```
SELECT IS_SRVROLEMEMBER ('sysadmin')
```

```
--
1
```

2. Find if the current user is a member of the specified database role:

```
SELECT IS_MEMBER ('scientists')
```

```
--
1
```

String:

1. Return a specified number of characters from the left and right of the supplied character string:

```
SELECT LEFT('Andromeda',3), RIGHT('Pegasus',4)
```

```
____    ____
And     asus
```

2. Replaces all occurrences of the second supplied string expression in the first string expression with a third expression:

```
SELECT REPLACE('Pluto','u','a')
```

```
_____
Plato
```

System:

1. Find the number of rows affected by the last SQL statement:

```
UPDATE authors SET city = 'Oakland'
  WHERE state = 'CA'
SELECT @@ROWCOUNT
```

```
___
15
```

2. Convert one datatype to another using the ANSI SQL-92 standard CAST function and the Transact-SQL CONVERT function:

```
PRINT CAST (@Ivar1 AS VARCHAR(10))
```

```
PRINT CONVERT (CHAR(10),@Ivar1)
```

In conjunction with the *style* parameter, the CONVERT function also has the capability to format dates:

```
SELECT CONVERT(CHAR(10),GETDATE(),103)
```

01/10/1998

System Statistical:

1. Find the number of disk writes performed by SQL Server since it was started:
    ```
    SELECT @@TOTAL_WRITE
    ```

    83

Text and Image:

1. Find the starting position of the first occurrence of a pattern in a specified expression:
    ```
    SELECT PATINDEX('%muckraking%', notes) FROM TITLES
    WHERE title_id = 'PC8888'
    ```

    --

    1

5.4.7   The CASE Function

The CASE function can be used to substitute data values within, for example, a SELECT statement. There are two forms of the CASE function—*simple* and *searched*. The simple case function allows a simple equality test to be performed:

```
SELECT au_id,
    CASE contract
        WHEN 1 THEN 'Under Contract'
        WHEN 0 THEN 'No Contract'
        ELSE 'Unknown'
    END
    AS 'Contract Status'
FROM authors

au_id           Contract Status
-----------     ---------------
172-32-1176     Under Contract
213-46-8915     Under Contract
238-95-7766     Under Contract
```

```
267-41-2394      Under Contract
274-80-9391      Under Contract
341-22-1782      No Contract
409-56-7008      Under Contract
                 ⋮
                 ⋮
899-46-2035      Under Contract
998-72-3567      Under Contract
```

Instead of printing a fairly meaningless 0 or 1 value, the CASE expression substitutes meaningful text for these values. The searched CASE expression takes this concept a stage further and allows more powerful comparisons to be made:

```
SELECT title_id,
  CASE
      WHEN ytd_sales IS NULL THEN 'Not yet sold'
      WHEN ytd_sales < 500 THEN 'Low Sales'
      WHEN ytd_sales >= 500 AND ytd_sales < 4000 THEN 'Good Sales'
      ELSE 'Keep Authors Happy!'
  END
  AS 'Sales Comment'
FROM titles
WHERE type = 'psychology'
```

```
title_id      Sales Comment
--------      -------------
PS1372        Low Sales
PS2091        Good Sales
PS2106        Low Sales
PS3333        Keep Authors Happy!
PS7777        Good Sales
```

5.5   Adding Data to a Table

There are various methods of putting new data into a database, that is, adding new rows to tables. In Transact-SQL this is usually accomplished with the INSERT statement but can also be accomplished with a variation of the SELECT statement. Before looking at these methods it is useful to introduce the concept of a transaction.

5.5.1   **Working with Transactions**

Transactions will be dealt with in more detail in Chapter 7, however, we need to introduce the concept of a transaction here as operations that change the data in a table, such as inserting, modifying, and deleting rows, can be executed within the scope of a transaction. A transaction is an atomic unit of work; either all the operations within a transaction are performed or none are. In Chapter 7 we will see how this rule applies to stored procedures and triggers, but for now let us consider that a transaction is an all or nothing event.

By default, if a statement such as INSERT is executed it will either succeed or fail. Once it succeeds the result of the insert is made permanent and the only way to remove the change made to the table by the insert is to execute a compensating statement such as a DELETE. If a series of inserts is made and one fails, perhaps because the server crashes, the inserts made prior to the failure will be unaffected—they will have succeeded as shown below:

```
insert row₁      OK

insert row₂      OK

insert row₃      OK

insert row₄      <====server crashes during this insert
```

The insert of row 4 will not execute partially; the statement itself will be rolled back. However, if these insertions formed part of a higher-level business transaction it may not make sense to allow some of the inserts to succeed and some to fail. If money were being transferred between bank accounts, the integrity of the operation would normally require that debits and credits must all happen successfully or none of them must happen.

Note: The default behavior of committing a transaction initiated by a Transact-SQL statement such as INSERT is known as *autocommit* mode. This is not ANSI SQL-92 behavior, which leaves the transaction open to be subsequently committed explicitly. To turn on the ANSI SQL-92 behavior use SET IMPLICIT_TRANSACTIONS ON.

We will therefore introduce the concept of an explicit transaction. An explicit transaction is a group of statements that must all succeed or must all fail. If a failure occurs during an explicit transaction, the database is restored to its state at the point at which the explicit transaction started. In other words, all the statements in the explicit transaction are rolled back. In the previous example, the server machine crashed during the insert of row 4. If these operations had been performed within an explicit transaction, the insertion of rows 1, 2, and 3 would be subsequently rolled back.

```
start an explicit transaction here

    insert row₁      OK

    insert row₂      OK

    insert row₃      OK

    insert row₄      <====server crashes during this insert

*** all inserts rolled back ***
```

To start an explicit transaction in Transact-SQL the BEGIN TRANSACTION statement is used. To end a transaction and make the changes to the database permanent, the COMMIT TRANSACTION statement is used, and to force a transaction rollback during a transaction a ROLLBACK TRANSACTION statement is used. To support the ANSI SQL-92 standard, COMMIT WORK and ROLLBACK WORK may be used instead.

5.5.2 Using INSERT to Add Rows to a Table

Now that the concept of a transaction has been introduced we can look at changing the database with various statements such as INSERT. If you execute a BEGIN TRANSACTION before changing the data in the database you can then execute a ROLLBACK TRANSACTION to remove the changes. This will allow you to *leave a database as you found it!*

Hint: Write locks are held on database objects for the length of a transaction, as discussed in Chapter 10. Be very careful when experimenting with changing data that you do not lock out other users. The authors suggest that your own test database be used.

The INSERT statement takes three common forms. The first is used when the values for the columns of the row to be inserted are explicitly specified. The second is used when the values for the columns of the row to be inserted are obtained from the result of a SELECT statement, that is, the values already exist somewhere. The third form is used when the values for the columns of the row to be inserted are obtained from the result of the execution of a stored procedure that returns a result set, often because it contains a SELECT statement. Let us look at the first form:

```
INSERT authors
  VALUES ('674-23-8877', 'Brown','Jim','603-786-8877','23
  Acacia Av.','Nashua','NH','03055',1)
```

In this example we have specified a value for all the columns and so we did not need to provide a *column list*. The number of values we have specified is the same as the number of columns in the table and they are in the same order.

Note: It is also permissible to use the optional keyword INTO as in INSERT INTO . . .

If we only wished to supply values for a subset of the columns we would need to provide a column list:

```
INSERT authors (au_id, au_lname, au_fname, phone, contract)
  VALUES ('774-49-5653', 'Green','Sue','415-332-5541',1)
```

Note that omitting columns can only be done if a table column was defined to allow NULL values, a default value was associated with it, the column had the IDENTITY property, or its data type was TIMESTAMP, otherwise an error would occur:

```
INSERT authors (au_id, au_lname, au_fname, phone)
  VALUES ('569-32-7675', 'Smith','Margaret','301-999-8888')
```

```
Server: Msg 515, Level 16, State 2
Cannot insert the value NULL into column 'contract', table
'pubs.dbo.authors'; column does not allow nulls. INSERT fails.
The statement has been aborted.
```

Note: To force defaults to be inserted into columns use the DEFAULT and DEFAULT VALUES keywords.

The second form of the INSERT statement uses a SELECT clause in order to retrieve rows from other tables or views and store them in the target table. Suppose we had created a new table to contain those authors who live in California and that new table was identical to the *authors* table:

```
CREATE TABLE ca_authors
  (
  au_id      ID,
  au_lname   VARCHAR(40)      NOT NULL,
  au_fname   VARCHAR(20)      NOT NULL,
  phone      CHAR(12),
  address    VARCHAR(40)      NULL,
  city       VARCHAR(20)      NULL,
  state      CHAR(2)          NULL,
  zip        CHAR(5)          NULL,
  contract   BIT
  )
```

We could easily populate the new table with the following INSERT statement:

```
INSERT ca_authors
  SELECT * FROM authors WHERE state = 'CA'
```

Often the target table is not identical to the source table and so slightly different formats are used for the INSERT statement. For example, suppose we decide that the *state* column is now superfluous so it is not present in the *ca_authors* table. If we attempted to use the same INSERT statement as in the above example we would receive an error message:

```
INSERT ca_authors
  SELECT * FROM authors WHERE state = 'CA'
```

```
Server: Msg 213, Level 16, State 5
Insert Error: Column name or number of supplied values does not
match table definition.
```

In this example we can specify a column list on the SELECT statement:

```
INSERT ca_authors
  SELECT au_id, au_lname, au_fname, phone, address, city, zip,
contract
  FROM authors WHERE state = 'CA'
```

We might decide that the new table has an extra column *author_status* and that once the table is populated, this column will be updated as the information becomes available. We must, in this case, supply a column list on the INSERT statement omitting this column or the column list in the table and the column list on the SELECT statement will no longer agree:

```
INSERT ca_authors (au_id, au_lname, au_fname, phone, address,
city, zip, contract)
```

```
SELECT au_id, au_lname, au_fname, phone, address, city, zip, contract
FROM authors WHERE state = 'CA'
```

The new column must have been defined to allow NULL values or have a default value defined.

The source of the data to be inserted into a table may be the result set from a stored procedure. The stored procedure will typically contain a SELECT statement and the discussion about matching column lists with INSERT...SELECT apply. One advantage of using a stored procedure is that is can be executed on a remote server so data from a database table other that tables on the local server can be used as a data source. Stored procedures will be discussed in Chapter 6 but an example of a table insertion that used this mechanism would be:

```
INSERT ca_authors EXECUTE faraway.pubs.dbo.usp_ca_authors
```

The stored procedure *usp_ca_authors* would execute on the remote server *faraway* and return the result set to the local server to be used as the source of the data for the INSERT.

Note: With the new capabilities in SQL Server 7.0 to allow Transact-SQL statements to execute against remote objects, such as tables, this INSERT...EXECUTE capability is less useful that it was in SQL Server 6.5.

5.5.3   Using SELECT INTO to Add Rows to a Table

A special form of the SELECT statement, SELECT INTO, can be used to load data from a table, a table join, or a view into another table and to automatically create the target table before inserting the data. This operation, unlike operations using the INSERT statement, is not logged in SQL Server's transaction log and therefore there are important considerations for recovery when using this version of the SELECT statement to create a permanent table.

Simply put, the database administrator will not be able to backup the transaction log. This is discussed in more detail in Chapter 8.

To use the SELECT INTO statement, a special database option, *select into/ bulk copy,* must be set on the database using the *sp_dboption* system-stored procedure or SQL Server Enterprise Manager. The only users who can change database options are members of the *sysadmin* fixed server role or the *db_owner* fixed database role for the database on which the option is to be changed.

Note: Often this construct is used to create temporary tables and pull data into them from other sources, in which case no option needs to be set.

Before setting the option you can easily check to see if it is already set. This can be achieved by using the system-stored procedure *sp_helpdb*:

```
sp_helpdb BankingDB
```

name	db_size	owner	dbid	created	status
BankingDB	200.00MB	sa	8	Sep 301998	no options set

We can immediately see that there are "no options set" in the status column. To see the options that can be set we can execute *sp_dboption* with no parameters:

```
sp_dboption


Settable database options:
_____

ANSI null default
ANSI nulls
ANSI warnings
auto create statistics
auto update statistics
autoclose
autoshrink
concat null yields null
cursor close on commit
dbo use only
default to local cursor
merge publish
offline
published
quoted identifier
read only
recursive triggers
```

```
select into/bulkcopy
single user
subscribed
torn page detection
trunc. log on chkpt.
```

To set the database option we can use *sp_dboption* with one of the above options, the value for the option, and the database name of the database for which we wish to set the option:

```
sp_dboption pubs, 'select into/bulkcopy', 'TRUE'
```

We are now able to run the SELECT INTO statement in the *pubs* database and create a permanent table:

```
SELECT au_fname, au_lname INTO ca_authors FROM authors WHERE
state = 'CA'
```

The resulting table will contain two columns - *au_fname* and *au_lname*.

We can create an empty table by specifying a condition in the WHERE clause that will not result in any rows being returned:

```
SELECT au_fname, au_lname, city INTO #empty_authors FROM authors
WHERE state = 'ZZ'
```

5.5.4   Modifying Data in a Table

It is often the case that one or more rows in a table need to be changed. This is achieved with the Transact-SQL UPDATE statement:

```
UPDATE authors
  set au_fname = 'Katy' WHERE au_fname='Katie' AND au_lname = 'Brown'
```

It can be seen that the UPDATE statement has a WHERE clause like a SELECT statement and this is used to specify the rows that are to be changed.

More than one column can be changed:

```
UPDATE authors
  SET   au_fname = 'Smith',
        au_lname = 'Joe'
  WHERE au_id = '893-72-1158'
```

The UPDATE statement can use arithmetic expressions such as in the example below where all the book prices are increased by 10%:

```
UPDATE titles SET price = price*1.1
```

> **Hint: To find the number of rows updated by the UPDATE statement check the @@ROWCOUNT function described earlier in this chapter.**

5.5.5   Deleting Data from a Table

The removal of data from a table is achieved with the Transact-SQL DELETE statement:

```
DELETE authors
```

The above example removes all the rows from the authors table. Like the UPDATE statement, the DELETE statement has a WHERE clause that is used to specify the rows that are to be removed:

```
DELETE authors WHERE au_id = '267-41-2394'
```

> **Note: It is also permissible to use the optional keyword FROM as in DELETE FROM . . .**

The DELETE statement, like the INSERT and UPDATE statements, logs each delete in the transaction log. If many rows are to be deleted, this can cause the transaction log to grow significantly. Another means of deleting all the rows from a table is provided in Transact-SQL with the TRUNCATE TABLE statement:

```
TRUNCATE TABLE ca_authors
```

This statement removes all the rows from a table by deallocating space used by the table (and its indexes) without logging the individual row removals to the transaction log. A TRUNCATE TABLE statement cannot be used on a table that is referenced by foreign key constraints and it will not fire a delete trigger. Foreign key constraints and triggers are described in Chapter 7.

6

Advanced Database Manipulation

6.1   Introduction

The previous chapter discussed elements of the *Data Manipulation Language* (DML). This chapter will take this subject further and look at some more advanced DML features. The features covered will be:

◆   Control-of-Flow

◆   Cursors

◆   Stored Procedures

◆   System-Stored Procedures

◆   Extended Stored Procedures

6.2   Control-of-Flow

As opposed to executing a single line of Transact-SQL, SQL Server supports the concept of batches of Transact-SQL statements. SQL Server also provides Transact-SQL language syntax to support flow control.

6.2.1   Transact-SQL Batches

It is possible with Transact-SQL to issue a group of Transact-SQL statements as a unit known as a *batch*. This is most commonly done when executing Transact-SQL from a script through ISQL, OSQL, or the Query Analyzer. SQL Server executes the statements in a script when it sees an *end-of-batch* terminator, which by default is *go* but may be altered on the OSQL or ISQL command line using the -c flag.

An example of a batch would be as follows:

```
SELECT MAX(price) AS 'Max Price' FROM titles
SELECT COUNT(*) AS 'Num Publishers' FROM  publishers
```

```
GO

Max Price
_____

22.9500

Num Publishers
_____

8
```

There are various rules that specify what Transact-SQL statements are allowed in a batch alongside other Transact-SQL statements and what operations are allowed in the same batch. Statements that must be on their own in a batch are:

* CREATE PROCEDURE
* CREATE RULE
* CREATE DEFAULT
* CREATE TRIGGER
* CREATE VIEW

The following example violates this rule by placing two CREATE VIEW statements in a batch:

```
CREATE VIEW v1 AS SELECT * FROM authors
CREATE VIEW v2 AS SELECT * FROM titles
GO

Server: Msg 156, Level 15, State 1, Procedure v1, Line 2
Incorrect syntax near the keyword 'CREATE'.
Server: Msg 111, Level 15, State 1, Procedure v1, Line 2
'CREATE VIEW' must be the first statement in a query batch.
```

The correct form would be to use two batches:

```
CREATE VIEW v1 AS SELECT * FROM authors
GO
CREATE VIEW v2 AS SELECT * FROM titles
GO
```

A table cannot be altered and then the new columns referenced in the same batch:

```
ALTER TABLE authors
  ADD birthdate DATETIME NULL
```

```
UPDATE authors
  SET birthdate = '10-Jan-1950'
  WHERE au_id = '998-72-3567'

Server: Msg 207, Level 16, State 1
Invalid column name 'birthdate'.
```

Another common restriction is that the execution of a stored procedure must be performed with an EXECUTE statement unless the stored procedure is the first statement in the batch. This works:

```
sp_help
SELECT COUNT(*) FROM sales
```

But this does not:

```
SELECT COUNT(*) FROM sales
sp_help
```

Apart from the above rules, for repetitive jobs, Transact-SQL statements can happily be placed in files and executed through OSQL or ISQL, which is an extremely useful time-saving capability. The OSQL or ISQL command line flag -i can be used to specify an input file containing batches of Transact-SQL statements:

```
osql -E -i script.sql -o outputfile.rpt
```

The above example executes a file named *script.sql,* containing Transact-SQL statements using a trusted connection to gain access to SQL Server.

6.2.2   Transact-SQL Flow Control

Like many languages, Transact-SQL provides various statements to support flow control. These statements are commonly used in scripts, stored procedures (described later in this chapter), and triggers, described in Chapter 7. Transact-SQL also provides the ability to define local variables. The flow control statements, in alphabetic order are:

+ BEGIN...END
+ GOTO
+ IF...ELSE
+ PRINT
+ RAISERROR
+ RETURN
+ WAITFOR
+ WHILE

To describe these statements, the alphabetic order will be discarded in favor of a more logical order.

PRINT

Print returns a user-defined message to the client's message handler:

```
PRINT 'Where is Dave?'
```

```
Where is Dave?
```

Sometimes the string you wish to print contains quotes:

```
PRINT 'Dave's not here'
```

```
Server: Msg 170, Level 15, State 1
Line 1: Incorrect syntax near 's'.
Server: Msg 105, Level 15, State 1
Unclosed quote before the character string ''.
```

The solution is to add another quote:

```
PRINT 'Dave''s not here'
```

```
Dave's not here
```

The PRINT statement can be used with functions:

```
PRINT 'Hello ' + UPPER('dave')
```

```
Hello DAVE
```

The PRINT statement can also be used with variables as described shortly.

IF...ELSE

The IF and ELSE keywords are used frequently as this is a useful mechanism for performing conditional processing. As in many languages, the SQL statement following the IF is executed when the IF condition is true, otherwise the SQL statement following the ELSE is executed assuming that an ELSE has been specified:

```
IF (SELECT MAX(price) FROM titles) > 30
   PRINT 'There are books costing more than $30'
ELSE
   PRINT 'There are no books costing more than $30'
```

```
There are no books costing more than $30
```

Note that a single Transact-SQL statement follows the IF and the ELSE. It is possible to execute a number of Transact-SQL statements instead of just one and to do this the BEGIN and END keywords must be used.

BEGIN...END

A group of Transact-SQL statements can be delimited by the BEGIN and END keywords and such a group is known as a *statement block*:

```
IF (SELECT MAX(price) FROM titles) > 30
  PRINT 'There are books costing more than $30'
ELSE
  BEGIN
  PRINT 'There are no books costing more than $30'
  SELECT AVG(price) AS 'Average price of a book' FROM titles
  END


There are no books costing more than $30
Average price of a book
  _____

14.7662
```

Note: BEGIN...END blocks may be nested.

WHILE

The WHILE statement is used in a similar fashion to that found in many languages, with some action or group of actions being performed as long as some condition is true:

```
WHILE (SELECT MIN(price) FROM titles) > 1
  BEGIN
    UPDATE titles SET price = price - 1
  END
```

In the above example, as long as the price of the books stays above one dollar, a dollar is subtracted from each price repeatedly. The test first sees if the minimum price of the books is greater than one dollar and, if it is, all the books will have their prices updated. The test will then be made again and so on until the minimum price is not greater than one dollar.

One application you may find for the WHILE statement is to facilitate the loading of test data into your tables.

The BREAK and CONTINUE keywords can be also used in conjunction with the WHILE statement. The BREAK forces a premature exit from the WHILE loop, whereas the CONTINUE causes a return to the beginning of the WHILE loop without executing subsequent Transact-SQL statements:

```
WHILE (SELECT MIN(price) FROM titles) > 1
  BEGIN
    UPDATE titles SET price = price - 1
    IF (SELECT price FROM titles WHERE title_id = 'PS2106') = 6
      BEGIN
        PRINT 'Back to the while test without doing the next step'
        CONTINUE
    END

    IF (SELECT AVG(price) FROM titles WHERE type = 'BUSINESS') < 20
      BEGIN
        PRINT 'Exit stage right...'
        BREAK
      END
  END
```

In the above example there are extra tests made. If the price of the book with *title_id* PS2106 becomes equal to six dollars, the WHILE loop is continued without executing the second test. The second test checks to see if the average price of the business books has become less than twenty dollars, and if it has, the WHILE loop is immediately exited.

GOTO

The GOTO statement is used in a similar fashion to that found in many languages, with a code branch to a label being taken if some condition is true:

```
IF (SELECT MAX (qty) FROM sales) > 1000
  GOTO hi_fi_shop
```

The label *hi_fi_shop* would appear in the Transact-SQL with a colon:

```
hi_fi_shop:
```

Note: A GOTO statement cannot jump outside the batch in which it is executing.

RETURN

This causes an exit and is normally used within a stored procedure as we shall see shortly:

```
    :
    :
stored procedure body
    :
IF  (SELECT COUNT(*)  FROM authors) > 10
   RETURN
    :
```

RAISERROR

The RAISERROR statement can be used to return a user-defined message that it retrieves from the *sysmessages* system table in the master database, and sets the @@ERROR system flag to record that an error has occurred. The RAISERROR statement can also be used to construct a message dynamically with user-specified severity and state information:

```
RAISERROR ('She''s breaking up captain',16,1)
```

```
Server: Msg 50000, Level 16, State 1
She's breaking up captain
```

Note that ad-hoc messages such as in the previous example raise an error number of 50,000. Error numbers for user-defined error messages should be greater than 50,000, while error numbers less than 50,000 are reserved for Microsoft. User-defined error messages can be added to the *sysmessages* system table in the master database by using the SQL Server Enterprise Manager or the *sp_addmessage* system-stored procedure.

A RAISERROR statement can then pick up an entry from the *sysmessages* table:

```
RAISERROR (50005, 16, 1)
```

```
Server: Msg 50005, Level 16, State 1
The widgets have dropped below 1000.
```

The severity level of a message can range from 0 to 25. Severity levels from 0 to 18 inclusive can be used by any user, however, severity levels of 19 to 25 inclusive can only be used by members of the *sysadmin* fixed server role. The *sysadmin* fixed server role is described in Chapter 9.

The state of a message is a number between 1 and 127 inclusive that can be used to provide extra information about the error.

If there is a requirement that the error message is written to the Windows NT application event log and the SQL Server error log, then the WITH

LOG option may be used. This ensures that, regardless of the severity of the message, the message will be logged.

```
RAISERROR (50005, 16, 1) WITH LOG

Server: Msg 50005, Level 16, State 1
The widgets have dropped below 1000.
```

For severity levels 19 to 25 the WITH LOG option is mandatory. Severity levels 20 through 25 are termed fatal. If a fatal severity level occurs, the client connection is broken after receiving the message and the error is logged in the SQL Server error log and the Windows NT application event log.

Suppose we take our earlier example:

```
RAISERROR (50005, 16, 1)

Server: Msg 50005, Level 16, State 1
The widgets have dropped below 1000.
```

This message is a little inflexible. We might want to generate a message that warns us that the widgets have dropped below 500. Rather than create a second message in the *sysmessages* table, it would be useful if SQL Server let us substitute the widget level into the message without us having to hard-code it. SQL Server allows us to do exactly this. Using formatting like the PRINTF format style used in the C language, we can add a message to the message file such as:

```
The widgets have dropped below %u
```

The *%u* character type represents an unsigned integer. Other character types include *%d* for signed integer and *%s* for string.

All we now need to do is supply the value in the RAISERROR:

```
RAISERROR (50005, 16, 1, 500)

Server: Msg 50005, Level 16, State 1
The widgets have dropped below 500
```

WAITFOR

The WAITFOR statement causes a wait to occur for a specified delta-time, for example 10 minutes, or an absolute time, for example 10:23. The WAITFOR statement has been largely superseded by the scheduling capabilities of the SQL Server Agent, as described in Chapter 8.

```
WAITFOR DELAY '00:00:10'
PRINT 'Your 10 seconds is up...'
```

```
WAITFOR TIME '12:50'
PRINT 'Lunchtime approaching...'
```

The first example waits for 10 seconds before displaying a message and the second waits until 12:50.

DECLARING VARIABLES

Transact-SQL is capable of defining local variables in a similar fashion to most programming languages. Variables, in conjunction with the flow control constructs we have seen, allow for a level of programming to be performed with Transact-SQL.

Local variables are found everywhere, for example they are often found in stored procedures and triggers. They are created with the DECLARE statement:

```
DECLARE @college CHAR(30)

DECLARE @counter_1 SMALLINT
```

Note that the variable name must begin with an @ symbol. A number of variables may be declared with one DECLARE statement:

```
DECLARE @college   CHAR(30),
        @counter_1 SMALLINT,
        @prize     MONEY
```

Variables are assigned values with a SELECT or SET statement:

```
DECLARE @planet   CHAR(30)
DECLARE @star     CHAR(30)

SELECT  @planet = 'Mercury'
SET     @star   = 'Sirius'
```

A number of variables may be assigned values with one SELECT statement (SET can only assign a value to one variable):

```
SELECT  @college   = 'Queen Elizabeth',
        @counter_1 = 0,
        @prize     = 1000
```

Local variables must be used in the same procedure or batch where they are declared:

```
DECLARE @planet   CHAR(30)
SELECT  @planet = 'Pluto'
PRINT   @planet
GO
```

```
PRINT @planet
GO


Pluto
Server: Msg 137, Level 15, State 2
Must declare the variable '@planet'.
```

In the above example the second PRINT statement attempts to use the variable outside the batch in which it was declared.

Variables may be used in flow control statements:

```
DECLARE @num_authors SMALLINT
SELECT @num_authors = COUNT(*) FROM authors
IF @num_authors < 100
  PRINT '*** Recruit more authors ***'


*** Recruit more authors ***
```

EXECUTE

The EXECUTE statement can be used to run a stored procedure and we shall see examples of this later in the chapter. The EXECUTE statement also has the ability to allow the execution of a character string that is dynamically created at execution time:

```
EXECUTE ('DROP TABLE ' + @Tname)
```

However, there is a more efficient way to build Transact-SQL statements at run time and execute them under SQL Server 7.0. This involves the use of the *sp_executesql* system-stored procedure.

The *sp_executesql* system-stored procedure supports parameter substitution similar to that described in RAISERROR earlier in this chapter and it also supports Unicode strings. The following example shows how this works:

```
DECLARE @SQLStr NVARCHAR(100)
DECLARE @ParamDef NVARCHAR(100)
DECLARE @StateVariable NCHAR(2)

SET @SQLStr = N'SELECT * FROM pubs.dbo.authors WHERE state
= @StateCode'

SET @ParamDef = N'@StateCode NCHAR(2)'

SET @StateVariable = 'CA'

EXECUTE sp_executesql @SQLStr, @ParamDef, @StateCode =
@StateVariable
```

The first parameter to the *sp_executesql* system-stored procedure is the Transact-SQL statement that is to be executed. Note that this Transact-SQL statement can contain parameters, in this case *@StateCode*. The second parameter to the *sp_executesql* system-stored procedure is a single string that contains the definitions of all the parameters that have been embedded in the Transact-SQL statement. The third parameter is a value for the first parameter defined in the parameter string. If there were a second parameter defined in the parameter string, then there would be a fourth parameter supplying its value and so on. There must be a parameter value supplied for every parameter included in the Transact-SQL statement.

The benefit of using the *sp_executesql* system-stored procedure in preference to the EXECUTE statement is that the text of the Transact-SQL statement in the *sp_executesql* system-stored procedure does not change between executions of *sp_executesql*. This means that it is highly likely that the query optimizer will match the Transact-SQL statement in the second execution with the execution plan generated for the first execution. This means that the second statement will not incur the overhead of query compilation. For example, a second execution of the Transact-SQL statement to search for authors from Oregon would only need to be stated as:

```
SET @StateVariable = 'OR'

EXECUTE sp_executesql @SQLStr, @ParamDef, @StateCode =
@StateVariable
```

Note: The full name of the table must be specified to reuse the original query plan.

6.3   Cursors

A cursor is a mechanism that allows an application to process the result set from a SELECT statement one row at a time. This provides the capability to update and delete the row on which the cursor is positioned and to navigate around the result set.

Database APIs such as ADO, OLEDB, and ODBC provide cursor capabilities. However, we are focusing on Transact-SQL and so we will look at the cursor capabilities of Transact-SQL. Transact-SQL cursors are typically used in stored procedures, triggers, and scripts and as they are executed on the server, they are known as server cursors.

The general approach to defining and processing Transact-SQL cursors is:

- Define the cursor in terms of a SELECT statement and specify other cursor properties using the DECLARE CURSOR statement.
- Populate the cursor using the OPEN statement.
- Retrieve single rows with the FETCH statement.
- Finish with the cursor by closing it with a CLOSE statement and freeing up remaining resources with the DEALLOCATE statement.

6.3.1   Declaring a Cursor

The DECLARE CURSOR statement is used to create the cursor. Before SQL Server 7.0, the syntax supported was based on the SQL-92 standard, but SQL Server 7.0 now also supports syntax that, while not found in the standard, provides a greater ability to specify the cursor properties. The SQL-92 syntax is shown below:

```
DECLARE cursor_name [INSENSITIVE] [SCROLL] CURSOR
FOR select_statement
[FOR {READ ONLY | UPDATE [OF column_name [,...n]]}]
```

A cursor defined with the keyword INSENSITIVE is implemented by copying the result set to tempdb. Changes cannot be made to the result set by the connection processing the cursor, nor can this connection see any changes made by other connections. The connection processing the cursor can see updates and deletions made by other connections if INSENSITIVE is not used, as long as those changes are committed.

If the SCROLL keyword is used, the FETCH statement can navigate around the result set in any direction. If SCROLL is not used, FETCH can only navigate in a forward direction.

The READ ONLY keywords turn the cursor into a cursor that cannot be updated. The UPDATE keyword allows updates to be made to all the columns in the cursor, unless a list of columns is also included, in which case only those columns may be updated.

The Transact-SQL syntax allows a finer level of control over the definition of the cursor. The syntax is shown below:

```
DECLARE cursor_name CURSOR
[LOCAL | GLOBAL]
[FORWARD_ONLY | SCROLL]
[STATIC | KEYSET | DYNAMIC | FAST_FORWARD]
[READ_ONLY | SCROLL_LOCKS | OPTIMISTIC]
[TYPE_WARNING]
```

```
FOR select_statement
[FOR UPDATE [OF column_name [,...n]]]
```

The LOCAL and GLOBAL keywords define the scope of the cursor. Before SQL Server 7.0, cursors created in a stored procedure on a connection could be accessed by another stored procedure executing on that connection. In fact, any Transact-SQL statement executing on that connection could reference the cursor. The cursor was global to the connection. Because of this global scope, SQL Server 7.0 refers to such cursors as GLOBAL cursors.

This global scope on the connection could cause problems. If a global cursor was not properly closed, no other cursor could be created on the connection of that name. Similarly, Transact-SQL statements executing outside of the stored procedure that created the cursor could accidentally change it. SQL Server 7.0 allows a developer to also define cursors with a local scope. These are known as LOCAL cursors. The scope of a local cursor is the stored procedure, trigger, or batch in which it is created. Local cursors will often be safer to use, as they cannot be accessed outside the stored procedure, trigger, or batch in which they are created. Global and local cursors of the same name can exist. Statements that access cursors can specify whether they wish to access a local or global cursor.

So, when creating a cursor, the LOCAL or GLOBAL keywords are used to specify its scope. If no keyword is used, the setting of the database option *default to local cursor* is used. If it is *true*, the scope of the cursor created will be local. The default value of this database option is *false.*

The FORWARD_ONLY keyword specifies that the cursor can only be navigated from the first row to the last row. The only FETCH statement supported is FETCH NEXT. Forward only cursors are dynamic cursors unless this behavior is overridden with the STATIC and KEYSET keywords. The behavior of the SCROLL keyword is the same as defined above in the SQL-92 syntax. If neither FORWARD_ONLY nor SCROLL is specified and the cursor type is specified—STATIC, KEYSET, or DYNAMIC—the cursor will be a scroll cursor, otherwise it will be a forward cursor.

The STATIC, KEYSET, DYNAMIC, and FAST_FORWARD keywords specify the type of cursor to be created. The STATIC keyword defines a cursor that is implemented by copying the result set to tempdb. Changes cannot be made to the result set by the connection processing the cursor nor can this connection see any changes made by other connections. This is like the INSENSITIVE keyword in the SQL-92 definition.

In the case of a cursor defined with the KEYSET keyword, when the cursor is opened a set of keys that uniquely distinguish the rows is stored in tempdb.

This is known as a *keyset*. Because the keyset is built when the cursor is opened, the rows that make up the cursor and their order are defined at this point. Updates and deletes to rows in the keyset made by the connection processing the cursor or made by other connections are visible, but not inserts. Note that an update to the key that defines the keyset appears like a delete because the row will have moved position. A fetch from a cursor of a deleted row (a corpse!) can always be checked by using the function @@FETCH_STATUS. If this returns –2, the fetch has retrieved a deleted row.

The keyword DYNAMIC specifies that a cursor is created whose attributes are to allow all changes to be seen to the result set, including inserts.

The keyword FAST_FORWARD defines a cursor that is both forward only and read only. As its name suggests, this type of cursor is performance optimized.

The keyword READ_ONLY turns the cursor into a cursor that cannot be updated. The keywords SCROLL_LOCKS and OPTIMISTIC effectively control cursor locking. Locking is described in Chapter 10.

The SCROLL_LOCKS keyword ensures that positioned updates or deletes made through the cursor will not find that another connection has already changed the row. This is because the use of this keyword ensures that the rows are locked as they are retrieved by the cursor in order to block any other connection.

The OPTIMISTIC keyword ensures that positioned updates or deletes made through the cursor do not succeed if another connection has changed the row since it was retrieved into the cursor. If the row contains a timestamp column, a "before" and "after" comparison of the column is made. If there is no timestamp column, a checksum value is used.

The TYPE_WARNING keyword displays a warning message if the cursor is implicitly converted from the requested type to another. For example, if a keyset cursor is requested for a table with no unique indexes it will be implicitly converted.

The following example declares a forward only keyset cursor using optimistic locking:

```
DECLARE AuthorsCACurs CURSOR GLOBAL
    FORWARD_ONLY
    KEYSET
    OPTIMISTIC
    TYPE_WARNING
```

```
      FOR SELECT * FROM authors WHERE state = 'CA'

OPEN AuthorsCACurs

FETCH NEXT FROM AuthorsCACurs
   :
   :

CLOSE AuthorsCACurs
DEALLOCATE AuthorsCACurs
```

Following the opening of the cursor the rows are retrieved one at a time with the FETCH statement and they can then be individually processed. When the required rows have been processed the cursor is closed. It can be reopened but no fetches are possible while it is closed. Finally, the cursor is deallocated, which deletes the cursor and removes any memory structures and resource associated with it.

As the above cursor is a forward only cursor, the FETCH statement can only move forward through the result set. To move about the result set a scroll cursor can be declared:

```
DECLARE AuthorsCACurs CURSOR GLOBAL
   SCROLL
   KEYSET
   OPTIMISTIC
   TYPE_WARNING
   FOR SELECT * FROM authors WHERE state = 'CA'

OPEN AuthorsCACurs
   :
FETCH FIRST FROM AuthorsCACurs
   :
FETCH LAST FROM AuthorsCACurs
   :
FETCH PRIOR FROM AuthorsCACurs
   :
FETCH ABSOLUTE 5 FROM AuthorsCACurs
   :
FETCH RELATIVE -3 FROM AuthorsCACurs
   :
CLOSE AuthorsCACurs

DEALLOCATE AuthorsCACurs
```

Absolute N returns the *Nth* row within the results set. *N* can be negative, in which case the row returned will be the *Nth* row counting backwards from the last row of the results set.

Relative N returns the *Nth* row after the row that has just been fetched. *N* can be negative, in which case the row returned will be the *Nth* row counting backwards from the row that has just been fetched.

The first row in the result set is addressed by N set to one, that is, ABSOLUTE 1. FETCH ABSOLUTE and FETCH RELATIVE can also work with a variable:

```
FETCH ABSOLUTE @rowpos
```

Note: The ABSOLUTE form of the FETCH statement cannot be used with a dynamic cursor.

A fetch statement can place the column data returned into variables:

```
FETCH NEXT FROM MyCurs INTO @var1, @var2
```

6.3.2   Retrieving Information about Cursors

There are a number of functions and stored procedures that can be used to retrieve information about cursors.

The following functions can be used:

* @@FETCH_STATUS
* @@CURSOR_ROWS
* CURSOR_STATUS

The following stored procedures can be used:

* sp_cursor_list
* sp_describe_cursor
* sp_describe_cursor_columns
* sp_describe_cursor_tables

The function @@FETCH_STATUS can be used to check if a FETCH statement has attempted to fetch a row outside of the result set, for example, beyond the end of the result set (@@FETCH_STATUS = -1). It can also be used to check to see if the FETCH statement has attempted to fetch a row that has been deleted (@@FETCH_STATUS = -2).

The function @@CURSOR_ROWS can be used to check how many rows are in the current cursor. If the cursor is a dynamic cursor the value returned will always be –1.

The function CURSOR_STATUS returns information that allows the caller of a stored procedure to determine whether or not the procedure has returned a cursor and result set.

```
SELECT CURSOR_STATUS ('GLOBAL','AuthorsCACurs')
```

For example, if the function returns –1, the cursor is closed.

The system-stored procedure *sp_cursor_list* returns the properties of server cursors currently open on the connection. The *sp_describe_cursor* system-stored procedure describes the attributes of a cursor, for example, is it a keyset cursor? The system-stored procedure *sp_describe_cursor_columns* describes the attributes of the columns in the cursor result set and *sp_describe_cursor_tables* describes the tables used by the cursor.

6.4 Stored Procedures

Now that we have covered many aspects of Transact-SQL we can look at stored procedures. What is a stored procedure? A stored procedure is like a Transact-SQL program that is stored in an SQL Server database. It is comprised of a number of Transact-SQL statements and often includes variables and flow control statements.

What is the advantage of using stored procedures? There are, in fact, a number of benefits in using stored procedures.

- Encapsulation of business logic
- Performance
- Security

From an *encapsulation of business logic* perspective, stored procedures enable the designer to place an action or group of actions together in a database. The alternative might be to store the logic either in the client application or a middle tier, if an *n* tier architecture is being used. An advantage of stored procedures is that they can effectively *hide* the complexity of the function being performed by the stored procedure. They can also hide the structure of the database from the client application. This means that database schema structures can be modified and the stored procedure code changed while maintaining the same interface to the client application. The ability to keep the stored procedure code in one place—the database—and the ability to minimize client application changes while modifying the database schema means that the use of stored procedures can reduce application maintenance effort.

From a *performance* perspective, stored procedures provide a number of benefits. Imagine a business function that required 100 Transact-SQL statements to be executed every time it was invoked. If we placed these Transact-SQL statements in the client application, each statement would be sent down to the server for processing and a result sent back to the client. This would clearly result in many messages being sent from the client and back from the server that would impact the network, as shown in Figure 6.1.

Figure 6.1
Executing Multiple
Transact-SQL
Statements on the Client

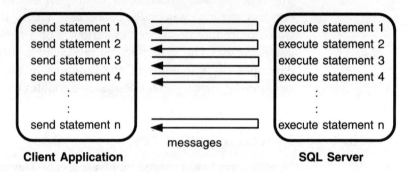

Client Application   SQL Server

If, on the other hand, these 100 Transact-SQL statements resided in a stored procedure on the server, then the client would issue a Transact-SQL statement to execute the stored procedure, the stored procedure would execute on the server, and would pass information back. This reduced message traffic would lessen the network load and would improve performance, especially where the network was busy, as shown in Figure 6.2.

Figure 6.2
Executing a Stored
Procedure on the Server

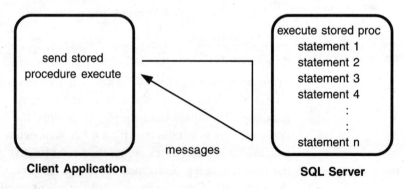

Client Application   SQL Server

Stored procedures also provide another performance benefit. SQL Server processes a stored procedure when it is first executed and uses the query optimizer to create an efficient query execution plan, which it then keeps in a memory cache known as the *procedure cache*. The subsequent execution of the stored procedure by that or another connection therefore happens very quickly as the query optimization need not be performed again. In other words, once the query plan has been placed in the procedure cache, it can be used by anyone executing that stored procedure and he or she will not suffer the overhead of query optimization.

From a *security* perspective, users can execute stored procedures to which they have been given EXECUTE permission. This means that they can perform set actions in a database even though they have no access to the base objects, such as tables, referenced in the stored procedure.

Stored procedures are not unlike the procedures found in other programming languages as they can be called with input and output parameters and they themselves can call other stored procedures. If required, stored procedures can return a status, which may indicate the success or failure of the stored procedure.

However, unlike the procedures found in many languages, stored procedures that reside on remote SQL Servers can also be called relatively easily. A typical configuration is shown in Figure 6.3.

Figure 6.3
*Calling
Remote Stored
Procedures*

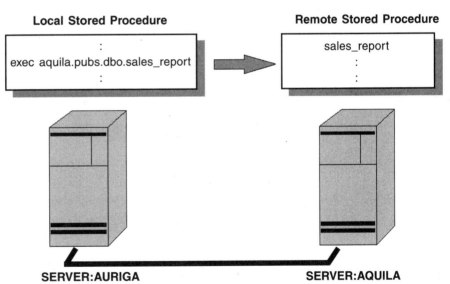

6.4.1 Creating Stored Procedures

Stored procedures are defined in Transact-SQL with the CREATE PROCEDURE or CREATE PROC statement:

```
CREATE PROCEDURE usp_AuthorsFromCA AS
SELECT * FROM authors WHERE state = 'CA'
```

The simple example above creates a stored procedure named *usp_AuthorsFromCA* that retrieves the authors from California. We have chosen to use the prefix *usp* to designate this as a user-written stored procedure (as opposed to *sp* for a system-stored procedure as discussed later in this chapter). How do we execute this stored procedure? We use the EXECUTE statement or EXEC for short:

```
EXEC usp_AuthorsFromCA
```

It is possible to omit the EXEC statement, but this can only be done if the stored procedure execution is the only or first statement in a batch because, if not, the batch might fail:

```
SELECT * FROM STORES ORDER BY stor_id
usp_AuthorsFromCA


Server: Msg 170, Level 15, State 1
Line 2: Incorrect syntax near 'usp_AuthorsFromCA'.
```

Note: Executing a stored procedure on a remote server is a simple matter of supplying the server name on which the stored procedure resides:

```
EXEC aquila.pubs.dbo.usp_AuthorInState UT
```

Of course, the configuration of the local and remote server security must have been set up to allow this remote stored procedure invocation to succeed.

There are important considerations for recovery when using remote stored procedures; because they cannot be rolled back, they are not treated as part of a transaction unless the *Microsoft Distributed Transaction Coordinator (DTC)* is used.

The *usp_AuthorsFromCA* stored procedure is very simple as it does not take any parameters. Stored procedures may take a number of parameters up to a maximum of 1024:

```
CREATE PROCEDURE usp_AuthorInState @state_code CHAR(2) AS
SELECT au_id, au_fname, au_lname FROM authors WHERE state =
@state_code
```

In this example the *usp_AuthorInState* stored procedure accepts a single input parameter, the state code:

```
EXEC usp_AuthorInState UT

au_id          au_fname  au_lname
_____     _____ _____

899-46-2035 Anne        Ringer
998-72-3567 Albert      Ringer
```

Suppose that we were to omit the parameter:

```
EXEC usp_AuthorInState

Server: Msg 201, Level 16, State 2, Procedure
usp_AuthorInState, Line 0
Procedure 'usp_AuthorInState' expects parameter
'@state_code', which was not supplied.
```

As we can see, SQL Server displays an error message. One way around this is to supply a default value for the parameter. Another way around this is to test for the existence of any required parameters:

```
CREATE PROCEDURE usp_AuthorInState @state_code CHAR(2) = 'UT'
AS
SELECT au_id, au_fname, au_lname FROM authors WHERE state =
@state_code
```

The above example assigns a default value of *UT* to the *@state_code* parameter.

```
EXEC usp_AuthorInState

au_id          au_fname  au_lname
_____     _____ _____

899-46-2035 Anne        Ringer
998-72-3567 Albert      Ringer
```

To test for the omission of a parameter it is convenient to give the parameter a value of NULL and then to test the parameter value for NULL:

```
CREATE PROCEDURE usp_AuthorInState @state_code CHAR(2) =
NULL
AS
  IF @state_code IS NULL
    PRINT '*** You forgot to enter a state code, please try
    again ***'
  ELSE
    SELECT au_id, au_fname, au_lname FROM authors WHERE
    state = @state_code
```

If we now omit the parameter:

```
EXEC usp_AuthorInState
```

```
*** You forgot to enter a state code, please try again ***
```

If more than one parameter is needed by a stored procedure it is important to know the order in which parameters are specified on the call to execute the stored procedure.

An alternative way of supplying parameters to a stored procedure is to use the parameter names as in the following format:

```
EXEC usp_AuthorInState @state_code = MI
```

au_id	au_fname	au_lname
712-45-1867	Innes	delCastillo

This method of entering parameters removes the need to ensure that the position of the parameters is correct, which is important when more than one parameter is used:

```
EXEC ComplexCalculation @num1 = 10, @num2 = 7
```

This is equivalent to specifying the parameters the other way around:

```
EXEC ComplexCalculation @num2 =7, @num1 = 10
```

It is important for the Transact-SQL that called a stored procedure to be able to test if the stored procedure was successful or not, and this is achieved by virtue of the fact that a stored procedure can return a status value that may then be tested. The integer value returned may be set by SQL Server itself or by the stored procedure developer. SQL Server reserves the range of values -1 to -99 to indicate a failure and 0 to indicate success.

```
DECLARE @StatusCode   INT
EXEC @StatusCode = usp_AuthorInState KS
```

The above example declares a variable to receive the return status. It then executes the stored procedure using syntax that will pass the return status into the variable.

To pass a value in the return status code the RETURN keyword is used with the status code value:

```
CREATE PROCEDURE usp_AuthorInState @state_code CHAR(2) = NULL
AS
   IF @state_code IS NULL
    RETURN 1
   ELSE
```

```
SELECT au_id, au_fname, au_lname FROM authors WHERE state
= @state_code
```

Instead of printing a message as before, the *usp_AuthorInState* stored procedure now returns a status code of 1 if no parameter value is supplied. The calling Transact-SQL can test this:

```
DECLARE @StatusCode  INT
EXEC @StatusCode = usp_AuthorInState
    IF (@StatusCode = 1)
    PRINT '*** Forgot again didn''t we!! ***'
```

We have just seen that stored procedures can return information in the form of a result set from a SELECT statement and a value through the RETURN statement. SQL Server also allows us to return values in parameters and these are known as *output parameters.* Output parameters are defined in the same way as the input parameters we have already seen but with the OUTPUT keyword:

```
CREATE PROCEDURE usp_AddNumbers @num1 INT, @num2 INT,
@answer INT OUTPUT
AS
SELECT @answer = @num1 + @num2
```

To execute this stored procedure we could enter the following Transact-SQL:

```
DECLARE @TheSum INT
EXEC usp_AddNumbers 5, 18, @TheSum OUTPUT
```

Stored procedures can also be created using the SQL Enterprise Manager:

⇨ Expand the server group and expand the server.

⇨ Expand *Databases* and right-click the database in which the stored procedure is to be created.

⇨ Click *New* and *Stored Procedure.*

⇨ Enter the code of the stored procedure.

⇨ Click *OK.*

The SQL Server Enterprise Manager does not really assist the developer very much when creating a stored procedure, as it only presents a window in which Transact-SQL can be typed, as shown in Figure 6.4. This is more useful when editing a stored procedure once it has been created.

SQL Server also provides a *Create Stored Procedures* wizard. This can be used to create three stored procedures—insert, update, and delete—for any table in a specified database. It is shown in Figure 6.5.

Figure 6.4

Creating Stored Procedures in
the SQL Enterprise Manager

Figure 6.5

Using the Create Stored
Procedure Wizard

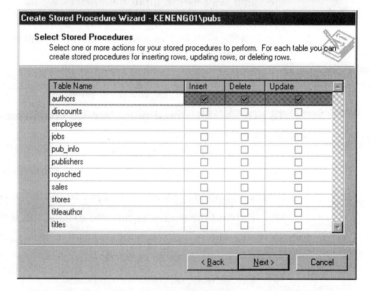

Another feature available to the developer when creating a stored procedure is the ability to encrypt the stored procedure definition so the Transact-SQL used to create the stored procedure will not be available to anyone else. The WITH ENCRYPTION clause can be used to achieve this:

```
CREATE PROCEDURE usp_AuthorInState @state_code CHAR(2) = NULL
WITH ENCRYPTION
AS
   IF @state_code IS NULL
     RETURN 1
   ELSE
```

```
SELECT au_id, au_fname, au_lname FROM authors WHERE state
= @state_code
```

6.4.2   Managing Stored Procedures

It is highly likely that a stored procedure will, at some point, need to be changed. Perhaps code needs to be modified or parameter definitions altered. A stored procedure can always be dropped and recreated but this does mean that any permissions associated with the stored procedure will have to be redefined. To avoid having to redefine permission lists it is usually easier to just modify the stored procedure using the ALTER PROCEDURE or ALTER PROC statement:

```
ALTER PROCEDURE usp_AuthorInState @state_code CHAR(2) = NULL
AS
  IF @state_code IS NULL
    RETURN 1
  ELSE
    SELECT au_id, au_fname, au_lname FROM authors
    WHERE state = @state_code
    ORDER BY au_lname
```

To remove a stored procedure use the DROP PROCEDURE or DROP PROC statement:

```
DROP PROCEDURE usp_AuthorInState
```

To rename a stored procedure use the *sp_rename* system-stored procedure:

```
EXEC sp_rename usp_AuthorInState, usp_WriterInState
```

The altering, removing, and renaming of stored procedures can also be performed through the SQL Server Enterprise Manager.

6.4.3   Finding Information about Stored Procedures

The stored procedures that are present in a database can be listed by using the *sp_help* system-stored procedure:

```
EXEC sp_help
```

Name	Owner	Object_type
authors_names	dbo	view
:		
:		
usp_AddNumbers	dbo	stored procedure

```
usp_AuthorsFromCA  dbo      stored procedure
usp_WriterInState  dbo      stored procedure
```

Information can also be obtained about an individual stored procedure using *sp_help* with the stored procedure name:

```
EXEC sp_help author_in_state
```

Name	Owner	Type	Created_datetime
usp_AddNumbers	dbo	stored procedure	1998-10-11 10:47:49.887

Parameter_name	Type	Length	Prec	Scale	Param_order
@num1	int	4	10	0	1
@num2	int	4	10	0	2
@answer	int	4	10	0	3

The Transact-SQL used to create a particular stored procedure can be obtained using *sp_helptext*:

```
EXEC sp_helptext usp_AddNumbers
```

Text
_____

```
CREATE PROCEDURE usp_AddNumbers @num1 int, @num2 int, @answer
INT OUTPUT
AS
SELECT @answer = @num1 + @num2
```

Note: Although *sp_helptext* can be used to view the source code of a stored procedure, it is far clearer to view the code through the SQL Server Enterprise Manager.

Suppose the developer has encrypted a stored procedure definition:

```
EXEC sp_helptext usp_AddNumbers
```

```
The object comments have been encrypted.
```

To display information concerning the objects referenced by a stored procedure, the system-stored procedure *sp_depends* can be used:

```
EXEC sp_depends usp_MonthlyReport
```

```
In the current database, the specified object references
the following:
```

name	type	updated	selected	column
dbo.publishers	user table	no	no	pub_id
dbo.titles	user table	no	no	title_id
dbo.titles	user table	no	no	pub_id
dbo.sales	user table	no	no	qty
dbo.sales	user table	no	no	title_id
dbo.publishers	user table	no	no	pub_id
dbo.titles	user table	no	no	title_id
dbo.titles	user table	no	no	pub_id
dbo.sales	user table	no	no	qty
dbo.sales	user table	no	no	title_id

```
In the current database, the specified object is referenced
by the following:
```

Name	type
dbo.usp_PublishersReport	stored procedure

To display dependency information using the SQL Server Enterprise Manager:

⇨ Expand the server group and expand the server.

⇨ Expand *Databases* and click the *Stored Procedures* folder.

⇨ Right-click the target stored procedure.

⇨ Select *All Tasks* and *Display Dependencies*.

The stored procedure *dependencies* window is shown in Figure 6.6.

Figure 6.6

Stored Procedure Dependencies

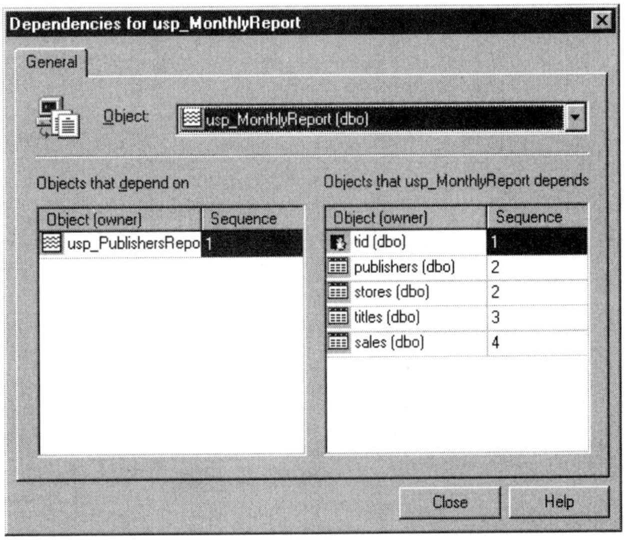

6.4.4   Creating Temporary Stored Procedures

It is possible to create *local* and *global temporary stored procedures*. As with temporary tables discussed in Chapter 4, they are created by preceding the stored procedure name with a *#* for local temporary procedures or a *##* for global temporary procedures:

```
CREATE PROCEDURE ##usp_AuthorInState @state_code CHAR(2)
AS
SELECT au_id, au_fname, au_lname FROM authors WHERE state =
@state_code
```

Again, as with temporary tables, local temporary procedures are visible in the current session only and global temporary procedures are visible to all sessions. Both types of temporary stored procedure are created in tempdb.

6.4.5   Marking Stored Procedures for Automatic Execution

Another useful stored procedure feature is the ability to mark stored procedures for automatic execution so that they are executed every time SQL Server starts. This can be useful to ensure that tasks are performed every time SQL Server is started. To mark a stored procedure for automatic execution, the system-stored procedure *sp_procoption* is used:

```
sp_procoption usp_StartupChecks, 'startup', 'on'
```

The option setting of *off* will unmark the stored procedure for automatic execution.

Note: To suppress the running of automatic execution stored procedures when SQL Server starts, use the server configuration option *scan for startup procs*.

6.5   System-Stored Procedures

System-stored procedures, often known as simply *system procedures*, are stored procedures that are supplied by Microsoft as part of SQL Server. The naming convention in SQL Server uses "*sp_*" to prefix the stored procedure name so that it is obvious that the stored procedure is a system-stored procedure. Often, system-stored procedures manipulate system tables because these should not be manipulated directly.

We have met system-stored procedures already, for example, *sp_help*, *sp_depends*, and *sp_rename*. There are many system-stored procedures in SQL Server and there are also *extended stored procedures* and *catalog stored procedures*. Extended stored procedures will be discussed shortly. Catalog stored procedures are merely system-stored procedures that provide a consistent interface to the system catalog (in practice the system tables) so that the routines present in the Microsoft SQL Server Open Database Connectivity (ODBC) driver or the Microsoft SQL Server OLEDB provider can interrogate an SQL Server.

It is worth setting aside some time to browse through the documentation to familiarize yourself with the system procedures so that you can make a mental note of which useful ones exist. It is also worth doing the same for the system tables. The system-stored procedures supplied with SQL Server in many cases use the same Transact-SQL statements and functions as user-written stored procedures, the only difference is that they access system tables. For most system tables there is no reason why you cannot write your own useful stored procedures, but it is recommended that you do not access the system tables directly; instead, access the information schema views described in Chapter 4.

Hint: It is worth spending some time looking at how the system-stored procedures are written. This is best accomplished using the SQL Server Enterprise Manager, and selecting the *Stored Procedures* folder in the master database. The definitions of selected system-stored procedures can then easily be read.

Here is a simple example of a stored procedure that lists the tables in the current database:

```
CREATE PROCEDURE usp_ShowTables
AS
SELECT table_name AS 'Table' FROM information_schema.tables
WHERE table_type = 'BASE TABLE'
ORDER BY table_name

EXEC usp_ShowTables

Table

--------

authors
```

```
discounts
employee
   :
   :
```

If you have been creating and using stored procedures, you may have noticed that in order to execute your stored procedure you must have set the database that you were working with to be the database in which your user stored procedures were created. Alternatively, you used the database name when executing your stored procedure:

```
EXEC pubs.dbo.usp_AuthorInState
```

However, the system-stored procedures that you have put to use executed successfully no matter which database you were using. This is because of the way in which SQL Server finds and executes stored procedures whose names begin with "*sp_*". The master database is always searched before the current database. This means that if you create a stored procedure named *sp_helpme* in your user database, SQL Server will check to see if this stored procedure resides in the master database before it looks in your user database (assuming it is your current database). If you create a stored procedure named *sp_help* in your user database, it will never be executed because SQL Server will find and execute *sp_help* in the master database first.

6.6   Extended Stored Procedures

SQL Server provides *extended stored procedures* that permit developers to write their own external routines. This means that developers are able to extend the functionality of SQL Server. Developers can write *extended stored procedures* using Microsoft's *Open Data Services* (*ODS*) API. As with conventional stored procedures, *extended stored* procedures are called and a return status and output parameters can be returned. Extended stored procedure run in SQL Server's memory space, that is, they run in-process.

Once an extended stored procedure has been written, a member of the *sysadmin* fixed server role (a system administrator) must add them to SQL Server and this is accomplished with the *sp_addextendedproc* stored procedure or the SQL Server Enterprise Manager.

```
EXEC sp_addextendedproc xp_cpu_usage, cpucalc
```

In the above example, *cpucalc* is the name of the dynamic link library that contains the function *xp_cpu_usage*. Extended stored procedures must be added to the master database.

To use the SQL Server Enterprise Manager:

⇨ Expand the server group and expand the server.

⇨ Expand *Databases* and right-click the master database.

⇨ Click *New* and *Extended Stored Procedure.*

⇨ Enter the name and path of the extended stored procedure.

⇨ Click *OK.*

Extended stored procedures are removed with the stored procedure *sp_dropextendedproc*. The stored procedure *sp_helpextendedproc* displays information about extended stored procedures:

```
EXEC sp_helpextendedproc
```

```
Name               dll
_____ -   _____ --

sp_bindsession     (server internal)
sp_createorphan    (server internal)
sp_cursor          (server internal)
   :
   :
```

Microsoft provides a number of extended stored procedures with SQL Server. Some of the more useful ones are described below.

The extended stored procedure *xp_cmdshell* allows a Windows NT command to be executed:

```
EXEC master..xp_cmdshell "print c:\feb_report.lis"
```

```
output
_____

C:\feb_report.lis is currently being printed
```

The extended stored procedure *xp_sendmail* sends a message (or the result of a query) to the specified recipients:

```
xp_sendmail 'db_admin', 'Transaction log backed up OK.'
```

```
xp_sendmail 'england', @query = 'EXEC my_report'
```

This is a very useful extended stored procedure as it allows the database administrator to send messages from within a stored procedure or trigger.

7

Data Integrity

7.1   Introduction

Maintaining data integrity in a database is clearly important. Once data integrity is compromised the data begins to lose its value to the organization and whether the performance of the database is good or bad becomes irrelevant—bad data is no good to anyone. It should be noted that attempts to enforce data integrity usually result in performance degradation, however small. If a parent table has to be read to ensure that a valid parent row exists for the row that is about to be inserted, extra disk I/O and CPU will be required as well as extra locking. Data integrity, therefore, is likely to be a trade-off between performance and reliable data.

Where should the integrity of the data in the database be enforced? As database servers are likely to provide data storage facilities for multiple clients residing on multiple platforms around the network, it seems reasonable to place integrity mechanisms at the database server level. This has a number of advantages:

- No matter what client generates input data and no matter where that client is, if integrity checking is done at the database server level, the input data can be validated and rejected if necessary.

- The integrity constraints are held in one place, that is, the database server. This can simplify maintenance considerably as a data integrity restriction only has to be changed, added, or removed in one place.

However, one also has to take network access into account. Some data checks may be sensibly done at the client even if they are also repeated in the database server, for example, is a U.S. state code valid? There are no correct or incorrect approaches; the best approach depends upon the requirements of the application. It is unusual, however, not to have at least some data integrity checking.

183

It is useful to be able to categorize integrity as follows:

* Entity integrity
* Domain integrity
* Referential integrity
* User-defined integrity

Entity integrity is concerned with ensuring that rows in a table can be uniquely identified. Domain integrity is concerned with making sure that data in a column lies within some specified range of valid values. Referential integrity enforces cross table integrity and user-defined integrity is the category that caters to complex integrity requirements that are not satisfied by the standard categories above.

Each category uses various mechanisms to enforce integrity. Some or all of these mechanisms may be used and these will be described in the rest of this chapter.

Entity integrity is typically enforced by defining a PRIMARY KEY constraint on one or more columns. These columns cannot allow NULL values. Often a database designer uses a PRIMARY KEY constraint in conjunction with a column that has an IDENTITY property used to populate it with automatically increasing numbers. The IDENTITY property is described in Chapter 4. Entity integrity can also be enforced with the help of UNIQUE KEY constraints.

Domain integrity is usually enforced with CHECK constraints, although defining a DEFAULT value for a column and a nullability for a column also play a part. The set of allowed values in a column can also be governed with a FOREIGN KEY constraint.

Referential integrity is defined using FOREIGN KEY constraints. A CHECK constraint can also further restrict FOREIGN KEY values. Referential integrity between tables in different databases can be enforced with triggers.

User-defined integrity can be enforced with any of the above mechanisms, however, complex integrity requirements can usually only be implemented using triggers and stored procedures because they are programmable.

Let us look at the facilities available within SQL Server that help the database designer enforce database integrity. These features are listed below:

* Constraints
* Default definitions
* Triggers
* Transactions

7.2   Primary Key Constraints

Primary key constraints can be defined using the CREATE TABLE or ALTER TABLE Transact-SQL statements or by using the SQL Server Enterprise Manager. There can only be a single PRIMARY KEY constraint defined on a table. The columns on which the PRIMARY KEY constraint is defined must not allow NULL values. The combination of these columns must only hold unique key values. If an attempt is made to create a PRIMARY KEY constraint on a set of columns that violate either of these restrictions, the PRIMARY KEY constraint creation will fail.

Note: A PRIMARY KEY constraint may be defined with a maximum of 16 columns.

Below is an example of a PRIMARY KEY constraint definition on the *publishers* table in the pubs database.

```
CREATE TABLE publishers
  (
  pub_id   CHAR(4)        NOT NULL
           CONSTRAINT PK_publishers PRIMARY KEY CLUSTERED,
  pub_name VARCHAR(40)    NULL,
  city     VARCHAR(20)    NULL,
  state    CHAR(2)        NULL,
  country  VARCHAR(30)    NULL    DEFAULT ('USA')
  )
```

The above example creates the *publishers* table and defines a PRIMARY KEY constraint on the *pub_id* column. As a primary key cannot contain NULL values, the column *pub_id* must be defined as NOT NULL.

Note: The above example has been simplified for clarity. The *publishers* table in the pubs database also defines a CHECK constraint on the *pub_id* column.

To ensure that the primary key contains only unique values, SQL Server automatically creates a unique index on the column or columns that constitute the PRIMARY KEY constraint. By default, this is clustered, but, if desired, a non-clustered index can be created instead. Also, if SQL Server detects that a clustered index is already present on the table, a non-clustered index is created by default (SQL Server only allows one clustered index per table—see Chapter 10).

Note: If the SQL Server Enterprise Manager is used to create a PRIMARY KEY constraint, the index created by default is a non-clustered index.

As the PRIMARY KEY constraint is a single column it can be defined as part of the column definition in the table and, as such, is known as a *column level* constraint.

In the *titleauthor* table in the pubs database, the PRIMARY KEY constraint consists of multiple columns. It cannot be defined as part of a column definition, therefore, and so it is defined as a *table level* constraint:

```
CREATE TABLE titleauthor
  (
  au_id      ID
  title_id   TID
  au_ord     TINYINT    NULL,
  royaltyper INT        NULL,
  CONSTRAINT PK_titleauthor PRIMARY KEY CLUSTERED(au_id, title_id)
  )
```

Note: The above example has been simplified for clarity. FOREIGN KEY constraints have been removed.

A PRIMARY KEY constraint enforces entity integrity by disallowing duplicate key values. If an attempt is made to insert a duplicate key value into a table, the PRIMARY KEY constraint will cause the INSERT statement to fail:

```
INSERT publishers VALUES ('1622', 'Mystic Publishing',
'Remulade', 'WA', 'USA')

Server: Msg 2627, Level 14, State 1
Violation of PRIMARY KEY constraint 'PK_titleauthor'.
Cannot insert duplicate key in object 'publishers'.
The statement has been aborted.
```

The above example shows that the PRIMARY KEY constraint will stop any attempt to insert a row that will result in the primary key column holding non-unique values.

To alter an existing table to add a PRIMARY KEY constraint, the ALTER TABLE statement is used:

```
ALTER TABLE publishers
  ADD CONSTRAINT PK_publishers PRIMARY KEY CLUSTERED (pub_id)
```

The creation of the constraint will fail if a duplicate key value is present in the existing data:

```
ALTER TABLE publishers
  ADD CONSTRAINT PK_publishers PRIMARY KEY CLUSTERED (pub_id)
```

```
Server: Msg 1505, Level 16, State 1
CREATE UNIQUE INDEX aborted because a duplicate key was
found. Most significant primary key is '0877'.
Server: Msg 1750, Level 16, State 1
Could not create constraint. See previous errors.
```

A PRIMARY KEY constraint can be created when creating or modifying a table using the SQL Server Enterprise Manager. For example, to add a PRIMARY KEY constraint to an existing table:

⇨ Expand the server group and expand the server.

⇨ Expand *Databases* and expand the database holding the table to be changed.

⇨ Expand the *Tables* folder and right-click the table to be changed.

⇨ Click *Design Table*.

⇨ Select the column that is to become the PRIMARY KEY column. If more than one column is to become the PRIMARY KEY column, hold down the CTRL key while selecting the columns.

⇨ Right-click one of the selected columns and choose *Set primary key*.

⇨ Close the *Design Table* dialog box, saving the changes.

An example of the *Design Table* dialog box with a PRIMARY KEY constraint defined is shown in Figure 7.1.

A PRIMARY KEY constraint must be removed and recreated in order to change its attributes (except its name that can be changed with the system-stored procedure *sp_rename*). Changing its attributes can be performed with the SQL Server Enterprise Manager; however, the PRIMARY KEY constraint is dropped and recreated in the background.

Figure 7.1

*Adding a PRIMARY
KEY Constraint*

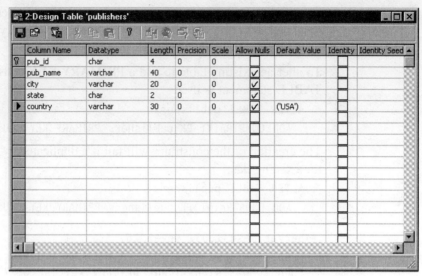

To drop a PRIMARY KEY constraint the SQL Server Enterprise Manager
or the Transact-SQL ALTER TABLE statement can be used. A PRIMARY
KEY constraint cannot be removed if it is referenced by FOREIGN KEY
constraints. FOREIGN KEY constraints are discussed shortly. To drop a
PRIMARY KEY constraint using the SQL Server Enterprise Manager:

⇨   Expand the server group and expand the server.

⇨   Expand *Databases* and expand the database holding the table to be
    changed.

⇨   Expand the *Tables* folder and right-click the table to be changed.

⇨   Click *Design Table*.

⇨   Right-click anywhere in the table definition and choose *Properties*.

⇨   Choose the *Index/Keys* tab and select the PRIMARY KEY constraint
    to be removed.

⇨   Click *Delete* and *Close*.

⇨   Close the *Design Table* dialog box, saving the changes.

The *Index/Keys* tab is shown in Figure 7.2.

To drop a PRIMARY KEY constraint using the ALTER TABLE statement:

```
ALTER TABLE publishers
    DROP CONSTRAINT PK_publishers
```

Of course, if the table is dropped, any constraints defined on the table are
dropped automatically.

Figure 7.2

The Index/Keys Tab

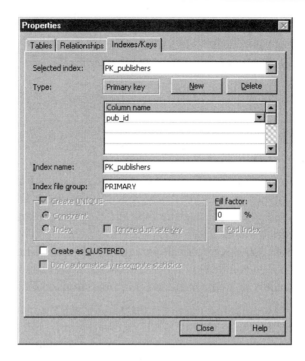

7.3 **Foreign Key Constraints**

Foreign key constraints can be defined using the CREATE TABLE or AL-
TER TABLE Transact-SQL statements or by using the SQL Server Enterprise Manager. There can be a maximum of 253 FOREIGN KEY constraints
defined on a table referencing a maximum of 253 tables that must be in the
same database. The columns on which the FOREIGN KEY constraint is
defined may allow NULL values. The FOREIGN KEY constraint must reference columns in the PRIMARY KEY or UNIQUE KEY constraint.

Below is an example of two FOREIGN KEY constraint definitions on the
sales table in the pubs database.

```
CREATE TABLE sales
(
stor_id     CHAR(4)      NOT NULL
CONSTRAINT FK_sales_stores REFERENCES stores(stor_id),
ord_num     VARCHAR(20)  NOT NULL,
ord_date    DATETIME     NOT NULL,
qty             SMALLINT     NOT NULL,
payterms    VARCHAR(12)  NOT NULL,
title_id    TID
```

```
CONSTRAINT FK_sales_titles REFERENCES titles(title_id),
CONSTRAINT PK_sales
PRIMARY KEY CLUSTERED (stor_id, ord_num, title_id)
)
```

The above FOREIGN KEY constraints reference columns in the *stores* and *titles* table PRIMARY KEY constraints respectively

SQL Server does not create an index on the FOREIGN KEY constraint columns. If there is no index created on the FOREIGN KEY constraint columns, any deletion from the PRIMARY KEY constraint table will have to table scan the FOREIGN KEY constraint table. The PRIMARY KEY constraint table and the FOREIGN KEY constraint table may be accessed together with a join. This operation is likely to benefit from an index on the FOREIGN KEY constraint columns. On the whole, then, you should create your own indexes on FOREIGN KEY constraint columns. Indexes are described in Chapter 10 and join operations in Chapter 5.

In a similar fashion to the PRIMARY KEY constraint described previously, because the FOREIGN KEY constraint is a single column it can be defined as part of the column definition in the table and, as such, is known as a *column level* constraint. If the FOREIGN KEY constraint consists of multiple columns, it cannot be defined as part of a column definition and so it is defined as a *table level* constraint.

A FOREIGN KEY constraint enforces referential integrity by ensuring that a row cannot be inserted into the child table with a FOREIGN key value that does not exist in the parent table. For example, a sales row cannot be entered for a non-existent store or a non-existent title. If an attempt is made to insert such a row, the FOREIGN KEY constraint will cause the INSERT statement to fail:

```
INSERT sales VALUES ('8765', 'QHZ 6871', '1994-09-14',5,
'Net 60', 'BU1032')

Server: Msg 547, Level 16, State 1
INSERT statement conflicted with COLUMN FOREIGN KEY constraint
'FK_sales_stores'. The conflict occurred in database 'pubs',
table 'stores', column 'stor_id'.
The statement has been aborted.
```

The above example shows that the FOREIGN KEY constraint will stop any attempt to insert a row in the child table that has no match in the parent table. The FOREIGN KEY constraint will also prevent the deletion of a row from the parent table, which is referenced by a child table.

```
DELETE stores WHERE stor_id = '6380'
```

```
Server: Msg 547, Level 16, State 1
DELETE statement conflicted with COLUMN REFERENCE constraint
'FK_sales_stores'. The conflict occurred in database 'pubs',
table 'sales', column 'stor_id'.
The statement has been aborted.
```

The FOREIGN KEY constraint also prevents the update of key values in the parent or child table that would leave orphaned child rows.

To alter an existing table to add a FOREIGN KEY constraint, the ALTER TABLE statement is used:

```
ALTER TABLE sales
  ADD CONSTRAINT FK_sales_stores
  FOREIGN KEY (stor_id) REFERENCES stores(stor_id)
```

Assuming the FOREIGN KEY constraint had not been defined as part of the CREATE TABLE statement, the above statement will add it.

The creation of the constraint will fail if a foreign key value is not present in the PRIMARY KEY constraint of the referenced table:

```
ALTER TABLE sales
  ADD CONSTRAINT FK_sales_stores
  FOREIGN KEY (stor_id) REFERENCES stores(stor_id)
```

```
Server: Msg 547, Level 16, State 1
ALTER TABLE statement conflicted with COLUMN FOREIGN KEY
constraint 'FK_sales_stores'. The conflict occurred in
database 'pubs', table 'stores', column 'stor_id'.
```

However, a FOREIGN KEY constraint can be added to a table while specifying existing data is not to be checked:

```
ALTER TABLE sales
  WITH NOCHECK
  ADD CONSTRAINT FK_sales_stores
  FOREIGN KEY (stor_id) REFERENCES stores(stor_id)
```

Existing FOREIGN KEY constraints can be flagged as NOCHECK to insert data that would not normally pass the constraint check. Clearly, disabling constraints is not normally a good idea!

To drop a FOREIGN KEY constraint using the ALTER TABLE statement:

```
ALTER TABLE sales
  DROP CONSTRAINT FK_sales_stores
```

Of course, if the table is dropped, any constraints defined on the table are dropped automatically.

To create a FOREIGN KEY constraint with the SQL Server Enterprise Manager, the database diagramming tool is used:

⇨   Expand the server group and expand the server.

⇨   Expand *Databases* and expand the database holding the table to be changed.

⇨   Expand the *Diagrams* folder and right-click the diagram to be changed. If a database diagram has not been previously created click *New Database Diagram* and follow the instructions in the wizard.

⇨   Click *Design Diagram.*

⇨   Click a primary key column in the parent table and drag over to the child table.

⇨   Modify attributes as required in the *Create Relationship* dialog box.

⇨   Click *OK* and save the diagram.

The *Create Relationship* dialog box in the database diagram is shown in Figure 7.3.

Figure 7.3

The Create Relationship Dialog Box

When the FOREIGN KEY constraint has been created, the database displays the relationship between the tables as shown in Figure 7.4.

To drop the FOREIGN KEY constraint in the database diagram, the relationship line can be right-clicked and *Delete Relationship from Database* chosen. To change the attributes of the relationship, right-click the relationship line and choose *Properties.*

Figure 7.4

*The Relationship between
Tables in a Database Diagram*

Note: A FOREIGN KEY constraint may reference the table on which
it is created because the FOREIGN KEY constraint columns can reference other columns in the same table. This is known as a *reflexive* relationship.

7.4   Unique Key Constraints

A table may have only one primary key constraint. However, there still may
be a requirement to enforce uniqueness in another column or a group of
columns that do not define the PRIMARY KEY constraint. This can be
achieved using UNIQUE constraints. UNIQUE constraints can be defined
using the CREATE TABLE or ALTER TABLE Transact-SQL statements
or by using the SQL Server Enterprise Manager. Up to 249 UNIQUE constraints can be created on a table. The columns on which the UNIQUE
constraints are defined may allow NULL values but a column containing
NULL is considered to be holding the same "value" as another column
holding NULL and so these two columns would be treated as not unique.
The combination of columns in a UNIQUE constraint must only hold unique
key values. If an attempt is made to create a UNIQUE constraints on a set
of columns that violate the uniqueness restriction, the UNIQUE constraint
creation will fail.

Note: A UNIQUE constraint may be defined with a maximum of 16
columns.

Suppose in the pubs database it was decided that the uniqueness of the store name should be enforced. There is already a PRIMARY KEY constraint defined using the *stor_id* column so we must use a UNIQUE constraint.

Below is an example of the UNIQUE constraint definition on the *sales* table in the pubs database.

```
CREATE TABLE stores
    (
    stor_id        CHAR(4)            NOT NULL
       CONSTRAINT  PK_stores PRIMARY KEY CLUSTERED,
    stor_name      VARCHAR(40)        NULL
       CONSTRAINT  UC_stores UNIQUE NONCLUSTERED,
    stor_address   VARCHAR(40)        NULL,
    city           VARCHAR(20)        NULL,
    state          CHAR(2)            NULL,
    zip            CHAR(5)            NULL
    )
```

The above example creates the *stores* table and defines a PRIMARY KEY constraint on the *stor_id* column and a UNIQUE constraint on the *stor_name* column.

To ensure that the UNIQUE constraint contains only unique values, SQL Server automatically creates a unique index on the column or columns that constitute the UNIQUE constraint. As the UNIQUE constraint is a single column it can be defined as part of the column definition in the table and, as such, is defined as a *column level* constraint. If it contains multiple columns, it cannot be defined as part of a column definition, therefore it is defined as a *table level* constraint.

To alter an existing table to add a UNIQUE constraint, the ALTER TABLE statement is used:

```
ALTER TABLE stores
    ADD CONSTRAINT UC_stores UNIQUE NONCLUSTERED (stor_name)
```

A UNIQUE constraint can be created when creating or modifying a table using the SQL Server Enterprise Manager. For example, to add a UNIQUE constraint to an existing table:

⇨ Expand the server group and expand the server.

⇨ Expand *Databases* and expand the database holding the table to be changed.

⇨ Expand the *Tables* folder and right-click the table to be changed.

⇨ Click *Design Table.*

⇨ Right-click anywhere in the table definition and choose *Properties.*

⇨ Choose the *Index/Keys* tab and select *New.*

⇨ Add the attributes of the UNIQUE constraint ensuring that *Create UNIQUE* and *Constraint* are checked.

⇨ Click *Close.*

⇨ Close the *Design Table* dialog box, saving the changes.

An example of the *Index/Keys* tab dialog box is shown in Figure 7.2.

A UNIQUE constraint must be removed and recreated in order to change its attributes (except its name, which can be changed with the system stored procedure *sp_rename*). Changing its attributes can be performed with the SQL Server Enterprise Manager; however, the UNIQUE constraint is dropped and recreated in the background.

To drop a UNIQUE constraint the SQL Server Enterprise Manager or the Transact-SQL ALTER TABLE statement can be used. A UNIQUE constraint cannot be deleted if it is referenced by FOREIGN KEY constraints. To drop a UNIQUE constraint using the SQL Server Enterprise Manager:

⇨ Expand the server group and expand the server.

⇨ Expand *Databases* and expand the database holding the table to be changed.

⇨ Expand the *Tables* folder and right-click the table to be changed.

⇨ Click *Design Table.*

⇨ Right-click anywhere in the table definition and choose *Properties.*

⇨ Choose the *Index/Keys* tab and select the UNIQUE constraint to be removed.

⇨ Click *Delete* and *Close.*

⇨ Close the *Design Table* dialog box, saving the changes.

To drop a UNIQUE constraint using the ALTER TABLE statement:

```
ALTER TABLE sales
    DROP CONSTRAINT UC_stores
```

Of course, if the table is dropped, any constraints defined on the table are dropped automatically.

7.5   Check Constraints

CHECK constraints are used to ensure that the range of values stored in a column is valid. CHECK constraints can be defined using the CREATE TABLE or ALTER TABLE Transact-SQL statements or by using the SQL Server Enterprise Manager. There can be more than one CHECK constraint defined on a column and this can refer to other columns in the table.

Below is an example of a CHECK constraint definition on the *publishers* table in the pubs database.

```
CREATE TABLE publishers
(
pub_id     CHAR(4)           NOT NULL
  CONSTRAINT PK_publishers PRIMARY KEY CLUSTERED
  CONSTRAINT CK_publishers CHECK
(pub_id in ('1389', '0736', '0877', '1622', '1756') OR
pub_id like '99[0-9][0-9]'),
pub_name   VARCHAR(40)       NULL,
city       VARCHAR(20)       NULL,
state      CHAR(2)           NULL,
country    VARCHAR(30)       NULL DEFAULT ('USA')
)
```

The above example creates the *publishers* table and defines a CHECK constraint on the *pub_id* column. The CHECK constraint ensures that the *pub_id* only contains values from the list (IN) or values of the form (LIKE) 99NN where N is a numeric digit. The IN and LIKE operators are discussed in Chapter 5.

As the CHECK constraint is a single column it can be defined as part of the column definition in the table and, as such, is defined as a *column level* constraint. It can also refer to multiple columns and, if so, is defined as a *table level* constraint.

A CHECK constraint enforces entity integrity by disallowing illegal values. If an attempt is made to insert an illegal value into a column, the CHECK constraint will cause the INSERT statement to fail:

```
INSERT publishers VALUES ('8877', 'Rustic Publishing',
'Remulade', 'WA', 'USA')

Server: Msg 547, Level 16, State 1
INSERT statement conflicted with COLUMN CHECK constraint
'CK__publishers.
```

```
The conflict occurred in database 'pubs', table 'publishers',
column 'pub_id'.
The statement has been aborted.
```

The above example shows that the CHECK constraint will stop any attempt to insert a row that will result in the column holding illegal values. This also applies to the UPDATE statement, which cannot change a column to an illegal value.

To alter an existing table to add a CHECK constraint, the ALTER TABLE statement is used:

```
ALTER TABLE sales
  ADD CONSTRAINT CK_sales CHECK (qty > 0)
```

The creation of the constraint will fail if an illegal value is present in the existing data.

A CHECK constraint can be created when creating or modifying a table using the SQL Server Enterprise Manager. For example, to add a CHECK constraint to an existing table:

⇨ Expand the server group and expand the server.

⇨ Expand *Databases* and the database holding the table to be changed.

⇨ Expand the *Tables* folder and right-click the table to be changed.

⇨ Click *Design Table.*

⇨ Right-click anywhere in the table definition and choose *Properties.*

⇨ Choose the *Tables* tab and select *New.*

⇨ Add the attributes of the CHECK constraint.

⇨ Click *Close.*

⇨ Close the *Design Table* dialog box, saving the changes.

An example of the *Tables* tab dialog box is shown in Figure 7.5.

A CHECK constraint must be removed and recreated in order to change its attributes (except its name, which can be changed with the system-stored procedure *sp_rename*). Changing its attributes can be performed with the SQL Server Enterprise Manager; however, the CHECK constraint is dropped and recreated in the background.

To drop a CHECK constraint the SQL Server Enterprise Manager or the Transact-SQL ALTER TABLE statement can be used. To drop a CHECK constraint using the SQL Server Enterprise Manager:

⇨ Expand the server group and expand the server.

⇨ Expand *Databases* and the database holding the table to be changed.

Figure 7.5

Adding a CHECK Constraint

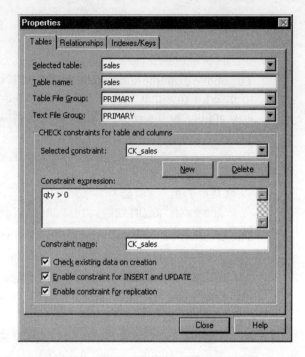

⇨   Expand the *Tables* folder and right click the table to be changed.

⇨   Click *Design Table*.

⇨   Right-click anywhere in the table definition and choose *Properties*.

⇨   Choose the *Tables* tab and select the CHECK constraint to be removed.

⇨   Click *Delete* and *Close*.

⇨   Close the *Design Table* dialog box, saving the changes.

As with FOREIGN KEY constraints, a CHECK constraint can be added to a table while specifying existing data is not to be checked:

```
ALTER TABLE sales
  WITH NOCHECK
  ADD CONSTRAINT CK_sales CHECK (qty > 0)
```

Existing CHECK constraints can be flagged as NOCHECK to insert data that would not normally pass the constraint check. This is not normally a good idea.

To drop a CHECK constraint using the ALTER TABLE statement:

```
ALTER TABLE sales
  DROP CONSTRAINT CK_sales
```

Of course, if the table is dropped, any constraints defined on the table are dropped automatically.

7.6   DEFAULT Definitions

A default value is a value that is stored in a column if the INSERT statement that inserted the row did not supply a value for the column. If no default value is defined for a column and the INSERT statement that inserted the row did not supply a value for the column, SQL Server will store NULL in the column as long as the column allows NULL values. If the column does not allow NULL values and there is no default value defined for the column, the INSERT statement will fail.

A DEFAULT definition can be defined using the CREATE TABLE or ALTER TABLE Transact-SQL statements or by using the SQL Server Enterprise Manager. There can only be a single DEFAULT definition specified for a column and the column must not be a data type of TIMESTAMP or have the IDENTITY property. A DEFAULT definition can be a constant value or a system function.

Below is an example of a DEFAULT definition on the *authors* table in the pubs database.

```
CREATE TABLE authors
    (
    au_id       ID,
    au_lname    VARCHAR(40)    NOT NULL,
    au_fname    VARCHAR(20)    NOT NULL,
    phone       CHAR(12)       NOT NULL
      DEFAULT ('UNKNOWN'),
    address     VARCHAR(40)    NULL,
    city        VARCHAR(20)    NULL,
    state       CHAR(2)        NULL,
    zip         CHAR(5)        NULL,
    contract    BIT            NOT NULL
    )
```

The above example creates the *authors* table and defines a DEFAULT definition for the *phone* column.

Note: The above example has been simplified for clarity. The *authors* table in the pubs database also defines a PRIMARY KEY constraint and CHECK constraints.

To alter an existing table to add a DEFAULT definition, the ALTER TABLE statement is used:

```
ALTER TABLE authors
    ADD DEFAULT 'UNKNOWN' FOR phone
```

Note: Unlike the constraints we have met in this chapter where it is recommended to specify a name with the CONSTRAINT keyword, this is not usually used in SQL Server 7.0 with a DEFAULT definition.

A DEFAULT definition can be created when creating or modifying a table using the SQL Server Enterprise Manager. For example, to add a DEFAULT definition to an existing table:

⇨   Expand the server group and expand the server.

⇨   Expand *Databases* and the database holding the table to be changed.

⇨   Expand the *Tables* folder and right-click the table to be changed.

⇨   Click *Design Table*.

⇨   In the *Default Value* add a constant or system function that defines the default value for the column.

⇨   Close the *Design Table* dialog box, saving the changes.

An example of the *Design Table* dialog box with a DEFAULT definition is shown in Figure 7.1.

To drop a DEFAULT definition the SQL Server Enterprise Manager or the Transact-SQL ALTER TABLE statement can be used. To drop a DEFAULT definition using the SQL Server Enterprise Manager:

⇨   Expand the server group and expand the server.

⇨   Expand *Databases* and the database holding the table to be changed.

⇨   Expand the *Tables* folder and right-click the table to be changed.

⇨   Click *Design Table*.

⇨   Delete the default value.

⇨   Click *Close*.

⇨   Close the *Design Table* dialog box, saving the changes.

To drop a DEFAULT definition using the ALTER TABLE statement:

```
ALTER TABLE publishers
    DROP CONSTRAINT DF_authors
```

Of course, if the table is dropped, any DEFAULT definitions defined on the table are dropped automatically.

7.7   Triggers

It is possible in SQL Server to ensure that predefined actions take place when an event occurs such as an INSERT, UPDATE, or DELETE statement being executed. The initiation of predefined actions is made possible through database objects known as *triggers*. A trigger can *fire* when, for example, a row from a particular table is deleted. The trigger then executes Transact-SQL statements as specified by the database designer.

One of the most useful aspects of triggers is that, no matter how an event is initiated, the trigger will always fire. For example, a row may be updated by the use of the Query Analyzer, a Microsoft Access client application, a Visual Basic program, or another application. The important fact is that the update of the row fires the trigger. This has important implications for the enforcement of database integrity as triggers make it possible to enforce database integrity outside of the applications in one central place—the database.

Triggers are created and stored in the database and are associated with particular tables. They are usually classified as one of three types:

*   INSERT
*   UPDATE
*   DELETE

A trigger may be defined to fire for any combination of the above statements. For example, a trigger may be defined as both an INSERT trigger and a DELETE trigger. More than one trigger on a table may be defined to fire when an INSERT, UPDATE, or DELETE statement executes. Two important points to note concerning triggers are:

*   A trigger fires once in response to the Transact-SQL statement that caused it to fire, for example, a DELETE statement. It does not matter if the DELETE statement deleted zero rows or a million rows—the trigger fires once.

*   The trigger and the statement that caused it to fire form a single transaction that can be rolled back from within the trigger. This is shown in Figure 7.6.

Figure 7.6
Transactions and Triggers

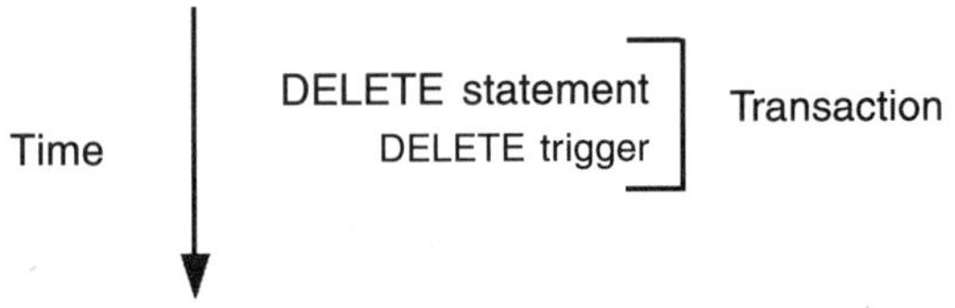

Triggers are created with the CREATE TRIGGER statement:

```
CREATE TRIGGER publishersTRG_I ON publishers
  FOR INSERT
  AS
  PRINT 'A new publisher has been inserted'
```

The above trigger will fire when a row is inserted into the *publishers* table. Note that individual INSERT statements will each cause the trigger to fire, whereas the single INSERT statement INSERT INTO ... SELECT * FROM ... will only cause the trigger to fire once.

Note: The use of the PRINT statement is convenient for debugging triggers but is not used normally, as applications would need to be written to handle its output.

```
CREATE TRIGGER publishersTRG_U ON publishers
  FOR UPDATE
  AS
  PRINT 'A publisher has been updated'
```

The above trigger will fire when a row is updated in the *publishers* table. Again, individual UPDATE statements will each cause the trigger to fire, whereas a single UPDATE statement that updates many rows will only cause the trigger to fire once.

Note: A WRITETEXT statement will not cause the firing of an IN-SERT or UPDATE trigger.

```
CREATE TRIGGER publishersTRG_D ON publishers
  FOR DELETE
  AS
  PRINT 'A publisher has been deleted'
```

The above trigger will fire when a row is deleted from the *publishers* table. Individual DELETE statements will each cause the trigger to fire, whereas a single DELETE statement that deletes many rows will only cause the trigger to fire once.

Note: A TRUNCATE TABLE statement will not cause the firing of a DELETE trigger.

```
CREATE TRIGGER publishersTRG_IUD ON publishers
  FOR INSERT, UPDATE, DELETE
  AS
  PRINT 'A publisher has been inserted, updated or deleted'
```

The above trigger will fire when a row is inserted, updated, or deleted from the *publishers* table. This trigger therefore fires when any event occurs, and is useful when the same set of actions are to be performed, whatever the event.

Note that in the above examples, even if the INSERT INTO ... SELECT * FROM, UPDATE, or DELETE statements did not process any rows, the triggers would still have fired as in the example below:

```
DELETE publishers WHERE state = 'NH'

A publisher has been inserted, updated or deleted

(0 row(s) affected)
```

Like views and stored procedures, trigger definitions may be encrypted with the WITH ENCRYPTION clause:

```
CREATE TRIGGER publishersTRG_IUD ON publishers
  WITH ENCRYPTION
  FOR INSERT, UPDATE, DELETE
  AS
  PRINT 'A publisher has been inserted, updated or deleted'
```

In the above examples simple PRINT statements have been used. In practice, triggers would contain many Transact-SQL statements to execute complex actions; however, some Transact-SQL statements cannot be put inside a trigger. These are listed in Table 7.1.

Triggers may not be defined on views, system tables, or temporary tables.

A trigger that accesses another table may cause a trigger to fire that is associated with that table. This is allowed in SQL Server but only to a maximum nesting of 32 levels. Setting the *nested triggers* server configuration option to 0 with the *sp_configure* system stored procedure will disable trigger nesting. The ability to nest triggers is a server-wide option. The option may also be set through the SQL Server Enterprise Manager in the *Server Properties-Server Settings tab.*

Table 7.1
Transact-SQL Statements That Cannot Be Placed Inside a Trigger.

ALTER DATABASE	ALTER PROCEDURE	ALTER TABLE
ALTER TRIGGER	ALTER VIEW	CREATE DATABASE
CREATE DEFAULT	CREATE INDEX	CREATE PROCEDURE
CREATE RULE	CREATE SCHEMA	CREATE TABLE
CREATE TRIGGER	CREATE VIEW	DENY
DISK INIT	DISK RESIZE	DROP DATABASE
DROP DEFAULT	DROP INDEX	DROP PROCEDURE
DROP RULE	DROP TABLE	DROP TRIGGER
DROP VIEW	GRANT	LOAD DATABASE
LOAD LOG	RESTORE DATABASE	RESTORE LOG
REVOKE	RECONFIGURE	
TRUNCATE TABLE	UPDATE STATISTICS	

Triggers can call themselves recursively. This can be *direct* recursion when a trigger performs an action that causes itself to fire again, or *indirect* recursion when the trigger causes another trigger to fire, which then performs an action that causes the original trigger to fire. Trigger recursion requires that the database option *Recursive Triggers* is set.

Trigger code can test to see if a specific column or columns are affected by an UPDATE or INSERT statement:

```
CREATE TRIGGER publishersTRG_IU ON publishers
  FOR INSERT, UPDATE
  AS
  IF UPDATE (state)
  PRINT 'The state has been updated'
```

If the *state* column is updated through the use of an INSERT or UPDATE statement, the PRINT statement will execute:

```
INSERT publishers VALUES ('1622', 'Smith & Brown', 'Boston',
'MA')

The state has been updated
```

If the *state* column is not updated through the use of an INSERT or UP-DATE statement, the PRINT statement will not execute:

```
INSERT publishers (pub_id, pub_name, city) VALUES ('1756',
'Bloggs and Soap', 'Nashua')
```

The IF UPDATE may involve multiple columns:

```
CREATE TRIGGER publishersTRG_IU ON publishers
  FOR INSERT, UPDATE
  AS
  IF UPDATE (state) OR UPDATE (city)
  PRINT 'The state or city has been updated'

UPDATE publishers SET city = 'Alton' WHERE pub_id = '1622'

The state or city has been updated
```

Note: SQL Server 7.0 has also introduced the *IF COLUMNS_ UP-DATED()* test to check if columns have been updated.

7.7.1   Trigger Test Tables

It is often useful while executing Transact-SQL statements inside a trigger to have access to column values that are potentially changed by the statement that caused the trigger to fire. For example, an UPDATE statement may change the values of one or more columns so there will be an old pre-update value for a column and a new post-update value.

To facilitate access to these old and new values from the Transact-SQL statements executing inside the trigger, SQL Server provides two tables. These tables are known as the *deleted* table and the *inserted* table and are written to by SQL Server during INSERT, UPDATE, and DELETE statements. The Transact-SQL statements executing inside the trigger can read these tables but not change them. The type of statement that fired the trigger, whether INSERT, UPDATE, or DELETE, governs the way in which the tables are used.

The Deleted Table

The *deleted* table is written to when a DELETE statement causes the trigger to fire. It holds the rows that have been deleted from the user table and its column structure is identical to the table on which the trigger is defined. As an UPDATE statement is logically treated by SQL Server as a DELETE plus INSERT combination, it too writes the rows that have been deleted from the user table to the *deleted* table.

The INSERT statement does not access the *deleted* table.

The Inserted Table

The *inserted* table is written to when an INSERT statement causes the trigger to fire. It holds copies of the rows that have been inserted into the user table and its column structure is also identical to the table on which the trigger is defined. Again, as an UPDATE statement is logically treated by SQL Server as a DELETE plus INSERT combination, it writes the rows that it inserts into the user table also into the *inserted* table.

The DELETE statement does not access the inserted table. Hence, the *inserted* table can be seen by trigger code executing inside an INSERT trigger and an UPDATE trigger. In an INSERT trigger the rows in the *inserted* table are an exact copy of the rows inserted into the user table by the INSERT that caused the trigger to fire.

The *deleted* table can be seen by trigger code executing inside a DELETE trigger and an UPDATE trigger. In a DELETE trigger the rows in the *deleted* table are an exact copy of the rows deleted from the user table by the DELETE that caused the trigger to fire.

The UPDATE trigger can see both tables. There is one row in the *inserted* and *deleted* table for every row affected by the UPDATE statement that caused the trigger to fire. The *inserted* table holds the new values of the columns and the *deleted* table holds the old values of the columns.

The *deleted* and *inserted* tables are extremely useful. Without them it would be very difficult to know in the trigger which rows had just been inserted or deleted. They are, in fact, an abstraction of the transaction log records held in memory ready to be flushed to the transaction log.

7.7.2   Using Triggers for Auditing

It is often useful to keep an audit trail by writing changes made to a table into an associated audit table, together with perhaps the date and time the change was made and the person who made the change. The following trigger inserts a row into an audit table for every row that is inserted into the *publishers* table. This example uses the *inserted* table.

The definition of the audit table is as follows:

```
CREATE TABLE PublishersAudit
    (
    pub_id      CHAR (4),
    pub_name    VARCHAR (40)      NULL,
    city        VARCHAR (20)      NULL,
    state       CHAR (2 )         NULL,
```

```
change_date DATETIME,
change_user NVARCHAR(128)
)
```

The definition of the trigger on *publishers* is as follows:

```
CREATE TRIGGER publishersTRG_I ON publishers
  FOR INSERT
  AS
  BEGIN
  INSERT PublishersAudit
    SELECT pub_id, pub_name, city, state, getdate(),
    user_name() FROM INSERTED
  END
```

Again, this is a fairly simple trigger. Even if the INSERT statement inserts many rows, such as in an INSERT INTO ... SELECT ... statement, each inserted row will be copied to the audit table.

7.7.3 Using Triggers for Integrity Enforcement

We have discussed constraints as a means of enforcing database integrity. Even though they are the preferred method of doing this, they have limitations. For example, tables in other databases cannot be referenced by a FOREIGN KEY constraint. Because triggers can be programmed, they can be more flexible and they can access tables in other databases.

As an example of using triggers to enforce cross table integrity, let us use the *stores* and *sales* tables as an example.

Enforcing referential integrity between the *stores* and *sales* tables would require that the following could not occur:

1. A *sales* row is inserted into the *sales* table with a *stor_id* value that does not exist in the *stores* table.

2. A *sales* row is updated such that the *stor_id* value in it is given a value that does not exist in the *stores* table.

3. A store is deleted from the *stores* table while sales exist for that store.

4. A store has its *stor_id* changed while sales exist for that store.

If any of the above were allowed to happen the database would contain sales for a nonexistent store, which would indicate nonsensical data in the database. Note, however, these are business rules, and it might be reasonable to record sales for a store that did not exist in the database, however strange!

There are a number of tables in the database that are related; we will, however, just focus on the *stores* and *sales* tables. Let us first of all look at a trigger to ensure that (1) above does not occur. We will need to check that the appropriate store exists when we insert a sale:

```
CREATE TRIGGER salesTRG_I ON sales
  FOR INSERT
  AS
  IF (SELECT COUNT(*) FROM inserted INNER JOIN stores
    ON inserted.stor_id = stores.stor_id) <> @@ROWCOUNT
  BEGIN
    ROLLBACK TRANSACTION
    PRINT 'A stor_id does not exist in the stores table -
    statement cancelled'
  END

INSERT sales VALUES ('2323', 'TZ87YY', '1994-09-14', 30,
'Net 30', 'MC2222')

A stor_id does not exist in the stores table - statement
cancelled
```

How does this trigger work? The SELECT statement performs an inner join between the *inserted* table and the *stores* table using the common *stor_id* column. The *inserted* table contains copies of all the inserted rows, and therefore contains the same number of rows as the number of rows inserted that is obtained from the system function @@ROWCOUNT provided by SQL Server.

However, if the *stor_id* of any of the rows in the *inserted* table does not have a corresponding row in the *stores* table, then the number of rows returned from the inner join will be less than the number of rows inserted. Therefore, the COUNT(*) result will not equal the value of the number of rows inserted that is held in @@ROWCOUNT, and the IF statement will be evaluated as TRUE. The transaction will be rolled back and all the inserts performed by the INSERT statement that fired the trigger will be cancelled. Note that the PRINT statement is only used to display a message for this example. It would not be used in the live, production trigger.

This example is a little coarse in that we might have inserted many sales and only had one insertion that compromised integrity, but the trigger still cancels all the inserts. The trigger can be fine-tuned to allow the inserts that do not compromise integrity to succeed:

```
CREATE TRIGGER salesTRG_I ON sales
FOR INSERT
AS
IF (SELECT COUNT(*) FROM inserted INNER JOIN stores
  ON inserted.stor_id = stores.stor_id) <> @@ROWCOUNT
BEGIN
  DELETE sales FROM sales INNER JOIN inserted
    ON inserted.stor_id = sales.stor_id
    WHERE inserted.stor_id NOT IN (SELECT stor_id FROM stores)
END
```

The above trigger does not impede the inserts that do not compromise integrity but it deletes the inserts that do. The trigger does not cause the transaction to rollback.

Now let us look at a trigger to ensure that integrity violation (2) listed previously does not occur. We will need to check that the appropriate store exists when we update the *stor_id* in a row held in the *sales* table:

```
CREATE TRIGGER salesTRG_U on sales
FOR UPDATE
AS
IF (SELECT COUNT(*) FROM inserted INNER JOIN stores
  ON inserted.stor_id = stores.stor_id) <> @@ROWCOUNT
BEGIN
  ROLLBACK TRANSACTION
  PRINT 'A stor_id does not exist in the stores table -
statement cancelled'
END

UPDATE sales SET stor_id = '8765' WHERE ord_num = 'N914008'

A stor_id does not exist in the stores table - statement
cancelled'
```

How does this trigger work? It works in a similar fashion to the INSERT trigger we looked at earlier. The SELECT statement performs an inner join between the *inserted* table and the *stores* table using the common *stor_id* column. The *inserted* table contains copies of all the rows that resulted from the update, and therefore contains the same number of rows as the number of rows updated that is obtained from the system function @@ROWCOUNT.

However, if the *stor_id* of any of the rows in the *inserted* table does not have a corresponding row in the *stores* table then the number of rows returned from the inner join will be less that the number of rows updated. Therefore, the COUNT(*) result will not equal the value of the number of rows updated that is obtained from @@ROWCOUNT, and the IF statement will be evaluated as TRUE. The transaction will be rolled back and all the changes made by the UPDATE statement that fired the trigger will be cancelled.

Again, this example is a little coarse in that we might have updated many sales and only had one update that compromised integrity, but the trigger still cancels all the updates. This trigger can also be fine-tuned to allow the updates that do not compromise integrity to succeed in a similar way to the INSERT trigger.

Now let us look at a trigger to ensure that integrity violation (3) listed previously does not occur. We can deal with this by either disallowing the DELETE statement and rolling it back if any sales exist for the store we are deleting, or we could *cascade* the delete operation. Cascading removes any rows in the *sales* table that reference the store we are deleting.

The following trigger disallows the DELETE if any sales exist for the store we are deleting:

```
CREATE TRIGGER storesTRG_D ON stores
FOR DELETE
AS
IF (SELECT COUNT(*) FROM deleted INNER JOIN sales
  ON deleted.stor_id = sales.stor_id) > 0
BEGIN
  ROLLBACK TRANSACTION
  PRINT 'Sales exist for the stor_id that is to be deleted
- - statement cancelled'
END
```

This trigger works the following way. The SELECT statement performs an inner join between the *deleted* table and the *sales* table using the common *stor_id* column. The *deleted* table contains copies of all the deleted rows that resulted from the DELETE statement. If the *stor_id* of any of the rows in the *deleted* table have a corresponding row in the *sales* table, then the number of rows returned from the inner join will be greater than zero. Therefore, the IF statement will be evaluated as TRUE. The transaction will be rolled back and all the changes made by the DELETE statement that fired the trigger will be cancelled.

Again, this example is a little coarse in that we might have deleted many stores and only had one delete that compromised integrity, but the trigger still cancels all the deletes. Again, the trigger can be fine-tuned to allow the deletes that do not compromise integrity to succeed.

The following trigger cascades the DELETE operation if any sales exist for the store we are deleting:

```
CREATE TRIGGER storesTRG_D ON stores
FOR DELETE
AS
DELETE sales
  WHERE stor_id IN (SELECT stor_id FROM deleted)
```

In practice we would need to put in a little more effort than this. First of all, a DELETE trigger on the *stores* table would need to delete any rows from the *discount* table that referenced the *stores* that were being removed from the *stores* table. Second, we would probably want to audit some information from the deleted rows into an audit table so that information about sales involving the deleted store could be kept.

Triggers can be, and typically are, much more complex that the examples shown above. However, it is only a matter of using the Transact-SQL constructs we have already seen and perhaps stored procedures to create very powerful triggers. A trigger can even include an extended stored procedure as shown below:

```
CREATE TRIGGER discountsTRG_D ON discounts
FOR DELETE
AS
EXEC master.dbo.xp_cmdshell "PRINT c:\feb_report.lis"
```

Triggers can also be created and edited using the SQL Server Enterprise Manager. To do so:

⇨ Expand the server group and expand the server.

⇨ Expand *Databases* and expand the database holding the table to be changed.

⇨ Expand the *Tables* folder and right-click the table to be changed.

⇨ Click *All Tasks* and *Manage Triggers.*

⇨ Type in the trigger definition.

⇨ Click *OK.*

An example of the *Manage Triggers* dialog is shown in Figure 7.7.

Figure 7.7

Managing Triggers in the SQL Server Enterprise Manager

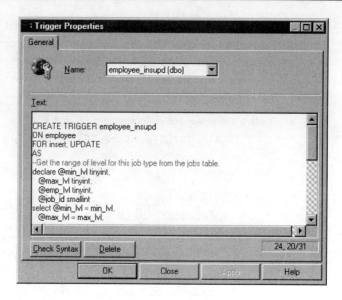

7.7.4   Managing Triggers

If a table that has triggers associated with it is dropped, then the triggers are also dropped. Triggers may be dropped explicitly with the DROP TRIGGER statement:

```
DROP TRIGGER storesTRG_D
```

Triggers can also be dropped using the SQL Server Enterprise Manager. To do so, choose the trigger to be deleted in the *Manage Triggers* dialog box and click *Delete*.

Triggers may be renamed with the *sp_rename* system-stored procedure:

```
EXEC sp_rename storesTRG_D, shopsTRG_D
```

Like stored procedures, triggers may be affected if the objects they reference are renamed. To display information concerning the objects referenced by a trigger, the system-stored procedure *sp_depends* can be used:

```
EXEC sp_depends storesTRG_D
```

```
In the current database, the specified object references
the following:
```

Name	type	updated	selected	column
dbo.sales	user table	yes	no	NULL
dbo.sales	user table	no	yes	stor_id

The SQL Server Enterprise Manager can also be used to view dependencies:

⇨ Expand the server group and expand the server.

⇨ Expand *Databases* and expand the database holding the table to be changed.

⇨ Expand the *Tables* folder and right-click the table to be changed.

⇨ Click *All Tasks* and *Display Dependencies.*

⇨ Choose the trigger from the *Object* list; dependency information will then be displayed.

⇨ Click *Close.*

The *Dependencies* window is shown in Figure 7.8.

Figure 7.8

Trigger Dependencies

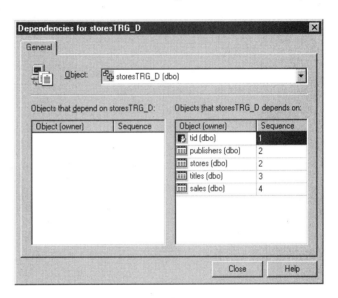

Triggers may be altered without dropping and recreating them. Triggers can be altered with the ALTER TRIGGER Transact-SQL statement or the SQL Server Enterprise Manager.

```
ALTER TRIGGER storesTRG_D ON stores
FOR DELETE
AS
DELETE sales
  WHERE stor_id IN (SELECT stor_id FROM deleted)
```

In the SQL Server Enterprise Manager the trigger can be altered in the *Manage Triggers* dialog box.

7.7.5   Showing Trigger Details

The system-stored procedure *sp_help* provides a list of the triggers in the current database:

```
EXEC sp_help
```

Name	Owner	Object_type
:		
:		
titles	dbo	user table
employee_insupd	dbo	trigger
storesTRG_D	dbo	trigger
:		

The system-stored procedure *sp_helptrigger* may be used to check the types of triggers on a table, that is, INSERT, UPDATE, and DELETE:

```
EXEC sp_helptrigger stores
```

trigger_name	trigger_owner	isupdate	isdelete	isinsert
storesTRG_D	dbo	0	1	0

The system-stored procedure *sp_helptext* displays the Transact-SQL used to create the trigger (unless it is encrypted):

```
EXEC sp_helptext storesTRG_D
```

Text
_____

```
CREATE TRIGGER storesTRG_D ON stores
FOR DELETE
AS
DELETE   sales
  WHERE stor_id IN (SELECT stor_id FROM deleted)
```
_____

Note: Although *sp_helptext* displays the trigger source code, it is much easier to view this through the SQL Server Enterprise Manager.

7.8   Transactions

The concept of a transaction being an *atomic* unit of work was introduced in Chapter 5. We will revisit transactions here as they are essential for maintaining database integrity. The fact that all the Transact-SQL statements that change the database in some way can be grouped together so that all the changes succeed or none do is clearly an important feature. For example, we can debit one bank account and credit another, confident in knowing that should a failure occur, we will not be in a position where only one account has been changed.

SQL Server 7.0 classifies transactions as:

- Explicit transactions
- Autocommit transactions
- Implicit transactions

Explicit transactions are started by executing a BEGIN TRANSACTION statement and must be completed by executing a COMMIT TRANSACTION or ROLLBACK TRANSACTION.

Autocommit transactions are started when a Transact-SQL statement such as DELETE is executed and committed when the statement successfully completes. This is the normal SQL Server behavior when managing single Transact-SQL statements.

Implicit transactions are transactions that start on a connection where the statement

```
SET IMPLICIT_TRANSACTIONS ON
```

has been executed. This ensures that any of the Transact-SQL statements in Table 7.2 starts a transaction if one is not already active.

Table 7.2
Transact-SQL Statements That Start a Transaction

ALTER TABLE	FETCH	REVOKE
CREATE	GRANT	SELECT
DELETE	INSERT	TRUNCATE TABLE
DROP	OPEN	UPDATE

However, an implicit transaction must be manually completed with a COMMIT TRANSACTION or ROLLBACK TRANSACTION statement. If not, the active transaction is rolled back when the connection is disconnected and the changes made in the transaction are undone.

To return to autocommit mode, execute the statement:

```
SET IMPLICIT_TRANSACTIONS OFF
```

Note: The statement SET ANSI_DEFAULTS ON turns implicit transaction mode on.

In the case of both a COMMIT and a ROLLBACK, all resources held by the transaction such as locks are released. In the case of COMMIT, changes occurring during the transaction are made permanent to the database, whereas a ROLLBACK discards these changes.

The following Transact-SQL can be used to start and complete a transaction. BEGIN TRANSACTION and BEGIN TRAN are equivalent, as are COMMIT TRANSACTION and COMMIT TRAN, and ROLLBACK TRANSACTION and ROLLBACK TRAN. Also, to be compatible with the SQL-92 standard, completing a transaction may also be achieved with COMMIT WORK or COMMIT, and ROLLBACK WORK or ROLLBACK. The SQL-92 statements are equivalent to the traditional Transact-SQL statements with the exception that the traditional statements can refer to a user-defined transaction name.

The following example shows a ROLLBACK taking place:

```
BEGIN TRANSACTION
  SELECT price FROM titles WHERE title_id = 'MC2222'
  UPDATE titles SET price = $10.99 WHERE title_id = 'MC2222'
  SELECT price FROM titles WHERE title_id = 'MC2222'
ROLLBACK TRANSACTION
SELECT price FROM titles WHERE title_id = 'MC2222'

price
_____

19.99

price
_____

10.99

price
_____

19.99
```

In the above example of an explicit transaction, it can be seen that the ROLLBACK TRANSACTION statement has returned the price changed by the UPDATE statement to its original value.

Pairs of BEGIN TRANSACTION and COMMIT TRANSACTION statements can be nested, although the successful ending of the transaction is caused by the outermost COMMIT TRANSACTION. This nesting usually occurs when a trigger or stored procedure that is executed within a user transaction itself has a pair of BEGIN TRANSACTION and COMMIT TRANSACTION statements.

To check the user transaction nesting level the system function @@TRANCOUNT may be used. SQL Server sets the nesting level in @@TRANCOUNT automatically:

```
BEGIN TRANSACTION
  BEGIN TRANSACTION
    BEGIN TRANSACTION
    SELECT @@TRANCOUNT
    COMMIT TRANSACTION
  COMMIT TRANSACTION
COMMIT TRANSACTION
```

———

3

The behavior of user transactions in which stored procedures are called and triggers fired needs a little further discussion. Suppose a trigger or stored procedure executes a ROLLBACK TRANSACTION statement—how will this affect other Transact-SQL statements in the batch?

```
CREATE PROCEDURE usp_roll_them_back AS
BEGIN TRANSACTION
ROLLBACK TRANSACTION
```

In the example below the stored procedure *usp_roll_them_back* issues a ROLLBACK TRANSACTION statement:

```
BEGIN TRANSACTION
  SELECT price FROM titles WHERE title_id = 'MC2222'
  UPDATE titles SET price = $10.99 WHERE title_id = 'MC2222'
  SELECT price FROM titles WHERE title_id = 'MC2222'
EXEC usp_roll_them_back
SELECT price FROM titles WHERE title_id = 'MC2222'
COMMIT TRANSACTION
```

```
price
_____

19.9900

price
_____

10.9900

Server: Msg 266, Level 16, State 2, Procedure
usp_roll_them_back, Line 3
Transaction count after EXECUTE indicates that a COMMIT or
ROLLBACK TRANSACTION statement is missing. Previous count =
1, current count = 0.

price
_____

19.9900

Server: Msg 3902, Level 16, State 1
The COMMIT TRANSACTION request has no corresponding BEGIN
TRANSACTION.
```

The ROLLBACK TRANSACTION statement in the stored procedure causes all the Transact-SQL statements between it and the first BEGIN TRANSACTION in the batch that called the stored procedure to be rolled back. This means that the ROLLBACK TRANSACTION statement in the stored procedure causes a rollback past the BEGIN TRANSACTION statement in the stored procedure. In other words, more than one nesting level is rolled back, so an error message is displayed that specifies the change in nesting levels.

Note that because this has occurred, the last COMMIT TRANSACTION has no explicit transaction to commit and so another error message is also displayed.

The above is also true of triggers that contain a ROLLBACK TRANSACTION statement. However, there is a fundamental difference between triggers and stored procedures in this respect. While a ROLLBACK TRANSACTION statement in a stored procedure does not affect subsequent statements in the batch, a ROLLBACK TRANSACTION statement in a trigger does. In fact, all the subsequent Transact-SQL statements in the batch are cancelled. In the previous example the third SELECT statement in the batch executed. In the next example, which fires a trigger containing a rollback, the SELECT statement following the UPDATE does not execute:

```
CREATE TRIGGER roll_them_back_TRG_U ON titles
FOR UPDATE
AS
BEGIN TRANSACTION
  PRINT 'rolling back...'
ROLLBACK TRANSACTION

BEGIN TRANSACTION
  SELECT price FROM titles WHERE title_id = 'MC2222'
  UPDATE titles SET price = $10.99 WHERE title_id = 'MC2222'
  SELECT price FROM titles WHERE title_id = 'MC2222'
COMMIT TRANSACTION

price
_____

19.9900

rolling back...
```

Note that the execution of a nested COMMIT statement merely decrements the transaction nesting level by one. Only the outermost COMMIT statement actually commits the changes made by Transact-SQL statements.

In any discussion of user transactions the subject of locking should be raised. Locking is discussed in detail in Chapter 10, however, it should be noted that certain classes of locks, particularly write locks, once placed on a table, database page, or row, will remain until the user transaction is committed or rolled back. This will have important ramifications when considering the multi-user aspects of an application. In general, user transactions should be kept as short as possible.

8

Database Administration

8.1   Introduction

This chapter discusses some of the major topics that an SQL Server database administrator will need to perform. The topics discussed are:

- Backing up a database.

- Managing alerts, jobs, and operators (automating database administration).

- The Web Assistant.

- The SQL Server Profiler.

Other chapters discuss database administration activity such as security.

8.2   Database Backups

Perhaps the most important activity that a database administrator has to perform is a database backup. The obvious reason to do this is to ensure that the data held in the database is copied and placed in a secure location so that, in the event of a media failure, the database and its data can be recovered. This section looks at the different options provided by SQL Server to backup and restore databases.

8.2.1   When to Backup?

There are a number of events after which a database backup is recommended. These are:

- The creation of a database.

- The creation of an index.

- A non-logged operation.

Note: If any files are added or removed from a database, the database should be backed up immediately.

If you create a database that you wish to recover in the event of a media failure, you must back it up. SQL Server will not allow you to perform transaction log backups until you have performed a full (complete) backup.

When you create indexes, many index entries are inserted into index pages. To increase performance and reduce the amount of information written to the transaction log, SQL Server only logs the fact that the index was created (actually it also logs page allocation information, too). This means that a recovery from a media failure would encounter the index creation step in the transaction log backup it was processing and recreate the index. If it took one hour to create the original index, then it would take one hour to recreate it during recovery. To avoid this recovery overhead, take a full backup of the database after a large index is created. In the event of a media failure, the full backup taken after the index creation can be restored. This will contain the complete index and so the index will not need to be created during recovery.

Non-logged operations, as the name suggests, are operations that do not write information to the transaction log. Such operations include the WRITETEXT and SELECT INTO Transact-SQL statements. When these operations are performed, SQL Server will suspend the capability to backup the transaction log. As a transaction log backup is a key operation in many companies' backup strategies, this is not normally acceptable. If a full database backup is performed after a non-logged operation, however, the non-logged changes will be backed up and SQL Server will allow transaction log backups to resume.

An SQL Server backup is an intelligent backup in that it understands SQL Server internal structures and file structures and can thus offer more capabilities than a simple file backup utility, such as the NTBACKUP utility. It is very important to note that file backup utilities cannot generally backup SQL Server files because while SQL Server is running, these files are in use. The exception to this rule is where the file backup vendor offers an add-on SQL Server backup agent. These agents usually run SQL Server backup under the covers.

SQL Server backup can backup SQL Server files when they are being used. Users can be reading and writing to the database that is being backed up. SQL Server 7.0 backup has been designed to minimize the impact of its execution on users but it is best run at a quiet time. There are some operations that cannot be run concurrently with SQL Server backup and these are:

* Adding or removing database files.

* Shrinking a database or file.

* Creating an index.

* Non-logged operations such as bulk load, SELECT INTO, WRITETEXT, and UPDATETEXT.

If a backup is already in progress when one of the above operations is initiated, the operation fails.

8.2.2   Backup Destinations

Regardless of the type of backup performed, a backup destination must be chosen. Three types of backup destinations are supported by SQL Server 7.0:

* Disk

* Tape

* Named pipe

A disk backup device is a disk file resident on a hard disk like any other Windows NT operating system file. It can be created on a local disk or on a network share. The size of the file is dynamic and it will grow and shrink as necessary. A tape backup device is similar to a disk backup device; however, it must be connected physically to the server on which SQL Server is running. Tape backups can span tapes, so if a tape fills another one will be requested. Named pipes are used by third-party backup utility vendors.

Backup devices can be referred to by a logical or physical name. An example of a logical name would be *BankingFull* whereas *F:\backups\ BankingFull.BAK* would be an example of a physical name. If logical names are to be used in the BACKUP or RESTORE statements, then a named backup device must be created through the SQL Server Enterprise Manager or the system-stored procedure *sp_addumpdevice.*

```
EXEC sp_addumpdevice 'disk', 'BankingFull',
'F:\backups\BankingFull.BAK'
```

Information about the named backup device *BankingFull* is now held in system tables in the master database together with its physical location. The backup would then be initiated by the statement:

```
BACKUP BankingDB TO BankingFull
```

If a backup is to be made to a physical backup device, the full physical location must be specified:

```
BACKUP PayrollDB TO
DISK='D:\databasebackups\PayrollFull.BAK'
```

8.2.3   Types of Backup

SQL Server 7.0 offers three types of database backup:

*   Full—sometimes referred to as complete

*   Transaction log

*   Differential

The basic backup strategy is to use a regular full backup. Most SQL Server sites will wish to embellish this with transaction log backups, differential backups, or both.

Full Database Backup

A full database backup strategy is the simplest database backup strategy. Recovery only requires a single restore of the latest full backup. However, there is often no way to recover any changes made to the database after the most recent database backup was completed. For this reason, a backup strategy that only consists of full database backups is usually not adequate for most companies.

There are some databases for which such a backup strategy may be adequate. These include:

*   Databases that do not hold important data, such as development test databases.

*   Databases that are updated infrequently.

*   Database that are updated via batch loads from files that can easily be replayed.

When a full backup of a database executes, every database page that contains data is backed up, even if it has not changed since the last backup. An example of performing a full backup would be:

```
BACKUP DATABASE BankingDB TO BankingFull
```

If a full backup strategy is being used with no transaction log backups, the transaction log will fill, at which point applications will not be able to make changes to the database. Normally, transaction log backups free up space in the transaction log. It is recommended, therefore, that the database option *trunc. log on chkpt.* is set to TRUE so that space is automatically and continually freed up in the transaction log. Another option would be to backup the transaction log with the TRUNCATE_ONLY option, which effectively discards the transaction log records of completed transactions, thus freeing up space in the transaction log.

Transaction Log Backup

The transaction log keeps a log of all changes that have been made to a database. In conjunction with full database backups, transaction log backups may make it possible to recover a database to the point where it failed. Transaction logs also allow recovery to a point in time.

An example of performing a transaction log backup would be:

```
BACKUP LOG BankingDB TO BankingTXN
```

A typical backup scenario using a full database backup and a transaction log backup would be to back up the database every night and back up the transaction log every hour through the working day. If a media failure occurred such that a data file was lost but the primary data file and transaction log was still available, a typical recovery scenario would then be to:

1. Backup the active transaction log (using the NO_TRUNCATE qualifier on BACKUP LOG);

2. restore the database from the last full backup; and

3. restore the transaction log backups in sequence, with the transaction log backup from step (1) being applied last.

Note that the database option *trunc. log on chkpt.* must not be set to TRUE if a transaction log backup strategy is required.

Differential Backup

Differential backups are new in SQL Server 7.0. A differential backup backs up only those database pages that have changed since the last full backup. If few pages have been updated since the last full backup, even if those pages have been updated frequently, the differential backup will be much smaller that the full backup and will perform more quickly.

Differential backups must be used in conjunction with full backups. If a transaction log backup strategy is being used, differential backups can also be used alongside transaction log backups. Unlike a transaction log-based recovery strategy, differential backups cannot be used to recover to a specific point in time, as they only capture the latest update that was made to a page.

An example of performing a differential backup would be:

```
BACKUP DATABASE BankingDB TO BankingDiff WITH DIFFERENTIAL
```

8.2.4   Backup Using the SQL Server Enterprise Manager

As well as using the BACKUP statement, backups can be performed using the SQL Server Enterprise Manager.

⇨ Expand the server, right-click *Databases*.

⇨ Click *All Tasks*.

⇨ Click *Backup Database*.

⇨ Enter the required information such as the database name and backup type.

⇨ Click *OK*.

The *SQL Server Backup* dialog box is shown in Figure 8.1.

Figure 8.1

Backing up a Database with the SQL Server Enterprise Manager

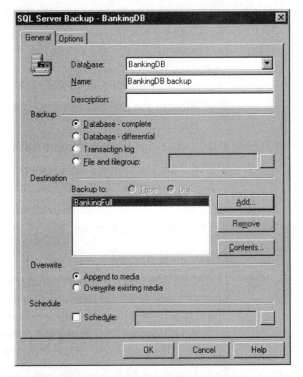

Various options can be specified when backing up a database. In the *General* tab the type of backup to be performed and the backup device can be specified. Whether the backup overwrites any existing backups held in the database backup or not can be specified. If desired, instead of overwriting existing backups, the new backup may be appended to the backup device. Instead of backing up immediately, as a single one-off operation, the backup may be scheduled to run once in the future or at some regular interval.

Note: **Individual files and filegroups may be backed up. This must be done in conjunction with transaction log backups. Various restrictions apply to which files and filegroups may be backed up independently of other files and filegroups.**

The *Options* tab can be used to specify more attributes of the backup. These attributes include whether the backup file is verified after the backup, and various media options. The *Options* tab is shown in Figure 8.2.

Figure 8.2

The Backup Options Tab

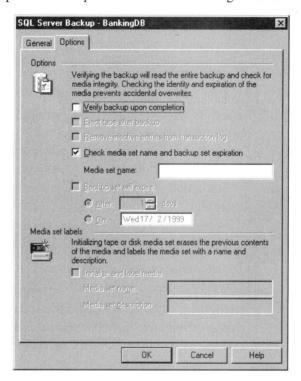

8.2.5 Backing up System Databases

It is very important for the database administrator to back up system databases as well as user databases, in particular, master and msdb. Model may need to be backed up if it has been modified. Tempdb does not need to be backed up as it is recreated when SQL Server is started.

The master database holds vital information that is key to the proper functioning of SQL Server, such as the location of user databases and security logins. The msdb database holds information that is key to the proper functioning of the SQL Server Agent service, such as jobs and alerts.

Master is modified when, for example, a user database is created. Msdb is modified when an alert is created. If regular backups of these databases are not performed, vital information may be lost if they have to be restored. We recommend that these databases be backed up at least daily using a scheduled job. They are small, so a backup takes a minute or so.

Note: If Data Transformation Services (DTS) packages are stored in the msdb database or in the repository, which in turn is stored in msdb, msdb may grow significantly.

8.2.6 Restoring Databases

A database restore operation will create a new database using files that are exactly as they were defined in the original database. Cross-platform backup and restore is supported. There are various options available on the RESTORE statement to allow this default behavior to be modified. One option allows the database administrator to restore the database files to new locations:

```
RESTORE DATABASE BankingDB FROM BankingFull
WITH
MOVE 'BankingData' TO 'e:\mssql7\data\BankingData.mdf'',
MOVE 'BankingLog' TO 'g:\mssql7\log\BankingLog.ldf''
```

To determine the file names to use, issue a RESTORE FILELISTONLY statement, which will be described shortly.

By default, SQL Server performs some safety checks to make sure that existing databases are not accidentally overwritten by the restore. To override the safety checks, a REPLACE option can be used. The safety checks do not stop a restore operation from overwriting a database that matches the database in the backup file; however, it does prevent a restore operation from overwriting a database of the same name if either:

(a) the database name is different from the name in the backup set OR

(b) the database files are different from the files in the backup set (except size).

Note: SQL Server 7.0 cannot restore backups from earlier versions of SQL Server.

When a database is restored, the default behavior is to roll back any uncommitted transactions. That is, the default behavior is to recover the database as if the RECOVERY option is used in the RESTORE statement. This results in a consistent database that can be accessed by users once the database restore has completed.

However, if the recovery plan is to restore a differential backup and/or transaction logs after the database restore, the NORECOVERY option should be specified. This leaves the database inconsistent but in a state where it is able to have subsequent recovery take place. An example sequence follows:

```
RESTORE DATABASE BankingDB FROM BankingFull WITH NORECOVERY

RESTORE DATABASE BankingDB FROM BankingDiff WITH RECOVERY
```

Note that the RECOVERY option in the second restore is actually redundant, as it is the default behavior.

If the last restore operation on a database used NORECOVERY (perhaps in the case of applying transaction logs to a standby server) and database access is now required, it can be made accessible by specifying:

```
RESTORE DATABASE PayrollDB WITH RECOVERY
```

It is not necessary to specify a backup device.

There is another option that can be taken when a database is restored. The STANDBY=*undofilename option* allows a database to be made accessible in a read-only mode between transaction log restores. This is useful when implementing a warm standby server.

8.2.7 Restoring a Database with the SQL Server Enterprise Manager

Databases can be restored via the SQL Server Enterprise Manager. If *Restore database and transaction logs* is chosen, the backup history of the database is displayed. This can be used to easily restore from a full backup, differential backups, and/or transaction log backups, as shown in Figure 8.3.

The *Options* tab allows various options to be set as shown in Figure 8.4.

These include the ability to restore a database to a new physical location.

8.2.8 Finding Information from the Backup Media

It is often useful to be able to interrogate the backup device to find information about the backups contained in it. Various options on the RESTORE statement make this possible.

Figure 8.3

Restoring a Database Using the
SQL Server Enterprise Manager

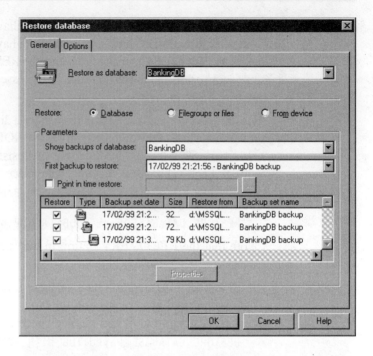

Figure 8.4

The Restore Options Tab

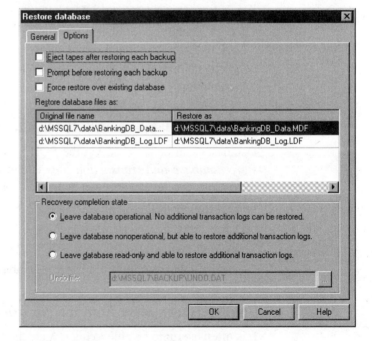

```
RESTORE FILELISTONLY FROM <backup_device>
```

Returns a result set with a list of the database and log files contained in the backup set.

```
RESTORE HEADERONLY FROM <backup_device>
```

Retrieves all the backup header information for all backup sets on a particular backup device.

```
RESTORE LABELONLY FROM <backup_device>
```

Returns a result set containing information about the backup media identified by the given backup device.

Another option allows the backup to be verified. It checks to see that the backup set is complete and that all volumes are readable, but it does not attempt to verify the structure of the data.

```
RESTORE VERIFYONLY FROM <backup_device>
```

8.2.9   Restoring System Databases

If the msdb or model database is lost, it can be restored like any other database. If master is not critically damaged, it can be restored from its latest backup like any other database also. However, to stop other users from accessing master, SQL Server should be started in single user mode. From the command prompt issue:

```
sqlservr -m
```

However, if the master database is critically damaged, SQL Server is probably not functioning. In this case the master database must be rebuilt using the *rebuildm* utility. This utility creates a new master database but it will contain only the information it contained when SQL Server was newly installed. Therefore, the latest backup of the master database needs to be restored after it is rebuilt. If there is no current backup of master, it is still possible to make user databases known to the master database with the *sp_attach_database* system-stored procedure, which will be described shortly. However, security logins will be lost as will other system data.

Note: Rebuilding the master database also rebuilds msdb and model so they may need to be restored also. When running *rebuildm*, the SQL Server installation files need to be available. *Rebuildm* itself is present in MSSQL7\BINN and must be run from the command prompt.

8.2.10   Database Integrity Checking

Due to architectural changes in SQL Server 7.0, the requirement to run DBCC to check integrity has lessened. However, DBCC integrity checks in SQL Server 7.0 are much faster than in previous releases.

There are a number of DBCC statements that can be run to check integrity, but we recommend that DBCC CHECKDB be run because it detects and repairs the widest possible errors. DBCC CHECKDB now has a number of repair options:

```
DBCC CHECKDB
      ('database_name'
                [, NOINDEX
                      |   {REPAIR_ALLOW_DATA_LOSS
                      |   REPAIR_FAST
                      |   REPAIR_REBUILD
                      }]
      ) [WITH {ALL_ERRORMSGS | NO_INFOMSGS}]
```

8.2.11   Attaching and Detaching Databases

Attaching and detaching databases is a new facility in SQL Server 7.0. A database can be detached from a server using *sp_detach_db* and then attached to the same server or another server using *sp_attach_db*.

```
sp_detach_db ResearchDB

sp_attach_db ResearchDB,
      'd:\mssql7\data\ResearchDB_Data.mdf',
      'd:\mssql7\data\ResearchDB_Log.ldf'
```

The system-stored procedure *sp_attach_single_file_db* can be used when there is no log file because it builds a new one.

```
sp_attach_single_file_db ResearchDB,
      'd:\mssql7\data\ResearchDB_Data.mdf'
```

8.3   Management of Alerts, Jobs, and Operators

8.3.1   Scheduled and Unattended Operations

One of the key features of SQL Server 6.x was the ability to schedule operations to execute without the intervention of an operator and the ability to send alerts when certain events occur within the server. The integration of

SQLMAIL via the MAPI interface enabled these alerts to be sent as mail messages or pager messages, expanding the scope of the more traditional alert systems.

SQL Server 7.0 has seen an improvement in these services. The first thing is the renaming of tasks to jobs. In fact, with version 7.0 the following job types can be created:

- Stand-alone or multiserver jobs.

- Single-step or multistep jobs.

Jobs themselves can comprise of the following job *types:*

- *CmdExec* task type is an operating system command or .EXE file. After completion, a suitable exit code needs to be returned to tell SQL Server the command has completed. There is a special Windows NT account SQLAgentCmdExec that allows the running of CmdExec jobs by others than the system administrator in this account context.

- *TSQL* is a Transact-SQL statement. Any variables need to be included in the script, but the GO batch terminator cannot be included.

- *Active scripting* is the execution of any scripting language such as VBScript or Jscript.

Replication jobs are automatically created for the replication agents. The following replication agents automatically have job steps built:

- Log Reader

- Distribution Agent

- Merge Agent

- Snapshot Agent

For further details on replication see Chapter 11.

Each SQL Server job has a set of core attributes that are stored in a system table called *sysjobs*. Static scheduling properties are stored in the *sysjobschedules* table. The *sysjobsteps* table contains the details on how the job runs and appropriate success or failure action and also contains execution history for local server jobs. By using job categories, it is possible to apply an administrative structure to the jobs for a better degree of manageability. The two default categories, Uncategorized (local) and Multiserver, allow for locally-created jobs or those created on a master server to be managed appropriately.

Recurring jobs can be scheduled at frequent intervals—daily, weekly, or monthly. The date of the job can be preset or left to be unending with no specified beginning and finish date. Parameters can be set for the tasks that include e-mail on event success or failure, Windows NT log entries on success or failure, and retry parameters to try and force through an execution. SQL Server 7.0 has introduced a novel job execution option for when the CPU is idle to use up those wasted cycles.

Each job needs to have a set of steps defined according to the action to be taken on success or failure. For example, on a step failure it might need to retry the step or quit the step in its entirety, reporting back either a success or failure. The success reporting action can be via e-mail, electronic paging, net send, or an NT alert. The job history is documented in the job history dialog box. The result of a job can be one of the following:

* Succeeded
* Failed
* Between Retry
* In Progress
* Cancelled
* Unknown

Creating a Scheduled Job

Each job needs to be configured with a number of attributes:

* Name. No more than 128 characters, it must be unique if more than one job of the same name is based on the same server. A job can be enabled or disabled at this point.
* Category. This is sometimes used to sort jobs into groups for easier management. SQL Server will automatically create jobs in the SQL Server Agent as uncategorized, database maintenance, full text, jobs from MSX, Web Assistant, or one of nine different replication categories. Local jobs will sit in the uncategorized category by default.
* Owner
* Description
* Job steps
* Schedules
* Notifications

The procedure for creating and defining a job are:

⇨ To create a job, right click *Jobs* and then click *New Jobs*.
⇨ On the *general* tab enter the *job name*, disabling it if you don't want the job to run immediately.

⇨ Under *source*, select the target server as either local or multiple servers. If you choose *target multiple servers* then select *change* and in the *change job target servers* dialog select the *targeted server*.

⇨ In the *new job properties*, select the *owner* from the owner list. If this option is not available then you are not logged on as sysadmin.

⇨ Enter a *job description* and then select *steps* to give the job at least one step to use for execution.

Figure 8.5
Creating a Backup Job on the Server

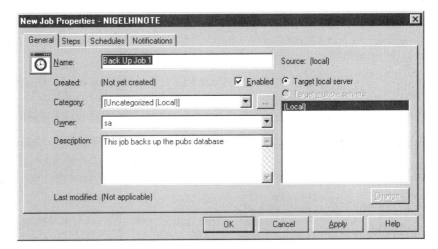

Figure 8.6
Defining the Actions to Take When the Job Completes

8.3.2   Multiserver Jobs

SQL Server now uses the concept of a Master SQL Server Agent (MSX) that can be used to manage a network of target servers called TSX within SQL Server. A SQL Server job can be defined and then given the target servers that it needs to run on. On a periodic basis the TSXs will check the MSX and see if there are any jobs that they need to carry out. Once a job has been completed or if it should fail, then the appropriate report is sent back to the MSX. Both the MSX and TSX servers are identical, and have the same *msdb* database schema. The good news is that the domain can grow as quickly as the organization needs it to as the MSX needs no special preparation. In a similar fashion, TSX servers can be moved to another MSX by a process known as *defection.*

8.3.3   Alerts

SQL Server events can be trapped by the Windows NT event log, which in turn is monitored by the SQL Agent. If an event occurs that has been set up as requiring an alert to be executed, the SQL Agent ensures a mail message, pager alert, or executable event is initiated to inform the appropriate person.

The following events will be trapped by the Windows NT event viewer and are therefore most suitable for initiating an alert:

- *sysmessages* with a severity greater than 19.
- Non sysmessages and errors with severity between 120 and 130.
- Any RAISERROR invoked by the WITHLOG syntax.
- Any event logged by *xp_logevent.*
- *sysmessage* errors modified with *sp_altermessage.*

There is a tremendous amount of flexibility available to the system administrator to specify alerts based on error messages. The SQL Server error message repository can be searched for messages containing a particular string to facilitate the setting up of the new alert.

Creating a Simple Alert Using an Error Number

⇨ Right click onto *Alerts* and then click *new alert*. Enter a name in the *new alert* properties box and select *enabled* to enable the alert to run.

⇨ Select the error number you want to trap.

⇨ Select the *database name* of the database the alert refers to and if you wish, enter a key word or character string into the *Error message contains this text box.*

⇨ Select *response* and define the *alert response.*

Figure 8.7

Alert Properties Dialog

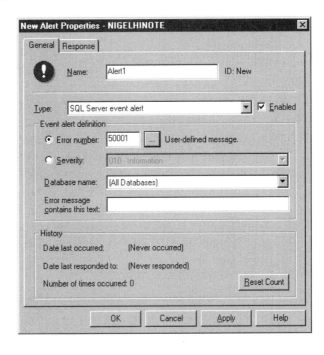

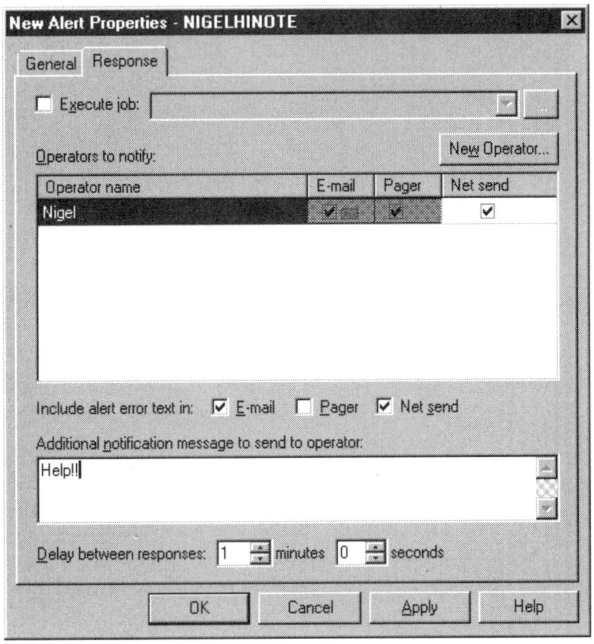

Figure 8.8

Defining the Response to the Alert

8.3.4   Operators

Automated systems are all very well, but they can only go so far. The lynch pin of any SQL Server installation is the Systems Administrator (SA), who may or may not also be an operator. The idea of operators really comes from the days of managing large mainframe-type installations, where teams of operators were needed just to manage the machine on a daily basis. SQL Server does not need such manpower, but occasionally operators need to be setup to manage the unusual. System communication with the operators is via e-mail, paging software, or net send network communication methods. Obviously the system will need to have appropriate software or hardware installed to make the most of this. The great flexibility with SQL Server is the ability to set up operators with a very high degree of granularity—pager on duty times, event history, alert events—and manage them appropriately.

Creating an Operator

⇨   Right-click *operator* and select *New Operator.*

⇨   Enter the *operator name* in the dialog box.

⇨   Define a notification mechanism; *Pager, E-mail,* or *Net Send.*

Figure 8.9

This Operator Has Long Duty Hours

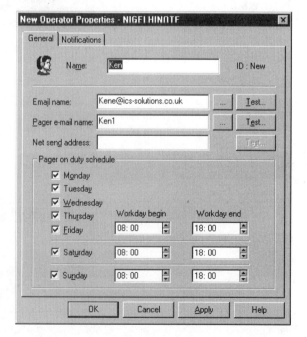

Figure 8.10

Setting up Which Errors Are Notified by Which Mechanism

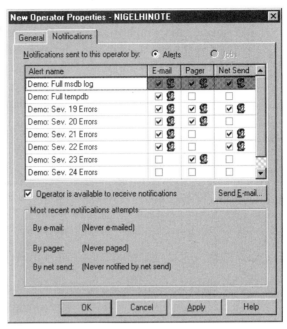

8.4   SQL Server Web Assistant

The SQL Server Web Assistant was introduced in version 6.5 of SQL Server, alongside the general move to "HTMLize" Microsoft products. The Web Assistant enables you to create data in Hypertext Markup Language (HTML) format from Transact-SQL queries and stored procedures. This process can either be a one-off task or scheduled for later execution as a task. On that

Figure 8.11

Using the Web Assistant Is Easy. Here We Are Using the Pubs Database to Publish Information from Selected Tables

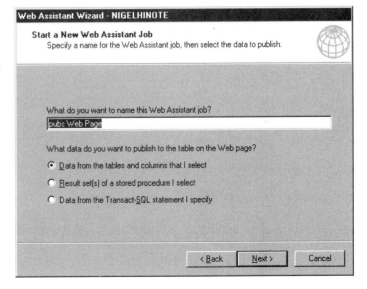

basis, a developer may design an SQL Server application that may, for instance, take a nightly download of products in store from the database and export it onto an intranet or Internet website. This approach lends itself very well to decision support or Data Warehouse solutions that produce read-only reports. Using extended stored procedures, information can be gathered from sources outside of SQL Server and published in the same way.

The Web Assistant is based on the popular wizard format, making it a lot easier to use. Essentially the user selects the appropriate data source and

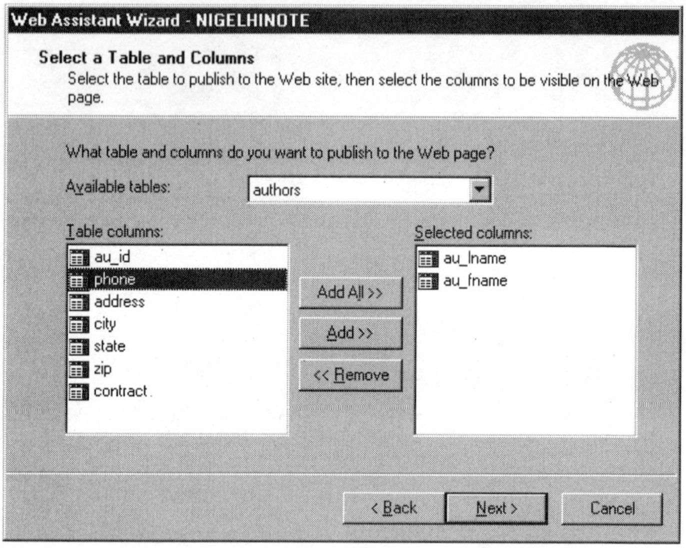

Figure 8.12
Selecting the Columns from the Table

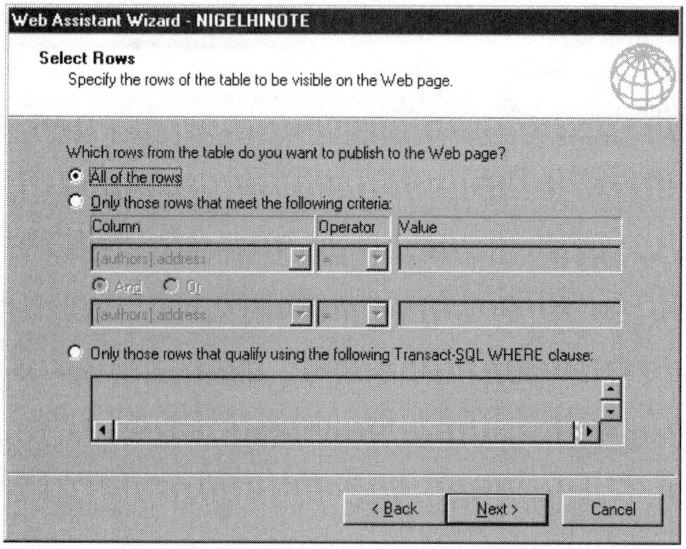

Figure 8.13
You Can Select a Subset of the Data According to Some Criteria. In This Case We Are Selecting to See All of the Rows

then builds either a query or other select statement to retrieve data. The user must have the appropriate rights to access the underlying data, and the rights will be authenticated by the server. It is also possible to install the Web Assistant on 32-bit clients for use locally.

The scheduled web publishing can be set according to all the usual parameters, such as a certain time or certain day of the week, but probably more interesting is the option to publish data when the source data changes. This will lend itself very well to the publishing of stock levels—maybe across an extranet (an intranet open to select third parties).

Figure 8.14

Scheduling the Job

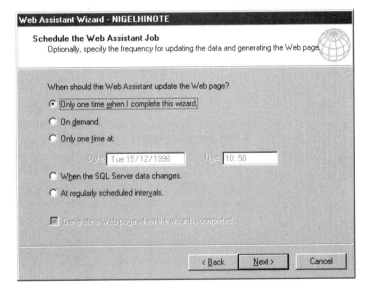

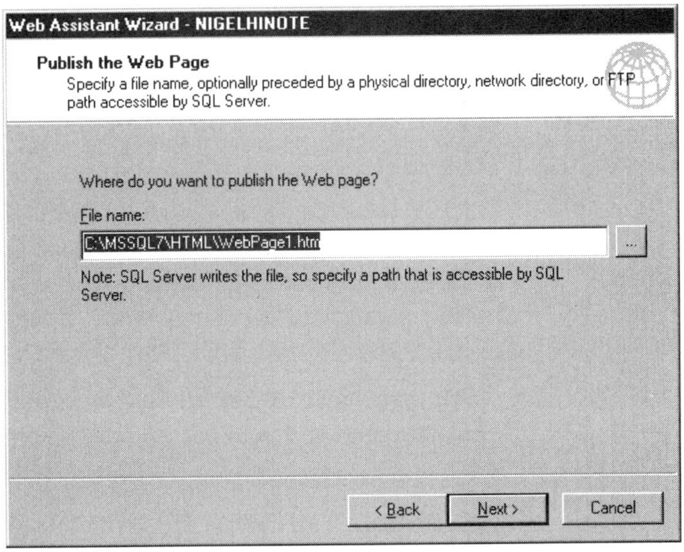

Figure 8.15

Selecting the Location to Publish to. The Default Directory is \MSSQL7\HTML

Figure 8.16
*After Running through Some
HTML Formatting Screens, the
Final Screen Confirms the Action.
Note the Button to Write a T-SQL
File*

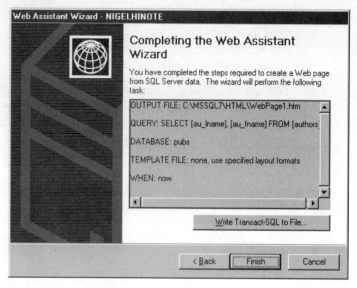

8.5   The SQL Server Profiler

The SQL Server Profiler allows database administrators and developers to monitor events that happen in SQL Server. There are many events that can be monitored, such as the execution of a Transact-SQL statement or the acquisition of a lock, and these can be captured in a number of ways.

Building on the SQL Server 6.5 SQL Trace tool, the SQL Server Profiler is an invaluable aid for performance monitoring and troubleshooting. In fact, we find a new use for this tool every day. The following sections will describe the SQL Server Profiler.

8.6   The SQL Server Profiler Architecture

SQL Server 7.0 generates events known as event classes. Examples of SQL Server components that generate events, known as *event producers,* are the query processor, storage engine, lock manager and log manager. Event classes can also be user-defined. The events are accessed via *event consumers.* Examples of event consumers would be a file, database table, and the SQL Server Profiler GUI. This is shown graphically in Figure 8.17.

The events may also be filtered. For example, only queries of above a particular duration would be captured. Examples of events are:

♦   Login successes and failures.

♦   SELECT, INSERT, UPDATE and DELETE statements.

Figure 8.17
The SQL Server Profiler Architecture

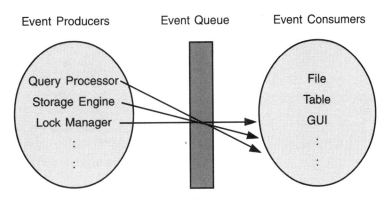

Event Producers   Event Queue   Event Consumers

Query Processor
Storage Engine
Lock Manager

File
Table
GUI

♦   The start or end of a stored procedure.

♦   An error written to the SQL Server error log.

♦   A lock acquired or released on a database object.

Traces can be defined using the SQL Server Profiler GUI, extended stored procedures, or the SQL Server Profiler wizard. The overhead of the SQL Server Profiler is not high; however, it may not be wise to trace every access to every object.

An SQL Server Profiler trace is defined by the event classes that are captured, what information is captured about those classes, what is filtered, and what the destination for the information is. If the SQL Server Profiler GUI is to be used to define a trace, four tabs are used to represent the trace definition. These tabs and the information specified in them will be discussed in the next sections.

Note that the SQL Server Profiler is started from the Windows NT or Windows 95/98 *Start* menu. Choose *Programs → Microsoft SQL Server 7.0 → Profiler*.

8.7   Tracing Event Classes

The SQL Server Profiler can trace many event classes. For convenience, they are grouped together in *Event Categories*. For example, the *Objects* event category groups together operations executed against database objects. By default, not all are displayed in the SQL Server Profiler GUI. To display all the event categories choose *Tools →Options →Commonly Traced Event Classes*.

When an event category or event class is selected, help information concerning the category selected is displayed. To add an event class to the trace, merely select the event category and click *Add*.

The *Events* tab showing the categories is shown in Figure 8.18.

Figure 8.18
The SQL Server Profiler Events Tab

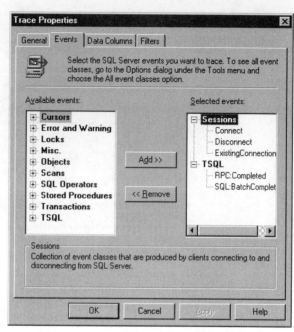

A brief description of the event categories is shown in Table 8.1:

Table 8.1
Event Categories

Event Category	Description
Cursors	Event classes that are generated by cursor activity
Error and Warning	Monitors many SQL Server errors and warnings
Locks	Monitors SQL Server lock activity
Miscellaneous	Monitors events not found in other categories
Objects	Monitors when an object, e.g., table, is opened, created, deleted, or used
Scans	Monitors table or index scans
Sessions	Monitors user connections
SQL Operators	Monitors when a SELECT, INSERT, UPDATE, or DELETE executes
Stored Procedures	Monitors the execution of stored procedures
Transactions	Monitors transactions
TSQL	Monitors Transact-SQL statements, batches, and RPCs
User Configurable	Monitors user-defined events

When a new trace is created, the SQL Server Profiler automatically selects the *Sessions* event category and some event classes from the TSQL event category.

The SQL Server Profiler can capture much information about each event class. These are represented as data columns. By default, not all are displayed in the SQL Server Profiler GUI. To display all the data columns choose *Tools→Options →Commonly Captured Data Columns*.

The Data Columns tab is shown in Figure 8.19.

Figure 8.19

The SQL Server Profiler Data Columns Tab

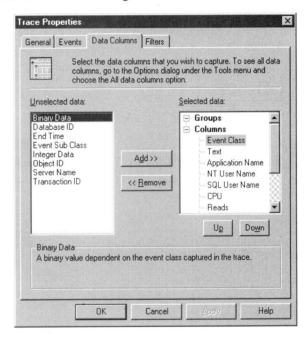

When a data column is selected, help information concerning the data column selected is displayed. To add a data column to the trace, merely select the data column and click *Add*. The trace can be grouped by one or more data columns to make the trace display easier to read.

Some data columns, for example *Application Name,* represent the same measure regardless of the event class being traced. However, some data columns are event class-specific. For example, the *Text* data column for the *ErrorLog* event class is the text of the error message, whereas, for the *SQL:StmtCompleted* event class it is the Transact-SQL statement source code. Similarly, the *Integer Data* data column for the *SQL:StmtCompleted* event class is the actual number of rows returned, whereas, for the *Exception* event class it represents an error number.

Filters are used to reduce the amount of data that is collected. There are three kinds of filters:

- Name filters—Used to include or exclude SQL Server or Windows NT users and applications.

- Range filters—Used to specify a range of values, such as the minimum and maximum duration of a Transact-SQL statement.

- Identification numbers—Used to include a specific ID number, such as a server process ID (SPID) or connection ID.

Note: System-stored procedures that manage passwords, for example, *sp_password*, are never monitored for security reasons.

The Filters tab is shown in Figure 8.20.

Figure 8.20

The SQL Server Profiler Filters Tab

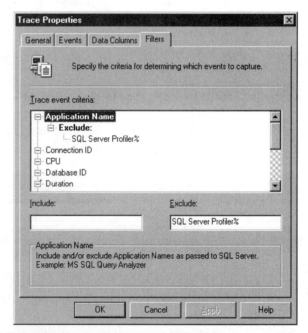

The destination(s) for the trace data can be specified on the *General* tab. The two destinations that can be specified through the SQL Server Profiler GUI are file and database table.

The obvious advantage of capturing data in persistent storage such as a file or table is that it can be analyzed later as many times as is required. However, there are other advantages. Captured trace data in a file or table can be used as input to the Index Tuning Wizard. Captured trace data in a file or table can be used to troubleshoot problems or send the data to a support provider. Captured trace data in a table can be analyzed with Transact-SQL statements. Data is always appended to the file or table. The file extension of a trace file is .trc.

If extended stored procedures are used to define traces, it is possible to define the Windows NT Application Event Log as a destination, or another server can be defined as an event-forwarding server. To do this, use the extended stored procedure *xp_trace_setqueuedestination*.

Note: To capture data in a table the *Application Name* data column must be traced.

The *General* tab is also used to name the server to be traced and specify whether the trace should be *Shared* or *Private*. Shared means that other users can use the trace. Private means that only the trace creator can use the trace.

Figure 8.21 shows the *General* tab.

Figure 8.21

The SQL Server Profiler General Tab

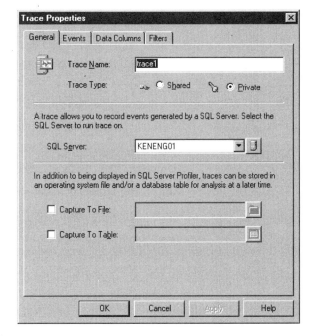

Note that the definition of the trace can be saved and exported to other computers. The file extension of a trace definition file is .tdf.

The SQL Server Profiler contains a *multithreaded playback engine* that can be used to reproduce the activity captured in a trace to the same or another server. The multithreaded nature of this engine allows it to simulate multiple user connections.

When replaying a trace, debugging capabilities such as break points, run-to-cursor, and single-stepping is available.

There are requirements that need to be satisfied before replaying traces. Depending on the activity being replayed, certain event classes must be captured. However, the *Connect, Disconnect, ExistingConnection, RPC:Starting*, and *SQL:BatchStarting* event classes must be captured regardless of the activity being replayed. The following data columns must also be captured: *Application Name, Binary Data, Connection ID or SPID, Database ID, Event Class, Event Sub Class, Host Name, Integer Data, Server Name, SQL User Name, Start Time,* and *Text.*

An example trace definition (TSQL for Replay) is provided by Microsoft to make the trace definition for replay easier to define.

If the activity is to be replayed against another server, other requirements apply. For example, logins must exist on the target server. When replaying, synchronization and replay rate can also be specified.

Although the SQL Server Profiler can be used to monitor a variety of situations, it is likely that the database administrator will use it for some situations over and over again. These common scenarios are:

- Monitoring Transact-SQL activity per user.
- Monitoring Transact-SQL activity by application.
- Finding the worst-performing queries.
- Identifying the cause of a deadlock.
- Monitoring stored procedure performance.
- Identifying scans of large tables.

The *Create Trace Wizard* can be used to define the trace definitions that can monitor these scenarios.

9

Security

9.1　Introduction

Most database applications require security of one kind or another. This is typically done to ensure that users do not accidentally or willfully view or change sensitive data to which they should not have access. Developers have a number of methods by which to implement security. For example, they can create a customized security mechanism in the application itself, or make use of the facilities available in SQL Server. There are advantages and disadvantages to both methods.

If a customized security mechanism in the application itself is used, users will be authenticated via the application software and, if validated, will be connected to SQL Server. This has the advantage of offering great flexibility as the security mechanism used is not general purpose but is designed specifically for a particular application. However, creating a customized security mechanism does have disadvantages. It requires extra design and coding effort on the part of the developer and does not address the needs of other application software on the system. Often customized security mechanisms, having validated a user, connect to SQL Server via one SQL Server account name that makes auditing and tracing from the database side very difficult. Typically the user will also have to remember his or her Windows NT account name and password and also an application username and password.

There are a number of advantages to using the security mechanisms provided by SQL Server. The developer can rely on a tried and trusted security mechanism and will therefore not have to reinvent the wheel. The SQL Server security mechanism is highly integrated with Windows NT and so the user will only need to remember his or her Windows NT account name and password. Once set up, the security plan is valid for all applications that use the SQL Server, whether they are home-grown applications or off-the-shelf applications such as Microsoft Excel or Microsoft Access.

There is a downside to using SQL Server's security mechanism. A customized security mechanism in the application itself is typically more flexible than SQL Server's security mechanism, but this is much less the case in SQL Server 7.0 than it was in SQL Server 6.5. In SQL Server 6.5, due to architectural limitations, developers often found that they had to put in extra effort to overcome various idiosyncrasies, such as the fact that users could be a member of only one database group. The SQL Server 7.0 security mechanism is much more powerful and flexible and is much better integrated with Windows NT security.

There is no reason why only one approach needs to be adopted, as a hybrid of the two approaches may be more appropriate for some applications, and those applications that use Microsoft Transaction Server (MTS) also have extra security facilities at their disposal. However, this is a handbook on SQL Server and so it is on SQL Server's security mechanism that we will focus.

9.2   Architecture

Before data can be retrieved and modified or stored procedures can be executed, a user must successfully pass through a number of barriers that SQL Server uses to protect itself. First of all, a user must gain access to SQL Server itself; in other words, a user must be authenticated to use SQL Server. This in itself does not enable the user to do very much. Typically a user will not be able to gain entry to any databases managed by the SQL Server. To gain entry to a database the user must be "known" in that database; in SQL Server terminology the user must have a *database user account* in the database to which they want to gain access.

Note: In SQL Server 6.5 terminology this was usually referred to as a *database username.*

Having gained entry to a database the user can still typically do very little. Unless he or she has permission to access tables and views or execute stored procedures, he or she will be unable to do so.

The user's database user account must be given permissions or he or she must be a member of a database *role* that has itself been given appropriate permissions. Roles will be discussed shortly.

Note: An SQL Server 7.0 database role is not unlike an SQL Server 6.5 database group but, as we shall see, an SQL Server 7.0 database role offers much more flexibility.

Figure 9.1
SQL Server Security Architecture

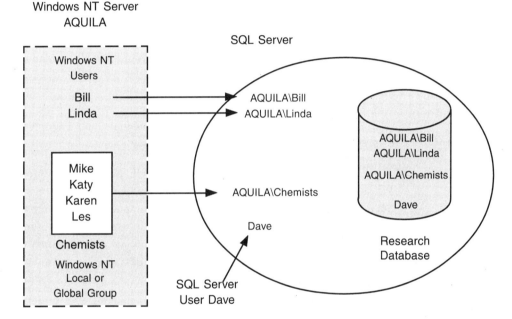

In Figure 9.1, we can see that individual Windows NT users and Windows NT groups (both local and global) can be granted access to SQL Server. To gain access to the database Research, the granted logins must be given database user accounts in that database. These database user accounts, which may relate to individual Windows NT users or groups, may then be given permission to access database objects such as tables and stored procedures. Also shown is an SQL Server login, Dave. The SQL Server 7.0 security architecture supports standard SQL Server logins for backward compatibility. Standard SQL Server logins do not have a relationship with Windows NT users and groups. The concepts shown in the figure will be described in detail in the rest of this chapter.

As can be seen from the above, gaining access to the interesting parts of your server means that you must pass through a number of security checks on the way. This is not unlike gaining access to a secure government building.

You gain access to the building by being authenticated by the guard at the entrance to whom you show your ID card. You can then wander aimlessly through the building unless you have been given access to specific rooms. Perhaps being given access to a room means you successfully pass through a retinal scan, because an image of your retina is associated with that room. Finally, having entered the room, you wish to view some documents in a filing cabinet. Unless you can open the filing cabinet, you have wasted your time. We can consider the building to be SQL Server, which contains rooms that are analogous to databases that contain filing cabinets that represent tables.

To gain access to the building you needed an ID card. To gain access to SQL Server your ID card is in the form of a Windows NT account name and password or an SQL Server login ID and password. So let us now focus on gaining access to SQL Server.

9.3 Gaining Access to SQL Server

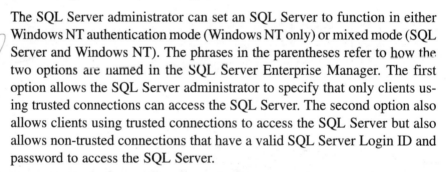

The SQL Server administrator can set an SQL Server to function in either Windows NT authentication mode (Windows NT only) or mixed mode (SQL Server and Windows NT). The phrases in the parentheses refer to how the two options are named in the SQL Server Enterprise Manager. The first option allows the SQL Server administrator to specify that only clients using trusted connections can access the SQL Server. The second option also allows clients using trusted connections to access the SQL Server but also allows non-trusted connections that have a valid SQL Server Login ID and password to access the SQL Server.

Using an SQL Server Login ID and password to access the SQL Server is a legacy from the past. There may be applications written for versions of SQL Server prior to SQL Server 7.0 that use this approach to allow access to SQL Server, and so for backward compatibility reasons this has to be provided.

Note: Windows NT authentication mode is similar to the *Integrated* security mode in prior versions of SQL Server. Mixed mode is similar to *Mixed* mode in prior versions of SQL Server. The old *Standard* mode, which completely ignored Windows NT security, has no direct equivalent in SQL Server 7.0.

A key concept to emphasize here is that we are talking about gaining access to SQL Server or, in our analogy, gaining access to the building. Irrespective of the security mode used, once a user is permitted to access SQL Server, then access to databases and objects within those databases is treated the same way. In the building analogy, it does not matter whether the guard asks to see your ID card or you have a security chip embedded in some dark corner of your body. Once you have been granted entry into the building, the mechanisms to gain entry to the rooms and filing cabinets are the same.

9.3.1   Windows NT Authentication Mode

The idea behind Windows NT Authentication Mode is that a user who successfully logs onto Windows NT with his or her Windows NT account name and password, and is therefore authenticated by Windows NT, is recognized as that Windows NT account by SQL Server. SQL Server does not need to authenticate the user again because it trusts Windows NT to have done so. SQL Server can interrogate Windows NT to find who the user is and which Windows NT groups the user has membership of, as well as other security characteristics.

Knowing this information, SQL Server can then check to see if the Windows NT account or any Windows NT group that the Windows NT account is a member of has been granted access to SQL Server. If access has been granted then that user will successfully be logged into SQL Server.

An obvious advantage of the Windows NT Authentication Mode is that no other username or password needs to be specified. There are other advantages. Windows NT authentication offers a number of features to facilitate security management. For example, when a Windows NT account is created characteristics can be specified such as:

*   Password expiration
*   Minimum password length
*   Password uniqueness
*   Account lockout after login failure
*   Auditing

To login using Windows NT Authentication Mode the client must login over a trusted connection.

9.3.2   SQL Server Authentication Mode

As mentioned previously, SQL Server Authentication Mode is provided mainly for backward compatibility. If a user logs into SQL Server from a non-trusted connection he or she must provide a valid SQL Server login ID and password. SQL Server will validate the user by checking for a matching entry in the *syslogins* system table in the master database.

Note: As well as backward compatibility, SQL Server Authentication Mode must be used for non-trusted clients and Internet clients.

What happens if the SQL Server is set up to use SQL Server Authentication Mode and a user logs in over a trusted connection? Assuming the Windows NT account or any Windows NT group that the Windows NT account is a member of has been granted access to SQL Server, the user will login to SQL Server as his or her Windows NT account name. However, if the application software allows the user to specify an SQL Server login ID and password, and the user enters a valid SQL Server login ID and password, that is who he or she will be logged in as. The SQL Server Query Analyzer is an example of such software. A user can elect to connect using Windows NT authentication or SQL Server authentication.

9.3.3   Setting the SQL Server Authentication Mode

The authentication mode can be set using the SQL Server Enterprise Manager.

⇨   Expand the server group in which the server resides.

⇨   Right-click the server and click *Properties.*

⇨   Click the tab labeled *Security.*

⇨   Select the appropriate authentication option: *SQL Server and Windows NT* or *Windows NT only.*

⇨   Click *OK.*

The Security tab in the Properties page is shown in Figure 9.2. For the new authentication mode to take effect, the SQL Server must be restarted.

9.3.4   Allowing Access to SQL Server for Windows NT Users and Groups

Apart from the reasons mentioned previously, such as backward compatibility, most sites will benefit from using Windows NT Authentication Mode. Assuming that the Windows NT administrator (who may or may not be the SQL Server administrator) has created appropriate Windows NT users and groups, the SQL Server administrator can give individual Windows NT users and Windows NT groups access to SQL Server. In many instances it

Figure 9.2

The Security Tab in the Server Properties Page

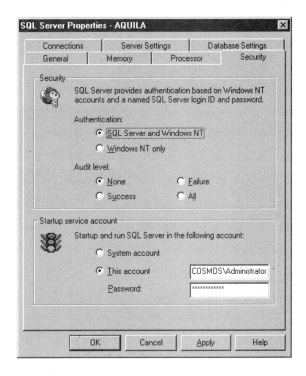

is better to give access to groups because this facilitates administration. This way, a number of individuals can be managed as a whole.

Note: When using Windows NT Authentication Mode, users and groups are created under Windows NT. By comparison, when SQL Server Authentication Mode is used, the SQL Server login is created within SQL Server. There is no relationship with a Windows NT user account.

To add a Windows NT user or group to SQL Server, the SQL Server Enterprise Manager or the Transact-SQL system-stored procedure *sp_grantlogin* can be used.

To use the SQL Server Enterprise Manager:

⇨ Expand the server name.

⇨ Right-click *Logins* and then click *New Login.*

⇨ Select *Windows NT Authentication.*

⇨ In the *Name* box enter the Windows NT account name or group name.

⇨ Choose the require computer name or domain name.

⇨ Ensure that *"Grant Access"* is selected.

⇨ Optionally specify a default database and/or language to be set for this account.

⇨ Click *OK*.

Figure 9.3

Adding a New Login to SQL Serve

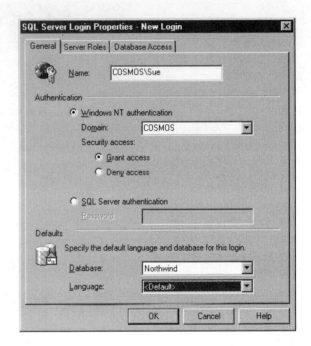

The *New Login* dialog box is shown in Figure 9.3. In this example access is being given to a Windows NT user and so *Windows NT Authentication* is selected. Note that the Windows NT account name or group name must be qualified with a Windows NT domain name or computer name. The *Domain* list box helps you to choose the domain, which then automatically appears in the *Name* box. Access to SQL Server can also be granted to a built-in Windows NT group, in which case the name *BUILTIN* should be used, as in *BUILTIN\Administrators*. Under *Defaults*, a database can be chosen that will be the database the login is connected to after successful login.

Note: Choosing a database as a default database does not give the login permission to access that database. Permission must be given explicitly either as part of adding the new login or later. SQL Server will issue a warning if you attempt to create a login that has a default database to which you have not yet been granted permission.

To use the Transact-SQL system-stored procedure:

```
EXEC sp_grantlogin 'Europe\SmithF'

EXEC sp_grantlogin 'Aquila\Biochemists'
```

Or, if preferred:

```
EXEC sp_grantlogin [Europe\SmithF]
```

Note: Using the SQL Server Enterprise Manager or *sp_grantlogin* to add a Windows NT login will cause a row to be added to the *syslogins* table in the master database if the row does not already exist. A single row will be added if an individual Windows NT account is specified. In the case of a Windows NT group being specified, a single row is also added, not one row for each individual in the group. The only exception to this is when an individual user account in the group creates an object in a database such as a table or view.

Can anyone add a Windows NT account or group to SQL Server? This is an operation that grants access to the SQL Server, so it is restricted to those SQL Server accounts that belong to the *sysadmin* or *securityadmin* fixed-server roles. Fixed-Server roles will be discussed later in this chapter.

9.3.5 Disallowing Access to SQL Server for Windows NT Users and Groups

Inevitably, it will become necessary to disallow access to SQL Server to selected Windows NT users and groups. A Windows NT user, however, can gain access to SQL Server by a number of routes. The user could have been granted access because their Windows NT user account has been granted access, or the user could have been granted access because he or she is a member of Windows NT groups that have been granted access. Disallowing access to SQL Server therefore has two interpretations. The Windows NT user can be disallowed access through a particular route by removing that route or disallowed access through all possible routes.

For example, suppose the Windows NT user "aquila\mike" is a member of the Windows NT groups "aquila\biologists" and "aquila\chemists." Suppose also that access to SQL Server has previously been allowed to "aquila\mike," "aquila\biologists," and "aquila\chemists." If the Windows NT user "aquila\mike" is removed from SQL Server, then access to SQL Server will still be available to Mike because he is a member of the two Windows NT groups that still have access. However, SQL Server access can be disallowed to this Windows NT user completely irrespective of the Windows NT group membership if desired.

To remove a Windows NT user or group from SQL Server, the SQL Server Enterprise Manager or the Transact-SQL system-stored procedure *sp_revokelogin* can be used.

To use the SQL Server Enterprise Manager:

⇨   Expand the server name.

⇨   Click *Logins* and then in the *Details* pane, right-click the login to remove.

⇨   Click *Delete* and confirm the operation when prompted.

To use the Transact-SQL system-stored procedure:

```
EXEC sp_revokelogin 'Europe\SmithF'


EXEC sp_revokelogin 'Aquila\Biochemists'
```

Note: Using the SQL Server Enterprise Manager or *sp_revokelogin* to remove a Windows NT login will cause a row to be deleted from the *syslogins* table in the master database.

Can anyone remove a Windows NT account or group from SQL Server? This is an operation that removes access to the SQL Server, so it is restricted to those SQL Server accounts that belong to the *sysadmin* or *securityadmin* fixed-server roles.

To deny a Windows NT account or group access to SQL Server completely, the SQL Server Enterprise Manager or the Transact-SQL system-stored procedure *sp_denylogin* can be used.

To use the SQL Server Enterprise Manager:

⇨   Expand the server name.

⇨   Click *Logins* and then in the *Details* pane, right-click the login to deny access.

⇨   Click *Properties* and select *Deny Access*.

⇨   Click *OK*.

To use the Transact-SQL system-stored procedure:

```
EXEC sp_denylogin 'Europe\SmithF'

EXEC sp_denylogin 'Aquila\Biochemists'
```

Note: Using the SQL Server Enterprise Manager or *sp_denylogin* to deny a Windows NT login will cause a row to be inserted into the *syslogins* table in the master database. If a row already exists for the login, it will be modified. The effects of *sp_denylogin* can be reversed with *sp_grantlogin*.

Can anyone deny a Windows NT account or group from SQL Server? This is an operation that removes access to the SQL Server, so it is restricted to those SQL Server accounts that belong to the *sysadmin* or *securityadmin* fixed-server roles.

9.3.6 Allowing Access to SQL Server by Creating an SQL Server Login

When operating in mixed mode the SQL Server administrator may wish to create SQL Server logins. There is no relationship between these SQL Server logins and Windows NT accounts and they are created through SQL Server.

To add an SQL Server login the SQL Server Enterprise Manager or the Transact-SQL system-stored procedure *sp_addlogin* can be used. To use the SQL Server Enterprise Manager:

⇨   Expand the server name.

⇨   Right-click *Logins* and then click *New Login.*

⇨   Select *SQL Server Authentication.*

⇨   In the *Name* box enter the login name.

⇨   In the *Password* box enter a password.

⇨   Optionally specify a default database and/or language to be set for this login.

⇨   Click *OK.*

The *New Login* dialog box is shown in Figure 9.4. Note that the SQL Server login name is not qualified by a domain name as it is not a Windows NT account or group name.

To use the Transact-SQL system-stored procedure:

```
EXEC sp_addlogin Jones, secret, payroll
```

This creates a SQL Server login of "Jones" with a password of "secret" and a default database of "payroll."

Note: Using the SQL Server Enterprise Manager or *sp_addlogin* will cause a row to be added to the *syslogins* table in the master database.

Figure 9.4

Creating a SQL Server Login

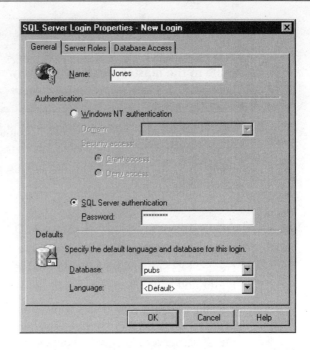

Can anyone create an SQL Server login? Again, this is an operation that grants access to the SQL Server, so it is restricted to those SQL Server accounts that belong to the *sysadmin* or *securityadmin* fixed-server roles.

9.3.7   Disallowing Access to SQL Server by Dropping an SQL Server Login

To remove a SQL Server login from SQL Server, the SQL Server Enterprise Manager or the Transact-SQL system-stored procedure *sp_droplogin* can be used. Unlike the case of Windows NT accounts and groups, there is no concept of revoking access versus denying access because an SQL Server login can only gain access through one route—the entry in *syslogins* for that specific login.

To use the SQL Server Enterprise Manager:

⇨   Expand the server name.

⇨   Click *Logins* and then in the *Results* pane, right-click the login to remove.

⇨   Click *Delete* and confirm the operation when prompted.

To use the Transact-SQL system-stored procedure:

```
EXEC sp_droplogin 'Jones'
```

Note: Using the SQL Server Enterprise Manager or *sp_droplogin* to remove a SQL Server login will cause a row to be deleted from the *syslogins* table in the master database.

Only members of the *sysadmin* or *securityadmin* fixed-server role can drop an SQL Server login.

9.4   Allowing Access to Databases

When a user has gained access to SQL Server he or she will need to access databases. Unless the user is given permission to do so, he or she will not be able to access any databases unless a *guest* database user account has been created in a database. The guest database user account will be discussed shortly.

To gain access to a database, a *database user account* must be created in the database and associated with the Windows NT login or SQL Server login. In the case of a Windows NT login, an individual Windows NT account can be associated with a database user account. If all the members of the Windows NT group are going to be performing the same tasks in the database then only the Windows NT group needs to be associated with a database user account.

To create a database user account in a database, the SQL Server Enterprise Manager or the Transact-SQL system-stored procedure *sp_grantdbaccess* can be used.

To use the SQL Server Enterprise Manager:

⇨   Expand the server name.

⇨   Click on + to expand the databases.

⇨   Click on + to expand the database of interest.

⇨   Right-click *Users* and then click *New Database User.*

⇨   Select an entry from the *Login Name* list box.

⇨   Choose a different entry in the *User Name* box if desired.

⇨   Choose database role membership if desired.

⇨   Click *OK.*

The concept of a *database role* will be discussed shortly. The *New User* dialog box is shown in Figure 9.5.

Figure 9.5

Creating a New Database User Account

To use the Transact-SQL system-stored procedure:

```
EXEC sp_grantdbaccess 'Europe\SmithF'
```

```
EXEC sp_grantdbaccess 'Europe\SmithF', Fred
```

In the first example the database user account will be named "Europe\ SmithF." In the second the database user account will be named "Fred."

Can anyone create a database user account in a database? This is an operation that grants access to a database, so it is restricted to members of the *db_accessadmin* or *db_owner* database roles only.

Note: Using the SQL Server Enterprise Manager or *sp_grantdbaccess* will cause a row to be added to the *sysusers* table in the database to which the database user account is being added.

So, once a user has successfully logged into SQL Server, he or she can access a database as long as he or she has a database user account in that database. If the user does not have a database user account in a database, then he or she cannot gain access to it. This is fine, but suppose you had hundreds of users who log into SQL Server and had database user accounts in various databases, but they all needed the same access to one special database in a limited fashion. Perhaps the database contains information on allowable business expenses that all the employees need to reference. A database user account could be created for each user, but this seems a little over the top. Instead we can make use of the special database user account *guest*.

Guest allows a login without a database user account to access a database. If a user who is successfully logged into SQL Server accesses a database in which he or she has no database user account, he or she will be associated with the guest database user account and will enjoy any permissions given to that account. If the guest database user account does not exist in a database, the user must have a database user account in the database in which access is required.

Note: The master and tempdb databases always contain a guest database user account.

So how is a guest database user account created? In the same way that any other database user account is created. However, the *Login Name* as shown in Figure 9.5 is left blank, as the guest database user account is not associated with any specific login.

9.5   Disallowing Access to Databases

A database user account may have been created in a database so that a Windows NT user or group can gain access to the database. It may have now become necessary to disallow access to the database. Database user accounts can easily be removed from a database as long as they do not own objects in the database.

To remove a database user account from a database, the SQL Server Enterprise Manager or the Transact-SQL system-stored-procedure *sp_revokedbaccess* can be used.

To use the SQL Server Enterprise Manager:

⇨   Expand the server name.

⇨   Click on + to expand the databases.

⇨   Click on + to expand the database of interest.

⇨   Click *Users* and then right-click the Database User Account to remove.

⇨   Click *Delete*.

⇨   Click *OK*.

To use the Transact-SQL system-stored procedure:

```
EXEC sp_revokedbaccess 'Europe\SmithF'
```

In the example the database user account "Europe\SmithF" will be removed from the current database.

Can anyone remove a database user account from a database? This is an operation that removes access to a database, so it is restricted to members of the *db_accessadmin* or *db_owner* database roles only.

Note: Using the SQL Server Enterprise Manager or *sp_revokedbaccess* will cause a row to be deleted from the *sysusers* table in the database to which the database user account is being removed.

9.6   Database and Object Ownership

Having created database user accounts, its worth mentioning a few words about database and object ownership. If you have been adding database user accounts you will have noticed that there is a database user account already created named DBO. This database user account stands for "database owner" and represents the owner of the database. The DBO database user account enjoys full permissions in the database because the database belongs to the DBO. How do you become the DBO? In other words, how does a login get mapped to this rather important database user account?

There are, in fact, a number of ways that this can happen. If a login creates a database, assuming that it has permission to do so, it will be mapped to the DBO database user account in that database. It can become the DBO of a database by being given the privilege. A member of the *sysadmins* fixed-server role can change the ownership of a database and bestow it on another login. This is achieved with the system-stored procedure *sp_changedbowner*:

```
EXEC sp_changedbowner 'COSMOS\Sue'
```

Finally, any member of the *sysadmins* fixed-server role is a DBO in a database.

All objects in a database such as tables and stored procedures have an owner. Typically, the creator of an object becomes its owner. By default, database user accounts should not have permission to create objects and it is a good practice to ensure that all objects in a database have the same owner—

usually DBO. Unlike previous versions of SQL Server, database object ownership can be changed. This is accomplished with the system-stored procedure *sp_changeobjectowner*:

```
EXEC sp_changeobjectowner MyTable, Marge
```

In this example, the database user account "Marge" becomes the owner of the object "MyTable."

Let us now look at how database user accounts can be grouped into roles inside an SQL Server database.

9.7   User-Defined Database Roles

In many ways, user-defined database roles are similar to Windows NT groups. Both offer an easier way to manage the permissions given and removed from individual users. Before we look at user-defined database roles let us look at the reasons why using Windows NT groups for permission management is a good idea.

Imagine a situation where a research organization had many researchers who were each individual Windows NT users. Many of the researchers are chemists and biologists. The chemists need access to a specific set of tables and stored procedures and the biologists need access to a different set. What approaches could be taken to assigning appropriate permissions?

Each individual Windows NT user could be given access to SQL Server, given a database user account in the research database, and then each of these database user accounts could be given a set of permissions. This would work but could be a nightmare to administer. Each new chemist or biologist would have to be individually granted access to SQL Server, given a database user account and given, perhaps, a complex set of permissions. What would happen if the chemists needed access to a new table? Each individual chemist's access would need to be changed.

A far simpler approach is to collect the individuals together who have the same set of access requirements and put them in a Windows NT group. In our example we would then have a Windows NT group Chemists and a Windows NT group Biologists. Individual Windows NT users would be placed in their respective groups, the group would be given access to SQL Server, and a database user account would be created in the research database for the group. That single database user account representing the group would be then be given permissions. As researchers joined and left the company their Windows NT accounts would be added to or removed from the appropriate Windows NT group.

Figure 9.6
*A Single Permission List
for the Chemists Role*

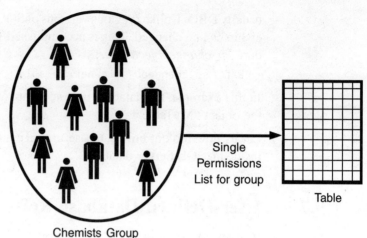

Single
Permissions
List for group

Table

Chemists Group

If the chemists needed access to a new table, the new permission would be implemented once on the single database user account associated with the Chemists group. As you can see, this is a far easier way to administer permissions to multiple individuals with the same access requirements.

So, using Windows NT groups is great but it does assume that something is true. It assumes that the SQL Server administrator is the same individual as the Windows NT administrator. In other words, the SQL Server administrator is free to create Windows NT groups as required and has the permission to do so. This is often not the case and this is where user-defined database roles help us out. User-defined database roles allow the SQL Server administrator to group individual database user accounts into roles within SQL Server.

Note: A database administrator setting up groups will have to decide whether to set the group up as a Windows NT group or as a database role. As mentioned above, the approach may be decided by the fact that the database administrator is not a Windows NT administrator. Another consideration might be the scope of the group. A database role has only the scope of a single database.

In our example above there may be a localized requirement in the research database to give a number of chemists and biologists extra permissions to work on a special project known as ProjectX. The SQL Server administrator can create a user-defined database role, perhaps called ProjectX, place the selected chemists and biologists in this role and then assign permissions to the role.

> **Note: A user-defined database role is specific to a given database. User-defined database roles do not span databases.**

If you are familiar with previous versions of SQL Server, you are probably thinking that roles sound a lot like database groups. They are similar in that both group users together, but that's pretty much where the similarity ends. User-defined database roles are much more powerful and flexible.

An annoying restriction in previous versions of SQL Server with database groups was that a database user could only be a member of one database group. This is not the case with user-defined database roles. A database user account can be a member of many user-defined database roles and, thus, the role model is the same as the Windows NT group model. Another way of thinking about this is that user-defined database roles overlap.

This is shown in Figure 9.7. As can be seen, not only do user-defined database roles overlap, but they can contain other user-defined database roles so hierarchies can be modeled.

Figure 9.7
Database Roles

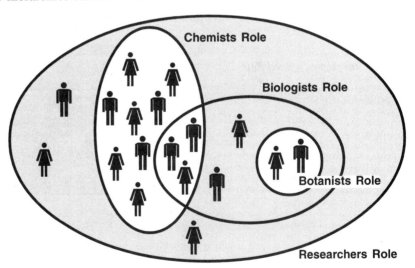

As can be seen in Figure 9.7, a database user account can be a member of more than one role and roles can contain roles. Some researchers are members of both the Chemists and Biologist roles. The Botanists role is a member of the Biologists role and the Chemists; Biologists and Botanists roles are members of the Researchers role.

9.7.1   Creating User-Defined Database Roles

To create a user-defined database role in a database the SQL Server Enterprise Manager or the Transact-SQL system-stored procedure *sp_addrole* can be used.

To use the SQL Server Enterprise Manager:

⇨   Expand the server name.

⇨   Click on + to expand the databases.

⇨   Click on + to expand the database of interest.

⇨   Right-click *Roles* and then click *New Database Role*.

⇨   Enter a name for the database role.

⇨   Designate the role as a *standard* role.

⇨   Add database user accounts or other roles into the role being created.

⇨   Click *OK*.

The *New Role* dialog box is shown in Figure 9.8. The user-defined database roles we have been discussing are designated as *Standard* in the *New Role* dialog box. *Application* roles will be discussed shortly.

Figure 9.8

Adding a New User-Defined Role

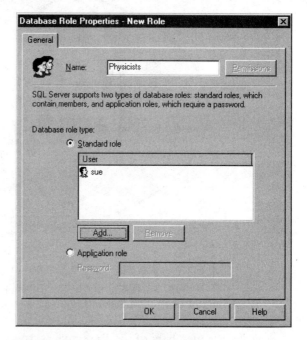

To use the Transact-SQL system-stored procedure:

```
EXEC sp_addrole Physicists
```

Can anyone create a user-defined database role in a database? This is an operation that is restricted to members of the *db_securityadmin* or *db_owner* database roles only.

Note: Using the SQL Server Enterprise Manager or *sp_addrole* will cause a row to be added to the *sysusers* table in the database to which the role is being added.

9.7.2   Removing User-Defined Database Roles

To remove user-defined database roles in a database, the SQL Server Enterprise Manager or the Transact-SQL system-stored procedure *sp_droprole* can be used.

To use the SQL Server Enterprise Manager:

⇨   Expand the server name.

⇨   Click on + to expand the databases.

⇨   Click on + to expand the database of interest.

⇨   Click *Roles*.

⇨   In the *Details* pane, right-click on the role to be removed.

⇨   Click *Delete*.

⇨   Click *OK*.

To use the Transact-SQL system-stored procedure:

```
EXEC sp_droprole Physicists
```

There are some restrictions concerning role dropping. Roles cannot be dropped if they contain members. The members must be removed from the role first as discussed in the next section. The *public* role cannot be dropped from a database. Also, fixed-database and server roles, described shortly, cannot be dropped.

Dropping a database role is an operation that is restricted to members of the *db_securityadmin* or *db_owner* database roles only.

Note: Using the SQL Server Enterprise Manager or *sp_droprole* will cause a row to be removed from the *sysusers* table in the database from which the role is being dropped.

9.7.3   Adding Members to User-Defined Database Roles

A user-defined database role can contain Windows NT users and groups, SQL Server logins, and other user-defined database roles. User-defined database roles are local to a database and so a user-defined database role cannot include a user-defined database role or database user account from another database.

To add a member to a user-defined database role in a database, the SQL Server Enterprise Manager or the Transact-SQL system-stored procedure *sp_addrolemember* can be used.

To use the SQL Server Enterprise Manager:

⇨   Expand the server name.

⇨   Click on + to expand the databases.

⇨   Click on + to expand the database of interest.

⇨   Click *Roles*.

⇨   In the *Details* pane, right-click the target role then click *Properties*.

⇨   Under *User*, click *Add* and select the users or roles to add to the target role.

⇨   Click OK to close the *Add Role Members* window.

⇨   Click *OK*.

The *Database Role Properties* dialog box is shown in Figure 9.8.

To use the Transact-SQL system-stored procedure:

```
EXEC sp_addrolemember Biologists, 'Aquila\Katy'
```

The above example adds the Windows NT user "Aquila\Katy" to the *Biologists* user-defined database role created previously.

```
EXEC sp_addrolemember Biologists,ExoBiologists
```

The above example adds the user-defined database role *ExoBiologists* to the Biologists user-defined database role.

Can anyone add a member to a user-defined database role in a database? Role owners can execute *sp_addrolemember* to add a member to any SQL Server role they own.

Note: Using the SQL Server Enterprise Manager or *sp_addrolemember* will cause a row to be added to the *sysmembers* table in the database to which the role member is being added.

9.7.4 Removing Members from User-Defined Database Roles

To remove a member from a user-defined database role in a database, the SQL Server Enterprise Manager or the Transact-SQL system-stored procedure *sp_droprolemember* can be used.

To use the SQL Server Enterprise Manager:

⇨ Expand the server name.

⇨ Click on + to expand the databases.

⇨ Click on + to expand the database of interest.

⇨ Click *Roles.*

⇨ In the *Details* pane, right-click the target role then click *Properties.*

⇨ Under *User*, select the user or role to remove and click *Remove.*

⇨ Click *OK.*

The *Database Role Properties* dialog box is shown in Figure 9.8.

To use the Transact-SQL system-stored procedure:

```
EXEC sp_droprolemember Biologists, 'Aquila\Katy'
```

The above example removes the Windows NT user "Aquila\Katy" from the *Biologists* user-defined database role created previously.

```
EXEC sp_droprolemember Biologists,ExoBiologists
```

The above example drops the user-defined database role *ExoBiologists* from the *Biologists* user-defined database role.

Only members of the *db_owner* or *db_securityadmin* roles or the role owner can execute *sp_droprolemember*.

Note: Using the SQL Server Enterprise Manager or *sp_addrolemember* will cause a row to be removed from the *sysmembers* table in the database to which the role member is being added.

9.8 Fixed-Database Roles

As well as the user-defined database roles that were discussed above, there exists a set of *fixed-database roles* in every database. Each of the fixed-database roles has a set of capabilities and membership of a fixed-database role grants these capabilities to the member. A member of a fixed-database role can be a Windows NT user, Windows NT group, SQL Server user, or user-defined database role.

A fixed-database role cannot itself be a member of a user-defined database role or another fixed-database role. The fixed-database roles are shown in Table 9.1.

Table 9.1
Fixed-Database Roles

Fixed-Database Role	Description
db_owner	Is able to perform the actions of all database roles as well as other maintenance and configuration activities in the database.
db_accessadmin	Is able to add or remove Windows NT groups, Windows NT users, and SQL Server users in the database.
db_datareader	Is able to read any data from all user tables in the database.
db_datawriter	Is able to add, modify, or delete data from all user tables in the database.
db_ddladmin	Is able to add, modify, or drop objects in the database.
db_securityadmin	Is able to manage roles and members of SQL database roles, and is able to manage statement and object permissions in the database.
db_backupoperator	Is able to back up the database.
db_denydatareader	Is not able to read any data in the database, but can make schema changes.
db_denydatawriter	Is not able to change any data in the database.

To view in detail the permissions associated with a fixed-database role, use the system-stored procedure *sp_dbfixedrolepermission*.

9.8.1 Adding Members to Fixed-Database Roles

To add a member to a fixed-database role in a database, the SQL Server Enterprise Manager or the Transact-SQL system-stored procedure *sp_addrolemember* can be used. In other words, the procedure is the same as adding a member to a user-defined database role.

To use the SQL Server Enterprise Manager:

⇨ Expand the server name.

⇨ Click on + to expand the databases.

⇨ Click on + to expand the database of interest.

⇨ Click *Roles.*

⇨ In the *Details* pane, right-click the target fixed-database role then click *Properties.*

⇨ Under *User*, click *Add* and select the users or roles to add to the fixed-database role.

⇨ Click OK to close the *Add Role Members* window.

⇨ Click *OK.*

The *Database Role Properties* dialog box is shown in Figure 9.8.

To use the Transact-SQL system-stored procedure:

```
EXEC sp_addrolemember db_backupoperator, 'Aquila\Kate'
```

The above example adds the Windows NT user "Aquila\Kate" to the *db_backupoperator* fixed-database role.

```
EXEC sp_addrolemember db_ddladmin, Biologists
```

The above example adds the user-defined database role *Biologists* to the *db_ddladmin* fixed-database role.

Can anyone add a member to a fixed-database role in a database? Only members of the *db_owner* role can execute *sp_addrolemember* to add a member to a fixed-database role.

Another database role that is created by SQL Server in each database is the *public* role. The public role contains every database user account and role within a database and, as such, it provides a useful mechanism to grant everyone some general permissions. Every database contains a public role and this role cannot be dropped. It provides the same function as the public group in previous versions of SQL Server.

9.8.2 Removing Members from Fixed-Database Roles

The method of removing members from fixed-database roles is identical to that used for removing members from user-defined database roles, that is, using the SQL Server Enterprise Manager or *sp_droprolemember*. Note that members cannot be removed from the *public* role. Only a member of the *db_owner* role can remove members from a fixed-database role.

9.9 Fixed-Server Roles

As well as fixed-database roles that are present in each database, there exists a set of *fixed-server roles* present at the server level, that is, independent of databases. Each of the fixed-server roles has a set of capabilities and membership of a fixed-server role grants these capabilities to the member. A member of a fixed-server role can be a Windows NT user, Windows NT group, or SQL Server login.

The fixed-server roles are shown in Table 9.2.

Table 9.2
Fixed-Server Roles

Fixed-Server Role	Description
sysadmin	Is able to perform any activity in SQL Server.
serveradmin	Is able to configure server-wide settings.
setupadmin	Is able to install replication and manage extended procedures.
securityadmin	Is able to manage server logins.
processadmin	Is able to manage processes running in SQL Server.
dbcreator	Is able to create and alter databases.
diskadmin	Is able to manage disk files.

9.9.1   Adding Members to Fixed-Server Roles

To add a member to a fixed-server role, the SQL Server Enterprise Manager or the Transact-SQL system-stored procedure *sp_addsrvrolemember* can be used.

To use the SQL Server Enterprise Manager:

⇨   Expand the server name.

⇨   Expand the *Security* folder.

⇨   Click on *Server Roles*.

⇨   In the *Details* pane, right-click the required fixed-server role and then click *Properties*.

⇨   On the *General* tab, click *Add* and select the logins to add to the fixed-server role.

⇨   Click OK to close the *Add Members* window.

⇨   Click *OK*.

To use the Transact-SQL system-stored procedure:

```
EXEC sp_addsrvrolemember 'Aquila\Mike', sysadmin
```

The above example adds the Windows NT user "Aquila\Mike" to the *sysadmin* fixed-server role.

Figure 9.9

Adding a Member to a Fixed-Server Role

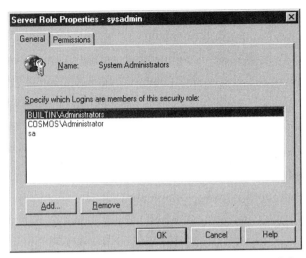

Can anyone add a member to a fixed-server role? Only members of the fixed-server role can execute *sp_addsrvrolemember* to add a member to that fixed-server role.

Note: Using the SQL Server Enterprise Manager or *sp_addsrvrole-member* will cause the *syslogins* table in the master database to be modified for the member.

9.9.2   Removing Members from Fixed-Server Roles

To remove a member to a fixed-server role the SQL Server Enterprise Manager or the Transact-SQL system-stored procedure *sp_dropsrvrolemember* can be used.

To use the SQL Server Enterprise Manager:

⇨   Expand the server name.

⇨   Expand the *Security* folder.

⇨   Click on *Server Roles.*

⇨   In the *Details* pane, right-click the target fixed-server role and then click *Properties.*

⇨   On the *General* tab, select the logins to remove and click *Remove.*

⇨   Click *OK.*

To use the Transact-SQL system-stored procedure:

```
EXEC sp_dropsrvrolemember 'Aquila\Mike', sysadmin
```

The above example removes the Windows NT user "Aquila\Mike" from the *sysadmin* fixed-server role.

Only members of the fixed-server role the member is being dropped from can execute *sp_dropsrvrolemember*.

Note: Using the SQL Server Enterprise Manager or *sp_dropsrvrole-member* will cause the *syslogins* table in the master database to be modified for the member.

9.10 Application Roles

The roles we have discussed so far revolve around the fact that permissions will be granted to collections of users to allow them to access a variety of database objects such as tables and stored procedures (the granting of permissions will be discussed later). It does not matter what application is used to access the objects—a Microsoft Visual Basic program, Microsoft Excel or the Query Analyzer, to mention a few—the permissions stay the same.

Sometimes, however, it becomes necessary to grant permissions on an individual application basis. Take the example shown in Figure 9.10.

Figure 9.10

The Sales Order Application

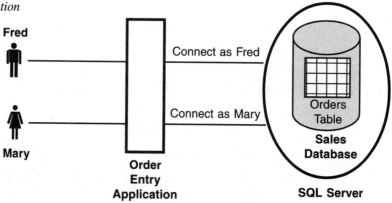

Suppose Fred and Mary are sales order clerks. They take orders on the telephone and enter order details into a Microsoft Visual Basic program that stores the information in an SQL Server database. The organization in which Fred and Mary work have adopted an integrated security approach, so Fred and Mary log into Windows NT in the morning, and when the application connects to SQL Server when they start it, they are logged into SQL Server as their Windows NT user accounts.

To allow Fred and Mary to perform their tasks, they must have been given permissions on the Orders table, such as INSERT, so that the application can insert new rows into it.

Mary has become a bit of an expert at Microsoft Excel and her supervisor decides that it would be useful if Mary could use Microsoft Excel to produce ad-hoc charts. So Mary is given access to Microsoft Excel from her desktop.

The problem is that when Mary connects to SQL Server using Microsoft Excel, she will have all the permissions given to her in order to support the execution of the Order Entry application. The permissions are associated with her user account and the roles in which it is a member—not the application. There is no problem accessing the database through the Order Entry application as it is a "captive" application and only provides certain functions to the user. In Microsoft Excel, Mary can browse any table to which she has permission. What we need is some way of granting permissions on an application basis. This is where *application roles* help out.

Application roles, like user-defined database roles, are database specific—they do not span databases. Also like database roles, application roles are granted permissions on database objects. However, there is a major difference. Application roles do not contain any members.

The way they are used is as follows. When an application connects to SQL Server, an application role can be activated by the execution of a system-stored procedure. The application role is then active on that connection. When an application role is activated on a connection, the connection permanently loses all permissions associated with the user login and the database roles to which it is a member. This state of affairs exists only for the lifetime of the connection.

In return, the connection acquires the permissions associated with the application role for the database in which the application role exists.

So let us relate this to our example. We want Fred and Mary to be able to execute the Order Entry application, which needs INSERT permission on the Orders table, but we want Mary to have few permissions when accessing data through Microsoft Excel.

We can create an application role named *OrderEntryAppRole* and grant INSERT to the Orders table and any other required permissions. We can remove the permissions granted to Fred and Mary previously, just leaving some low-level permissions to allow Mary to do her Microsoft Excel work.

In the Order Entry application, just after the connection to SQL Server is made for the user starting the application, the *OrderEntryAppRole* is activated. The connection loses its default permissions but gains the permissions of the application role. The application role has sufficient permissions to allow the Order Entry application to function correctly and for Fred and Mary to perform their work.

Now Mary starts Microsoft Excel. As the application role is not activated, she just enjoys her low-level default permissions that allow her to browse non-sensitive data but not to change it.

Fine, but how is an application role activated? When an application role is created, as described shortly, a password is associated with it. To activate an application role, this password must be supplied. Application role activation is performed by the application executing the system-stored procedure *sp_setapprole*.

```
EXEC sp_setapprole 'OrderEntryAppRole', 'secretpassword'
```

This example shows the application role *OrderEntryAppRole* being activated by supplying the password. The idea is that the application, not the user, knows about the password so it can activate the application role. In our example, the Order Entry application knows the password; perhaps it encrypts it and stores it in the registry, but Mary does not know it so she cannot activate the application role through Microsoft Excel. The Order Entry application merely executes the *sp_setapprole* system-stored procedure after it connects to SQL Server. The permissions obtained by activating the application role stay until the connection terminates.

9.10.1   Creating Application Roles

Application roles can be created using the SQL Server Enterprise Manager or Transact-SQL.

To create an application role in the SQL Server Enterprise Manager:

⇨   Expand the server name.

⇨   Click on + to expand the databases.

⇨   Click on + to expand the database of interest.

⇨   Right-click *Roles* and then click *New Database Role*.

⇨   Enter a name for the database role.

⇨   Designate the role as an *application* role.

Figure 9.11

Creating an Application Role

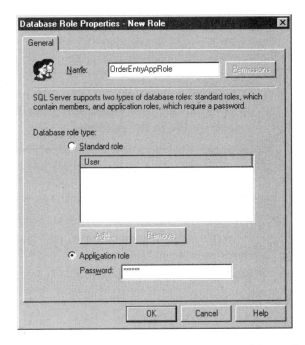

To use Transact-SQL, the system-stored procedure *sp_addapprole* is used:

```
EXEC sp_addapprole 'OrderEntryAppRole', 'secretpassword'
```

9.10.2 Removing Application Roles

To remove an application role in a database the SQL Server Enterprise Manager or the Transact-SQL system-stored procedure *sp_dropapprole* can be used.

To use the SQL Server Enterprise Manager:

⇨ Expand the server name.

⇨ Click on + to expand the databases.

⇨ Click on + to expand the database of interest.

⇨ Click *Roles*.

⇨ In the *Details* pane, right-click on the role to be removed.

⇨ Click *Delete*.

⇨ Click *OK*.

To drop an application role with the system-stored procedure *sp_dropapprole*:

```
EXEC sp_dropapprole 'OrderEntryAppRole'
```

Creating and dropping an application role is an operation that is restricted to members of the *db_securityadmin* or *db_owner* database roles only.

Note: Using the SQL Server Enterprise Manager, *sp_addapprole* or *sp_dropapprole* will cause a row to be added or removed from the *sysusers* table in the database.

9.11 Permissions

The ultimate goal of SQL Server security is to allow and disallow users and roles the ability to, for example, read and write data, execute stored procedures, and create tables.

It is useful to group the different types of permissions into the following categories:

+ Object Permissions.
+ Statement Permissions.
+ Implied Permissions.

9.11.1 Object Permissions

Object permissions are required when objects such as tables, views, and stored procedures need to be accessed. When an object is created, its owner is the database user account that created it and only the owner can access it.

To allow other users to access the object, the owner must grant permissions to that user on the object. The list of permissions that can be granted to objects is shown in Table 9.3:

Table 9.3
Objects and Object Permissions

Object Permission	Relevant Objects
SELECT	Table, view, columns
UPDATE	Table, view, columns
INSERT	Table, view
DELETE	Table, view
REFERENCE	Table
EXECUTE	Stored procedure

It can be seen that different objects support different permissions. For example, tables and views support SELECT permission, whereas stored procedures only support EXECUTE permission. The SELECT and UPDATE permissions can be set at the column level, whereas INSERT and DELETE permissions can only be granted at the table or view level.

Note: From a security management perspective, setting permissions at the column level can be complex to administer. It is better to create views that contain only those columns to which access is to be granted.

The REFERENCES permission allows the owner of a table to use columns in a table owned by another user as the target of a REFERENCES FOREIGN KEY constraint. FOREIGN KEY constraints are described in Chapter 7.

9.11.2   Statement Permissions

To allow users to perform tasks such as creating a stored procedure or table or backing up a database requires the use of statement permissions. Unlike object permissions, statement permissions do not refer to any objects. The statement permissions are shown below:

```
CREATE DATABASE     CREATE RULE
CREATE DEFAULT      CREATE PROCEDURE
CREATE TABLE        CREATE VIEW
BACKUP DATABASE     BACKUP LOG
```

9.11.3   Implied Permissions

There are a number of tasks for which there are no explicit permissions that can be granted. The authority to perform these tasks is granted by virtue of the fact that the user or role is a member of a fixed-server role or is in fact the owner of an object. For example, members of the *sysadmin* fixed-server role can configure the SQL Server or shut it down. A table owner can create an index on the table.

9.11.4   Granting Permissions

Object and statement permissions can be granted by using the SQL Server Enterprise Manager or the Transact-SQL GRANT statement.

To use the SQL Server Enterprise Manager to grant object permissions:

⇨   Expand the server group and expand the server.

⇨   Expand *Databases* and then expand the database.

⇨   Click the type of object required, for example, *Tables*.

⇨   Right-click the object, and then click *All Task*s.

⇨   Click *Manage Permissions* and select the required permissions

⇨   Click *OK*.

Figure 9.12 shows the permissions grid with which object permissions can be granted. Granting object permission is performed by mouse-clicking the appropriate object permission next to the appropriate object.

Figure 9.12

Granting Object Permissions

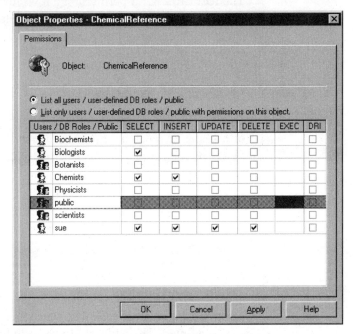

Note that the symbol showing two users represents a database role—user-defined or application. The single user symbol represents a database user account that may be mapped to a Windows NT user or Windows NT group or a SQL Server login.

To grant statement permissions using the SQL Server Enterprise Manager:

⇨   Expand the server group and expand the server.

⇨   Expand *Databases* and right-click the database.

⇨   Click *Properties* and click the *Permissions* tab.

⇨   Select the required statement permissions.

⇨   Click *OK*.

Figure 9.13 shows the permissions grid with which statement permissions can be granted. Granting permission is performed by mouse-clicking the appropriate statement permission next to the appropriate database user account or role.

Figure 9.13

Granting Statement Permissions

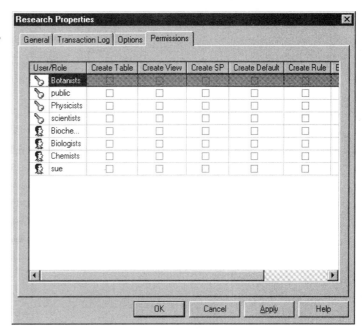

Granting object permissions and statement permissions with Transact-SQL is accomplished by means of the GRANT statement.

To grant object permissions:

```
GRANT DELETE ON ChemicalReference TO [aquila\chemists]
```

This statement grants the database user account [aquila\chemists] the authority to delete rows from the *ChemicalReference* table.

```
GRANT ALL PRIVILEGES ON ChemicalReference TO
[aquila\biologists]
```

This grants the database user account [aquila\biologists] the authority to select, insert, update, and delete rows from the *ChemicalReference* table. Basically, the ALL keyword grants all permissions on the object.

```
GRANT SELECT ON ExperimentalResults TO public
```

This gives the *public* role the authority to select from the *ExperimentalResults* table. This means that every database user account and role in the database can select from this table.

```
GRANT SELECT ON ChemicalReference TO [aquila\labtechs] WITH
GRANT OPTION
```

This fourth statement grants the database user account [aquila\labtechs] the authority to select rows from the *ChemicalReference* table. The WITH GRANT OPTION clause gives the database user account [aquila\labtechs] the ability to grant SELECT permission to others, that is, the ability to grant the permission is granted as well as the permission itself.

To grant statement permissions:

```
GRANT CREATE PROCEDURE, CREATE TABLE TO [aquila\chemists]
```

The statement gives the database user account [aquila\chemists] the authority to create tables and stored procedures.

```
GRANT ALL TO [aquila\biologists]
```

This gives all the statement permissions to the database user account [aquila\biologists].

Note: Granting permission causes a row to be inserted in the *sysprotects* system table present in the user database.

9.11.5   Revoking and Denying Permissions

Once an object or statement permission has been granted to a database user account or role, it can be revoked, which means that the permission is taken away. In terms of the *sysprotects* system table in the user database, the row that was inserted by the GRANT statement is deleted by the REVOKE statement. This is fine, but if the user is a Windows NT user who is a member of a Windows NT group that also has been granted permissions on the object, or is a member of a database role that has permissions on the object, then the user will still be able to access the object. This is because of permissions gained through the Windows NT group or database role membership.

Therefore, it is also possible to use the DENY statement to deny permissions. If a database user account or role is denied permissions, then no matter what permissions are obtained through Windows NT group or database role membership, the database user account will be denied them. Normally the database user account receives the union of the permissions granted to the Windows NT groups and database roles that it is a member of.

Revoking and denying permissions through the SQL Server Enterprise Manager is the same as granting permission. Granting permission is performed by mouse-clicking the appropriate permission next to the appropriate database user account, so that a tick appears in the checkbox. Revoking permissions is performed in the same way, making sure that the check box is cleared. Denying permission in achieved by clicking the checkbox such that a red cross appears.

Note: Denying permission adds a row to the *sysprotects* system table or modifies the appropriate row if it is already present.

Using Transact-SQL to revoke permissions is shown below:

```
REVOKE DELETE ON ChemicalReference FROM [aquila\chemists]
```

This revokes the authority to delete rows in the *ChemicalReference* table from the database user account [aquila\chemists]. They may still be able to delete rows in the *ChemicalReference* table if database roles that they are members of have DELETE permission on the table.

```
REVOKE ALL PRIVILEGES ON ChemicalReference FROM
[aquila\chemists]
```

This revokes the authority to select, insert, update, and delete rows in the *ChemicalReference* table from the database user account [aquila\chemists]. They may still be able to manipulate data in the *ChemicalReference* table if database roles that they are members of have permissions on the table.

```
REVOKE CREATE PROCEDURE, CREATE TABLE FROM
[aquila\chemists]
```

This statement revokes the authority to create tables and stored procedures from the database user account [aquila\chemists]. They may still be able to create tables and stored procedures if database roles that they are members of have these statement permissions.

Using Transact-SQL to deny permissions is shown below:

```
DENY DELETE ON ChemicalReference TO [aquila\chemists]
```

The statement denies the authority to delete rows in the *ChemicalReference* table from the database user account [aquila\chemists]. They will not be able to delete rows in the *ChemicalReference* table even if database roles that they are members of have DELETE permission on the table.

```
DENY ALL PRIVILEGES ON ChemicalReference TO [aquila\chemists]
```

This statement denies the authority to select, insert, update, and delete rows in the *ChemicalReference* table from the database user account [aquila\chemists]. They will not be able to manipulate data in the

ChemicalReference table even if database roles that they are members of have permissions on the table.

```
DENY CREATE PROCEDURE, CREATE TABLE TO [aquila\chemists]
```

This statement denies the authority to create tables and stored procedures from the database user account [aquila\chemists]. They will not be able to create tables and stored procedures even if database roles that they are members of have these statement permissions.

9.11.6   Permission Chains

We have already met the concept of a view in Chapter 4. A view is a very useful object as far as security is concerned because it enables a database designer to hide sensitive information. For example, the following view only contains non-sensitive columns in its definition:

```
CREATE VIEW AuthorsNamesVW
      AS SELECT au_id, au_lname, au_fname
      FROM authors
```

Using the permissions mechanism we have just met, we can set up a powerful and flexible security mechanism using views. We could, for example, grant users SELECT permission on the *AuthorsNamesVW* view but not give them SELECT permission on the base table. They could only then access the data through the view, not directly from the table.

The same approach can be used with stored procedures. A database user account or database role can be given EXECUTE access to a stored procedure, but no access to the objects it accesses. In this way, a stored procedure can be written to insert, update, and delete data, but the user has no authority to do this directly—he or she can only execute the stored procedure.

Of course, views can be based on views, and stored procedures can call stored procedures that access views, so how does this all work together?

As long as the underlying objects have the same owner as the view or stored procedure to which the database user account has permission, then SQL Server will not check permissions on these underlying objects. This is known as an *ownership chain*. If an underlying object has a different owner, then the ownership chain is *broken* and SQL Server will have to do an explicit permission check on the affected underlying objects. This is a good reason to ensure that all objects in the database have the same owner.

10

Indexing, the Query Optimizer, and Locking

10.1   Introduction

We have previously discussed how data can be inserted into and retrieved from a table using Transact-SQL statements. SQL Server can be accessed using many products other than Transact-SQL. Examples of such products from Microsoft are Microsoft Access and Microsoft Visual Basic.

Workloads may be characterized as online transaction processing (OLTP) or decision support. OLTP transactions are usually short-lived, access few tables, and often result in writes to the database. Decision support transactions are usually long-lived and complex, access many tables, and rarely write to the database. Real-life workloads are usually a mixture of the two.

Irrespective of the tool used or the workload type, the database designer will want to minimize the time and system resources needed to access the requested data. Therefore, in this chapter we will look at indexing and the query optimizer. Getting your indexing strategy correct so that the query optimizer chooses the most efficient plan for your query can result in massive query performance improvements. Conversely, choosing a poor index design can mean that queries that should take seconds take minutes or even hours. We will also look at locking in this chapter. Using the correct locking approach when accessing data can be critical to performance in a multi-user application.

10.2   Indexed Access

Suppose we execute the following Transact-SQL statement:

```
SELECT * FROM accounts WHERE account_no = 122345
```

How would SQL Server find the appropriate row? It could search the *accounts* table from the start of the table to the end of the table looking for rows that had an account number that contained the value 122345. This might be fine for small tables containing just a few rows, but if the table contained millions of rows the above query would take a very long time to complete. This is like searching through a book page by page looking for the mention of a particular topic. You would have to start at page one and you would carry on searching until you reached the last page of the book.

What is needed is a fast and efficient way of finding the data that conforms to the query requirements. In the case of a book there is usually an index section whereby the required topic can be found in an alphabetically sorted list and the numbers of the pages that feature that topic can then be obtained. The required pages can then be directly accessed in the book.

The method used to directly retrieve the required data from a table in SQL Server is not unlike that used with books. An object called an index may be created on a table, which enables SQL Server to quickly look up the *database pages* that hold the supplied key value, in our example the value 122345 for the *account_no* column.

Unlike a book, which normally has one index, a table may have many indexes. These indexes are based on one or more columns from the table. If an index is based on a particular column or group of columns, then a query that features the same columns in its WHERE clause may be able to retrieve the required data via the index. The ultimate decision as to whether an index is used or whether a complete scan of the table is performed is made by a component of SQL Server known as the *query optimizer,* which we shall discuss later in this chapter.

If queries can be assisted by indexes, why not create lots of indexes on every table? Unfortunately, like so many areas in database technology, there are pros and cons concerning the use of indexes. On one hand indexes can speed up access to data, but on the other hand, they can slow down table insertions, updates, and deletions. This is because SQL Server has more work to do maintaining all the indexes to ensure that they always truly reflect the current data in the table. Indexes also take up disk space.

Clearly, if disk space is plentiful and the database is predominantly read-only, there are good reasons to create many indexes. In reality, most databases experience a mixture of read and write activity, so the correct choice of indexes is critical to good performance. The choice of appropriate indexes should be a product of good up-front design and transaction analysis.

SQL Server supports two types of indexes that may be created on a table.

- Clustered
- Nonclustered

10.2.1   Clustered Indexes

One clustered index may be created per table. Creating a clustered index forces the data rows in the table to be reordered on disk such that they are in the same order as the index key. For example, if we were to create a clustered index on the *au_lname* column of the *authors* table, the data rows would be sorted so that their physical order on the disk was in ascending order of the last name. That is, "Bennet" would appear in a database page that preceded the database page that held "White."

This order would be maintained as long as the clustered index was present. SQL Server would ensure that the insertion of a new data row would cause the row to be placed in the correct physical location. In the authors example, the insertion of an author "England" would cause the new row to be stored between the "Bennet" and "White" rows and the subsequent insertion of an author "Stanley" would cause the new row to be stored between the "England" and "White" rows.

A clustered index, then, is tightly coupled with the underlying table rows. The order of the rows on disk is governed by the index. Also, if a clustered index is created in a filegroup separate to that of its table, the table will migrate automatically to the filegroup containing the clustered index.

To create a clustered index in Transact-SQL, the CREATE INDEX statement is used:

```
CREATE UNIQUE CLUSTERED INDEX CI_account_no  ON accounts
(account_no)
```

The above example creates a clustered index on the *account_no* column of the *accounts* table. The *unique* clause ensures that more than one row cannot have the same key value, in this case *account_no*. Note that the table may or may not already contain data. If it does and there are duplicate values in the *account_no* column the above CREATE INDEX statement will fail:

```
CREATE UNIQUE CLUSTERED INDEX CI_account_no  ON accounts
(account_no)

Server: Msg 1505, Level 16, State 1, Line 1
CREATE UNIQUE INDEX terminated because a duplicate key was
found. Most significant primary key is '105000'.
```

Similarly, once the index has been successfully created, an attempt to insert or update a row that would result in a duplicate key value will fail:

```
INSERT ACCOUNTS
  (account_no, customer_no, branch_no, balance, account_notes)
  VALUES
(1000, 1005, 1001, 101.27, 'Never Overdrawn')
```

```
Server: Msg 2601, Level 14, State 3, Line 1
Cannot insert duplicate key row in object 'accounts' with
unique index 'CI_account_no'.
The statement has been terminated.
```

This is fine because we want the *account_no* column to contain no duplicate values since this is the way we uniquely identify an account. Suppose instead, we wish to create a clustered index on the customer table using the customer name as a key. We will want to create an index that does not enforce unique values:

```
CREATE CLUSTERED INDEX CI_customer_name ON customers
(lastname, firstname)
```

As the above example shows, we accomplish this by merely omitting the UNIQUE keyword. The above example also shows that an index may be created consisting of more than one table column. This is known as a *composite* index. An index can be created consisting of no greater that 16 columns that in practical terms is a limit few people are likely to hit. Also, the sum of the column sizes in the index cannot be greater than 900 bytes.

As mentioned previously, only one clustered index can be created on a table, which makes sense because data can only be physically sorted in one order. Any attempt to create a second clustered index will fail.

```
CREATE CLUSTERED INDEX CI_customer_no  ON accounts
(customer_no)
Msg 1902, Level 16, State 1
Server: Msg 1902, Level 16, State 3, Line 1
Cannot create more than one clustered index on table 'ac-
counts'. Drop the existing clustered index 'CI_account_no'
before creating another.
```

Let us look at the structure of a clustered index in more detail. Figure 10.1 shows the structure of a simple clustered index defined on the *last_name* column of a customer table.

The data pages contain rows from the *Customers* table and in the above example we have chosen to show just the *lastname* and *firstname* columns in the table rows. In a clustered index, the *leaf level* is considered to be the data pages containing the table rows. Note that the data rows are in the same key sequence as the clustered index.

Above the data pages are *index pages* that contain entries that point to the data pages. This is a traditional hierarchical index structure with a top level index page (the root) pointing to intermediate index pages that eventually point to the data page level. Note that the index pages at the same level in

Figure 10.1
The Structure of a Clustered Index

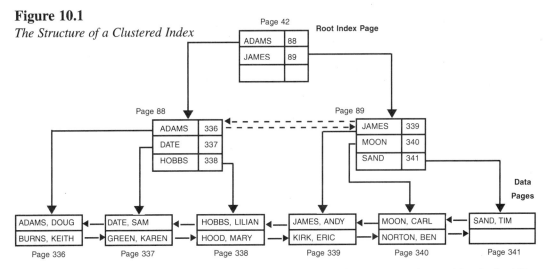

the index structure are linked by *next* and *previous* pointers (the dashed line arrows) in key sequence order. This enables SQL Server to easily process index pages at the same level in ascending or descending key sequence order. In a clustered index, the data pages are also linked by *next* and *previous* pointers (the dashed line arrows) in key sequence order to enable the data pages to be processed in ascending or descending key sequence order.

Note that in a clustered index only the first table row in the data page is pointed to. Because the table rows are in key sequence, it is not necessary to point to every table row in the data page. In the above example, the first table row in data page 337 has a key value of "Date." The first table row in the next data page, page 338, has a key value of "Hobbs." SQL Server knows that if a row is requested with a key value of "French" then it must be in data page 337.

Note: In reality, page numbers are not unique in a database. Instead, they are unique in a database file. The combination *File ID:Page Number* uniquely identifies a database page. The File ID has been left out of Figure 10.1 to simplify it.

10.2.2   Nonclustered Indexes

Unlike clustered indexes, many nonclustered indexes may be created per table. In fact up to 249 nonclustered indexes may be created. Creating a nonclustered index, unlike a clustered index, does not force the data rows in the table to be reordered on disk such that they are in the same order as the index key. For example, if we were to create a nonclustered index on the *branch_no* column of the *accounts* table, the data rows would not be moved.

Any order in the table rows would be maintained only if a clustered index was present; the nonclustered indexes present on the table have no influence on the order at all. If only nonclustered indexes were present on a table, data that was inserted would be placed at the end of the existing data (assuming there was no free space in pages at the beginning of the table).

A nonclustered index, then, is not tightly coupled with the underlying table rows and the order of the rows on disk is not governed by the index. Also, if a nonclustered index is created on a filegroup separate from the table, the table will not migrate automatically away from the filegroup it resides in to the nonclustered index filegroup as it would with a clustered index. If a clustered index is created or dropped on a table that already has nonclustered indexes created, then all the nonclustered indexes will also be automatically rebuilt.

To create a nonclustered index, the CREATE INDEX statement is used as it was for creating the clustered index, only in this case NONCLUSTERED is specified.

```
CREATE UNIQUE NONCLUSTERED INDEX NCI_customer_no
   ON customers (customer_no)
```

If neither CLUSTERED nor NONCLUSTERED is specified a nonclustered index is created.

Let us look at the structure of a nonclustered index in more detail. Figure 10.2 shows the structure of a simple nonclustered index.

The first observation that we can make is that every data row in the table has a pointer to it from the index leaf level (the dotted lines ending with a black circle). This was not the case with the clustered index in Figure 10.1 where the lowest level of index pages only contained pointers to the lowest keyed data row in each page. This means that nonclustered indexes are typically larger than their clustered counterparts because their leaf level has to hold many more pointers. If there were N customer rows per data page, the leaf level of the nonclustered index will need to hold N times more pointers. The typical effect of this is that a nonclustered index on a key will usually have one more level of index pages than a clustered index on the same key.

Note that, like a clustered index, the index pages at the same level in the index structure are linked by *next* and *previous* pointers (the dashed line arrows) in key sequence order. Unlike a clustered index, the data pages are

Figure 10.2

The Structure of a
Nonclustered Index

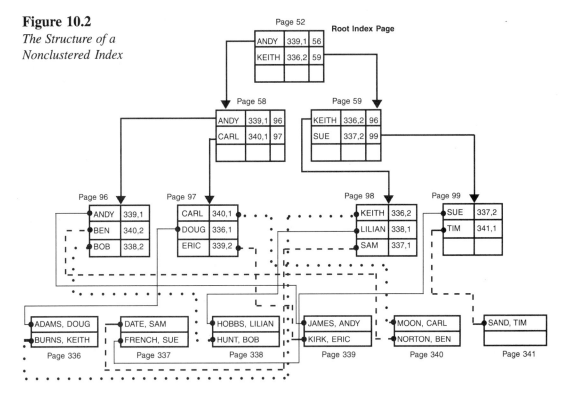

not linked by *next* and *previous* pointers.

What do the index entries in a nonclustered index look like? Like a clustered index, they contain a key value and a pointer to the relevant index page at the next lowest level. Eventually, the leaf level points to the data row. However, the pointer in the leaf level of a nonclustered index is a *row id* as long as there is no clustered index present on the table. A row id is a page number plus a row number. In Figure 10.2 the leaf level index page 96 has an entry for the key "Andy" that points to page 339, row number 1. The intermediate level index pages are similar to those found in a clustered index in that they contain a page pointer to the relevant index page at the next lowest level.

Note: As previously mentioned, a database page number is only unique within a file. Therefore, a row id is actually a combination of file ID, page number, and row number.

An important observation to make about Figure 10.2 is that, although the index levels are in key sequence order, the data is not. This means that any kind of range retrieval performed using the sorted index will have to issue a page request to follow each relevant leaf level pointer to the data rows themselves. Note also that once the leaf level has been accessed, SQL Server knows whether a row exists or not.

We have stated that the pointer in the leaf level of a nonclustered index is a *row ID* as long as there is no clustered index present on the table. A row ID is a page number plus a row number. What is the format of the pointer if there is a clustered index present on the table? The pointer is, in fact, the clustering key.

Figure 10.3

The Nonclustered Index Pointers in a Table with a Clustered Index

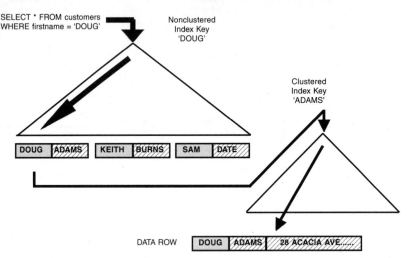

In our example, we have defined a nonclustered index on the *firstname* column of the *Customers* table and a clustered index on the *lastname* column.

Instead of the index pointer at the lowest level of the nonclustered index (the *leaf* level) being a *row ID*, it is now the clustering key; that is, it holds the *lastname* value for the row being referenced. This means that a query that uses the nonclustered index on the *firstname* column will traverse this index, obtain the clustering key, and use this to traverse the clustered index to the data row.

In Figure 10.3 we can see that the following query has been input:

```
SELECT * FROM customers WHERE firstname = 'Doug'
```

SQL Server traverses the nonclustered index, obtains the clustering key "Adams," and uses this to traverse the clustered index, which then points to the appropriate data row.

This may seem like a strange mechanism, but there are good reasons for implementing nonclustered indexes like this when there is a clustered index on the table. A clustered index forces the data to be placed in key sequence order. This requirement can be responsible for causing data pages to "split" to ensure that free space is available to store a new row in the correct key sequence location. Page splitting invariably results in rows migrating from their existing data page to a new data page, and so they change the page number on which they reside.

In the pre-SQL Server 7.0 mechanism, this meant that all nonclustered indexes defined for the table would have to have the relevant index entries modified because their row IDs changed. This "high cost" activity is eliminated in the SQL Server 7.0 mechanism because the row IDs are replaced by the clustering key and this is stable with respect to the page on which a row resides.

Note: SQL Server adds a number to a clustering key if duplicate values are present. This "uniqueifier" ensures that the index entries in the nonclustered index reference the correct data row via the clustering key. The "uniqueifier" is transparent to the application.

One consideration to make when designing indexes in SQL Server 7.0, however, is that a large clustered index key will be repeated in each nonclustered index on the table resulting in high space usage. Another consideration is the implication of creating and dropping a clustered index on a table. If a clustered index is created on a table, each existing nonclustered index will have to be rebuilt to use the clustering key. If the clustered index is removed, each existing nonclustered index will have to be rebuilt again to use row IDs. This will be discussed shortly.

10.2.3   CREATE INDEX Statement Options

As well as a CREATE INDEX statement specifying whether an index is to be unique, clustered, or nonclustered, other options can also be chosen. Let us now discuss some of these.

FILLFACTOR

The FILLFACTOR option specifies the packing density for a leaf level index page, that is, how much it should be filled when it is populated by the CREATE INDEX statement. If a leaf level index page is filled completely and a new index entry or row must be placed in it, the page will be *split* by SQL Server into two (or more) pages.

Note: By leaf level index page we mean the data pages in the case of a clustered index and the lowest level index pages (the level above the data pages) in the case of a nonclustered index.

Splitting a page is an expensive operation in terms of system resource and so, if page splitting can be minimized, it should be. One means of achieving this is to essentially reserve space in the index pages for future new entries and this can be done with the FILLFACTOR option. The FILLFACTOR is a value from 0 to 100. An index leaf level created with a FILLFACTOR of 100 will have its pages completely filled. This is useful if no data is to be entered into the table in the future.

An index created with a FILLFACTOR of 0 will have its leaf pages completely filled but other levels in the index will have enough space for a minimum of another index entry. An index created with a FILLFACTOR of between 0 and 100 will have its leaf pages filled to the FILLFACTOR percentage specified and, again, other levels in the index will have enough space for a minimum of another index entry.

The default FILLFACTOR value is 0 and this default value can be changed with the *sp_configure* system-stored procedure. Care should be taken when choosing a FILLFACTOR as its relevance will depend on the way the application uses the table data. For example, there is little point in reserving space throughout an index if the row inserted always has a key greater than the current maximum key value.

```
CREATE CLUSTERED INDEX CI_customer_name ON customers
(lastname, firstname)
WITH FILLFACTOR = 75
```

The above example creates an index with a FILLFACTOR of 75%. The FILLFACTOR only applies to the index creation. Over time, as rows are inserted into the table, the effectiveness of the FILLFACTOR value will vanish and so a planned rebuilding of critical indexes at periodic intervals should be considered.

An option that can be used with FILLFACTOR is PAD_INDEX. The addition of this option ensures that the FILLFACTOR percentage is applied to all the index pages in the index, not just the leaf pages.

IGNORE_DUP_KEY

The IGNORE_DUP_KEY option is useful when a unique clustered or unique nonclustered index is to be created on a table that might have rows with duplicate key values subsequently inserted into it as part of an INSERT...SELECT operation. If the IGNORE_DUP_KEY option is set, rows containing duplicate key values are discarded but the INSERT statement will succeed whereas, if the IGNORE_DUP_KEY option is not set, the INSERT will be aborted.

DROP_EXISTING

It was mentioned earlier that nonclustered indexes defined on a table would have to be rebuilt if a clustered index on the table were dropped. A clustered index being built on a table would also cause the nonclustered indexes to be rebuilt. It follows that, if a clustered index is dropped and recreated in order to rebuild it, each nonclustered index defined on the table would have to be rebuilt twice—once for the clustered index removal and once for its creation. This can be very expensive in terms of system resource.

To avoid this expensive operation, if a clustered index is to rebuilt, the index removal and creation can be replaced with a single CREATE INDEX statement using the DROP_EXISTING clause.

Note: To rebuild indexes that have been created automatically to support a PRIMARY KEY constraint or UNIQUE KEY constraint, use the DBCC DBREINDEX statement. This allows the index to be recreated without dropping the constraint.

STATISTICS_NORECOMPUTE

The STATISTICS_NORECOMPUTE option specifies that index statistics that are out-of-date are not automatically recomputed. Execution of the UPDATE STATISTICS statement omitting the NORECOMPUTE clause reverses this action. Index statistics are discussed shortly.

10.2.4 Creating Indexes Using the SQL Server Enterprise Manager

The SQL Server Enterprise Manager can be used to create indexes:

⇨ Expand the server group and expand the server.

⇨ Expand *Databases*, then expand the target database.

⇨   Click *Tables* and right-click the table on which the index is to be cre-
    ated.

⇨   Click *All Tasks* and *Manage Indexes*.

⇨   Click *New* to display the *New Index* dialog box.

⇨   Enter the index name, select the key columns and index options.

⇨   Click *OK* and *Close*.

The *New Index* Dialog Box is shown in Figure 10.4.

Figure 10.4

The New Index *Dialog Box*

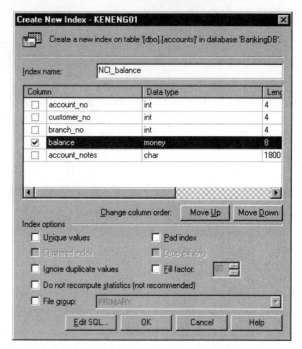

Indexes can also be created in the SQL Server Enterprise Manager through the
Design Table dialog box.

⇨   Expand the server group and expand the server.

⇨   Expand *Databases*, then expand the target database.

⇨   Click *Tables* and right-click the table on which the index is to be created.

⇨   Click *Design Table*.

⇨   Click the *Table and Index Properties* dialog box.

⇨   In the *Indexes/Keys* tab click *New* and enter the index details.

⇨   Click *Close* and save the changes.

The *Indexes/Keys* tab is shown in Figure 10.5.

Figure 10.5

The Indexes/Keys Tab

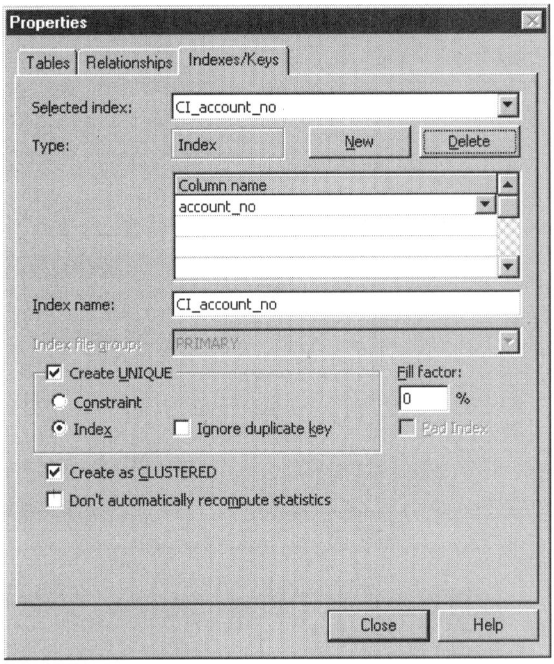

10.2.5 Using the Query Analyzer

Indexes may also be created through the Query Analyzer. If the graphical query plan is displayed, any table or index icon can be right-clicked and *Manage Indexes* chosen. If *New* is selected the *Create New Index* dialog box is chosen as shown in Figure 10.4.

10.2.6 Using the Create Index Wizard

An index may be created using the *Create Index Wizard*. This wizard takes you through a dialog where it shows you the existing indexes on the table, and then allows you to choose the columns that are to comprise the new index, index type, and fillfactor. An example is shown in Figure 10.6.

Another method of creating indexes is through the *Perform Index Analysis* option in the Query Analyzer. This is selected by right-clicking in the *Query* pane. The query (or queries) present in the *Query* pane will be analyzed. If SQL Server believes that an index would benefit the query, a CREATE INDEX statement is suggested, which can be accepted or discarded as shown in Figure 10.7.

Figure 10.6

The Create Index Wizard

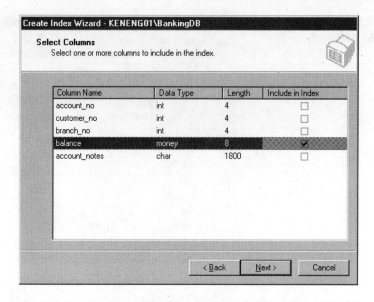

Figure 10.7

Performing a Query Analysis

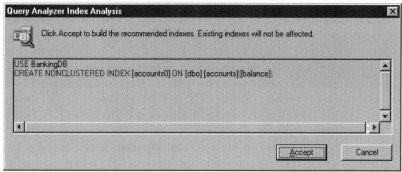

10.2.7   Dropping and Renaming Indexes

Both clustered and nonclustered indexes can be dropped with the DROP INDEX Transact-SQL statement:

```
DROP INDEX accounts.CI_account_no
```

Indexes may also be dropped by using the *Delete* button in the *Manage Indexes* dialog box, which is accessed through the SQL Server Enterprise Manager or Query Analyzer.

Indexes may be renamed by using the *sp_rename* system-stored procedure:

```
EXEC sp_rename 'accounts.CI_account_no', CI_account_num
```

Note the use of the single quotes.

Note: Indexes can be renamed through the SQL Server Enterprise Manager through the *Table and Indexes* dialog box in *Design Table*. However, if you examine the script generated you will see that the index is dropped and recreated—not the result you might wish!

10.2.8 Displaying Index Details

The indexes that are present on a table can be listed by using the *sp_helpindex* system-stored procedure:

```
EXEC sp_helpindex accounts
```

index_name	index_description	index_keys
CI_account_no	clustered, unique located on PRIMARY	account_no
NCI_balance	nonclustered located on PRIMARY	balance

10.3 The Query Optimizer

When we execute a query, whether by typing in a Transact-SQL statement or by using a Visual Basic program, it is highly likely we will be requiring that rows be read from one or more database tables. Suppose we require that SQL Server perform a join of two tables, table *A* containing a dozen rows and table *B* containing a million rows. How should SQL Server access the required data in the most efficient fashion? Should it access table *A* looking for rows that meet the selection criteria and then read matching rows from table *B*, or should it access table *B* first? Should it use indexes if any are present or do a table scan? If indexes are present and there is a choice of index, which indexes should SQL Server choose?

The good news is that SQL Server contains a component known as the *query optimizer,* which will automatically take a query passed to it and attempt to execute the query in the most efficient way. The bad news is that it is not magic and it will not come up with a great query plan if you do not write efficient queries or your indexing strategy is inadequate and does not support your workload. A database administrator should be aware of the factors that govern query optimization, what pitfalls there are, and how the query optimizer can be assisted in its job. Database administrators who know their data well can often influence the optimizer with the judicious use of indexes to choose the most efficient solution.

What do we mean by efficient in the context of the query optimizer? Basically, the query optimizer is looking to minimize the number of SQL Server resources required to fetch the required data. Resources include database page access and CPU.

10.3.1 Tools for Investigating Query Strategy

There are a number of tools at our disposal for checking what the query optimizer is doing. In the Query Analyzer we can request the display of the query optimizer strategy for a query with the following Transact-SQL statements:

* SET SHOWPLAN_TEXT
* SET SHOWPLAN_ALL

The SET SHOWPLAN_TEXT and SET SHOWPLAN_ALL statements display information showing how the query optimizer has decided to execute a query. The first statement outputs information in a form useful to MS-DOS applications such as the *osql* utility. SET SHOWPLAN_ALL returns more detailed output. Both these statements suppress the execution of the Transact-SQL statement or statements.

Here is an example of the output from the SET SHOWPLAN_TEXT statement:

```
StmtText
_____

SELECT * FROM accounts

StmtText
_____

    |-Table Scan(OBJECT:([BankingDB].[dbo].[accounts]))
```

We can see that the phrase *Table Scan* appears telling us that the query optimizer has chosen to scan the whole *accounts* table. The text of the Transact-SQL statement is also displayed.

Opposite is an example of the output from the SET SHOWPLAN_ALL statement.

As can be seen, the output is somewhat more verbose. This information includes cost information, such as CPU, and logical IO estimates (these are not absolute values but incorporate internal weightings). Again, we can see that the query optimizer has chosen a table scan strategy.

StmtText	StmtId
SELECT * FROM accounts	3
|—Clustered Index Scan(OBJECT:([BankingDB].[dbo].[accounts].[CI_account_no]))	3

NodeId	Parent	PhysicalOp	LogicalOp
1	0	NULL	NULL
3	1	Clustered Index Scan	Clustered Index Scan

Argument

NULL
OBJECT:([BankingDB].[dbo].[accounts].[CI_account_no])

DefinedValues

NULL
[accounts].[customer_no],[accounts].[branch_no],[accounts].[balance],
[accounts].[account_notes]

EstimateRows	EstimateIO	EstimateCPU	AvgRowSize	TotalSubtreeCost
10000.0	2.6323934	0.0110785	1838	2.6434717

OutputList

NULL
[accounts].[customer_no],[accounts].[branch_no],[accounts].[balance],
[accounts].[account_notes]

Warnings	Type	Parallel	EstimateExecutions
NULL	SELECT	0	NULL
NULL	PLAN_ROW	0	1.0

Note: The output has been broken onto multiple lines to aid clarity.

By far, the easiest way to view the query optimizer strategy is graphically in the Query Analyzer. This is accomplished in two ways. The *Display Estimated Execution Plan (CTRL + L)* button can be clicked that displays the graphical query plan without executing the query, or the *Execute Mode* button can be selected to enable the *Show Execution Plan (CTRL + K)* button to be clicked. This then causes the graphical query plan to be displayed in its own tab after the query has been executed. In other words, this option does not suppress query execution. Figure 10.8 shows an example of a graphical query plan. Figure 10.9 shows the same graphical query plan when the mouse cursor is passed over the table icon. Much detailed information is displayed concerning the query plan for the table. This information is similar to the information displayed by SET SHOWPLAN_ALL. The graphical execution plan must be read from right to left and from top to bottom.

Figure 10.8
A Graphical Query Plan

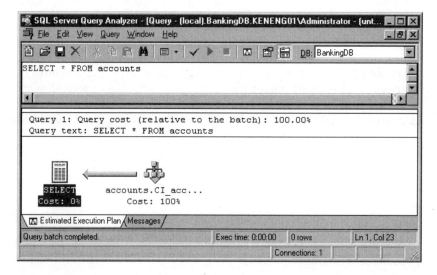

10.3.2   Example Query Strategies

Let us look at some queries:

Query 1: A query with a WHERE clause
```
SELECT * FROM accounts WHERE balance = 761.61
```

The query optimizer will attempt to use an index if there is an appropriate index present on the table. In this case, there are no indexes yet created on the table so a table scan is still performed, as shown in Figure 10.10.

Figure 10.9

Detailed Information from the Graphical Query Plan

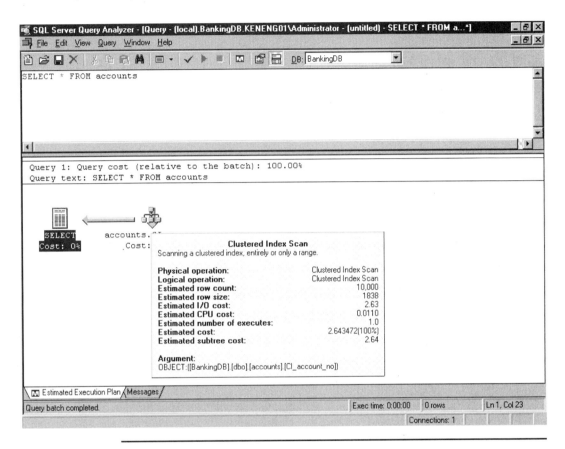

Note: The mouse can also be passed over the arrow symbol, in which case information is displayed showing the estimated number of rows returned from the operation at the start of the arrow.

Figure 10.10

The Graphical Query Plan for Query 1

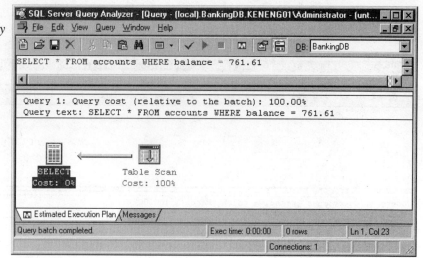

Figure 10.11

A Missing Statistics Warning

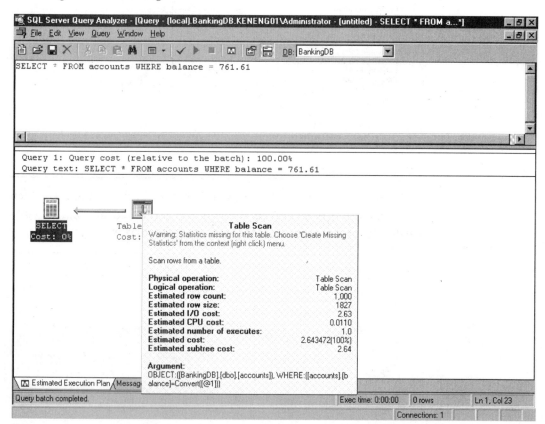

Although we cannot see it in the screenshot in Figure 10.10, the *Table Scan Cost : 100%* text is highlighted in red. There is a good reason for this visual warning. Let us pass the mouse pointer over the table graphic. The resulting display is shown in Figure 10.11.

We can see that the phrase *"Warning: Statistics missing for this table."* is displayed. SQL Server 7.0 can keep *distribution statistics* for the columns of tables. Unlike previous versions, these columns do not have to be part of an index key. Distribution statistics help the query optimizer estimate the cost of a query. Statistics can be created manually by right-clicking the table icon and choosing *Create Missing Statistics.* Or a database option *Auto create statistics* can be set that causes SQL Server 7.0 to automatically create distribution statistics for a column when a query is executed with a WHERE clause that specifies the column.

When an index is created, distribution statistics are created for the index column. Whether part of an index or not, SQL Server 7.0 will not update distribution statistics each time a row in the table is inserted, deleted, or updated—this would be too great a performance overhead. However, it will detect that distribution statistics have become out-of-date and automatically update them as long as this capability has not been turned off. This option can be turned off for the whole database, table, index, group of columns, or column.

The database administrator has no control over when an automatic statistics update will happen and how much data will be sampled in order to update the statistics. If the database administrator needs more control, he or she should update statistics manually by means of the graphical query plan or by using Transact-SQL. A table can be right-clicked in the graphical query plan and *Manage Statistics* chosen or the UPDATE STATISTICS Transact-SQL statement can be used.

Note: The system-stored procedure *sp_updatestats* **will execute the UPDATE STATISTICS Transact-SQL statement against all user tables in the current database.**

So, that's why we received a warning from the query optimizer. Let us now build an index on the *balance* column and issue the query again:

Query 2: A query with a WHERE clause supported by an index
```
SELECT * FROM accounts WHERE balance = 761.61
```

Figure 10.12 shows the new graphical display. We can immediately see that the icon has changed to something closely resembling an index. The rightmost icon represents an index seek and the index that is being used is named. The icon to the left of this is merely showing us that the pointer or pointers obtained from the index seek are now used to perform a lookup on the data. Indeed, an index named *NCI_balance* was created on the table prior to executing this query. Suppose we also create an index on the *customer_no* column and execute a query that also specifies this column.

Figure 10.12

Using an Index to Access Data

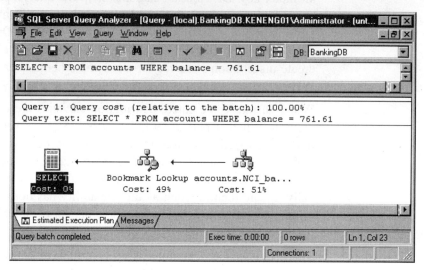

Query 3: A query with a WHERE clause supported by multiple indexes

```
SELECT * FROM accounts
WHERE
balance BETWEEN 750.00 AND 770.00
AND
customer_no BETWEEN 5 AND 100
```

Figure 10.13 shows the new graphical display. Instead of one simple left-to-right query plan, we can see that two streams come in from the right.

This is because the query optimizer has decided to make use of both indexes simultaneously. It has performed an *index intersection* in that it has obtained a set of pointers from the index on *balance* representing all the accounts with a balance between 750.00 and 770.00. It also obtained a set of pointers from the index on *customer_no* representing all the accounts with a customer number between 5 and 100 and discarded those pointers that are not present in each set.

It then uses the remaining pointers, which, by definition, represent accounts that satisfy both conditions, to access the account rows. As discussed previously in this chapter, an index pointer in a nonclustered index may be a row ID or a clustering key. There is no clustered index present on this table so the pointers will be row IDs. The *Hash Match/ Inner Join* is the technique used to internally find which pointers are members of both sets.

Figure 10.13
Using Multiple Indexes to Access Data

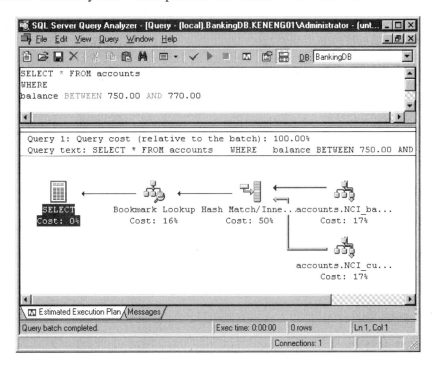

The benefit of the query optimizer's ability to use multiple indexes is that access to the data is minimized because candidate *accounts* table rows are eliminated before they are used to fetch a data row.

Query 4: A join query

The following query joins the *accounts* table with the *customers* table. An index has been created on the *customer_no* column on the *customers* table.

The query plan in Figure 10.14 shows a *Nested Loop* join operation processing the data streams from the two tables. Other join mechanisms are supported by SQL Server such as *hash* and *merge*.

Figure 10.14
Accessing Data from
Two Tables

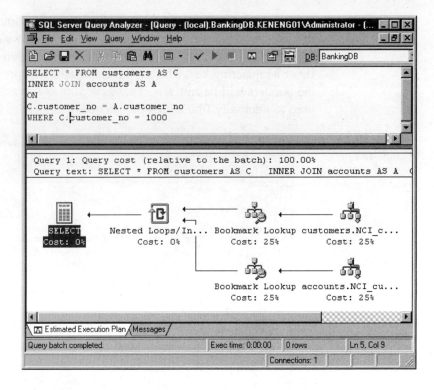

10.3.3   Vertical Table Partitioning

Another capability of the query optimizer is its support of *vertical table partitioning*.

Suppose that we have the following table in our database:

```
CREATE TABLE sales
    (
    ProductCode    CHAR(3),
    UnitSales      INT,
    SalesYear      CHAR(4)
    )
```

We might imagine that this table could contain hundreds of thousands of rows, perhaps millions, if we did not archive our rows but instead chose to keep the sales rows for the last few years. Probably our access to these rows would not be uniform. Perhaps 80% of accesses would be to this current year's data. It would be nice to be able to separate off the seldom-accessed data to other physical storage devices but we would want to maintain seamless access to the data for our applications.

We can achieve this by using more than one base table to hold the data and then using a view consisting of UNIONed SELECT statements to make the multiple physical tables appear as one table. For example, we could create the following tables:

```
CREATE TABLE sales97
  (
  ProductCode    CHAR(3),
  UnitSales      INT,
  SalesYear      CHAR(4)
   CHECK (SalesYear='1997')
  )

CREATE TABLE sales98
  (
  ProductCode    CHAR(3),
  UnitSales      INT,
  SalesYear      CHAR(4)
   CHECK (SalesYear='1998')
  )

CREATE TABLE sales99
  (
  ProductCode    CHAR(3),
  UnitSales      INT,
  SalesYear      CHAR(4)
   CHECK (SalesYear='1999')
  )
```

We could then create the following view definition:

```
CREATE VIEW AllSales AS
  SELECT * FROM Sales97
  UNION ALL
  SELECT * FROM Sales98
  UNION ALL
  SELECT * FROM Sales99
```

The CHECK constraint would ensure that no invalid data was entered into a table so, for example, the *sales99* table would only contain 1999 sales data.

Now, suppose we execute the following query:

```
SELECT * FROM AllSales
```

The graphical query plan is as shown in Figure 10.15.

Figure 10.15

*A Graphical Plan of
a Union View*

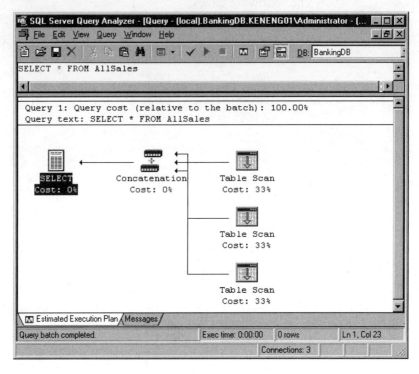

We can see that each table is accessed to retrieve the data and the results are
then UNIONed (concatenated) together. This is what we expect. However,
consider the following query:

```
SELECT * FROM AllSales WHERE SalesYear IN ('1998', '1999')
```

The graphical query plan for this query is shown in Figure 10.16.

The data to be concatenated is taken from just two tables. The query optimizer
has taken note of the CHECK constraints, and it therefore knows that it is
not possible that any of the sales data specified in the WHERE clause of the
query could be in the *sales97* table—so it does not waste time and resource
looking in it.

By carefully partitioning large tables in this way, performance gains can be
achieved.

Figure 10.16

A Graphical Plan of a Union View

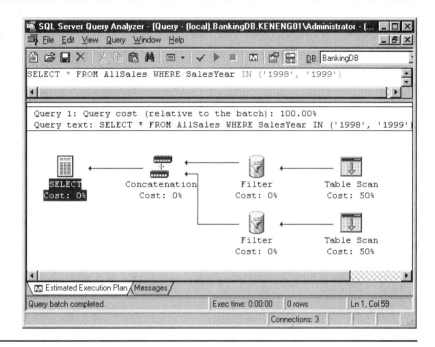

Note: It is possible for the database administrator to not validate the existing data in a table as part of the CHECK constraint creation. Also, CHECK constraints can be disabled. In these cases, the query optimizer will not consider the CHECK constraint to be a guarantee that a table does not contain relevant data, so it will search all tables when looking for rows that meet the selection criteria.

So, we have made a quick tour of the query optimizer. It is much more sophisticated in this version of SQL Server than in previous versions and probably deserves a book all to itself. The golden rule is to check the strategy adopted by the query optimizer to see that its chosen access method is what you expect—that it's not table scanning a million-row table when you thought you had created a great index!

Note: The query plan adopted by the query optimizer is also captured and displayed by the SQL Profiler. The SQL Profiler is discussed in Chapter 8.

We now need to delve into another important area as far as accessing data is concerned—locking.

10.4   SQL Server Locking

10.4.1   Why Lock Data?

A database that provides a multi-user environment where users are inserting, updating, and deleting data must provide a locking protocol, otherwise data inconsistencies may occur. Of course, if the environment is single-user, read-only, or both, a locking protocol is not necessary. However, many environments do not posses the read-only or single-user properties.

If an adequate locking protocol is not provided by a database management system, some classic inconsistency phenomena may occur. These phenomena are:

♦   Dirty read

♦   Buried update

♦   Non-repeatable read

♦   . Phantom read

A locking protocol of sufficient strictness should protect against all of these phenomena, however, it may be that many applications do not need to protect against all of these. The level at which transactions are protected against these phenomena is known as the *transaction isolation level*. This will be discussed in more detail shortly.

10.4.2   The Dirty Read Problem

In the example shown in Figure 10.17, Transaction 1 (Txn 1) makes a change to the stock level, subtracting 1000 items from the original 1100 items, leaving 100 items. Before Transaction 1 completes, Transaction 2 (Txn 2) is allowed to read the number of items in stock and retrieves the value 100.

Figure 10.17

The Dirty Read Phenomenon

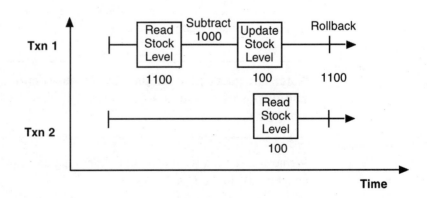

Transaction 1 now rolls back, the change is undone, and the stock level returns to 1100.

Transaction 2, by being allowed to see the uncommitted changes of Transaction 1, is now working with an erroneous copy of the data and possibly making ill-informed business decisions as a result.

This would not have happened if Transaction 2 had not been allowed to see the uncommitted changes of Transaction 1.

10.4.3   The Buried Update Phenomenon

In the example shown in Figure 10.18, Transaction 1 reads the stock level and retrieves the value 1100. Transaction 2 also reads the stock level and retrieves the value 1100.

Transaction 1 makes a change to the stock level, subtracting 1000 items from the original 1100 items, leaving 100 items.

Transaction 2 makes a change to the stock level, adding 200 items to the original 1100 items, giving 1300 items.

Now Transaction 1 writes its changed value of 100 to the database and commits its transaction. Shortly afterward, Transaction 2 writes its changed value of 1300 to the database and commits its transaction.

Figure 10.18
The Buried Update Phenomenon

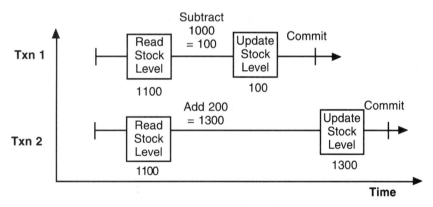

The change made by Transaction 1 has been lost or "buried." This probably has resulted in inconsistent stock levels in the database.

If the transactions had rechecked the stock levels before they made their change, Transaction 2 would have seen that there was a problem because the original value it read (1100) was no longer valid. Alternatively, by using locks, the problem could have been prevented.

10.4.4   The Non-Repeatable Read Phenomenon

In this example shown in Figure 10.19, Transaction 1 reads the stock level and retrieves the value 1100. Transaction 2 also reads the stock level and retrieves the value 1100.

Transaction 1 makes a change to the stock level, subtracting 1000 items from the original 1100 items, leaving 100 items.

Transaction 1 writes its changed value of 100 to the database and commits its transaction. Shortly afterward, Transaction 2 reads the stock level again and retrieves a value of 100.

When repeating its read, Transaction 2 has retrieved different values because another transaction had changed the value in between the reads.

Figure 10.19

The Non-Repeatable Read Phenomenon

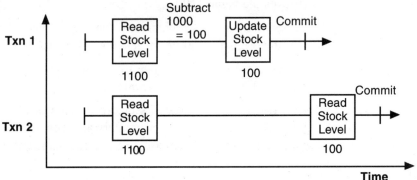

10.4.5   The Phantom Read Phenomenon

In the example shown in Figure 10.20, Transaction 1 counts the stock by its type and retrieves the value 10. Transaction 2 inserts a new stock item of type "X." Transaction 1 counts the stock by its type and retrieves the value 11.

The result has changed because Transaction 2 was allowed to add a new stock item.

This is similar in many ways to the non-repeatable read. However, the non-repeatable read is an update phenomenon, whereas the phantom read is an insert/delete phenomenon.

10.4.6   Transaction Isolation Levels

The previous section discussed the phenomena that can occur when adequate locking is not provided by the database management system. To protect against all these phenomena, a transaction must run at *serializable* isolation level. If transactions are serializable, then running them together

Figure 10.20

The Phantom Read Phenomenon

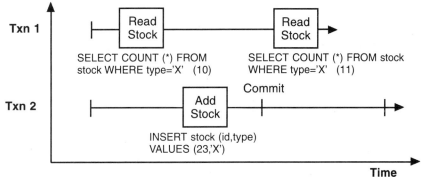

or running them in some serial order is guaranteed to produce the same result. This level of strictness is not needed by all applications because the type of work the application is performing means that some phenomena will not occur or it does not matter if they do.

The SQL-92 standard defines four transaction isolation levels that offer varying degrees of protection against the four phenomena. The four isolation levels are:

- Read Uncommitted.
- Read Committed.
- Repeatable Read.
- Serializable.

These transaction isolation levels protect against locking phenomena as shown in Table 10.1 below. A *Yes* means the phenomenon is allowed to happen. A *No* means it is prevented.

Table 10.1

Transaction Isolation Levels

Isolation Level	Dirty Read	Nonrepeatable Read	Phantom Read
Read Uncommitted	Yes	Yes	Yes
Read Committed	No	Yes	Yes
Repeatable Read	No	No	Yes
Serializable	No	No	No

SQL Server 7.0 supports all four levels. By default it runs at transaction isolation level Read Committed. The transaction isolation level can be set in a number of ways, as discussed later in this chapter.

10.4.7   Concurrency and Lock Granularity

In theory, locks could be taken out at the database level, table level, page level, row level, or column level. Locking at different levels provides more or less concurrency. Concurrency is a measure of sharing—how many users can share resources in the database at the same time. Low concurrency means low sharing—in a multi-user system this usually equates to low performance. High concurrency means high sharing. Many users are able to work together. This usually equates to high performance, as is shown in Figure 10.21.

Figure 10.21
Concurrency versus Locking Granularity

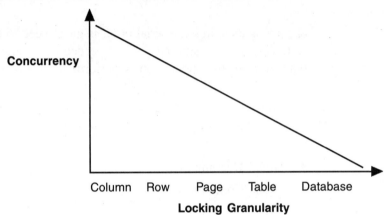

If the locking granularity is at the database level, a single lock can be used to control access to the database. When one user has the lock, he or she can change data in the database, but until he or she releases the lock, no one else can gain access to data and perform changes. Locking at the database level only provides low concurrency.

If the locking protocol is changed so that tables are locked instead of just the database, users are able to simultaneously change data in different tables but not in the same table. Concurrency has increased. Locking at the page level allows users to change data simultaneously in the same table but not in the same page. Locking at the row level allows users to change data simultaneously in the same page but not in the same row.

In theory, if locking individual columns were supported, this would provide the highest level of concurrency, as users would be able to simultaneously change data in rows but not the same column.

Locking at the database, then, provides the lowest level of concurrency, whereas locking at the row and column level provides the highest level of concurrency. So why not always lock at the column level?

Figure 10.22
System Resource versus
Locking Granularity

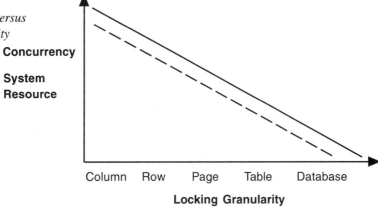

As Figure 10.22 shows, the finer the granularity of lock, the more system resource is used in terms of memory and CPU. Locking at the database level only uses one lock, whereas locking at the column level uses high numbers of locks and system resource.

Locking, therefore, is a compromise between concurrency and system resource. SQL Server 7.0 typically locks rows, pages, and tables. It does not lock columns, as doing so would probably mean using locks that were larger than the columns themselves! A database can be locked by putting it into single-user mode.

SQL Server 7.0 does not just lock at a given granularity, for example, rows. Instead, it locks at a granularity based on various factors, such as the amount of data accessed by the query. It does this to optimize the use of system resource. For example, if a query is going to change 100,000 rows, locking at the row level would cause 100,000 locks to be needed. It may be better to use a single lock to lock the whole table. The different locking granularities that SQL Server 7.0 can use are listed in Table 10.2, the coarsest granularity first.

Table 10.2
Locking Granularities

DB	The whole database.
Table	The whole table, including all data and indexes.
Extent	Contiguous group of eight data pages or index pages.
Page	An 8 KB data page or index page.
Key	A row lock in an index. Used to protect key ranges in serializable transactions.
RID	Short for row identifier. Used to lock a single row within a table.

SQL Server may take out locks at one level of granularity and subsequently escalate to another level of granularity. Locks can be escalated but cannot be de-escalated. The original granularity chosen by the lock manager is based on input from the query optimizer and other factors.

10.4.8   SQL Server Locking Modes

Depending on what a transaction is trying to achieve, for example update a row, SQL Server will use different lock modes. These lock modes determine what other transactions will be able to do. The lock modes are shown in Table 10.3.

Table 10.3
Lock Modes

Lock Mode	Use
Shared (S)	Used for read operations such as a SELECT statement.
Update (U)	Used on resources that can be updated. This lock is an optimization that prevents a common form of deadlock that can occur during updates.
Exclusive (X)	Used for operations that change data, for example, UPDATE, INSERT, and DELETE. This lock mode ensures that multiple transactions cannot change the same resource at the same time.
Intent	Used to establish a lock hierarchy. This enables SQL Server to avoid granting locks at a coarse level of granularity when other transactions hold finer grain locks. Intent locks include *intent shared* (IS), *intent exclusive* (IX), and *shared with intent exclusive* (SIX).
Schema	Used when an operation dependent on the schema of a table is executing. There are two types of schema locks— schema stability (Sch-S) and schema modification (Sch-M). For example, changes to a table definition may need to be blocked.
Bulk Update (BU)	Used when bulk copying data into a table and the *TABLOCK* hint is specified.

The lock modes described above are not all compatible with one another. For example, if a transaction is holding an exclusive (X) lock on a row, another transaction cannot take out an exclusive (X) lock or a shared (S) lock out on the row. In fact, the second transaction will be blocked. This stops it from reading or changing the uncommitted changes of the first transaction. The lock compatibility matrix is shown below in Table 10.4.

Table 10.4

Lock Compatibility Matrix

Lock mode already granted to Transaction 1:

	IS	S	U	IX	SIX	X
Transaction 2 requests lock mode						
Intent shared (IS)	Yes	Yes	Yes	Yes	Yes	No
Shared (S)	Yes	Yes	Yes	No	No	No
Update (U)	Yes	Yes	No	No	No	No
Intent exclusive (IX)	Yes	No	No	Yes	No	No
Shared with intent exclusive (SIX)	Yes	No	No	No	No	No
Exclusive (X)	No	No	No	No	No	No

This potential for one transaction to block others combined with the length of time that locks may be held can be a serious cause of performance problems in a multi-user application. In fact, locks using the most antisociable lock mode, exclusive (X), stay until the transaction completes with a commit or rollback. Database and application designers should always ensure that locks are held for the shortest possible time.

To support serializable transactions, SQL Server must be able to guard against inserts and deletes happening so that operations within the serializable transaction are repeatable. For example, if a query in a serializable transaction produces a range of values, perhaps by using a BETWEEN x AND y clause, and that query is run again within the transaction, it should return the same number of rows. That is, no inserts or deletes must have occurred in the range.

To protect against such inserts and deletes happening, SQL Server locks ranges of index rows. In the example above, all the index entries in the range x to y inclusive would be locked. This is known as *key range locking*.

Whatever the lock manager is requested to lock, for example, a page, table, or row, the lock manager treats each as just a named resource. Depending on the resource type, different information is held as part of the resource. This is shown in Table 10.5 below.

Table 10.5
Resource Information Used by the Lock Manager

For any given database ID, the resource is identified as:

Resource Type	Information Identifying Resource
RID	fileid:page:rid combination
KEY	Strange hexadecimal number used internally by SQL Server
PAG	fileid:page combination
EXT	First page number (fileid:page) in the extent being locked
TAB	The object ID of the table
DATABASE	The database ID of the database

In Table 10.5, a *fileid* is a unique number that identifies a file within a database. A database ID is a unique number that identifies a database on the server. A *rid* is the address of the row on the page.

10.4.9   Displaying Locking Information

Locking information is typically obtained using system-stored procedures or the SQL Server Enterprise Manager. The Performance Monitor and SQL Server Profiler can also return locking information.

The system stored procedure *sp_lock* displays information about locks held on the server. An example of the display is shown in Figure 10.23.

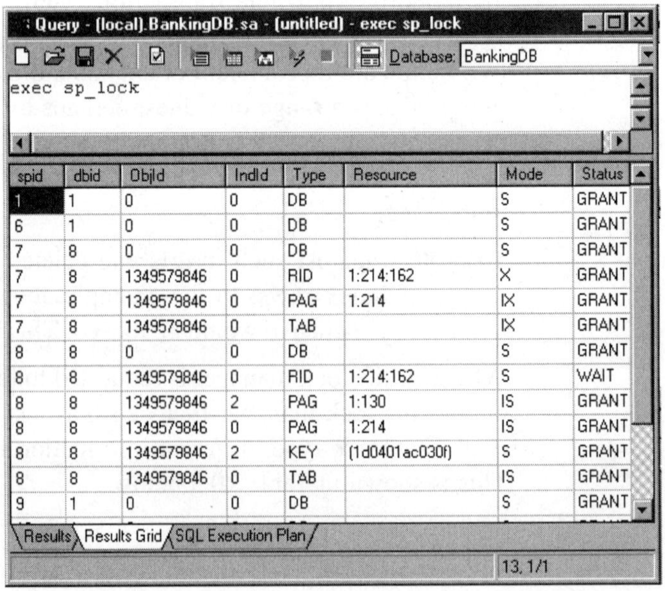

Figure 10.23
Information from the sp_lock System Stored Procedure

spid	dbid	ObjId	IndId	Type	Resource	Mode	Status
1	1	0	0	DB		S	GRANT
6	1	0	0	DB		S	GRANT
7	8	0	0	DB		S	GRANT
7	8	1349579846	0	RID	1:214:162	X	GRANT
7	8	1349579846	0	PAG	1:214	IX	GRANT
7	8	1349579846	0	TAB		IX	GRANT
8	8	0	0	DB		S	GRANT
8	8	1349579846	0	RID	1:214:162	S	WAIT
8	8	1349579846	2	PAG	1:130	IS	GRANT
8	8	1349579846	0	PAG	1:214	IS	GRANT
8	8	1349579846	2	KEY	(1d0401ac030f)	S	GRANT
8	8	1349579846	0	TAB		IS	GRANT
9	1	0	0	DB		S	GRANT

The *spid* specifies the connection holding the lock and the *dbid* holds the ID of the database to which the locked resource is associated. The *ObjId* specifies the table to which a locked resource belongs, for example a table, key, page, or row lock. The *IndId* specifies the index to which the resource belongs. The *Type* column specifies the type of resource and the *Resource* column has the resource specific information such as *fileid:page:rid*. The *Mode* column specifies the mode of the lock and the *Status* column shows whether it has been granted or is waiting to be granted, that is, blocked.

In the SQL Server Enterprise Manager, locking activity can be displayed by expanding the *Management* folder and selecting the Locks /Process ID option. Blocking and blocked locks are displayed as shown in Figure 10.24.

Figure 10.24

Lock Information from the SQL Server Enterprise Manager

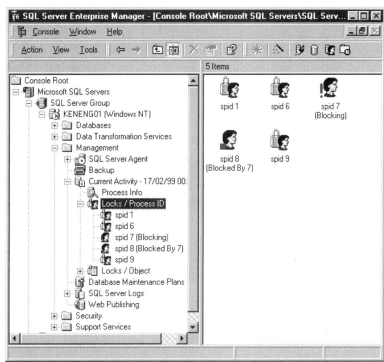

10.4.10 Modifying SQL Server Locking Behavior

The SQL Server locking behavior follows a default set of rules. These are suitable for most situations, but for those situations where they are not, the default behavior can be modified.

The following can be modified:

◆   Deadlock Behavior

◆   Lock Timeouts

- ◆ Transaction Isolation Level
- ◆ Resource to be Locked (via locking hints)
- ◆ Index Locking Granularity

Deadlock Behavior

A deadlock is caused when one user wants a resource locked by another user and that user wants a resource owned by the first user. If SQL Server did not detect deadlocks, then users participating in a deadlock would wait forever. A simple deadlock is shown in Figure 10.25.

Figure 10.25
A Simple Deadlock

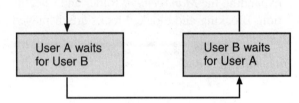

SQL Server does detect deadlocks and, if a deadlock is detected, a deadlock victim is selected. The victim's transaction is rolled back and it receives a 1205 error. SQL Server chooses the "least expensive" transaction as the victim.

This default behavior can be overridden by a connection specifically requesting that it be chosen as a deadlock victim if it participates in a deadlock. The SET DEADLOCK _PRIORITY Transact-SQL statement is used to change the deadlock priority of the connection.

To help reduce deadlocks, access objects in the same order, keep transactions short, and use as low an isolation level as possible.

Lock Timeouts

If a transaction requests a lock that is incompatible with a lock on the same resource held by another transaction, it will wait until the currently-granted lock is relinquished. If there is a problem with the application such that the granted lock is held for a long time, or perhaps forever, transactions requesting locks on the resource will start to queue, perhaps themselves becoming blockers.

SQL Server 7.0 now allows a connection to set a lock timeout value. This specifies a time limit on the lock wait. If this time limit is exceeded, the connection receives an error 1222 and the statement is cancelled. However, the transaction that contains the cancelled statement is not rolled back. It is the responsibility of the developer to trap this error and deal with the situation.

To set a lock timeout, specify the timeout in milliseconds:

```
SET LOCK_TIMEOUT 10000
```

This sets the timeout to 10 seconds. Setting the timeout value to -1 (the default) means that you will wait forever, as in SQL Server 6.5. Setting the timeout value to 0 means you will not wait at all. To check the lock timeout value set for a connection, use the function @@LOCK_TIMEOUT.

Transaction Isolation Levels

By default, SQL Server runs at transaction isolation level read committed. This is sufficient for many applications but it only prevents the dirty read phenomenon. Transactions can be made to run at any of the other three transaction isolation levels by using the SET TRANSACTION ISOLATION LEVEL statement or by using hints on the SELECT statement (see next section):

```
SET TRANSACTION ISOLATION LEVEL SERIALIZABLE
```

To find the transaction isolation level that transactions on a connection are running, use DBCC USEROPTIONS:

```
DBCC USEROPTIONS
```

Set Option	Value
textsize	64512
language	us_english
dateformat	mdy
datefirst	7
ansi_null_dflt_on	SET
isolation level	repeatable read

Locking Hints

Table-level locking hints can be specified on SELECT, INSERT, UPDATE, and DELETE statements to specify the type of locks to be used. A locking hint overrides the current transaction isolation level setting for the session for that Transact-SQL statement only. The locking hints are shown in Table 10.6 below.

Table 10.6

Locking Hints

Locking Hint	Description
HOLDLOCK	Keep a shared lock until completion of the transaction instead of releasing the lock as soon as the resource is no longer needed. HOLDLOCK is equivalent to SERIALIZABLE.
NOLOCK	Do not take out shared locks and do not honor exclusive locks. Dirty reads are therefore possible—can be used only with the SELECT statement.
PAGLOCK	Forces page locks to be used instead of a single table lock.
READCOMMITTED	Same as the transaction isolation level.
READPAST	Skips locked rows.
READUNCOMMITTED	Equivalent to NOLOCK and the transaction isolation level.
REPEATABLEREAD	Same as the transaction isolation level.
ROWLOCK	Forces row-level locks.
SERIALIZABLE	Same as the transaction isolation level.
TABLOCK	Forces a table lock.
TABLOCKX	Forces an exclusive lock on a table.
UPDLOCK	Forces update locks instead of shared locks while reading a table.

Index Locking Granularity

The lock manager automatically makes the best locking choice; however, there are situations when the database administrator may wish to override this, given the way an application behaves. Locking in an index can be customized with the *sp_indexoption* system-stored procedure.

```
EXEC sp_indexoption 'accounts.nci_account_no',
'AllowRowLocks', TRUE
```

The permitted options are *AllowRowLocks* and *AllowPageLocks*.

11

Distributing Data

11.1 Introduction

For some years now, there has been a move away from centralized systems toward more distributed systems. There are a number of reasons why this trend is growing and these are highlighted in the next section. To support the distribution of data it is necessary for database management systems to provide more and more distributed functionality, but without a corresponding massive increase in management or implementation complexity. Microsoft SQL Server has always provided a number of useful distributed capabilities and SQL Server 7.0 builds on these capabilities by enhancing data replication and providing heterogeneous distributed queries. This chapter will focus on these topics.

11.2 Why Distribute Data?

For some companies, distributing their data around the network makes no sense whatsoever. Their organizational structure is based around a centralized model and the way they do business works best with a central database running on a large minicomputer or mainframe. However, for some companies this centralized approach is not suitable and they have decided to place pieces of their database around their network. Some reasons why more and more companies may wish to distribute their databases are:

- Organizational Mapping
- Growth Flexibility
- Cost of Ownership
- Availability
- Performance

Many companies have a distributed organization and wish to model their data along similar lines. As their company expands (or contracts) they may wish to incrementally grow or shrink their computer resource and not have to knock down the computer room wall to completely replace the mainframe! Mainframes are expensive whereas, at least from a hardware perspective, more price performance can be obtained from multiple small servers.

If a company's data is spread over multiple servers, there is a greater chance that, at a given point in time, a server will not be functioning correctly. However, this will result in a small reduction in the overall system availability, as other servers will still be functioning. If a centralized database fails, it is likely that the overall system availability will be severely compromised.

If data is moved close to the users who need it most, then communication overheads will be reduced and performance will be increased. There may also be a cost benefit resulting from reduced network usage.

Let us look at the above reasons to distribute data from the perspective of a fictitious company. This company might have a number of distribution outlets around the country. It makes sense to place the data that is manipulated by the respective outlets at those outlets instead of in one centralized database. This has a number of advantages. As 80% of the data needed by each outlet is local to that outlet, the communication overhead of accessing a centralized database is largely removed with a corresponding increase in performance.

Since communication lines are usually one of the least reliable components in a system, reducing the reliance on them should increase overall system availability. If the company adds a new outlet, it merely adds a new server and local database. Unexpected company growth can be accommodated more easily.

However, we have made an important assumption, which is that data sharing is *low* between the outlets. Once the requirement to share data becomes *high*, the advantages that we have seen of the distributed approach are quickly eroded and a centralized approach becomes attractive again.

This highlights an important phenomenon concerning distributed systems, which is they are more attractive for systems that do not have a need to share most of the data in the database. This can be taken a step further. Distributed systems are more attractive for systems that do not have a requirement to share and update most of the data in the database.

To demonstrate this fact with our fictitious company, suppose that 80% of each outlet's data was frequently read by the other outlets. The communication overhead would rapidly increase, as each server would be in constant communication with every other server. As each server required constant communication with every other server, a communications failure or server failure would result in a severely degraded system. Incremental growth would not be as simple as before because the addition of a new server would have a greater effect on existing servers.

The above only demonstrates the negative effect of increased data sharing. We could make the distributed approach attractive again by keeping multiple copies of data at the outlets. When an outlet needed to look at another outlet's data it would find it locally. This is fine so long as we rarely wished to update the data, although in reality, this is often not the case. Most key data is constantly updated to reflect the state of a business at any given point in time. If we keep more than one copy of a piece of data on the network we are faced with the problem of synchronizing updates to the multiple copies.

What point are we trying to make here? Quite simply, distributing data around the network may not be the best approach for your company. There again, it may be the perfect solution to all your data access problems. Either way, you will have to think through the ramifications of data distribution extremely carefully. Do not just consider initial set up because, once your distributed system is ticking along smoothly, some user somewhere will want you to change it!

There are a number of ways of moving data around a network, perhaps using the Data Transformation Services (DTS) described in Chapter 13 or by using backup and restore. In this chapter we will focus on how SQL Server 7.0 provides the means to access remote data via distributed queries and the SQL Server 7.0 data replication facility.

11.3   Heterogeneous Distributed Queries

Before starting to look at this topic let us look at the terminology. By distributed we mean data that resides on multiple servers on the network. So when we talk of accessing distributed data we mean accessing data on another server on the network, that is, on a remote server. By heterogeneous we mean that the data need not be resident in a SQL Server 7.0 database. It can reside in another relational database management system or perhaps a file.

With SQL Server 6.5, statements such as SELECT, INSERT, UPDATE, and DELETE could only access local SQL Server data. The one exception to this was the INSERT statement, which could insert data into a table based on the result set of a remote stored procedure. Joins and unions could not cross servers and views could not be created that crossed servers. The local data that could be accessed had to be Microsoft SQL Server data.

With SQL Server 7.0, statements such as SELECT, INSERT, UPDATE, and DELETE can access remote SQL Server data. Joins and unions of tables residing on different servers can be performed and views of distributed joins and unions can be created.

However, SQL Server data is not the only data that can be accessed. By taking advantage of Microsoft's Universal Data Access standard, OLEDB, non-SQL Server data such as other relation databases and files can be accessed as if they were SQL Server tables.

OLEDB providers make their data available in tabular objects called rowsets. SQL Server 7.0 allows rowsets from OLEDB providers to be referred to in Transact-SQL statements as if they were an SQL Server table. Microsoft ships a number of OLEDB providers for data sources such as SQL Server and JET. There is also an OLEDB provider for ODBC that makes any data source with an ODBC driver available. There are likely to be many third-party OLEDB providers available over time.

The way that OLEDB can be used to access heterogeneous data is shown in Figure 11.1.

Figure 11.1
Accessing Heterogeneous Data via OLEDB

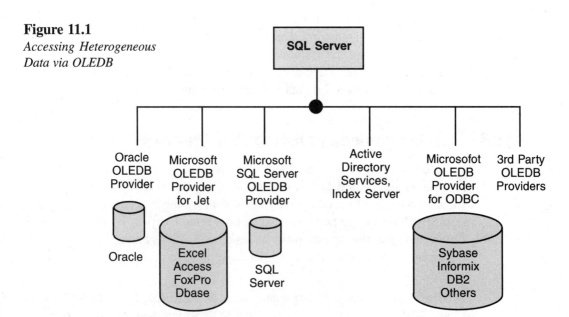

11.3.1 Accessing a Remote Data Source with OLEDB

Remote data can be accessed in an ad-hoc fashion or via a predefined *linked*
server. If a linked server is defined, Transact-SQL statements can use a
four-part naming scheme to access the remote data or the OPENQUERY()
rowset function. The linked server contains information such as the OLEDB
provider.

If no linked server is defined, the OPENROWSET() rowset function must
be used and all the information, such as the OLEDB provider, supplied at
that point.

The functions OPENQUERY() and OPENROWSET() are known as rowset
functions because they return an object that can be used in place of a table
reference in a Transact-SQL statement.

The advantage to using linked servers is that they provide central management of remote data. The linked server encapsulates various information,
such as the OLEDB provider and whether it can run in or out of process.
The use of linked servers with either a four-part naming scheme or the
OPENQUERY() function is likely to be the most useful approach to accessing remote data. The OPENROWSET() function is only likely to be
used for ad-hoc access of remote data.

Accessing a Remote Data Source Using a Linked Server

A linked server is a virtual server that has been defined to SQL Server with
all the information needed to access an OLEDB data source. A linked server
can be set up using the SQL Server Enterprise Manager or the *sp_add-
linkedserver* system-stored procedure. A diagram of the syntax follows:

```
sp_addlinkedserver [@server =] 'server'
[, [@srvproduct =] 'product_name'] [, [@provider =] 'provider_name']
[, [@datasrc =] 'data_source'] [, [@location =] 'location']
[, [@provstr =] 'provider_string'] [, [@catalog =] 'catalog']
```

This looks a little complex but the parameters are not all specified for a
given linked server definition. Rather, they are specific to the OLEDB provider that is being used and various parameters have specific meanings or a
given provider. The *server* parameter must be present and this specifies the
name of the linked server. The *srvproduct* parameter is the product name of
the OLEDB data source to add as a linked server, for example, *SQL Server*.
The use of *SQL Server* in the product name means that the other parameters
do not have to be specified. The *provider* parameter is the name of the
OLEDB provider. Other parameters provide information for the given provider. Here is an example of setting up a linked server to SQL Server 7.0:

```
EXEC sp_addlinkedserver @server ='FARAWAY', @srvproduct =
N'SQL Server'
```

Because the linked server refers to the product name of SQL Server, no other information needs to be supplied. Note that the SQL Server is named FARAWAY and the linked server will be named FARAWAY. If required, the linked server can be named differently from the SQL Server by naming the SQL Server in the *datasrc* parameter.

Note: The prefix *N* specifies that the string is Unicode.

The following linked server definition refers to a Microsoft Access data source:

```
EXEC sp_addlinkedserver @server ='AccessLink', @srvproduct
= 'Access 97',
@provider = 'Microsoft.Jet.OLEDB.4.0', @datasrc = 'f:\mydb.mdb'
```

Here, the provider name is specified as well as the data source. Note that the SQL Server 7.0 documentation provides many examples of accessing different types of OLEDB providers. A linked server can be set up using the SQL Server Enterprise Manager. To do this:

⇨   Expand the server group and expand the server.

⇨   Expand the *Security* folder.

⇨   Right-click the *Linked Servers* folder and choose *New Linked Server.*

⇨   Enter a name for the linked server and any other information as needed.

⇨   Click *OK.*

An example of setting up a linked server is shown in Figure 11.2.

Once a linked server has been set up and the appropriate security established (see later), Transact-SQL can use a four-part naming scheme to access the remote tables or rowsets:

```
SELECT * FROM faraway.pubs.dbo.authors
```

This naming is referred to as *linked_server.catalog.schema.object_name* and it is analogous to the more traditional *database.owner.object_name.*

Some OLEDB providers support the capability to pass the OLEDB provider a command that it can execute and expose the results of the command as a rowset. This is often known as a *pass-through* query. This is what the OPENQUERY() rowset function does:

```
SELECT * FROM OPENQUERY(ParisSvr, 'SELECT fname, lname FROM
customers')
```

Figure 11.2

Setting Up a Linked Server through the SQL Server Enterprise Manager

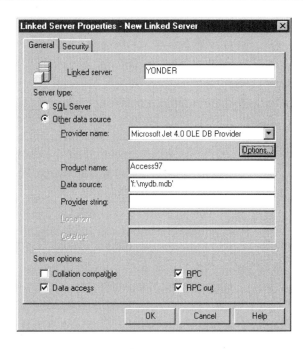

Accessing a Remote Data Source in an Ad-Hoc Fashion

The OPENROWSET() can be used to generate a rowset when ad-hoc access is needed to remote data. Because no information is encapsulated in a pre-defined linked server, all connection information needed to access the remote data must be specified. The OPENROWSET function can be referenced in the FROM clause of a query as though it is a table name:

```
SELECT aut.* FROM
OPENROWSET('SQLOLEDB','myserver';'sa';'secret','SELECT *
FROM pubs.dbo.authors')
AS aut
```

In the above example, the OLEDB provider is SQL Server, the server is *myserver* with the login ID as *sa* and the password *secret*. The string to be passed to the provider is *'SELECT * FROM pubs.dbo.authors'*.

Linked Server Security

From a security perspective, users cannot be allowed to access any linked server they desire. If a user executes a distributed query, the user must somehow login to the remote server. One mechanism to achieve this is to set up mappings between the local server and the remote server so that the local login is mapped to a remote login. However, if there is no mapping set up then the default behavior is to emulate the current security credentials of the login. That is, a person logged on as "sa" with a password of "secret" will be logged on with the same security credentials on the remote server.

However, depending on how the local user logged on to the local server, this may not function. If the user logged on using SQL Server authentication, the current local login and password is sent to the remote server and, if it exists, the user will successfully login to the remote server. However, if the user logged on using Windows NT authentication, the ability to emulate the security credentials of the current login is not possible under Windows NT 4.0 (this is known as *delegation*). This will be possible in the next version of Windows NT.

The alternative is to map to a remote login explicitly. This will work with either authentication mode assuming that the remote login exists and the password supplied is correct. The mapping can be made for the current login or all logins on the local server. Linked server security can be set up using the SQL Server Enterprise Manager or the *sp_addlinkedsrvlogin* system-stored procedure. A diagram of the syntax follows:

```
sp_addlinkedsrvlogin [@rmtsrvname =] 'rmtsrvname'
[,[@useself =] 'useself']
[,[@locallogin =] 'locallogin']
[,[@rmtuser =] 'rmtuser']
[,[@rmtpassword =] 'rmtpassword']
```

Setting up linked server security is achieved by specifying the linked server name and whether SQL Server authenticated logins use their own credentials to connect to the linked server. This happens if the *useself* parameter is *true*. A value of *true* for *useself* is invalid for a Windows NT authenticated login in a Windows NT 4.0 environment. A value of *false* for *useself* means that the *rmtuser* and *rmtpassword* arguments are used to connect to the linked server for the specified *locallogin*.

The *locallogin* parameter is a login on the local server. If *locallogin* is set to NULL then this mapping applies to all local logins that connect to the linked server. If not NULL, *locallogin* can be an SQL Server login or a Windows NT user. For example, a security mapping is established for the local login "sa"' to remote Microsoft Access data:

```
EXEC sp_addlinkedsrvlogin
@rmtsrvname = 'MyAccessLink',
@useself = false,
@locallogin = 'sa',
@rmtuser = 'Admin',
@rmtpassword = NULL
```

Linked server security can be set up using the SQL Server Enterprise Manager. To do this:

⇨ Expand the server group and expand the server.

⇨ Expand the *Security* folder.

⇨ Expand the *Linked Servers* folder.

⇨ Right-click the linked server whose security is to be defined and choose *Properties.*

⇨ Choose the *Security* tab and enter information as needed.

⇨ Click *OK.*

An example of setting up linked server security dialog box is shown in Figure 11.3 below.

Figure 11.3

Setting Up Linked Server Security through the SQL Server Enterprise Manager

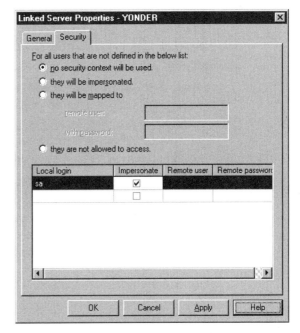

11.3.2   Considerations when Accessing Remote Data

When accessing linked servers a number of considerations need to be made. For example, how to access older versions of SQL Server and what Transact-SQL is valid. These considerations are described next.

Accessing SQL Server 6.x in Distributed Queries

There are two ways of accessing SQL Server 6.x servers with distributed queries. Since an SQL Server 6.x server can be always accessed via ODBC, the Microsoft OLEDB Provider for ODBC can be used.

It is more efficient, however, to use the SQL Server OLEDB Provider. To use this OLEDB provider against an SQL Server 6.x server requires that the catalog stored procedures on the SQL Server 6.x server are upgraded. To upgrade the catalog stored procedures, the INSTCAT.SQL script must be run. This can be run using the OSQL utility at the command prompt, for example:

```
C:\> OSQL -Usa -Psecret -Smy65server -
iC:\Mssql7\Install\instcat.sql
```

Supported Transact-SQL Statements

Many Transact-SQL statements are supported in distributed queries. There are, however, some restrictions. Although, SELECT statements are allowed, in the case of "SELECT ... INTO *newtable*" the *newtable* cannot be a remote table. INSERT, UPDATE, and DELETE statements are allowed as long as the OLEDB provider meets certain minimum criteria. READTEXT, WRITETEXT, and UPDATETEXT statements are not supported against remote tables.

Both static and keyset cursor types are supported when the OLEDB provider meets the minimum criteria. Dynamic or forward-only cursors requested with a distributed query are implicitly converted to keyset-driven cursors. A keyset-driven cursor is supported on a distributed query if all local and remote tables in the query have a unique key.

Data Definition Language (DDL) statements, for example CREATE, ALTER, or DROP, are not allowed against linked servers. Various other restrictions apply, particularly in the area of BLOB data types. Data type mappings may also be candidates for investigation.

Remote Query Optimization

If possible, the query optimizer will send the relevant predicate down to the OLEDB provider in order to eliminate as many rows as possible from the rowset before it is returned across the network. For example, consider the following query:

```
SELECT stor_name, qty FROM
    pubs.dbo.sales sa INNER JOIN fareast.pubs.dbo.stores st
    ON sa.stor_id = st.stor_id
    WHERE state = 'TX'
```

The WHERE state = "TX" predicate will be sent down to the *fareast* server to be executed instead of all the rows being returned to the local server and the filtering then being performed. Note that the linked server attribute *collation compatible* has an influence on what the query optimizer actually decides to do. If the *collation compatible* attribute is false, the data may be all returned to the local server for filtering.

11.4   Data Replication with SQL Server 7.0

If more than one copy of a piece of data must be held on the network, you, as a database designer, will also have to decide whether the copies are *loosely coupled* or *tightly coupled*—in other words, how and when are they synchronized.

11.4.1   Transactional Consistency and Convergence

If the data copies are tightly coupled, the *immediate transactional consistency* model is used. When one piece of data is updated all the other copies are also updated in real time. All the copies are updated in a single distributed transaction that cannot complete successfully until all the copies have been updated, irrespective of where they are on the network and how many copies are present.

If the data copies are loosely coupled, the *latent transactional consistency* model is used. One piece of data is updated and then the other copies are updated at some later point in time, which may be seconds or hours, after the first copy is updated. The copies are not now updated in a single distributed transaction.

There are advantages and disadvantages to both approaches. The advantage of the *immediate transactional consistency* model is that each copy of the data is always up-to-date. There is no *latency* involved with using tightly coupled data copies. This may be important, as it might be highly desirable that changes in the price of gold, for example, are made to each server database at the same instant in time.

There are a number of disadvantages to this approach. As previously stated, all the copies are updated in a single distributed transaction, which cannot complete successfully until all the copies have been updated. Each copy must, therefore, be available if the distributed transaction is to complete successfully. This means that each server must be available, which also means that the network must be available. In other words, there is low site *autonomy*—the sites are heavily dependent on one another and must be well connected. This might not be always the case. Another consideration is that the duration of the distributed transaction is the sum of the time it takes to update each copy. This means that the response time, as perceived by the user who issued the update, is unlikely to be good.

The more copies involved in the distributed transaction the higher the chance a server will be unavailable and the greater the transaction duration. This is why it is often stated that the immediate consistency model is not scalable. This does not mean that this approach is not practical, rather it has its place, which is likely to be updating a low number of copies on a fast local area network rather than a large number of copies on a slow wide area network.

It is worth mentioning that to implement the immediate consistency model requires the provision of a two-phase commit protocol (2PC). This protocol and, therefore, the ability to support distributed transactions is provided by the Microsoft Distributed Transaction Coordinator (DTC), which ships with SQL Server 7.0.

The advantage of the immediate consistency model is that each copy of the data is always up-to-date. The disadvantage of the latent transactional consistency model is that each copy of the data is not always up-to-date. Indeed there is usually some delay in updating all the copies. In the latent transactional consistency model, a designated primary copy of the data is updated and at some later point in time the secondary copies are updated (note that this does not necessarily mean that no other copy can be updated, as we shall see). The transaction that updates the primary copy completes the instant the copy is updated successfully.

This means that the response time, as perceived by the user who issued the update, is likely to be good. It also means that there is no requirement for all of the copies to be available. As long as some component of the system *remembers* the changes made to the primary copy, these can be propagated to an unavailable copy at some later time when the copy becomes available again. The latent transactional consistency model is therefore tolerant of network or server failure. The sites can be highly autonomous. As the updating of the multiple secondary copies is an asynchronous operation, tolerant of failures, the latent transactional consistency model is much more scalable than the immediate transactional consistency model and better able to function in a wide area network environment.

The immediate transactional consistency model and latent transactional consistency model share an important property. The participating sites are guaranteed to always see the same data values in the state that would have been achieved had all the work been done at a single site. In the case of the immediate transactional consistency model, the changes are seen at the exact same time and in the case of the latent transactional consistency model, there will be some delay.

However, there is also a model known as *data convergence*. With this model, like the previous models, all the sites may end up with the same values, but not necessarily the ones that would have resulted had all the work been done at only one site. This is a model that is used with SQL Server merge replication, described later, where the sites are highly autonomous and are usually disconnected. Every so often, they are synchronized and the changes made at each site are propagated to the other sites. In the case of a conflict, a site may have its value overwritten.

11.4.2 SQL Server Replication Terminology

SQL Server uses the *publisher/subscriber* model. The *publisher* is the server that makes data available to other servers engaged in replication. What is to be replicated is defined at the publisher.

A *subscriber* is a server that holds replicated data and receives updates. Unlike SQL Server 6.x subscribers, subscribers in SQL Server 7.0 can update replicated data.

A *distributor* is a server that manages the store and forward queue (distribution database) as well as other components.

What defines the data to be published? When specifying which data is to be published, an *article* is defined. An article is a whole table or a horizontal and/or vertical partition of a table, that is, a subset of the rows or columns or both. Which type of subset is allowed depends on the type of replication being defined (snapshot, transactional, or merge). An article can be thought of as a table or part of a table.

These articles may be grouped together into a *publication* and an article must always be part of a publication. Subscribers who wish to receive information subscribe to a publication.

When a subscriber subscribes to a publication, a *push* or *pull* subscription may be defined.

When a *push subscription* is set up, the publisher replicates the data changes to the subscriber. The subscriber does not need to request that the changes be sent. Often, push subscriptions are used when the subscriber is to receive the changes made at the publisher virtually as they happen. When a *pull subscription* is set up, the subscriber requests that it is updated with all the data changes made at the publisher since the last pull. Often, pull subscriptions are used when publications have a large number of subscribers as this moves the workload to the subscribers away from the distributor.

11.4.3   Replication Agents

Various agents are used in SQL Server 7.0 replication depending on the type of replication being performed:

◆   Snapshot

◆   Log Reader

◆   Distribution

◆   Merge

The *snapshot agent* creates a schema file, for example, containing a CRE-ATE TABLE statement, and a data file that is a copy of the published table. The snapshot agent essentially creates the files needed to get a subscriber started.

The *log reader agent* moves the committed transactions that must be repli-cated from a published database's transaction log to the distribution data-base—essentially the store and forward queue.

The *distribution agent* takes the jobs from the distribution database—essen-tially the store and forward queue—and applies the changes to the subscrib-ers. The distribution agent can run on the publisher or subscriber. It is not used by merge publications.

The *merge agent* moves and reconciles data changes between the publisher and the subscribers. It is not used by snapshot and transactional publica-tions.

11.4.4   SQL Server 7.0 Replication Types

The main replication types used in SQL Server 7.0 replication are:

◆   Snapshot

◆   Transactional

◆   Merge

These can be represented as replication solutions residing on different parts of the replication spectrum as shown in Figure 11.4.

On the right of the spectrum we have the lowest site autonomy—the sites must be well connected. At this end of the spectrum we find the immediate transactional consistency model (also known as the immediate guaranteed consistency model). At the other end of the spectrum we have the highest site autonomy. At this end of the spectrum we find merge replication.

Let us look at these different types of replication.

Figure 11.4
The Replication Spectrum

data convergence
latent guaranteed consistency
immediate guaranteed consistency

Merge Replication
Transactional Replication
Distributed Transaction Coordinator (2PC)

Snapshot Replication
Immediate Updating Subscribers

Snapshot Replication

Snapshot replication takes a "snapshot" of the data in a publication and sends this to the subscriber. The subscriber receives a complete refresh of the published table at intervals and because the whole table is sent to the subscriber, the publisher does not need to keep track of the changes made to the published table, for example, inserts, deletes, and updates. Therefore, there is less work for the publisher to do. Also, the network is not impacted by changes sent to subscribers continuously, however, the transmission of the whole publication may have an adverse impact on the network. Snapshot replication is a good approach for read-only subscribers when they do not need to see the most up-to-date values of data present at the publisher. Snapshot replication is shown in Figure 11.5.

Figure 11.5
Snapshot Replication

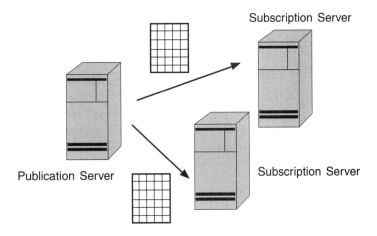

Subscription Server

Publication Server

Subscription Server

Transactional Replication

Transactional replication catches the events captured in the transaction log of the published database such as INSERT, UPDATE, and DELETE statements. These are stored in the distribution database, which provides the function of a reliable queue. Changes are then sent to subscribers and applied in the same order. The changes can be sent continuously or at scheduled intervals.

The snapshot agent creates a schema file, for example, containing a CREATE TABLE statement, and a data file that is a copy of the published table. The log reader agent monitors the transaction logs of published databases and transactions marked for replication are moved to the distribution database. The distribution agent moves the transactions and initial snapshot jobs held in the distribution database tables to the subscribers. Stored procedures may also be replicated. A simple transactional replication model is shown in Figure 11.6.

Figure 11.6

Simple Transactional Replication

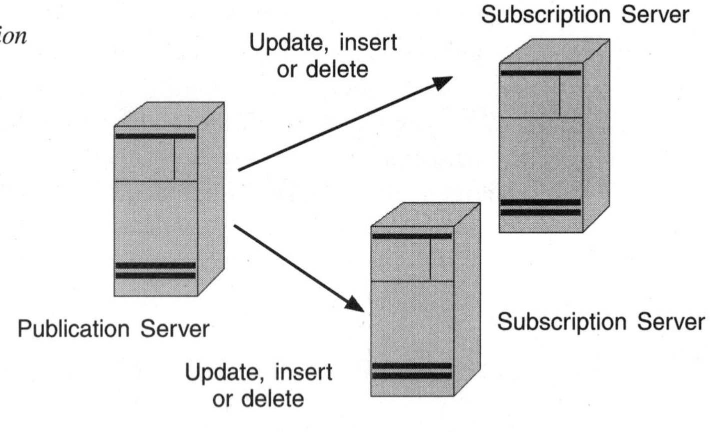

The model of transactional replication shown in Figure 11.6 has one publisher and multiple subscribers. The model of transactional replication shown in Figure 11.7 has a single, central subscriber and multiple publishers. This model is useful when, perhaps, multiple sales outlets are sending ordering information to a central site.

The model of transactional replication shown in Figure 11.8 has multiple publishers who are also subscribers. This model can be used to allow multiple sites to participate in transactional replication while allowing each site to publish data to the other sites and subscribe to data from the other sites. Conflicts, where two sites change the same data, are avoided by making sure that the data is partitioned across the sites.

For example, the London site may only be allowed to insert, delete, and update rows with an "L" in the location column. Paris may only be allowed to insert, delete, and update rows with a "P" in the location column. London would define an article horizontally partitioned so that only rows with an "L" in the location column were present in the article. Paris and the other sites would subscribe to the publication containing this article. Paris would define an article horizontally partitioned so that only rows with a "P" in the location column were present in the article. London and the other sites would subscribe to the publication containing this article, and so on.

In this way, changes to the London data would be sent to the non-London sites and changes to the Paris data would be sent to the non-Paris sites.

Figure 11.7

Multiple Publishers
—Single Subscriber

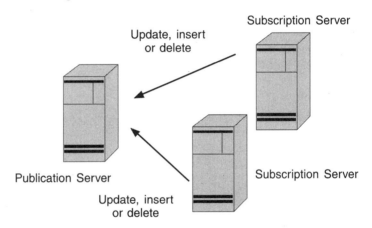

Figure 11.8

Multiple Publishers/Subscribers

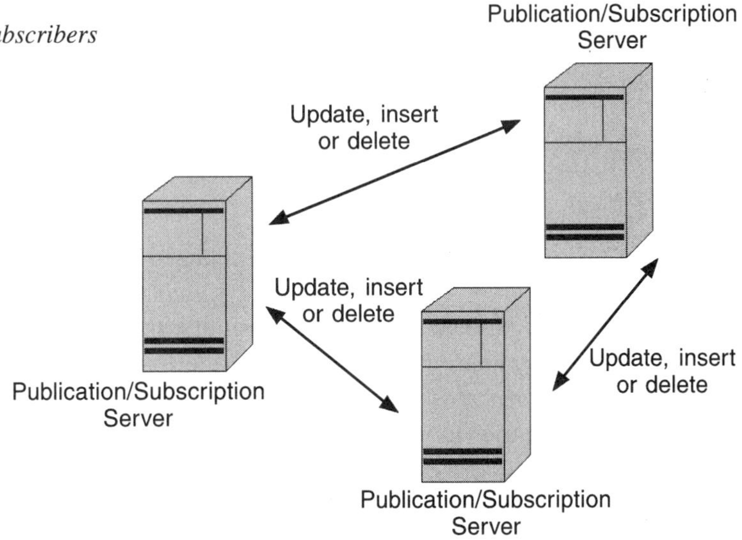

A powerful new transactional model (and snapshot model) supported by SQL Server 7.0 is the *updating subscribers* model. In this model, a subscriber is allowed to change data but only if it can simultaneously change the data at the publisher. If this can be done, then the change will be propagated from the publisher to the remaining subscribers using the normal transactional replication mechanisms. The implication here is that the subscriber must be connected to the publisher if it wants to change its data. If there is no connection then it cannot make the change. If the connection is present then the publisher is updated in a 2PC distributed transaction with the subscriber (transparently to the application). Conflicts are avoided (the publisher detects them) and so no conflict resolution is necessary. Updating subscribers is shown in Figure 11.9.

Figure 11.9

Updating Subscribers

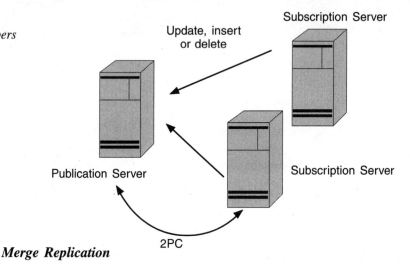

Merge Replication

The other type of replication is merge replication. In merge replication, the sites are highly autonomous. In many cases, the sites will be disconnected most of the time. Any site may update data and when the sites connect and the merge agent runs, the data changes are reconciled and changes are propagated to the appropriate sites, as shown in Figure 11.10.

Of course, two sites may have changed the same piece of data, in which case the merge agent must resolve the "conflict." This is done by using a priority-based mechanism that is built into SQL Server 7.0 replication. The site to which you have attached the highest priority wins. This priority-based mechanism is not a conflict resolution mechanism that everyone will wish to use, so you can specify your own conflict resolution mechanism if required.

Figure 11.10
Merge Replication

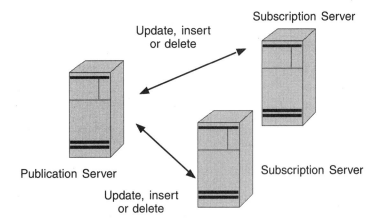

When merge replication is used to publish an article, the database schema definition is modified in three ways. First, a new column of data type UNIQUEIDENTIFIER is added to the table and this column is given the ROWGUID property and an index is created on it. The UNIQUEIDENTIFIER data type is discussed in Chapter 4. If a suitable column already exists in the table then SQL Server will use that. Second, insert, update, and delete triggers are added to the base table to track changes. Third, some new system tables are added to the database to track changes.

11.4.5   Setting Up Replication

There are various mechanisms that can be used to set up replication.

◆   Wizards

◆   SQL Server Enterprise Manager

◆   System-Stored Procedures

◆   Programming Interfaces

These all vary in the level of complexity and functionality offered.

Wizards

There are a number of wizards that can be used to set up and maintain replication. These wizards are:

◆   *Configure Publishing and Distribution*—used to set up and specify a server to use as a Distributor (see Figure 11.11 for the first page of this wizard).

◆   *Create Publication*—used to create a publication.

◆   *Push Subscription*—used to define a push subscription from the publication server to subscription servers.

- *Pull Subscription*—used to define a pull subscription to a publication.
- *Disable Publishing and Distribution*—disables publishing and/or distribution.
- *Replication Conflict Viewer*—views and resolves conflicts that happened during merge replication.

Figure 11.11
The Configure Publishing and Distribution Wizard

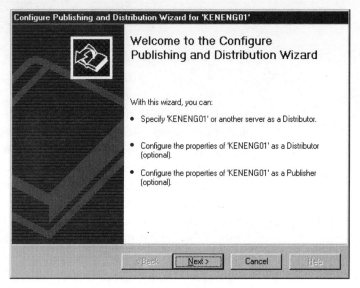

Having set up replication through wizards, the SQL Server Enterprise Manager can easily be used to make subsequent changes.

SQL Server Enterprise Manager

Through dialog boxes in the SQL Server Enterprise Manager, replication can be set up, maintained, and monitored. Replication can be chosen from the *Tools* menu option or *replicate data* can be chosen from the *Getting Started Taskpad*. The SQL Server Enterprise Manager also has a *replication monitor* that provides status and history information concerning the replication system. Figure 11.12 shows the SQL Server Enterprise Manager console tree containing the replication monitor.

It can be seen from Figure 11.12 that various folders allow publications and agents to be monitored. Various icons are used to show replication status.

Note: Even if wizards or the graphical interface of the SQL Server Enterprise Manager are used to set up replication, the definitions of the replication can be later scripted.

Figure 11.12

The Replication Monitor

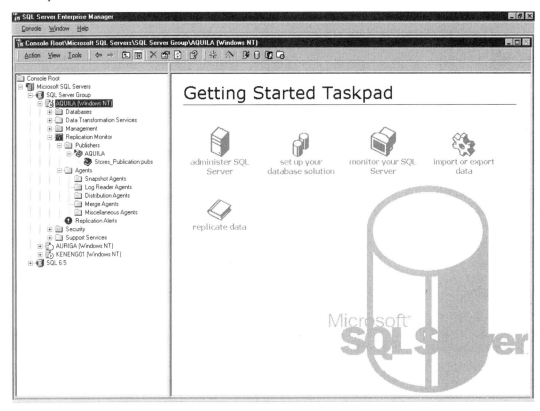

System-Stored Procedures

There are dozens of system-stored procedures that can be used to set up replication. If scripts are written to set up replication using system-stored procedures, then these scripts can be easily rerun and can be run on other servers for mass deployment. Rather than write the scripts from scratch it is often easier to set up replication on one server using the wizards and SQL Server Enterprise Manager and then script the replication set up. The script can then be edited as desired.

Programming Interfaces

The SQL-DMO (Distributed Management Objects) may be used to install and maintain replication. Applications can be written using Microsoft Visual Basic or C++ to configure or maintain a specific replication topology. Also available is the Replication Distribution interface and Microsoft ActiveX replication controls. The Replication Distribution interface can be used to replicate data from heterogeneous data sources, such as Oracle. ActiveX replication controls provide a mechanism to manage merge agent and distribution agent activity programmatically at a subscriber where there is a pull subscription defined.

12

Transaction Server and COM

12.1 Introduction

COM, the *Component Object Model,* and its distributed brother DCOM are the fundamental building blocks of Microsoft applications and many solutions based on Microsoft technology. While this book is primarily about Microsoft SQL Server, very few readers will use the product in isolation from other development tools or technologies. COM is the fundamental foundation that all developers will need to understand.

COM originated in the early days of Windows-based technologies with cut and paste, dynamic data exchange (DDE), and OLE, which matured into OLE 2. No discussion of COM is complete without a review of Microsoft Transaction Server technologies.

12.2 The Object-Oriented Paradigm

At the moment Object Orientation (OO) appears to be one of the fashionable areas of computing. Despite its current vogue, OO techniques have been around since the mid-1960s. Probably the earliest accepted OO programming language was the Scandinavian designed SIMULA or SIMUlated LAnguage, which was the basis for the now successful Smalltalk language.

There is currently a heated debate underway between Object-Oriented Programming (OOP) purists, who believe that an OO language must contain a specific set of features, and those who are happy with an object-oriented environment.

Generally, to be accepted as an object-oriented programming language, the following features need to be present:

- User definable classes
- Object class hierarchies

- ◆ Instantiation
- ◆ Inheritance
- ◆ Polymorphism
- ◆ Messaging
- ◆ Encapsulation

12.2.1   Classes, Objects, and Instances

Objects are abstract data types—the internal configuration and characteristics of an individual object need not be known by the developer. The internal data elements (data abstraction) and processes (process abstraction) can therefore, theoretically, be ignored and the developer can focus on the object interfaces.

A good example of this is the telephone receiver, where a user does not need to know its internal workings, only the ability to interface with the telephone by using the handset. This also demonstrates abstraction, the fact that the characteristics of an object differ according to the viewer. A layperson sees the telephone as a box with which conversations can take place, but an engineer may see the telephone as a complex assortment of electromechanical components, all interacting with each other.

A class is a special object containing data and procedural abstraction. It is a concept only, but this concept is delivered as an object. This class represents a set of objects that share a common structure and behavior, for example, all telephones enable communication to take place, but the design of the telephone may be upright, squat, wall-mounted, or a hands-free mobile in a car! Instantiation is the process of having multiple instances of an object that can be manipulated independently without effecting each one's functionality or attributes.

12.2.2   Containment and Inheritance

Containment is literally the containment of objects within each other. For example, a telephone object may contain a bell object, which in turn may contain a plunger object. Inheritance allows these objects to acquire some properties of other objects. Single inheritance or multiple inheritance indicates the number of parent objects that a child object can have.

12.2.3   Polymorphism, Messaging, and Encapsulation

Polymorphism is the ability for the system to determine the best way of executing code at runtime. The same or similar messages may be sent to different objects to achieve abstract results. For example the word OPEN is polymorphic. OPEN applied to a door will be interpreted differently to OPEN applied to an MS-DOS file.

Message passing is key to OO programming. It can be thought of as the application of methods to an object following a predetermined format, which in turn are handled in a very specific manner. For example, the message may change an object's data and, therefore, its behavior.

Encapsulation is the containment of the properties (or data) and the methods (or code) of an object. Objects that contain the same properties and methods are said to be of the same type. Objects have unique properties that are not shared with other objects, although other objects may have identical properties. In some languages, such as Smalltalk, the encapsulation happens at a physical level, using the syntax of the programming language. Smalltalk also offers the developer the ability to encapsulate methods, operations, and features to create a logical class. Using the telephone analogy again, the outer plastic casing of the phone encapsulates the internal implementation of the phone or object, effectively hiding its complexities.

12.3 Components

12.3.1 ActiveX

The *Component Object Model* (COM) is a binary standard specification for building code modules. Primarily aimed at C++ developers, it is increasingly used by programmers using other languages or tools. The advent of Visual Basic version 5.0 and later VB 6.0 gave Visual Basic developers the ability to fully enjoy COM by creating and deploying ActiveX objects. ActiveX was essentially the re-branding of Microsoft object technology. Early adopters of Visual Basic used third party "plug ins" such as Custom Controls, VBXs, and OCXs (32-bit VBX's!), but the advent of Microsoft's Internet strategy saw another renaming to ActiveX controls.

ActiveX controls are generally small applications or applets that run within the context of a web page, having been downloaded from a web server. ActiveX containers are COM-based programs that can run, load, and manage ActiveX controls, normally on the client and more often than not are a web browser. Interestingly, a component can act both as container and a control, for example Word for Windows can contain an embedded web browser.

To be a true ActiveX control certain criteria must be met. Download speeds need to be kept as reasonable as possible, and any Internet data access optimized to cope with low bandwidth connections. Users waiting for applets to download before using an application will soon get irritated. The size of a control is often a function of the number of COM interfaces implemented. ActiveX controls must only support one COM interface, IUnknown, which can be used by applications to query the control's functionality and allows freeing up of system resource when no longer needed by the control. Other COM interfaces can be implemented at the designer's discretion, reasonable download speed permitting. Data download is optimized by using a new system service called Asynchronous Moniker. The control can initiate the download, continue the download process, but inform the outer container when the download has been completed. By using the Asynchronous Moniker to receive status information, the control can place a suitable status bar or message on the screen.

The control must automatically make itself known to the system by registering itself, therefore preventing multiple downloads of the same version of the same component. The registering process includes the writing of the control's GUID (please note the use of *Global* Unique Identifier—the authors are of the opinion that nothing can be universally unique) and location of the executable to the client's registry. Additionally the control may be usable as another component form (i.e., OCX) and if so, this information will be written to the suitable component category.

The control needs to be accessible from client scripting languages such as VB Script or J Script. The control can then be manipulated or interacted with by the container application. This may be by requiring the user to enter name information or maybe data to be used in a calculation. The availability of a control's function is via OLE Automation. OLE Automation provides an enumeration mechanism whereby a control's functionality can be determined, for example the function name and associated parameter list. This is often supported by documentation supplied by the control designer.

ActiveX Component Download

Before a user can enjoy the functionality of an ActiveX control it needs to be downloaded to the client container.

When a page of HTML contains a tag indicating a component is required, the Internet Component Download Service (CDS) DLL, which is resident on the client machine, is called. The tag will contain the GUID of the control, its type, version, and URL location. The CDS DLL will undertake 4 tasks: determine if the download is required, control access to the source, download the code, and then install it.

1) Is download required?

As we know, ActiveX objects are registered on a client machine. The CDS DLL will check the GUID, version, name, and type with any objects in the local registry and if the same control exists then the new one will not be downloaded. Any version differences will invoke a new component download; therefore the developer can ensure version control is undertaken.

2) Access to the Source

The Internet Search Path contains the registry entries on the client machine. These entries include:

* Option to restrict any external control download, often set as a basic security measure by a network or systems administrator.

* List of alternative download locations, such as local Internet caches, to prevent unnecessary external downloads.

* List of URL locations to use after the source location has been accessed if the server should be unavailable or busy.

3) Control Download

Control source download is undertaken asynchronously, preventing system stoppage. The actual file downloaded may be packaged as a single file or with other multiple files. The single files used would have the extension .exe for binary executables, .OCX for 32-bit controls, or .DLL for dynamic link libraries. COM objects are often compiled as DLLs. Alongside the control binary, a set up file with the extension .INF will also be copied down. This file contains the setup and installation instructions for the control. For multiple control files, they are often compressed into a single "cabinet" file with the extension .CAB. This would be decompressed on the client machine and the files installed according to the instructions contained in the associated .INF file, also downloaded in the .CAB.

4) Control Installation

Assuming the control is verified by the Windows Trust Verification Service, the files are decompressed and installed into the appropriate area on the client machine's disk. DLLs would probably be loaded into the system path. As the distribution of ActiveX controls proliferates, it is envisaged that there will be system utilities removing unwanted (i.e., unused according to an LRU type algorithm) controls.

An in-depth discussion of trust and verification services is outside of the scope of this text.

12.4   Key COM Elements

12.4.1   COM Interfaces

COM provides a consistent memory structure and programming interface. The memory structures exist as tables of function pointers with COM treating each table as an interface, with a name prefaced by the letter "**I**". Once the interface has been implemented, the object agrees to a *contract* with it so that any object user will know what to expect from function calls to the interface.

Figure 12.1

COM Components All Use a Common Interface Like a Jigsaw

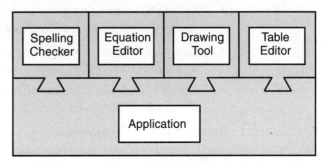

12.4.2   Monikers

Monikers are component objects that contain references to the location of a set of data. A compound document needs to understand the location of embedded data as soon as the user double-clicks on the embedded object. This is the job of the moniker, establishing connections between a data source and the data consumer.

12.4.3   Compound Files

COM specifies a format for the structured storage of information, based upon a hierarchical structure of storage objects. The benefit of this model is that small data changes can be made without affecting the overall compound file and rewriting large amounts of data.

12.4.4   Uniform Data Transfer

Using data objects, uniform data transfer provides a very efficient and powerful way of exchanging data, for example drag and drop, between applications. Used in conjunction with monikers, the user will be given an environment where they do not need to manage any links from a compound document to its underlying data.

12.4.5 Drag and Drop

Drag and drop is very similar to a cut and paste. Dragging an object will cut it and dropping an object will paste it. Any application that has utilized the Windows Clipboard in a cut and paste function is able to utilize the Drag and Drop feature of COM, and the code for using data objects in the clipboard is mostly reusable for implementing Drag and Drop.

12.4.6 Automation

Sometimes called *OLE Automation*, automation is a way to expose the attributes and functionality of an application. These properties and methods use the **IDispatch** interface to expose their automation objects. Once exposed, the application becomes an automation server and, with information about the application stored in a type library, users can examine an application without needing to load and run it.

12.4.7 Linking and Embedding

Embedded data is actually contained within the compound document but at times this may prove to be inefficient. In these circumstances, it is better to link to the data that is stored in another location. Once a linked object is activated the user can edit the data as if it were embedded.

12.4.8 In-Place Activation

Normally when an embedded or linked object is activated, the data server will generate another window with a set of separate toolbars and menus for the user to manipulate the object. *In-Place Activation* places its toolbars and menus within the compound document, removing the need to generate a separate window. This produces a better document-centric as opposed to an application-centric solution where the user is concerned about the application underlying the data.

12.4.9 Distributed Capabilities

OLE 2 implemented a local *lightweight* remote procedure call (LRPC) mechanism to transfer data and operations between objects on a single computer. DCOM, the second generation of OLE 2, has introduced interprocess communication between computers on a network using Microsoft RPC as opposed to LRPC. Microsoft RPC is compatible with the Open Software Foundation (OSF) Distributed Computing Environment (DCE) specification, enabling exchange of information with other DCE systems such as OpenVMS from Compaq and AS/400 from IBM.

Typically, creating a distributed object system is fraught with problems as the multitude of interfaces each need a unique name. Traditional naming conventions for modules, objects, classes, and methods is bound to produce problems of duplicated names within any reasonably large system. Any such duplication will cause failure of the software—despite the actual components being valid. To overcome this, COM uses a set of global unique identifiers (GUID) based upon 128-bit integers, which are virtually guaranteed to be unique, even in systems with millions of objects. Traditional names may be applied to these components, scoped locally they will not impact the overall naming convention.

12.5   COM+

Microsoft announced plans for a new version of COM called COM+ at the end of 1997. Designed to handle most of the repetitive or complex activities involved with COM-based programming, it builds on what was the specification for COM 3.0. COM+ will mostly be a Windows platform enhancement, enabling developers easier access to services such as Transaction Server and Message Queue. The delivery schedule for the full implementation of COM+ is expected to be after the release of Windows 2000 (NT 5.0).

12.5.1   New Features of COM+

Backward Support

All existing COM components and conventions will be supported by COM+

Easier COM Programming

Default implementations of IDispatch, IqueryInterface, and IUnknown will automatically be provided to an application on compile time, garbage collection will be made more automatic, and object creation tasks more streamlined by use of the runtime component.

Better Object Model

Class definitions will be formalized and variable data types provided with intrinsic types of variables.

Increased Extensibility

COM+ objects will no longer call each other directly as they do in COM. Instead COM+ invokes an interceptor between the objects that can intelligently undertake some preprocessing before an object receives the request. This can be utilized in an object performance monitoring application, and thus speed the performance of an application.

Better Access to Services

The days of writing large initialization scripts in code objects may be over with COM+. For example, to invoke support for transactions a single attribute may be all that is needed (i.e., transaction=required).

Improved Object Management

COM+ objects will be located and managed using the Active Directory Services in NT 5.0 and a central repository called the class store. This will remove the requirement to make manual registry changes if an object location is changed.

12.6 Microsoft Transaction Server

12.6.1 Introduction

In the authors' experience, more and more organizations are looking at ways of distributing their IT processing functions through out the organization, but still try to maintain the control and security that a central systems function has come to deliver. This immediately brings to the fore problems of managing transactions across multiple servers, ensuring data integrity is maintained, and business confidence survives. Microsoft has been developing transactional management software for a number of years, the first product delivered being the Distributed Transaction Coordinator (DTC), first released with SQL Server 6.5. Used for guaranteeing the integrity of cross-SQL Server transactions, this has now been joined by Microsoft Transaction Server (MTS). MTS and DTC work together to produce the transaction management services for Windows NT. Object requests are received via DCOM, with MTS managing the requests and resources and DTC invoking the transaction. MTS sits between the client and the object, monitoring everything that is happening—hence the term TP monitor. Once the client finishes with an object MTS will commit the transaction and free up resources.

12.6.2   Transaction Refresher

Most students of computer theory will study the role of transactions. Most will be familiar with the acronym ACID, used to explain the basic principles of a transaction. Interestingly, the origin of the acronym ACID is from a paper written by Dr Jim Gray, who (at the time of writing) heads up the Microsoft Bay Area Research Group.

◆   **Atomicity** ensures that all the updates completed under a specific transaction are committed (and made durable) or that they get aborted and rolled back to their previous state.

◆   **Consistency** means that a transaction is a correct transformation of the system state or data.

◆   **Isolation** protects concurrent transactions from seeing each other's partial and uncommitted results, which might create inconsistencies in the application state. RDBMs such as Microsoft SQL Server use transaction-based synchronization protocols to isolate the uncommitted work of active transactions.

◆   **Durability** means that committed updates to managed resources (such as a database record) survive failures, including communication failures, process failures, and server system failures. Transactional logging even allows you to recover the durable state after disk media failures. For a further discussion of this see Chapter 7.

A most simple explanation of the importance of transactional integrity is that of money transfer within a banking scenario. For a transfer of money from one account to another to take place, money needs to be deducted from one account and simultaneously credited to another. Failure at any stage of this process could result in money either being created or being lost in the system, neither of which would do much for the credibility of the bank concerned.

12.6.3   Why Transaction Server?

Accepting that transactional integrity is vital for this style of business application, what other benefits does Transaction Server give the database developer?

It is very difficult and time-consuming for developers to have to manage the server-based infrastructure that really has very little to do with the application "experience" they may be creating for users. Examples of typical infrastructure requirements include:

◆   Security management—ensuring those who are unauthorized don't access the solution.

- ◆ Tracking the user state, such as who they are and what they may or may not be doing.

- ◆ Managing system threads and server processes.

- ◆ Data access synchronization.

The cost in terms of development time spent coding and managing this infrastructure can be considerable. Some development teams have spent 40% of their time on server infrastructure-related issues rather than application functionality.

MTS has the following components:

- ◆ Transaction Server Executive—provides the server functionality for application components.

- ◆ Base processes—the clients that request work from the server.

- ◆ Resource dispensers—manages the shared state and database connections in a process.

Figure 12.2

Transaction Server Explorer, Showing Installed Packages and Objects

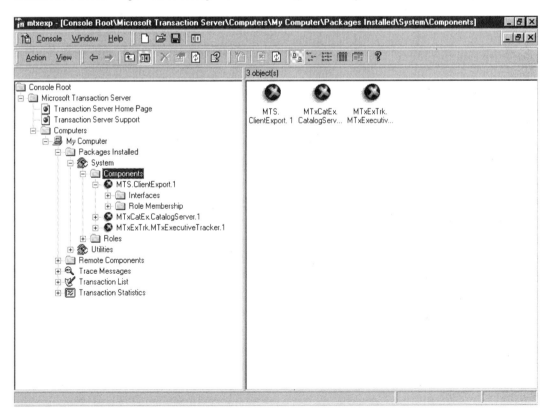

- ◆ Resource manager—the systems that manages the durable data, for example SQL Server.

- ◆ Application components—the objects, controls, or DLLs deployed into Transaction Server.

12.6.4   Tiered Application Development

The partitioning or splitting of application processing became in vogue as client-server computing matured. Developers were encouraged to split the application into logical layers such as the user interface, application processing, and data management. Indeed many client-server consultants became fat on the proceeds of such developmental advice! There is real benefit to this approach, despite what was originally seen as vendor hype.

Figure 12.3
Multiple Ways of Deploying Tiered Applications

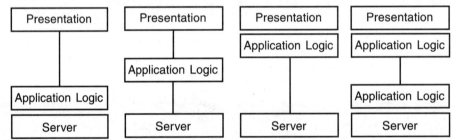

As client-server computing gained a hold, there was general acceptance that the three-tier model was most appropriate for business systems. With the three-tier approach, the client computer is responsible for presentation services, a mid-tier server holds business logic as objects, and the final layer is the persistent, durable data store RDBMS. The theory of a middle tier containing business logic is that changes to a business process can be made to the COM object, in one place, and those changes will be inherited throughout the system automatically, the next time users log to and use the system. The client is used for what it is good at, displaying the screens, and not much else. In reality, most developers will put some business logic on the client even if it is simple data validation or input checking to reduce network traffic.

This partitioning of the system lends itself rather well to web-based computing. The growth of interest in "thin computing" shows a move toward storing a minimum of local information. In fact some of the new thin device specifications, by definition, do not allow persistent storage anywhere on the client machine, may be taking tiered architectures a bit too far.

12.6.5 Packages and Components

To ease the process of deploying Transaction Server-based applications MTS uses the concept of a component package. Essentially, a component package contains components that:

♦ Execute in the same machine process as each other.

♦ Share a common security requirement.

♦ Can be released together as a single unit.

For example, the demonstration packages in version 1.0 of MTS included a banking scenario that contained a set of components that worked together in the same process, shared a common banking security requirement, and were deployed as a single unit to work together in the application. The other benefit of a package is the sub-partitioning available, to increase an application's scalability.

Figure 12.4
Packages Deployed into MTS

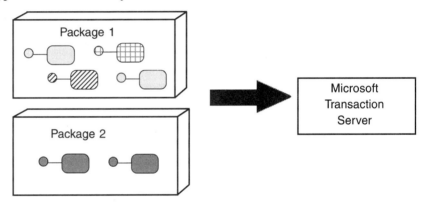

12.6.6 Developing Multitiered Applications with Microsoft Transaction Server

Before enjoying the benefits of Microsoft Transaction Server the developer is expected to commit to COM objects as the key foundation of his or her application. Once adopted and understood, Transaction Server can be usefully employed. Using their development tool, the developer will create a suitable COM object, and in this case we will discuss the use of objects stored as Dynamic Link Libraries (DLLs) created within Microsoft Visual Basic.

There are some basic programming interfaces that need to be learned by the developer. Visual Basic applications invoke Transaction Server applications by using the *Create Object* interface. The object then needs to make Transaction Server aware of its context by calling *GetObjectContext*. Once processing has completed successfully, then the object calls *SetComplete*, or if it has failed and requires a transactional rollback, then *SetAbort*.

For example:

```
Set ctxObject = GetObjectContext()

    Application code/business logic

Set ObjFoo = ctxObject.CreateInstance()

    Application code/business logic

If (OK)
    CtxObject.SetComplete
Else
    CtxObjectSetAbort
```

12.6.7   Database Connection Pooling

Anyone that has developed database applications will be familiar with the problem of database connections. There is application overhead involved in the connection, and often this can outweigh the data processing overhead, maintaining separate database connections for clients can hamper scalability, and establishing and maintaining multiple connections needs complex lock management. Contained within Transaction Server there is a Resource Dispenser that manages ODBC connections spawned by an application. The connections are efficiently shared and multiplexed, reducing the system overhead, all transparent to the system developer.

12.6.8   Thread and Process Management

Programming threads and thread management is a time-consuming task for the developer. The larger the number of users, the more threads that need to be created and managed. Often large multi-user systems will suffer poor performance due to poor thread management, especially if one system thread is allocated per user. MTS automatically manages the creation, allocation, and termination of threads with a thread pool that also addresses issues such as database dead locking and race conditions.

12.6.9   MTS and Internet Solutions

An obvious candidate for any scalable application must be one designed for the Internet. By its very nature, an Internet application may be accessed by many thousands of concurrent users. HTML-based web pages that use Active Server Pages as their base can invoke components running within MTS, which in turn allows the application to benefit from the scalable thread process management of MTS.

Figure 12.5
Typical MTS Internet Solution Architecture

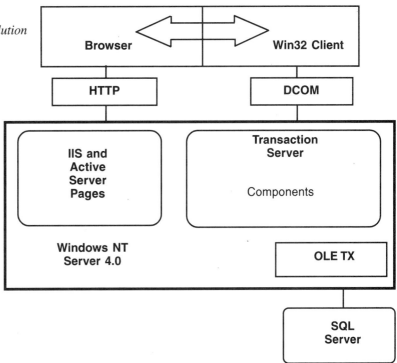

12.7   Microsoft Message Queue (MSMQ)

Many applications need a non-blocking asynchronous communication mechanism, rather than the synchronous mechanism provided by Microsoft Transaction Server. This is especially important when faced with a distributed application with inherent communication challenges.

MSMQ enables an application to send a message to another application without waiting for a response. If the receiving application is not loaded, then MSMQ will detect this and queue up messages until transmission can be completed. MSMQ works well with MTS as it supports transactions, with the sending and receiving of messages contained in an outer transaction that will be rolled back if the operation fails. MSMQ will also journal messages to provide an audit trail and automatically notify the calling application if the receiving application has been or has not been received.

12.8   Distributed Transaction Coordinator

The first release of Microsoft DTC was in Microsoft SQL Server 6.5, and
was the first deliverable of the team working on the Transaction Server
product. The DTC service enables an application to execute transactions
spanning multiple servers, but still ensures that the integrity of the transactions is retained.

The user interface of DTC contains three windows:

*   MS DTC Transactions

*   MS DTC Statistics

*   Microsoft DTC Trace

Figure 12.6
DTC Front Screen, Used to Start and
Stop the Service

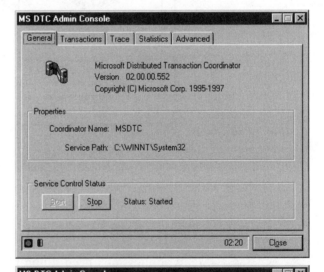

Figure 12.7
DTC Statistics Tab, Showing the Number
of Active and Aggregated Transactions

Figure 12.8

*DTC Advanced Settings Tab, Allowing
the DBA to Set a Log up to Trace
Transactional Activity*

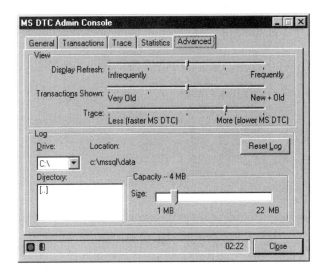

The MS DTC Transactions window lists the current transactions in which a local MS DTC participates. Specifically:

◆ Transactions whose status is in doubt.

◆ Transactions that have remained in the same state for a period of time as specified by the administrator in the MS DTC Configuration dialog box.

Inevitably there will be some problems with the transactions. Transactions that may need to be manually dealt with will normally fall into two categories:

◆ In-doubt transactions, normally caused by a communication failure.

◆ Transactions that have been committed but not "confirmed" by a SQL Server. This is probably caused by a log failure on the SQL Server.

Database locks will be maintained on one or more participating servers as long as a transaction remains unresolved, that is neither committed nor aborted. It may at times be necessary to manually resolve a transaction to release the locks and make database resources available to other users.

12.8.1 Transaction States

The condition of specific transactions is displayed to the administrator. The following states may at any one time apply to a set of transactions:

◆ **Active**—The transaction has been started and is working.

◆ **Aborting**—The transaction is aborting after failure.

◆ **Aborted**—The transaction has aborted.

- **Preparing**—The client application has issued a request to commit.

- **Prepared**—All participants have responded that they have prepared for the commit.

- **In Doubt**—The transaction is prepared, is coordinated by a different MS DTC, but the coordinating MS DTC is inaccessible, probably due to a communication failure.

- **Forced Commit**—The DTC administrator forced the transaction in doubt to commit.

- **Forced Abort**—The administrator forced the transaction in doubt to abort.

- **Notifying Committed**—The transaction has prepared successfully and the commit coordinator is notifying participants that the transaction has been committed.

- **Only Failed Remain to Notify**—The commit coordinator has notified all connected participants that the transaction has committed.

- **Committed**—The transaction has committed and all participants have been notified.

This chapter has explored the use of COM and COM+ with Microsoft Transaction Server. Combined with SQL Server, the developer can create some quite complex applications.

13

Data Warehousing with Microsoft SQL Server

13.1   Introduction

Data warehousing rapidly became the darling of the IT vendor community and the latest phase of client-server computing to be thrust upon IT customers during the late 1990s. Microsoft was not slow to catch on in this area and version 6.5 of Microsoft SQL Server contained some data warehousing features, probably the most notable being the CUBE and ROLLUP operators.

This chapter looks at the use of SQL Server as a data warehouse. We will look at the initial data warehouse functions in SQL Server 6.5, and then see how they have been updated with the new version 7.0 release. At the end of the chapter we will run through the import of data into SQL Server via Data Transfer Services and the building of a simple cube using the pubs database.

13.2   Microsoft SQL Server and the Data Warehouse

13.2.1   SQL Server Version 6.5: CUBE and ROLLUP

Probably the most significant data warehouse functions added to Microsoft SQL Server 6.5 were the grouping and aggregate functions CUBE and ROLLUP. These functions are useful to the data warehouse developer as he or she forces complex aggregate function processing onto the server. This, in turn, reduces server-to-client network traffic and hopefully uses the most powerful processor in the equation to undertake the bulk of the work. The CUBE and ROLLUP operators are discussed in detail in Chapter 5.

13.2.2   Data Transformation and Management

Removal of pure operational data is often the first process and would entail the removal of data "noise"—that is, data elements that are there for a purely one-off logistical reason that will never be needed again. An example could be the delivery company's transaction number, that for some reason was always stored on "the system," but is useless once a package has been delivered.

A time element would then need to be added to the data. If we look back to our definition of a data warehouse, we talk about "time variant" and this needs to be included in all of our data sets. Often data would have a suitable time column, such as delivery date, but often we may need to create an artificial value. An example of this artificial time variant may be the creation of an effective date for a customer account.

13.2.3   Data Warehouse Schemas

The data warehouse designer may often be mislead into thinking that a traditional approach to database design can be used to solve the data warehouse design problem. Data warehouses, by their very nature ("subject oriented") are often best modeled using a slightly different approach.

Relational databases typically use a cost-based optimizer. If a query contains multiple table joins or links, the optimizer will examine each combination of table joins in turn to determine the best execution plan. This can lead to many combinations being examined—for example a 4-table join has a total of 4 factorial (24) possible join combinations and a 10-table join has an amazing 3,628,800 possible join combinations! The query optimizer in SQL Server 7.0 has been changed to overcome this problem but is still subject to the limitations of the data structure.

Obviously, within a data warehouse environment, when a wide variety of queries can be executed the designer needs to try and preempt the user by reducing these table joins. This is achieved by using a star scheme, amalgamating commonly-used data into a single table.

Data merging to produce a star schema is a useful design tool when the following conditions are met:

♦   Tables share a common key.

♦   Data from the tables is used together on a frequent basis.

♦   Data insertion, if appropriate, is the same across the tables.

In fact, there is a slight difference between the star and snowflake structures. The snowflake structure has the surrounding dimension tables in a more normalized form, but for the purposes of this basic text we will deal with them identically.

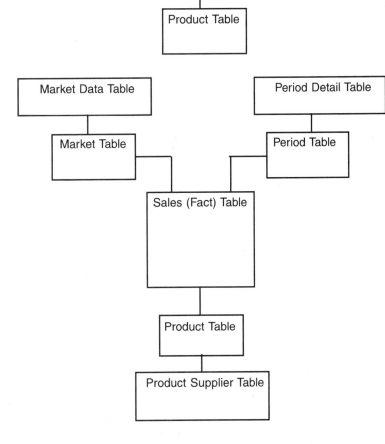

Figure 13.1
Star Structure Data Warehouse Schema Design

Figure 13.2
Snowflake Structure with Additional Tables to Add Detail

13.2.4   SQL Server 7.0 Data Warehouse Features

Data Transformation Services

Data transformation is the taking of data in one format and converting it for storage in a data warehouse. Data transformation can take on many forms, and the data warehouse designer has a number of tools in his or her armory, significantly improved with SQL Server 7.0. SQL Server Data Transformation Services (DTS) is a programmatic data transfer method based on OLEDB (see Chapter 11). It enables data to be brought into SQL Server and manipulated into the data warehouse schema.

DTS Wizard

Like most things in SQL 7.0, there is a wizard for the data transformation services allowing export, import, validation, and data transformation.

The DTS wizard will automatically check to see if the destination table exists and if it does not, then it will go through the steps of creating it. It will attempt to map appropriate data types between source and destination databases, but if an inappropriate choice is made then it can be changed manually by the developer. Naturally, limitations of specific data source/target products and OLEDB drivers cannot be overcome and the developer will have to work within product limitations. One of the most problematic areas is the BLOB, or binary large object data type, that has limitations when being exported to an ODBC destination (there can only be one BLOB column on the destination table and there must be a unique index).

Once data type issues have been resolved, the wizard will then step through the remaining processes such as job scheduling to set the transformation service up.

An Example of Using the DTS Wizard

In this example, we will get data from the Microsoft Access Northwind database and import it into the SQL Server Pubs database. This is a very simple example, but representative of using DTS to import data into SQL Server.

Prior to moving any data with DTS a number of parameters need to be set and configurations checked:

- Ensure the target and source (if appropriate) SQL Servers are running and accessible on the network.
- Backup crucial data.
- Build the target database if it does not already exist and ensure that it is large enough to cope with the new objects being imported.

- ◆ Ensure SELECT permission is granted on the source database if importing from SQL Server.

- ◆ Ensure that you are the DBO for the target database.

Passing through the initial wizard screen you are presented with a screen used to identify the source of the data. The drop-down source box lists all of the installed OLEDB providers available—that is, data sources that you can readily get to from the current SQL Server installation. In this case Access has been selected. The wizard will automatically select the appropriate data source parameters that need to be completed, such as login information or filename description.

Figure 13.3
Data Flow in the Data Warehouse

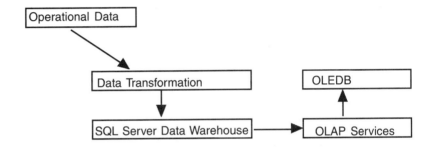

Figure 13.4
DTS Wizard Data Source Selector

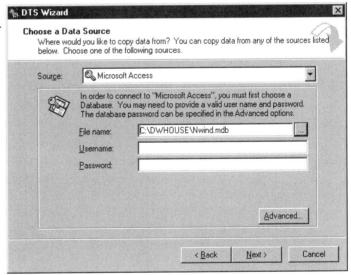

The destination dialog is virtually identical to the source dialog, and in this case we are going to our SQL Server. The advanced button gives access to advanced property settings that some OLEDB providers support, such as window handles, connections, and languages. Most developers or DBAs would not need to alter these settings.

Figure 13.5

*Destination Dialog,
Showing the Pubs
Database Selected as the
Import Database*

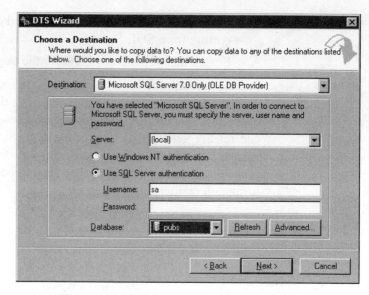

The next dialog enables the import to be a straight table import or involve a query to select specific data in the Access database.

Figure 13.6

*Copy the Table or Specifying
the User Query*

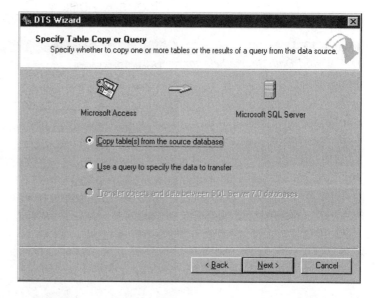

Once the table has been selected for import, the data type matchings are shown to the user. At this point you can decide whether to accept the default mappings that are derived by the OLEDB driver or fine-tune them to suit an individual circumstance. By clicking onto the transformations tab, a script can be created to actually scrub the data, for example change values in the source data to represent a new value in the target database, during the import process. It is important to note that transforming the data does not affect the source database—that data is left intact and dealt with as a read-only database.

Figure 13.7

Data Type Matching

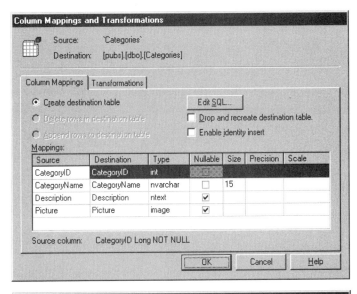

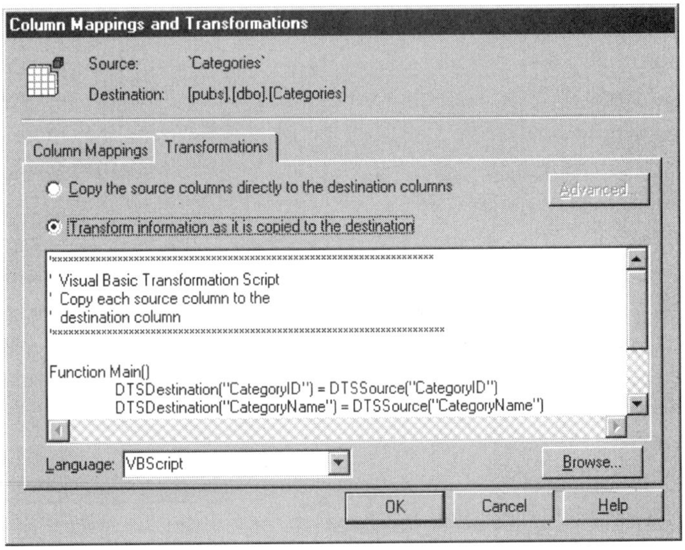

Figure 13.8

Data Transformation. In This Case Using VB Script To Do Very Simple Column Type Matching. At This Point Complex Transformations Can Be Applied

Once the final shape of the transformation has been decided on, the process can be executed immediately or scheduled for later execution. This is useful when a regular data upload is needed from operational systems.

Figure 13.9

Execute the Transformation
Now or Schedule for Later

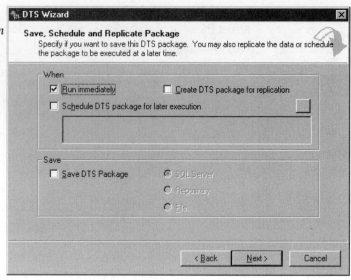

Finally, when the job has executed SQL Server will confirm the objects have been transformed.

Figure 13.10

Objects Successfully Transformed

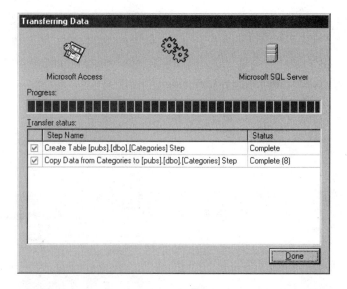

DTS Package

The DTS package is the coordinator that contains all of the steps required to carry out the transformation. Written in a suitable language and often stored as a COM storage file, it exists as a self-contained object. This containment makes for easier package distribution across a network using tools such as e-mail. A task is a piece of work carried out on the data during transformation, such as move from the originating source to the data warehouse or even launch an external application. Tasks are managed by step objects that maintain the correct sequence of events in the data "journey" from source to data warehouse. Only by completion of all steps can a task be said to be complete. This is rather analogous to a transaction. As expected on a multitasking operating system such as Windows NT, multiple tasks can be executed simultaneously and the Win32 thread priority tuned for the application.

DTS Package Security

The developer has the option of enabling encryption on the DTS package by using the Microsoft Crypto APIs. This will protect any username or passwords contained in the packages by only allowing the name, description, ID, version, and package CreationDate properties to be read.

Executing DTS Packages

The package can be executed using a command-line utility called dtsrun at the command line, which would probably be executed as an SQL Server job on a scheduled basis.

Figure 13.11
The DTS Package Designer, Showing a Simple Access to SQL Server Transformation

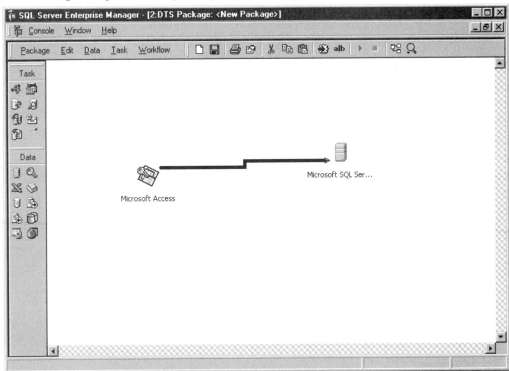

DTS Package Designer

The DTS Package Designer is an advanced tool used to create and edit packages. By using the Package Designer the user can create some complex workflows and data transformations between heterogeneous data sources, all wrapped up in a DTS package. The package is then stored in the repository MSDB database or as a COM storage file. The local folder shows objects stored as SQL Server objects with the repository folder showing those stored in the Microsoft Repository.

Microsoft Repository

The repository technology from Microsoft is fairly new. Essentially it comprises a set of interfaces and information models that define database schemas. Once a package has been put into the repository its data lineage can be traced—that is, the source and history of the data can be established. The repository forms part of the Microsoft Data Warehouse Framework, which outlines a set of standards used to integrate multiple data warehouse products into a single metadata model.

Each time OLAP Services creates an OLAP server, it creates a repository to store metadata such as cubes and dimensions. This is a Microsoft Access database .mdb file by default, contained in \program files\OLAP services\Bin\msmdrep.mdb. The Migrate Repository wizard is designed to move the data from the Access file into an SQL Server 7.0 file. This will enable the repository to scale better and enjoy the other benefits of sitting on an RDBMS. Once migrated to a SQL Server database, the repository cannot be taken back into Access.

The process of moving the repository is straightforward. Right-click the server that you wish to migrate and then select migrate repository. That will launch the wizard that will take you through the steps.

DTS Pump

The DTS Data Pump is an in-process COM server that uses OLEDB to access a wide variety of data in both relational and non-relational formats. The validation, conversion, or transformation of data happens as it passes through the Data Pump based upon scripts put together by the developer. As well as heterogeneous data access, the Data Pump provides access to other Microsoft SQL Server databases on Windows NT, Windows 9.x, and cross-architectural platforms such as Compaq Alpha and a way of importing/exporting that data. About the only data transfer task it cannot manage is the conversion of an SQL Server code page containing extended characters.

13.3   Microsoft OLAP Services

Code named PLATO in its development and beta test phase, Microsoft OLAP Services is Microsoft's entry into the lucrative $1.4 billion On Line Analytical Processing (OLAP) marketplace. OLAP was born out of work undertaken by relational database guru Ted Codd and Arbor Software. The entrance of Microsoft in the OLAP market was established with the purchase of OLAP technology from an Israeli company named Panorama in October 1996, and since then the technology has been enhanced and packaged as Microsoft OLAP Services. It is not the intention of the authors to give the reader a full description of building a data warehouse with OLAP Services, rather provide a basic foundation for further study.

13.3.1   OLAP, MOLAP, ROLAP, and HOLAP

OLAP is technology used to build and maintain data in a multidimensional format such as a cube. The source data is often stored in an underlying relational database in traditional rows and columns, and the cube built on top of that. MOLAP is the name given to conventional cube or multidimensional OLAP structures. This offers fast query performance as the data is prebuilt in the cube format, but often requires mass storage to store the aggregations—data explosion as it is called. ROLAP is seen to be a more scalable solution, and enables the data to remain on the RDBMS, but a skeletal cube structure will be built to house the aggregations when they are built on demand. HOLAP is the use of a hybrid storage structure, that is, data that combines both ROLAP and MOLAP data.

13.3.2   MOLAP? HOLAP? ROLAP? Which One Do I Use?

The cube is the central object in a multidimensional database containing dimensions and measures—dimensions being derived from underlying tables and columns and measures being the quantitative data derived from the columns. Dimensions should in any case be distinct categories added to the cube. Measures are usually time periods or geographical-based metrics often contained in a hierarchical structure, for example, hours roll into days, which roll into weeks.

The cube can hold a number of aggregations that can dramatically improve the efficiency and response time of a query. The scope of the aggregations can be massive, and the designer of a data warehouse needs to offset performance against storage space.

Table 13.1
Cube Storage Options

	Advantages	Disadvantages
MOLAP	· Data navigation, slicing, and analysis is quicker as the dimensions have all been precalculated and stored.	· Cube may take a while to process initially. · Cube needs to be managed on a regular basis as new data comes into the data warehouse.
ROLAP	· Data resides in the original data source, allowing changes to be reflected quicker. · Cubes are quicker to process.	· Data navigation may be slower.
HOLAP	· Best of both worlds, as the structure can be tuned to the business requirements for optimized performance.	· Administration and management may be cumbersome.

Figure 13.12
OLAP Services Creates Strategically Placed Aggregations To Maximize Performance against Data Warehouse Size

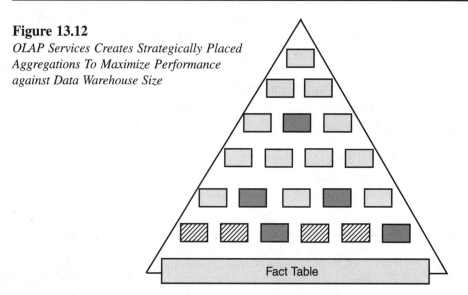

Figure 13.13
Top Level Aggregates Enable Other Aggregates To Be Calculated Quickly

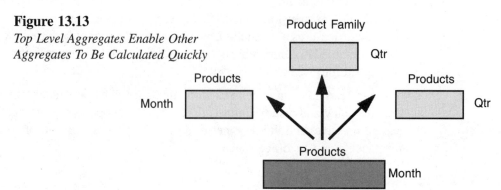

13.3.3   Building OLAP Applications with OLAP Services

The first step in building OLAP applications with OLAP services is to create a database. In the OLAP Manager, right-click database and then select new database. In the dialog, type in the database details and any comments that you want to document the data source.

Once the database is created, a root structure is built that will hold the cubes, virtual cubes, and a library of cube data sources, dimensions, and roles.

Figure 13.14

New Database Dialog

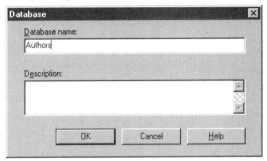

By right-clicking on the cube, the DBA is given the choice of using the cube wizard or cube editor. This example will use the editor since the concepts can be explained more easily, but the wizard is useful for new users wishing to create a quick cube.

The cube editor will load and present a dialog with a list of data sources, with appropriate tables that need to be selected that will form the fact table. The fact table is the base table that contains the core information that is needed in the cube, and in this case we will use the sales table in the pubs database. The fact table contains the measures—that is, the data that we wish to analyze, and normally it will be information such as sales quantity,

Figure 13.15

Selecting the Measure from the Fact Table

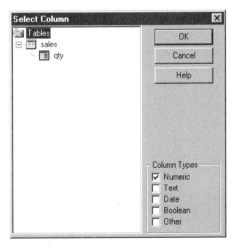

units sold, amount of revenue generated, and the like. In this case we select the qty column, which has actually been identified by OLAP Services by default, as it is the only column in the sales table with a numeric data type. Other column types can be selected, but normally only numeric data will be used as a measure.

We now need something to apply as a dimension against this measure, which enables us to analyze quantity sold by region or book title. The dimensions we are going to use are held in the stores and titles tables, because we wish to see how many books were sold across our regions.

Right-click the screen just above the fact table and select insert tables, selecting titles and stores from the dialog. The joins are automatically brought across from the database but these can be removed if need be by right-clicking them and selecting remove. In this case we will leave them on.

By now the screen should look like the following figure:

Figure 13.16
The Sales Fact Table, Linked To the Two Dimension Tables, Sales and Titles, from the Authors Database

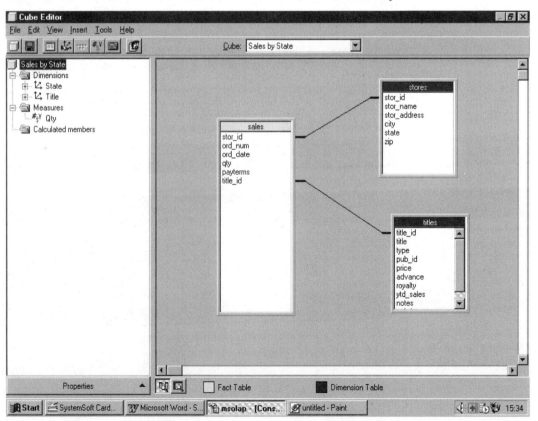

Right-click the dimensions folder and select private dimension. Private dimensions enable us to partition the data and offer a degree of security on the cube structure. Alternatively, a public dimension can be selected that will bring up the dimension wizard.

Select the store state from the stores table and book title from the titles table. Save the cube and then select process cube by right-clicking on the cube name. A dialog will appear warning you that aggregations have not been calculated and asking whether you wish to carry on.

Figure 13.17

Click on Yes To Start the Aggregation Wizard

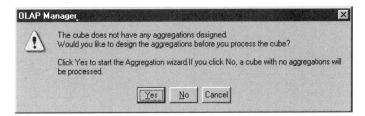

Figure 13.18

The Aggregation Wizard

The aggregation wizard is where you select the storage structure of your cube—MOLAP, ROLAP, or HOLAP.

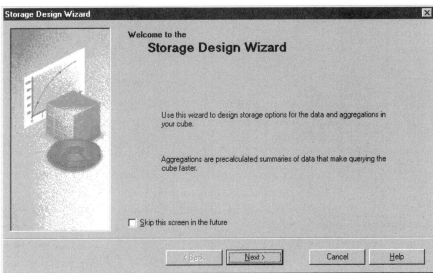

In this case we will select MOLAP because we want to have a multidimensional cube populated with data from the database.

We then get the storage size versus aggregation options. This is where OLAP Services will make smart choices on giving maximum performance versus optimized storage. It would be easy to aggregate all of the cube, but the storage requirements could be massive. Choose the best compromise and hit the start button to initiate the aggregation calculations.

Figure 13.19
MOLAP, ROLAP or HOLAP?

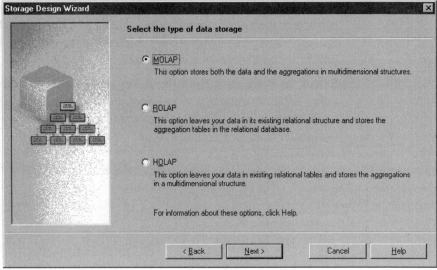

Figure 13.20
Using the 80/20 Rule, OLAP Services Will Determine the Optimum Performance versus Storage Size in the Data Warehouse Cube

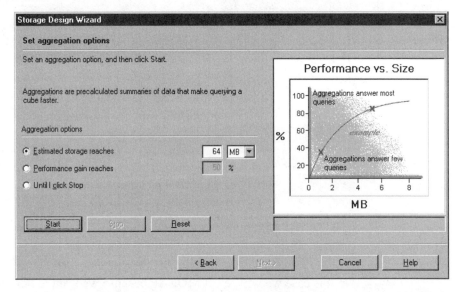

In this simple case there are only two aggregations so the optimization curve is vertical! If there were a potentially large cube to be processed, the next screen offers the choice of rescheduling the processing of the cube, maybe overnight if things are quieter then. Once processed, OLAP Services reports success.

Figure 13.21

This Is a Simple Cube Based on the Northwind Database. Note the Use of Transactions When the Build Was Happening

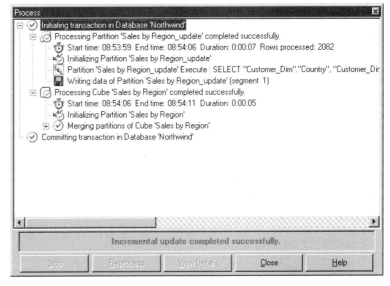

It is possible to incrementally update a cube when adding additional data that does not change the cube structure. As expected this would be quicker than running another process against the cube. If a large change has occurred, then the cube can be refreshed, which will recalculate the cube aggregations but still allow user access to the cube during the process. For improved storage and performance, an OLAP database can be physically separated or partitioned with its own storage structure—ROLAP, MOLAP, or HOLAP—which in turn can be fine tuned for performance.

Single-server partitions enable multiple partitions to be created on a single server, with a single DSN (data source name), with finely tuned aggregations. An example of this may be data that is needed on a regular basis is modeled in a MOLAP database, with maximum aggregations for improved performance, and the associated historical data in a ROLAP database, with a smaller number of aggregations to save on storage space.

Multiple server partitions enable queries to be processed in parallel (when using multiple DSN). Multiple servers can then be used for storing and processing OLAP data, often with a range of servers storing divisional data per server or maybe a year's worth of data per server. For this configuration to work, each server must have its own DSN, be registered in the database data source collection, and have identical data structures.

13.4   Cube Partitions

Partitions contain the cube's data, so all cubes have at least one partition. Further partitions can be built that contain subsets of data—for example, a cube may have a partition with the annual sales data, and then four further partitions for the quarterly data. On this basis the reader can see the dangers of incorrect data in partitions, so the developer needs to be absolutely certain that partitioned data is correct—or the annual figures may be different from the sum of the quarterly data! Partitions can be merged to avoid these problems, and as part of a data management strategy this may be an idea, but again the structures of the partitions need to be identical or incorrect data may be calculated. Luckily there is a partition wizard to help with the bulk of this work.

13.4.1   Virtual Cubes

Much as an SQL Server can have logical views on physical data, OLAP Services provide the developer with a virtual cube function. Essentially these are joins between physical cubes, but because they don't exist in reality, no extra storage space is required.

13.4.2   Viewing the Cube

Supplied with the OLAP Services product is a very simple tool that can be used to view cube data. This is not seen as a replacement for other front end tools, rather it is a useful utility for the DBA or developer to check a cube's structure and functionality. Dragging the dimensions from the quaintly named slicer pane to the grid and vice-versa changes the data grid row. Dimensions are drilled down by double-clicking on the dimension level. Slices are taken by selecting the appropriate dimension in the top pane. To prevent the chore of reprocessing the cube at each edit, the cube will deliver a set of sample data for browsing that will need to be reprocessed to view the live data.

13.4.3   Cube Security

OLAP Services supports a Windows NT security model enabling user access to be controlled in the cube. With this, Windows NT authenticates the user prior to connecting to the cube using the SSPI interface. Access rights can only be implemented on an NTFS based partition using standard Windows NT ACLs (access control lists)—this does not apply to FAT-based partitions. The OLAP manager explicitly supports read access to the data

Figure 13.22

Browsing the Cube Using the Simple OLAP Services Browsing Tool

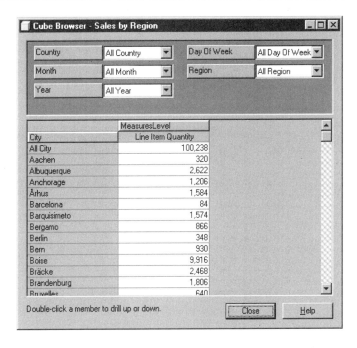

and implicitly supports administration access. You can also add roles to cubes, much in the same way as you add roles in an SQL Server database, to describe who can do what action with cube data.

13.4.4 Updating the Cube

Many of the changes to a cube will require the cube to be reprocessed to reflect the changes to the underlying cube data. A good example of this is a nightly reload of the data warehouse requiring a refresh of the cubes based on the new data. The cube can be reprocessed in three ways.

- Complete Process. This will do a complete restructure of the cube and its associated data. As it is a complete restructure it may be time consuming.

- Refresh Data. If the source data has changed but the structure remains the same, refresh will clear and reload the data, recalculating the aggregates.

- Incremental Update. This updates the aggregates and adds new data to a partition. None of the measures or dimensions is processed and the existing source data is left unchanged.

To incrementally update the cube:

⇨ Expand the *cubes* folder in OLAP Manager.

⇨ Right-click the cube and select *process*.

⇨ Select *incremental update* in the *process cube* dialog.

⇨ A wizard will be launched. Take the steps through the wizard. You will be asked to select a partition to update, select it, and if need be select another data source.

Figure 13.23
Reprocessing the Cube

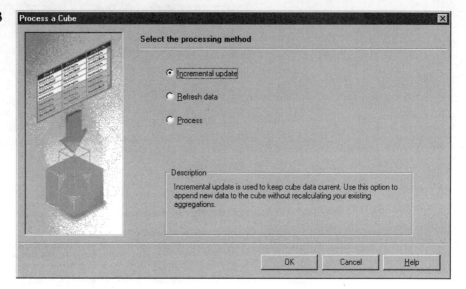

⇨ In the fact table box select the table that contains the data or use change to select another table. If another table is chosen it must have the same structure as the original fact table.

⇨ Specify a filter to limit the data added to the partition.

⇨ Click *Finish*.

To refresh the cube:

⇨ Expand the *cubes* folder in the OLAP Manager.

⇨ Right-click the cube and select *process*.

⇨ Click *Refresh data* and then *OK*.

13.4.5 Analyzing Usage of OLAP Services Cubes

Some of the more interesting tools in OLAP Services are those that can analyze the performance and usage of a cube. There are a number of reports that are available to the DBA:

♦ Query frequency table. This table shows the frequency that queries are run.

- Query run time table. Shows the time it takes to execute each of the queries, with the longest executing at the top.

- Active user table. Lists the users and the number of queries they have sent.

- Query by hour graph. Total number of queries processed, grouped by hour.

- Query response graph. Graph of the response time of each query executed.

- Query by date graph. Queries sent, ordered by date.

These reports are available from the Usage Analysis wizard, which is started by right-clicking the cube and selecting usage analysis.

13.4.6   Optimizing Usage of OLAP Services Cubes

Once analyzed, how are the cubes optimized based on usage? The Usage-Based Optimization wizard is designed to do exactly that, taking you through the steps to optimize the cube.

- Partition. The wizard will take you through the optimization of each partition of the cube. If there is a chance that you might merge partitions, then do not use the Usage-Based Optimization wizard, as it will change the underlying aggregations, preventing a merge, which must have identical aggregations.

- Queries. The wizard will select the queries to optimize. The wizard will use data from the query log, which by default will record one query in ten. To increase the sampling frequency of the log then go to the *properties* dialog box and then the *query log tab*.

Figure 13.24

Optimization of a Cube Based on Queries Between Certain Dates

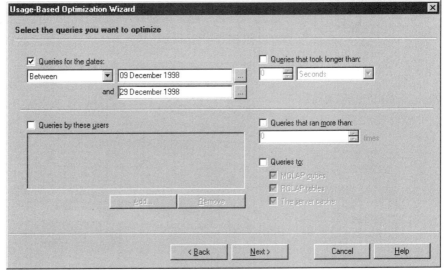

- Storage Option. If there are no aggregations or you wish to replace an aggregation, then Storage Option will enable you to redefine the storage of the cube into a new structure, for example, move from ROLAP to MOLAP.

- Aggregations. As discussed before, OLAP Services are quite clever in the storage of cube aggregations, which in turn can dramatically affect the volume of data stored and the performance of the cube. This option enables you to select the type of aggregation model for a cube.

13.4.7   Write Enabling Cubes

Although it may seem strange, and maybe a contradiction of the read-only nature of a data warehouse, but there may be some instances when users wish to update data in the data warehouse. A typical example may be a manager reviewing data and identifying a particular sales figure that is incorrect.

With a write-enabled cube, users that have the read/write permission level set can make changes to the cube, which are recorded in the *write-back table*. This is separate from the cube and its source data, and users are able to see the net effect of all changes in the write-back table for the associated cube.

13.4.8   Write-Enabling a Cube

⇨   Right-click the selected cube, and then click *Write-Enable*.

⇨   In the *write enable* dialog, enter a name for the write-back table in the *table name* box.

⇨   In the *data source* box select the data source and specify a new data source in the *data link* properties.

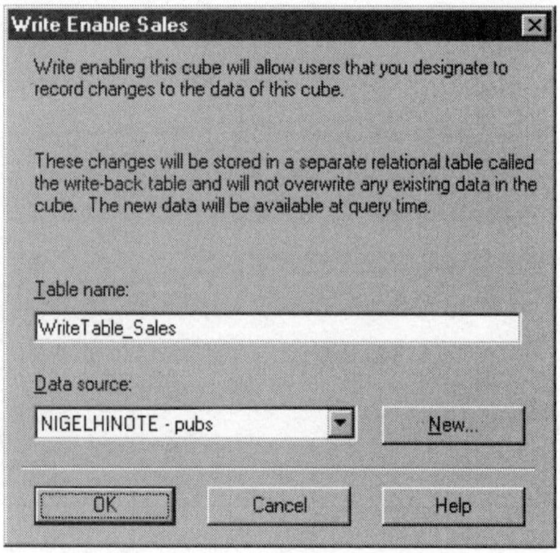

Figure 13.25
Write-Enabling a Cube.
Note the Table Name Box

13.4.9   Browsing and Deleting Write-Back Data

⇨   The contents of the cube's write-back table can be read by *right-clicking the cube*, selecting *write-back options* and then selecting *browse write-back data*.

⇨   To delete the write back data select *delete write-back data* in the *write back options*.

Once the data has been changed in the write- back table, it is possible to convert it into a cube partition.

13.4.10   Converting Write-Back Data to a Partition

When the data is converted back into a partition, all read/write permissions will be suspended and users will not be able to change the cube data. Additionally, the data in the write-back table is deleted.

⇨   Right-click the cube. Select *write-back options* and then *convert to partition*.

⇨   Enter a *name* for the partition and select an *aggregation design option*. At this point you can design aggregations immediately or later.

⇨   If needed, specify a *filter* on the write-back table to specify a subset of the data to be written back.

⇨   *Process* the new partition.

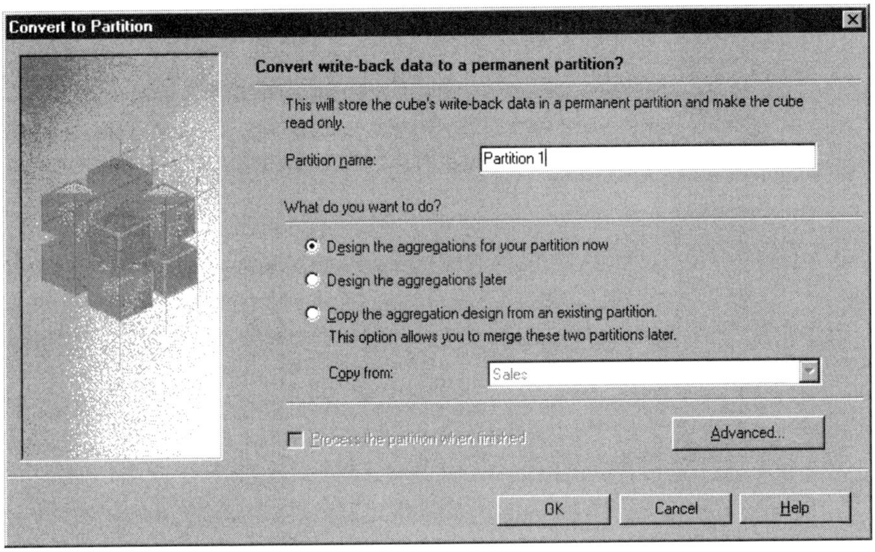

Figure 13.26
Converting the Write-Back Data to a Partition

14

Developing Applications with Microsoft SQL Server 7.0

14.1 Introduction

Very few—if any—organizations would use SQL Server as a business solution in its own right. SQL Server will always be used alongside a client development tool that is used to provide client services such as forms for data entry or query screens.

A wholesale discussion of application development with Microsoft SQL Server is out of the scope of this text. The authors have included this chapter as a way of describing a typical approach that may be taken, plus some clarification of the type of tool likely to be used in a business scenario. The chapter concludes with a review on migrating a Microsoft Access application to Microsoft SQL Server.

14.2 Distributed interNet Architecture (DNA)

Announced in late 1997, Distributed interNet Architecture (DNA) is Microsoft's future application development architecture designed to incorporate the often disparate world of client-server and Web-based development. It comes out of the latest Microsoft thinking that concerns the way organizations work and the use of IT in an organization's structure, called the Digital Nervous System.

14.2.1 DNA—The Key Features

- Users are demanding access to the communication capabilities of the Internet, while still enjoying the power of PC-based applications. With DNA, Microsoft intends to make this development easier.

- Most organizations have existing applications and databases that need to be integrated into newer systems. Very few would consider rewriting the software, instead they demand interoperability via open interfaces, which in turn need to be enhanced and developed in line with industry acceptance. Probably the best example of that is ODBC, which has come from an obscure API background into a mainstream, data connectivity component. DNA has further committed Microsoft to support industry API sets.

- Cost of ownership has become a new battle on the back of the NC versus NetPC debate. Every organization wants to reduce the overhead costs in building and managing systems, deploying software, and administration tasks. DNA is designed to make these tasks easier. The growth of the "device" marketplace, such as PDA (Personal Digital Assistants) and set-top boxes, is set to further fuel the PC cost of ownership argument, and some research organizations are now predicting a decline in PC sales in favor of more simple, task-oriented devices.

- Faster time to market—the ability for developers to create and ship robust software as quickly as possible—is increasingly more important. DNA will try to provide the structure to create these solutions, something that Microsoft had not been renowned for. One of the first examples of products in this area is Microsoft Transaction Server.

14.3 ODBC, OLEDB, DAO, RDO or ADO?

Connecting an application to SQL Server may at first appear a bit daunting due to the large number of acronyms and data object models. This is partly due to the evolution of Microsoft software over the years and the increasing requirement for Microsoft to maintain backward compatible software.

14.3.1 Database Connectivity—A Brief History

The proliferation of the personal computer in the workplace during the late 1980s lead to unprecedented demands from users to access data across the enterprise. Constantly frustrated by large IT departments that were seen to be obstructing the throughput of simple reports and requests for data, and wooed by the easy-to-use graphical user interface of the new Windows environment, users began to demand better and easier data access.

The myriad of solutions from the computing industry brought confusion to users and IT professionals alike. The use of a common protocol such as IBMs DRDA (Distributed Relational Database Architecture) was expensive, both in terms of money and local PC memory requirements. Common interface solutions abounded, for example, SQL-Link from Borland, DataLens from Lotus, and Data Access Language from Apple gave a confusing choice. Common gateway technologies again proved expensive.

Vendors soon realized that the customer base demanded a consistent, easy-to-use solution that was supported by a majority of software companies.

The SQL Access Group (SAG) was formed in 1988 from a group of vendors with a variety of backgrounds—diverse companies from the world of mainframe, mini, and PC computing. The SAG produced a Call Level Interface that is the basis for Open Database Connectivity (ODBC)—the ODBC SQL syntax is based on X/Open and the SAG SQL CAE specification (1992). In 1995 SAG moved to become a working group of X/Open.

ODBC from Microsoft is only implemented on the Windows and Apple Mac platforms, although other vendors are creating similar programming interfaces for other operating systems. ODBC is the data access component of Microsoft's Windows Open System Architecture (WOSA) architecture.

14.3.2 ODBC

ODBC was Microsoft's strategic data access application programming interface (API). Based upon an open standard generated by SAG, it has had good acceptance in the marketplace since its inception. This chapter is designed to give the developer a broad understanding of ODBC and how it can be used to create database solutions.

Introduction to Open Database Connectivity

The architecture of ODBC is, from a high level, surprisingly straightforward and is comprised of four separate layers:

- The application. This must have an ODBC compliant interface to the ODBC driver manager. An example of an ODBC client application includes Microsoft Access.

- ODBC Driver Manager. The driver manager maintains the latest information regarding which data sources the application can talk to, loads individual drivers when required, and generally looks after the ODBC connectivity interface.

- ODBC Driver. An appropriate driver has to be installed for each database that is to be connected. The driver undertakes some initial processing of the ODBC call from the application and will match datatypes with the underlying server database and return any results to the application.

♦   Database server or data source. This is the data repository that is stor-
    ing data to be accessed by ODBC.

All of the ODBC-specific software remains on the client PC; no extra software needs to be loaded onto the server.

Types of Drivers

Within ODBC there are three different types of ODBC driver and architecture:

♦   Single Tier drivers include those used to access ISAM-based data such
    as dBASE and Paradox. Due to the nature of ISAM (Indexed Sequen-
    tial Access Method) data, extra functionality has to be included in
    these drivers to translate SQL set orientated language into appropriate
    language that the ISAM data understands. These drivers are often said
    to contain an *engine in the box* to undertake this translation.

♦   Two Tier drivers are the standard client-to-server architecture, used
    with RDBMS data sources such as Microsoft SQL Server.

♦   Three Tier is used to describe the use of gateway servers to access
    remote data.

ODBC—The Future

ODBC gave the computer industry a database connectivity standard that
revolutionized the development of database applications. The life cycle of
ODBC is now coming to an end, to be replaced by OLEDB as discussed
later.

14.3.3   VBSQL

Initially Visual Basic used an API model called VBSQL. This was primarily because Visual Basic did not, originally, have an object model. VBSQL
was not difficult to use, rather it was too limiting as it was SQL Server-
specific at a time when SQL Server was very much a minor player in the
RDBMS marketplace. In fact, VBSQL was based on DB-Library, the proprietary C API for SQL Server and at that time SYBASE SQL Servers.

14.3.4   JET

JET, the Access database engine, was the best way for Visual Basic 3 developers to address ISAM-type files. Actually, despite some bad press at
the time, JET was an amazing piece of ISAM database technology and
could do some pretty neat things, albeit at times rather slowly. The other

benefit of JET was its ability to tackle RDBMS data via ODBC, which was at that time the emerging standard for relational database connectivity. DAO (Data Access Objects) was the object model built on top of JET, and was a remarkably easy-to-use interface. Developers who wanted to bypass the JET layer were offered ODBC access via the ODBC API, but that came with the difficulties of writing to a C language API set.

14.3.5   RDO and ODBCDirect

RDO (Remote Data Objects) was designed to give developers a lighter interface to SQL Server and Oracle and enable the developer to use stored procedures and other RDBMS objects for improved functionality and performance.

ODBCDirect was created for the Office developer's world, and is supported in applications such as Word and Excel. Prior to ODBCDirect, Office developers had to use the ODBC APIs, which is difficult. ODBCDirect is a DAO-type interface to RDO, giving developers DAO usability with RDO performance—a type of thin interface on top of the RDO thin interface. In fact, RDO and DAO have different object models due to the different data paradigm between ISAM and RDBMS data. ISAM databases are "table-centric"—the data is the main requirement—but with RDBMS the developer is more focused on stored procedures and other "programmer-centric" objects.

14.3.6   ADO and OLEDB

ActiveX Data Objects (ADO) is set to tidy up this real mixture of data access methods. Designed to be like both RDO and DAO in its object model, it will offer far more flexible access to data types from spreadsheets to relational database. It achieves this by creating an object interface to OLEDB. OLEDB is a data access interface that uses complex structures and pointers, both of which would be out of the scope of Visual Basic.

ADO 2.0, released with Visual Basic 6, is a superset of RDO 2.0. Visual Basic 6 has the ADO data control, a data environment designer for drag and drop ADO connections that has the ability to do dynamic data binding, so that settings can be made at runtime for better application control.

Microsoft has also dropped the name ActiveX from marketing activities, with ADO only being referred to by acronym rather than full name.

Although ADO is an emerging technology, the general recommendation when creating a new application is to consider ADO first. If that fails to offer you the functionality you require, then look at RDO or DAO. Using ODBC directly as an API is a very poor third choice. OLEDB is an emerging technology, and it is hoped that the service providers will continue to write interfaces in preference to ODBC, which is now seen as a static technology that has come to the end of its strategic life.

14.4   ADO Object Model

There are seven objects that form the backbone of ADO.

14.4.1   Connection Object

This object enables the developer to configure, create, and then terminate sessions with data sources. It can also identify an OLEDB provider, execute queries, manage transactions on an open connection, and choose a cursor library available to the data provider.

This example shows Visual Basic connecting to an SQL Server via the SQL Server OLEDB provider.

```
' You initialize variables here
Dim cn As New ADODB Connection
Dim provStr As String
' The OLEDB provider is specified here
cn.Provider = "sqloledb"
' This is the specific connection string on Open method.
ProvStr =
"Server=Auriga;Database=northwind;Trusted_Connection=yes"
cn.Open provStr
```

14.4.2   Command Object

The command object enables the developer to send commands to the data provider. Typically these will be query strings, prepared query strings, and all of their associated parameters. The individual OLEDB provider determines the scope of available options for the developer to use.

14.4.3   Recordset Object

Once connected to the data provider, the developer needs to manipulate the data. The record set object allows the developer to scroll through data sets and insert, update, and delete data.

14.4.4   Error Object

The errors collection contains the provider-specific errors generated by an operation. Each of the error objects relates to one error in the collection and by querying the error object properties via the connection object, error information can be returned.

14.4.5   Field Object

Field objects allow each column in the current record set to be accessed.

This example uses the field object to return the name, type, and values for each column in the current record.

```
Dim rs As New ADODB.Recordset
Dim fld As ADODB.Field
Dim cn As ADODB.Connection
Dim cmdText As String
cn.Provider = "sqloledb"
cn.Properties("Data Source").Value = "Auriga"
cn.Properties("Initial Catalog").Value = "pubs"
cn.Properties("Integrated Security").Value = "SSPI"
cn.Open
cmdText = "select * from authors"
rs.Open cmdText, cn
Set Flds = rs.Fields
Dim TotalCount As Integer
TotalCount = Flds.Count
For Each fld In Flds
Debug.Print fld.Name
Debug.Print fld.Type
Debug.Print fld.Value
Next
rs.Close
```

14.4.6   Parameter Object

If a query needs parameters, then the command object sends these via the parameter object.

14.4.7   Property Object

Connection, command, recordset, and field objects all report their property settings via the property object.

This example retrieves connection and time out properties:

```
Dim cn As New ADODB.Connection
Dim cmd As New ADODB.Command
Dim rs As New ADODB.Recordset
cn.Provider = "sqloledb"
cn.Properties("Data Source").Value = "Auriga"
cn.Properties("Initial Catalog").Value = "pubs"
cn.Properties("Integrated Security").Value = "SSPI"
cn.Open
' This is where we find out the connection time out property.
Debug.Print cn.Properties("ConnectionTimeout")
Set Cmd.ActiveConnection = Cn
cmd.CommandText = "titles"
cmd.CommandType = adCmdTable
Set rs = cmd.Execute
' This is where we find out the command time out property
Debug.Print cmd.Properties("CommandTimeout")
Debug.Print rs.Properties("Updatability")
```

14.5   Visual Interdev

Visual Interdev version 1 was introduced by Microsoft in March 1997. In the autumn of 1998, Microsoft had just released version 6, missing out on the interim 5 releases! Visual Interdev (VI) was Microsoft's first "proper" web development tool, designed to give developers a useful Visual Basic type-environment for web development. Up until the release of VI, the single most popular Web development tool was Notepad, the Windows-based text editor. Notepad was used by developers to write lines of Hypertext Markup Language (HTML) for publication. VI offers more than text editing. One of the major innovations in the product is the creation of Active Server Pages (ASP), which amount to pages of code that can host COM scripting components written in VB Script or something similar. Using this approach, the developer can build some fairly complex functionality into the application, which is then compiled and held in the ASP.

The ASP resides on Microsoft Internet Information Server and is accessed from the web client. In fact, Microsoft moved a lot of pages on the Microsoft.com website away from HTML to ASP—when you connect now you will connect to DEFAULT.ASP or INDEX.ASP rather than the more familiar DEFAULT.HTM or INDEX.HTM. Once connected, the browser will download the ASP, but the clever bit is that the ASP is dynamically translated into HTML during the download process—the browser only ever sees "pure" HTML, none of the embedded script. This delivers a couple of advantages. Firstly developers can embed complex functionality into their applications that would be beyond HTML as the language now stands, and secondly it automatically protects the source code—none of the code logic is downloaded, only the basic screen presentation details.

14.6 Visual Basic

Microsoft Visual Basic (VB) is a very popular application development environment based on the BASIC language, one of Microsoft's key development languages. Now at version 6.0, Visual Basic has a following of some 3 million developers world-wide—a considerable development base.

Visual Basic consists of an integrated development tool suite with a forms designer where the developer effectively *paints* a graphical screen and then attaches code behind screen objects, such as buttons or text fields. Visual Basic uses an event-driven model because Windows applications, by their very nature, can offer users a number of possible code paths at any one time. Using a procedural language to create this type of application is very complex and often not possible.

Visual Basic 5.0 is now available as a native 32-bit application for both the Intel and Compaq (formerly Digital) Alpha products.

The Visual Basic for Applications (VBA) edition is a version of the Basic language engine designed to be embedded with other applications such as Excel or Project. The embedding of the language element gives the developer access to an application's objects using VBA as a macro language, therefore freeing the developer from having to learn a multitude of different macro languages to link applications together.

14.7 VBA Architecture

The VBA code is organized into three separate components:

- ◆ Procedures
- ◆ Modules
- ◆ Projects

14.7.1 Procedures

Procedures are called using their name, and once called, the code block in the procedure is executed until the end of the procedure is reached. VBA has three different types of procedure:

- Sub
- Function
- Property

14.7.2 Sub Procedures

Sub procedures are excellent general-purpose code blocks that do not return any values. They are often used for tasks such as performing runtime screen changes and data input. A Sub procedure will always start with the Sub keyword followed by the Sub name and parenthesis that contain any arguments used in the procedure. If no arguments are used, then the parenthesis are left empty. The code block to be executed then follows, with the procedure terminating with an End Sub keyword:

```
Sub Procedure:

Sub Name (arguments)
    ...Code
End Sub
```

14.7.3 Function Procedures

The key difference between a Function and Sub procedure is that a Function will return a value to the calling code. An obvious use for this would be in mathematical calculations. Users of Excel are able to define functions and then call them as if they were native to the spreadsheet.

The Function construct is similar to a Sub:

```
Function Name (argument) As Returntype
    ...Code
    Name = value
End Function
```

One of the key differences between the Sub and the Function is that the Function can define the data type to be returned using the As keyword. The returning value is named after the Function name.

14.7.4 Property Procedures

Property procedures are an advanced feature of VBA. They enable a developer to call them by using the same syntax as used to set the value of a property.

14.7.5 Passing Arguments

Arguments can be passed to procedures using either conventional or named arguments. Conventional arguments pass the arguments to the procedure in the order in which they were defined, with any omitted argument being replaced by a space contained in commas:

```
DemoAddress (Town, County, Country)
```

This contains all of the arguments needed to allow the procedure DemoAddress to operate. If the developer decided not to include the county argument, then the example would look like this:

```
DemoAddress (Town, ,Country)
```

The alternative method is to use named arguments. Generally, named arguments are easier to read and allow the arguments to be passed in any order, irrespective of the order in which they were defined:

```
DemoAddress Country:="UK", Town:="Epsom"
```

Note the ":=" operator before any argument.

14.7.6 Variables

Variables are memory areas used to store information on a temporary basis by an application. Anything that contains a value has a data type that determines the type of, and legality of, data stored in that variable. Table 14.1 shows a sample of the data types available in VBA.

Table 14.1
Key VBA Data Types

Data Type	Description
String	1-byte text characters, maximum about 2 billion
Integer	2-byte, non-fractional numbers ranging from −32,768 to 32,767
Single	4-byte single precision floating point numbers
Boolean	2-byte true or false
Currency	8-byte scaled integer

If a data type is not assigned to a variable, then the variant data type is used by default. The variant data type can contain any numeric value up to the double range limit or any text character. Any change in the type of value stored in the variant data type is automatically managed by the code.

Any variables used in VBA are declared either explicitly in code written by the developer or implicitly when they are automatically given the variant data type.

Table 14.2
Declaration Statements

Statement	Comment
Dim	Used by variables shared in a module and to declare variables in procedures that are removed from memory when a procedure ends.
Static	Used for variables that are not removed from memory when a procedure ends.
Public	Used for all variables shared by all procedures in a project. This is the same as the Global statement in VB Professional and Standard, which it replaces.
Private	Used for variables that are available only in the module containing the procedures where it was declared.

Variables can be scoped, or made visible, at either the local, module, or public level. During execution the variables are evaluated according to scope, starting with local variables, through the module level, and then finally the public level.

Local variables are useful for temporary data storage in a procedure. As they have a narrow scope, they are only visible to the procedure in which they were created. Either the Dim or Static statements can be used to declare these variables, with the Dim variable not remaining in memory after the procedure has ended. Variables declared with the Static statement will remain in memory and can be used the next time the procedure is called.

Module Level variables are declared with the Dim, Static, or Private statements at the top of a module prior to the first procedure. This variable is then visible to all of the procedures in the module. If there is a conflict with a Local variable of the same name, then the Local variable will take precedence over the Module Level variable, which will be ignored.

Once declared with the Public statement, a Public variable is visible to all procedures in a project, irrespective of the module in which it was created.

14.8 Objects in Visual Basic for Applications

Each application supporting VBA has a file called an object library that contains information about the application's objects that are accessible from within VBA. These objects can be components of the application or other OLE objects from other external applications.

The interaction of these objects is the key to VBA. These objects can be manipulated by altering object properties, which are key attributes that control an object's behavior or appearance.

The setting of properties is a straightforward task. The object is named, with a period separating the object and the property that is to be altered. The new value of the property is entered after the "=" sign:

```
Form1.Visible = Yes
```

This will ensure that Form1 is visible.

14.8.1 Methods

A method is a characteristic of an object that it knows how to perform. Every object has a set of methods attached to it. An often-cited example of a method is the Save method with Microsoft Excel, which, when executed, will save the existing workspace or workbook changes. These methods may take arguments in the same way as a procedure, so a developer may, for example, specify the actual file name to be saved by the method.

14.8.2 Containment

Visual Basic offers the developer a framework for containment with the ability for a form to contain controls such as buttons and check boxes. VBA offers similar containment. For example, Excel is an object that contains workbook, worksheet, and range objects in, effectively, an object hierarchy.

14.8.3 Collections

A group of related objects can be contained in one object called a collection. Excel is a good example of this as the Worksheets collection object has a property that can be interrogated to establish some information about the worksheet, for example how many worksheets in a workbook.

14.8.4 Object Browser

The object browser is a special dialog that enables browsing of an application's objects, showing the names of all the objects and their associated methods and properties, names of projects, procedures, and modules.

14.8.5　Control Structures in VBA

VBA supports various code structures, including control and looping functionality. Probably the most commonly used control structures are the If...Then, If...Then...Else, and Select Case structures.

If...Then enables conditional execution of code based upon the validity of an expression, with false validity skipping code execution. The additional Else statement enables an extra scenario if all expressions are false, often used at the end of the code block if all expressions effectively fail.

Select ...Case is more focused on identifying matching values rather than a testing process used in If...Then.

Looping structures allow the iterative use of code that will be repeatedly executed until conditions are met.

For...Next enables use of a counter to determine the number of code cycles executed, with the developer specifying the number of cycles in a counter variable. Normally used in an incremental counting mode, decrementing is possible with the Step clause with a "-" sign prior to the step value.

Do...Loop will continue to process a code block iteratively, without the need for a counter until a determined condition is satisfied. The addition of the clause Until or While will ensure the code is executed until conditions are met, which can lead to interesting application functionality unless catered to by the developer!

14.9　SQL Server Distributed Management Objects (SQL-DMO)

Initially called SQL-OLE, the SQL Server Distributed Management Objects (SQL-DMO) bring the world of objects to the management of SQL Server. SQL Server has an object model with 40 separate objects containing 600 32-bit OLE interfaces that support the Visual Basic programming language. SQL DMO is implemented as a dual interface in-server process designed for developers who wish to create applications to undertake routine tasks or manage alerts, job execution, or SQL Server replication.

The object model is a hierarchy, with the primary SQL Server object containing databases that in turn contain tables, views, and stored procedure objects.

There are three basic object types in SQL DMO:

*   *Objects* that are stand alone and refer to a single SQL Server component.

◆ Container objects called *collections* that allow members to be added and removed.

◆ Container objects that have a fixed membership called *lists*.

14.9.1 Using SQL DMO

Developers familiar with Visual Basic will find the syntax for using SQL DMO straightforward. The following example uses Visual Basic to determine the name and space available for databases on a given server:

```
Dim NetServer as SQLServer
NetServer.Name = "AURIGA"
NetServer.Login = "sa"
NetServer.Connect
For each NetDB in NetServer.Databases
    Print NetDB.Name, NetDB.SpaceAvailable
    Next NetDB
NetServer.Disconnect
```

This example will declare the SQL Server object, connect to the server, and then for each database within the server, print the database name and the amount of available space remaining. The application will then disconnect from the server.

Each object has a multitude of methods and properties. The database object, for example, has many methods such as Dump and Load and many properties such as its Name and Owner. The Index object has methods such as Rebuild and UpdateStatistics and properties such as Name and FillFactor. Given the flexibility of VBA and SQL DMO, it can be seen that database administrators will be able to write very sophisticated scripts to assist them in their database administration tasks.

14.9.2 SQL Name Space (SQL-NS)

SQL-NS is designed to complement SQL DMO and allow access to the Enterprise Manager functions and features such as wizards and dialog boxes from Visual Basic or C++. With SQL-NS an application can programmatically traverse the Enterprise Manager console tree to a particular object and then execute a relevant command.

The main interface into SQL-NS is via the ISQLNamespace interface, that in turn enumerates the all of the objects in the namespace.

14.10   Migrating from Microsoft Access to SQL Server —"Upsizing"

14.10.1   Why Upsize?

Microsoft Access is a file server-based database as are most, if not all, PC-based databases in use today. A file server database is useful for creating applications designed for moderate amounts of data access, perhaps less then 100 MB, and for moderate numbers of concurrent users, perhaps less than 20. This is due to the database mechanisms that come into play when used in a PC network environment.

If a user executes a query or some other table access action, then the entire contents of that table may be brought across the network and loaded into memory on the client PC. This action is enough to bring an active PC network to its knees in no time at all! Multiply this by a number of users and the end result is obvious.

To overcome this type of performance limitation it is necessary to re-look at the access of data across the network. This is where client-server computing comes into its own. Reduction of network traffic is one of the important benefits of implementing an efficient client-server system.

Instead of entire tables of data brought over the network, client-server implementations are generally more intelligent and will return only the data that the users actually require.

There are a set of tools available to assist the user in migrating from Access to SQL Server 6.x. At the time of writing those tools are not supported with version 7.0 of SQL Server so the developer will need to resort to manual methods.

14.10.2   Objects in SQL Server 7.0 and Access 97

Access supports the use of spaces in object names, which are not supported in SQL Server naming conventions. The usual way of overcoming this is to insert an underscore character in the place of spaces, a technique often used by RDBMS developers when naming objects. The alternative is to use upper case letters to identify the different words. For example see Table 14.3.

Also note that SQL Server object names may be case-sensitive if that option is selected as part of the character set during installation. The default character set is dictionary order, case insensitive so in most installations this will not be an issue.

Table 14.3
Access and SQL Server Naming Conventions

Access Table	SQL Server Table
computer sales	ComputerSales
	Computer_sales

14.10.3 Table Design

Most Access developers are used to making ad hoc changes to table designs, but what they do not realize is that Access does not modify the existing tables, rather it builds a new table and will move data to it transparently. Changing table design has historically been very difficult with SQL Server. Version 7.0 makes this process a bit easier, because data is copied into the new structure as in Access. Even so, the developer may need to monitor this data transfer and be prepared to intervene if necessary.

14.10.4 Business Rules and Foreign Keys

The use of foreign keys in Access and SQL Server are basically the same, but Access cascade updates and deletes are not available in SQL Server. If you do need this type of functionality, then you will need to build UPDATE or INSERT triggers to do the work for you.

14.10.5 Typical SQL Server Trigger Use

Table 14.4
Typical SQL Server Trigger Use

Microsoft Access	SQL Server Triggers
Record and field validation, required property, referential integrity	UPDATE
Record and field validation, required property, referential integrity for child tables and counter data type	INSERT
Referential integrity	DELETE—Parent tables only

The usual place for business rules, especially if they are dealing with data, is at the SQL Server. Triggers and declarative referential integrity will enforce primary and foreign key constraints and unique indexes will enforce unique constraints. SQL Server also deals with rules and defaults differently from Access. In SQL Server it is possible to create a rule that is then bound to one or many tables or columns. In effect the developer can build a pool of rules that can be used by the SQL Server. Access uses rules applied to fields or as part of code modules. The obvious weak spot here is that some users may access tables directly bypassing these rules.

14.10.6 Indexes and Compacting Data

The Access developer will need to use the best index structure possible when moving to SQL Server. Access does not have the option of clustered or nonclustered indexes, and the developer will need to choose the best indexes for the type of application. See Chapter 10.

SQL Server does not have a utility for compacting the databases, instead it will rebuild indexes to recover empty space created by deletions and restructure the data pages in line with the chosen Fill Factor. A full database compaction is the equivalent to dropping and rebuilding all of the indexes in the database. This is most useful where a database is highly volatile—that is, it undergoes many updates and deletes in a given period. This can easily be scheduled via the SQL Server Agent.

14.10.7 Data Types

Data types define how the data is stored in a column. Access uses data types available to it from within Visual Basic; SQL Server uses C data types. When converting from Access to SQL Server, the data type matching shown in Table 14.5 occurs.

SQL Server does allow some changing of column data types, but there are some strict rules that apply. See ALTER TABLE in Chapter 4.

SQL Server timestamps are different from the use of timestamps in Access, and really the name timestamp is misleading. The SQL Server timestamp is a binary number that is updated automatically when a row is updated or inserted. DATETIME should be used if a readable value is needed to track an event on a column.

SQL Server has an auto-incrementing column feature called the identity column that is the same as an Access AutoNumber field. To import Access data into an SQL Server table with an identity column while preserving the original AutoNumber column values, turn off the identity column with the IDENTITY_INSERT function, copy the data in, and then turn it back on again with the same function.

Table 14.5
Access and SQL Server Datatype Matching

Access Data Type	SQL Server Data Type
Text	Varchar
Memo	Text
Replication ID	Varbinary
Date/Time	Datetime
Long Integer	Int
Currency	Money
Autonumber (Long Integer)	Int (Identity)
Byte	Smallint
Integer	Smallint
Single	Real
Double	Float
Yes/No	Bit
OLE Object	Image

14.10.8 Using Structured Query Language

Once the data has been moved to SQL Server, the developer needs to think through the different ways in which Access and SQL Server applications work.

The first tip is to limit the amount of data returned in any one query. Access lends itself well to browsing tables due to the generally small number of rows that are present. SQL Server is designed to store huge numbers of rows, so users need be restrained from browsing all of your 5 million records!

When updating data, SQL Server needs to be used effectively. In small Access applications individual rows can be updated easily, with minimum performance impact. With a large number of users on a big system, think about doing batch updates, for example:

```
UPDATE author SET royalty = 10 WHERE au_lname = "Stanley"

UPDATE author SET royalty = 10 WHERE au_lname = "England"

UPDATE author SET royalty = 10 WHERE au_lname = "Burns"

UPDATE author SET royalty = 10 WHERE au_lname = "Hobbs"
```

Should become:

```
UPDATE author SET royalty = 10 WHERE au_lname = "Stanley"
OR = "England" OR "Burns" OR "Hobbs"
```

This will incur one set of network traffic, rather than the previous four.

14.10.9   Functions and String Handling

Microsoft Access has the same string handling features as SQL Server, but
the keywords are slightly different, as are some of the math, dates, and
delimiters.

Table 14.6

Function and String Handling in SQLServer and Access

Access	SQL Server
asc(x)	ascii(x)
right$(x,y)	right(x,y)
mid$(x,y,z)	substring(x,y,z)
str$(x)	str(x)
ucase$(x)	upper(x)
len(x)	datalength(x)
ltrim$(x)	ltrim(x)
space$(x)	space(x)
lcase$(x)	lower(x)
chr$(x)	char(x)
rtrim$(x)	rtrim(x)

Table 14.7

Access and SQL Server Function Comparison: Conversion Functions

Access	SQL Server
cint(x)	convert(smallint,x)
clng(x)	convert(int,x)
csng(x)	convert(real,x)
cdbl(x)	convert(float,x)
cstr(x)	convert(varchar,x)
ccur(x)	convert(money,x)
cvdate(x)	convert(datetime,x)

Table 14.8
Access and SQL Server Date Functions

Access	SQL Server
now(x)	Getdate(x)
date(x)	Convert(datetime,convert(varchar, getdate(x)))
year(x)	Datepart(yy,x)
month(x)	Datepart(mm,x)
day(x)	Datepart(dd,x)
Weekday(x)	Datepart(dw,x)
hour(x)	Datepart(hh,x)
minute(x)	Datepart(mi,x)
second(x)	Datepart(ss,x)
datepart("<Access datepart>", x)	Datepart(<SQL Server datepart>, x)
dateadd("<Access datepart>", x, y)	Dateadd(<SQL Server datepart>, x, y)
datediff("<Access datepart>", x, y)	Datediff(<SQL Server datepart>, x, y)

Table 14.9
Access and SQL Server Mathematical Functions

Access	SQL Server
int(x)	floor(x)
sgn(x)	sign(x)

Table 14.10
Access and SQL Server Delimeters, Constants, Wildcards, and Operators

Description	Access	SQL Server
Date delimiter	#	'
String delimiter	"	'
Mod operator	mod	%
Concatenation operator	&	+
Wildcard character	?	_
Wildcard character	*	%
Constant	Yes	1
Constant	On	1

Description	Access	SQL Server
Constant	True	1
Constant	No	0
Constant	Off	0
Constant	False	0

14.10.10 Moving the Upsized Application Forward

Exporting tables to SQL Server will not instantly create a finely tuned client-server solution. There are a number of jobs that need to be undertaken to optimize the SQL Server and Access application.

14.10.11 Fine Tuning the Client

Record Locking

When using attached tables, the Record Locks property of any form used must be set to No Locks or Edited Record because any Dynaset used from a server cannot be opened in exclusive mode. Server tables are used with optimistic locking, with the appropriate page only being locked for the duration of the commit.

Event Ordering

Access validation occurs when the user leaves the appropriate field, but SQL Server triggers are not fired until the user leaves the row when used as attached tables. Applications that rely on validations when the user tabs from a field may need to be rewritten. Similarly, counter datatypes are incremented on field entry in Access and after row insert in SQL Server.

14.10.12 Security

Access cannot override the security model of SQL Server, so although the Access application may not be explicitly aware of SQL Server security, it cannot violate it. Indeed this is one of the strengths of this type of application—a strong security model. Users can log onto Access and then SQL Server separately, or alternatively Access will default to logging the user in with the Access login password and username and only prompt for another if this fails.

14.11   Optimizing an Access and SQL Server Solution

Microsoft Access gives the developer a number of ways of integrating with SQL Server, and indeed any other RDBMS via ODBC. Once an Access application has been upsized, the developer will need to optimize the system to ensure that it performs well.

14.11.1   Attached Tables

Using attached tables is the easiest and most efficient method of using remote data. Once the tables have been attached, they may be treated as local Access tables for most activities.

14.11.2   SQL Pass Through

Pass through is functionality that enables queries to be sent directly to the remote RDBMS, bypassing the Access query compilation process. There are a series of advantages and disadvantages that need to be taken into account before embarking on this route.

Advantages:

* Server-based functions, such as stored procedures with no Access equivalent, can be used directly.

* Queries are executed on the server, with less local processing and network traffic.

* Heterogeneous data sources can be joined at the SQL Server, reducing the amount of data returned locally to perform the join.

* Delete, Update, and Append queries using pass through are faster than action queries on attached tables.

Disadvantages:

* The code to access functions has to be typed in directly to the pass through window, with no syntax checking.

* Data is returned in Snapshots that are read-only views.

* Pass through queries cannot prompt a user for a parameter.

14.11.3   Optimizing Access Connection Utilization

Developers need to be aware of the connection techniques used by Access in a client-server application to improve performance of the system.

A connection is different from a user login; one user may have multiple connections or threads to the server database, which may, in some instances, prevent other users from logging onto the SQL Server because the maximum number of concurrent connections has been exceeded. Generally, the design of SQL Server allows an average of 2.5 connections per user logged on.

Access version 1.0 had considerable problems in some Access/SQL Server combinations due to overuse of available connections. This problem was overcome in later versions with the use of multiplexing within JET to release unused connections.

14.11.4   Dynasets

The best way of using a dynaset is to reduce the number of returned rows to less than 100. This way Access uses one connection, as opposed to two connections, when data chunks of larger than 100 rows are returned—one connection for the key values and one for the returned data. Normally, 100 rows are adequate for most applications. If other dynasets are created, then they can share the *data* connection but must create their own *key* connection.

Connections can be forced to close by using a TOP 100 PERCENT query to return all of the data or using an OPEN EVENT procedure in a form to explicitly close the data connection.

If a default time of 10 minutes expires with no activity between the client and the server, then the connection will be closed automatically. The connection will not be closed if a transaction or the results of a query are pending.

The connection timeout can be changed by setting the Connection-Timeout in the ODBC section of MSACC20.INI, the Access initialization file. To keep the connection closed, increase the Refresh Interval setting of the multiuser/ODBC category in the Options dialog box. The default setting is for 25 minutes (1500 seconds).

14.11.5   Optimizing Queries

The key to obtaining better performance in queries is to use indexes wisely and ensure the server is doing all or most of the processing.

Index any join fields in multi-table queries or fields used in the WHERE clause of the query. Chapter 10 describes the options available for choosing indexes.

14.11.6   Increasing Server Processing

When Access is required to query SQL Server, it will attempt to send all of the query to be processed to the server after evaluating any query clauses or expressions locally. To ensure that the query is processed on the server, there are some simple steps that can be taken:

- Avoid constructs that contain functions or operators specific to Access, such as TOP queries and multi-level grouping in reports.

- Avoid any user-defined Access Basic functions that use remote fields as their arguments.

- Avoid mixing text and numeric data types in UNIONS or expressions.

- Avoid heterogeneous joins, that is, those between different ODBC data sources. Access will either request all of the data from the remote table and perform the join locally or perform a remote index join where each key in the local table will be matched for data on the SQL Server.

- Avoid operations that cannot be contained in a single SQL statement, such as a FROM clause containing a totals query.

14.11.7   Deletions and Updates

Writing data to SQL Server in batches, by using Access Basic transactions, will improve both multi-user concurrency and the performance of updates. Transactions are effectively units of work, which either succeed or fail, never half completing. They should be kept as short as possible because an SQL Server lock will be generated preventing users from updating or reading the affected data used in the transaction.

An alternative application design is to have a holding table in Access to which all updates are written. These records can then be written to the SQL Server in a single Access Basic transaction.

14.11.8   Recordset Caching

The CacheSize property of a recordset allows the storage of between 5 and 1200 records in memory, which will spill into a temporary table should memory be filled. This caching will greatly improve the performance of datasheets and forms as cached records are retrieved from the client as opposed to the server, and therefore reduce network traffic. To recover memory used in a cache, the CacheSize method can be set to 0.

14.11.9   Error Trapping the Server

Since Access is connected to the SQL Server via ODBC, two error messages will be generated if an error is encountered—the first from Access and the second from SQL Server. The Access *Error$* function can be used to concatenate the Access and server error message together. This can then be parsed to determine the error created by the server.

Glossary

ADO (ActiveX Data Objects)

Object interface into the OLEDB (qv) programming interface.

Aggregate Functions

Functions in SQL that return a single value as a result of grouping together many rows, such as SUM or COUNT.

Aggregations

Precalculated data sets within an OLAP cube. Aggregations lead to an increase in data size, but an improvement in cube performance.

Alert

A response to an event occurring in SQL Server. Alert responses include e-mail, pager messages, net sends, and job execution.

ANSI

The American National Standards Institute, a leading force behind the SQL standard.

Application Role

A type of database role that provides the means to specify security on an application basis.

Article

A table or part of a table that can be replicated.

Ascending Order

A sorting order that starts with the lowest key value and proceeds to the highest value.

ASCII

A computer character set and collating sequence. Acronym for *American Standard Code for Information Interchange.*

Attribute

Another name for a column in a table.

Backup Device

A hard disk file or tape used to store database and transaction log backups.

Backup Set

The product of a distinct backup operation.

Batch File

A number of Transact-SQL statements executed together either interactively or from a file.

BCP

See *Bulk Copy Program.*

Blob

Binary Large Object. A datatype used for storing large amounts of data such as text, pictures, sound, or video. The actual datatypes used in SQL Server are the *text, ntext,* or *image* datatypes.

Boolean Expression

A string that specifies a condition that is either true or false.

Boolean Operator

A symbol or word that joins two or more Boolean expressions. Typical Boolean operators are AND, OR, and NOT.

B-tree

A balanced tree or sorted index structure for a specified table.

Bulk Copy Program

A command line utility for transferring data between an SQL Server table and a file.

Call Interface

A mechanism for a program to access components of a software product.

Cardinality

The number of rows in a table.

Catalog Stored Procedure

Stored procedures added to Microsoft SQL Server to provide a uniform catalog interface.

Check Constraint

A rule that defines the permitted values a column may take.

Checkpoint

A mechanism that ensures that completed transactions are written from cache to the database at frequent intervals.

Clustered Index

A type of index whereby the physical order of the data in the table is the same as the order in the index. There can only be one clustered index per table.

CODASYL

Acronym for *Conference on Data Systems Languages*. A network model database management system.

Collating Sequence

The sequence in which characters are ordered for merging, sorting, and comparing.

Column

A relational model term that equates to a field. Also called an *attribute*.

Commit

A statement that finishes a transaction and makes all changes on the database permanent.

Composite Key

Any type of key that is comprised of one of more columns.

Computed Column

A virtual field that appears in, for example, a table or view definition, but not physically in the table; therefore it occupies no space in the database.

Concurrency

The simultaneous use of a database by a number of users.

Consistency

The level to which a database system guarantees that tables being read by a user cannot be changed by another user at the same time.

Cross Operation

See *Join*.

Cube

A multi-dimensional data warehouse store.

Cursor

An object that is used to store the output of a query for subsequent row-by-row processing.

Data Definition Language

The statements that describe the metadata definitions.

Data Manipulation Language

The statements that allow data in an SQL Server database to be stored, retrieved, modified, or deleted.

Data Table

See *Table*.

Data Transformation Services (DTS)

An SQL Server data pump that allows data to be imported or exported from SQL Server while being scrubbed or massaged.

Database

A collection of related data. The database maintains its own data integrity and security. There can, and typically will be, be a number of databases per SQL Server.

Database Administrator

A person whose responsibility is the smooth running of the SQL Servers and their underlying databases. Will typically be responsible for ensuring that the database is backed up, DBCC is run regularly, performance is satisfactory, and there are no nasty surprises about to happen. Can be recognized by the bags under his or her eyes. Usually has the same expression on his or her face as that of parents of three-week-old quadruplets. See *System Administrator*.

Database Cache

An area of memory set aside to hold data and index pages read in from disk.

Database Consistency Checker

A database administration utility with many uses and options, such as checking database consistency and transaction log space usage.

Database File

An area of a hard disk used to store database data or a database transaction log. A database may consist of a minimum of two files but may reside on more.

Database Page

The structure used to store data or indexes within an SQL Server database. The database page size is fixed at 8KB.

Datatype

An attribute assigned to a column or field such as *char* or *int*. The datatype determines the storage space taken by the column and a range of allowable values. Datatypes that come with SQL Server are known as *system supplied datatypes*, whereas datatypes that are not created by SQL Server are known as *user-defined datatypes*.

DBA

See *Database Administrator*.

DBCC

See *Database Consistency Checker*.

DDL

See *Data Definition Language*.

Deadlock

The situation where two or more transactions request the same resources in an order that results in a deadly embrace. Nothing can be done to resolve the conflict, except aborting one of the transactions.

Default

A value stored in a column if no value is otherwise specified.

Denormalization

The reverse process of normalization.

Descending Order

A sorting order that commences with the highest value of a key and goes down to the lowest value.

Dimension Table

Table in a star or snowflake structure that contains measurement data, such as region or salesperson. When applied to the fact table, it enables data analysis such as sales by region by salesperson.

Distributed iNternet Architecture

A multi layered approach to software design architecture created by Microsoft. By using a DNA approach, developers separate the user interface from the business logic and database store.

Distributed Transaction Coordinator (DTC)

A service that manages transactions across multiple SQL Servers.

Distribution Database

An SQL Server database used as a staging post for those transactions that are being sent to subscription servers.

Distribution Server

An SQL Server where the distribution database resides.

DNA

See *Distributed iNternet Architecture*.

EBCDIC

Acronym for *Extended Binary Coded Decimal Interchange Code*, the computer set and collating sequence for IBM systems.

Embedded SQL

SQL code that is embedded in an application and precompiled before execution.

Equi-join

A join operation that matches a column from one table with a corresponding column in another table.

Error Log

The files in which SQL Server and SQL Server Agent write error and informational text.

Extended Stored Procedure

A special kind of stored procedure that provides a means of dynamically loading and executing functions.

Extent

A unit of data storage consisting of eight contiguous pages. An extend can be allocated to only one object (a uniform extent) or can supply single pages to more than one object (a mixed extent).

Fact Table

Table that contains the central data within a star or snowflake structure. Typically this will be a sales quantity or volume.

Filegroup

A named group of files. Objects such as tables can be explicitly placed in a filegroup.

Fill Factor

A value used when an index is created to reserve free space on each page of the index.

Fixed-Database Role

Built-in roles defined at the database level.

Fixed-Server Role

Built-in roles defined at the server level.

Foreign Key

A field in one table that is a primary key in another table.

Free Space

The space on a database page that is available for new data.

HOLAP (Hybrid OLAP)

The storing of OLAP data in a combination of ROLAP and MOLAP structures to give the best size/performance ratio for Data Warehouse cubes.

Index

A structure within the database that locates a row based on a key value.

Index Key

A column or columns that make up an index.

Integrated Security

The security model where SQL Server uses Windows NT security to authenticate users and bypasses the SQL Server login process.

Integrity

The correctness of the information in an SQL Server database. There are three types of integrity control: integrity constraints, concurrency control, and recovery during or after a system failure.

Isolation Level

Specifies how a transaction is affected by other transactions accessing the same data.

ISQL

A utility for command line-based SQL Server administration.

Join Operation

A relational operation that selects a row from a table, associates it with a row from another table, and presents them as though they were one table.

Joint Engine Technology (JET)

The database engine underlying Microsoft Access and Microsoft Visual Basic Professional Edition.

Journaling

The process of recording all operations applied to the database.

Key

A column in a table that is used to locate one or more rows.

Locking

A mechanism for protecting a transaction from interference from other concurrently executing transactions. In SQL Server, typically rows, pages, or tables can be locked.

Log Reader Process

A process that takes the relevant transactions from the transaction log of a publication database and moves them to a distribution database.

Logical Name

A user-specified name for a database file.

Master Database

Perhaps the heart of a SQL Server installation. The master database holds configuration information about the SQL Server and the objects in it. It also holds system tables and system-stored procedures.

Metadata

Data that is used to describe other data.

Microsoft Management Console (MMC)

The host for SQL Server Enterprise Manager and other Back Office administration tools.

Microsoft Transaction Server (MTS)

Software that manages the middle layer business objects in a DNA application.

Mixed Security

The security model where SQL Server uses Windows NT security and SQL Server security to authenticate.

Model Database

A template database used when SQL Server is asked to create a new database. A database administrator can modify some of the attributes of the model database that will then be copied to any databases created afterward. Such attributes include database configuration options, user-defined datatypes, rules, defaults, and privileges. There is one model database per SQL Server.

MOLAP (Multidimensional OLAP)

An OLAP storage cube that contains persistent data.

Multi-statement Transact-SQL

See *Batch File*.

Nonclustered Index

A type of index where the physical order of the data in the table is not the same as the order in the index. There can be 249 nonclustered indexes per table.

Normalization

The process of reducing a database to its simplest form and eliminating data redundancy.

Northwind Database

A learning database shipped with SQL Server representing a trading company.

Null

An indicator in SQL used to indicate that a value has not been supplied.

Object

Elements such as database files, login IDs, databases, tables, columns, and indexes.

ODBC

Microsoft's de facto standard for PC client access to database servers. Acronym for Open Database Connectivity.

OLAP (Online Analytical Processing)

The multidimensional view of a data set. Often used in the context of data warehouse cubes.

OLAP Services

The component of SQL Server that enables data warehouse cubes to be built and managed. Known as PLATO during SQL Server 7.0 development and beta test.

OLEDB

The preferred data access interface supported by Microsoft. Designed for accessing both relational and nonrelational data sources.

Online Transaction Processing (OLTP)

An environment that supports many users performing the same critical business functions. A typically OLTP system is made up of many simultaneous users, all performing the same function such as order taking or seat reservation.

Permissions

Determine which users can access which objects and execute which Transact-SQL statements.

Physical Name

An operating system name for a database file.

Primary Key

A column or group of columns that uniquely identifies a row. A primary key cannot be null or contain duplicates.

Privileges

See *Permissions*.

Procedure Cache

An area of memory set aside to hold stored procedures read in from disk and their query plans.

Publication

A set of tables that have been specified as being candidates for replication.

Publication Database

A SQL Server database from which replicated data originates. Sometimes known as the *primary* or *source* database.

Publication Server

An SQL Server where a publication database resides.

Pubs

Buildings, sometimes quaint, sometimes not, found in Great Britain where beers, spirits, and ales are consumed. A British institution. Also the location where this book was conceived. There is no connection with the pubs database shipped with SQL Server.

Pubs Database

A learning database shipped with SQL Server representing a publishing business.

Query Analyzer

A graphical utility for executing Transact-SQL and examining query plans.

Query Optimizer

The component of SQL Server that works out the most efficient way to execute a query.

Query Plan

The method that the query optimizer has decided is the most efficient way to execute a query.

Record

A table row.

Reflexive Join

An operation that joins a table to itself.

Relation

Another name for a table.

Relational Database

A database model that describes data as a set of independent tables. Within each table, the data is organized into rows and columns.

Remote Server

An SQL Server on the network accessible from the user's local server.

Replication

The process of copying data from a primary table to secondary tables around the network at various intervals.

Restore

The process of rebuilding a database from a database backup using RE-STORE DATABASE.

ROLAP (Relational OLAP)

A multidimensional cube structure that contains pointers to a data store. Eliminates the data explosion problem associated with MOLAP cubes.

Role

A useful mechanism granting and revoking permissions. Users can be assigned to database standard roles and then the role can have permissions granted, revoked, and denied.

Rollback

The Transact-SQL statement used to undo all changes made to the database since the last transaction was started.

Rollforward

The process of reapplying committed transactions from the transaction log to the database.

Row

The relational-model term for a record.

SA

See *System Administrator*.

Security

The protection of the data held in the database against unauthorized access.

Select Operation

The Transact-SQL operation for specifying which rows should be retrieved from the database.

Snowflake Structure

Similar to a Star structure (qv) but contains additional sublevels of the dimension tables.

Sort Key

A column used for sorting a table.

SQL

Structured Query Language. The standard query language for accessing relational databases. It is an official standard comprised of both a data definition and a data manipulation language.

SQL2

The name for SQL-92 while it was a working standard.

SQL3

The next revision to the SQL standard that is under discussion and review.

SQL 86

The original SQL standard.

SQL 89

Further enhancements to the original SQL standard.

SQL 92

Is a major enhancement to the SQL standard, which defines many new features and incorporates a number of features that have already been introduced into commercial relational database management systems. There are three levels to this standard: entry level, intermediate, and full.

SQL Agent

The component of SQL Server responsible for the management of administrative tasks such as the alerting of operators.

SQL Distributed Management Objects (SQL-DMO)

A layer of management objects forming a hierarchy, with the primary SQL Server object containing databases that in turn contain tables, views, and stored procedure objects. Used by the SQL Enterprise Manager and Visual Basic for Applications.

SQL Enterprise Manager

The graphical SQL Server management tool. Can be used to administer SQL Servers distributed around a network and to create and edit SQL Server objects such as databases, tables, and login IDs.

SQL-NS (SQL Name Space)

A complimentary service to SQL DMO allowing access to Enterprise Manager functions.

SQL Server Security

The security model where SQL Server uses a login ID and password to authenticate users.

Star Structure

A database schema that contains a central fact table surrounded by associated dimension tables.

Stored Procedure

A group of Transact-SQL statements defined as a procedure and stored in the system catalog.

Subscriber

See *Subscription Server*.

Subscription Database

An SQL Server database to which replicated data is sent. Sometimes known as the *secondary, destination,* or *target* database.

Subscription Server

An SQL Server where a subscription database resides.

System Administrator

The name often given to an administrator of a SQL Server installation. Any user who is a member of the fixed server role *sysadmins* is a system administrator.

System-Stored Procedure

A group of Transact-SQL statements defined as a procedure and stored in the system catalog in the master database. Supplied by Microsoft and typically used for managing an SQL Server and its underlying databases.

System Table

A table that contains information required for the operation of the SQL Server.

Table

A collection of rows and columns. Will typically contain the user data.

Tempdb Database

A temporary storage area that can be used for temporary tables and other scratch space requirements. There is one tempdb database per SQL Server.

Temporary Table

A table created in the tempdb database that will be removed when the user connection terminates. Temporary tables can be local or global.

Transaction

The grouping of a number of Transact-SQL statements together such that all their changes are applied to the database or none are.

Transaction Log

A file that contains all the data structures modified during a transaction. The transaction log file is used to reconstruct the database and maintain integrity during a system or application failure.

Transaction Processing

A style of computing supporting multiple users who are performing predefined tasks against a shared database.

Trigger

A type of stored procedure that is automatically executed when a table is changed. Triggers are associated with particular tables and there can be different triggers that execute if a row is inserted, updated, or deleted. Triggers are useful for maintaining integrity and keeping audit logs.

Tuple

Relational database terminology for a row or record.

User-Defined Datatype

A datatype not supplied by SQL Server but named and designed by a database administrator or database designer. User-defined datatypes are based on system-supplied datatypes.

View

A logical definition of a table that includes rows and columns from one or more physical base tables.

Windows NT

Microsoft's 32-bit server operating system.

Windows NT Performance Monitor

A graphical utility for monitoring various aspects of Windows NT and SQL Server performance.

WORM

Write once read many device.

X/Open

An independent, worldwide, open systems organization that is supported by most of the leading information system suppliers, software companies, and user organizations.

Index